SAMPLING TECHNIQUES FOR FOREST RESOURCE INVENTORY

SAMPLING TECHNIQUES FOR FOREST RESOURCE INVENTORY

BARRY D. SHIVER

BRUCE E. BORDERS

at University of Georgia

JOHN WILEY & SONS, INC.

New York / Chichester / Brisbane / Toronto / Singapore

ACQUISITIONS EDITOR Eric Stano
MARKETING MANAGER Rebecca Herschler
PRODUCTION EDITOR Tony VenGraitis
DESIGNER Kevin Murphy
MANUFACTURING MANAGER Dorothy Sinclair
ILLUSTRATION COORDINATOR Sandra Rigby
PRODUCTION SERVICE Graphic World Publishing Services
COVER PHOTO Carol Kohen/Image Bank

This book was set in Times Roman by Graphic World, Inc., printed by Courier/Stoughton and bound by Courier/Westford. The cover was printed by New England Book Components.

Recognizing the importance of preserving what has been written, it is a policy of John Wiley & Sons, Inc. to have books of enduring value published in the United States printed on acid-free paper, and we exert our best efforts to that end.

The paper in this book was manufactured by a mill whose forest management programs include sustained yield harvesting of its timberlands. Sustained yield harvesting principles ensure that the number of trees cut each year does not exceed the amount of new growth.

Library of Congress Cataloging-in-Publication Data

Shiver, Barry Dexter.
Sampling techniques for forest resource inventory/Barry D. Shiver, Bruce E. Borders.
p. cm.
Includes index.
ISBN 0-471-10940-1 (cloth: alk. paper)
1. Forest surveys—Statistical methods. 2. Forests and forestry—Statistical methods. 3. Sampling (Statistics) I. Borders, Bruce E. (Bruce Edward), 1956– . II. Title.
SD387.S86S48 1996
634.9′285—dc20 95-32955
CIP

Printed in the United States of America

10 9 8 7 6 5 4 3 2 1

DEDICATION

This book is dedicated to Lindsey, Brenton, and Clayton Shiver and Janet, Brandi, Sean, and Cole Borders and to the memory of Dr. Jerome L. Clutter.

PREFACE

The purpose for writing this book was to create a forest inventory textbook that clearly explains the sampling methods associated with the inventory of forest resources. There are several books available which do a good job of explaining the theory of the various sampling techniques used in forest inventory. However, the transition from theory to practice is not easily made without extensive course work in theoretical statistics and mathematics. This book provides thorough coverage of forest inventory topics for the practitioner rather than the theoretician and should be understandable to undergraduate forest resource students and professionals who must inventory forest resources.

Examples are used extensively throughout the book to illustrate various estimators and to demonstrate different uses for sampling methods. Problems are also included at the end of each chapter to help instructors and students.

Some of the topics discussed, such as point sampling and 3P sampling, were developed specifically for timber inventory. Other topics, such as mark-recapture methods were developed for inventory of mobile wildlife populations. Many of the topics, however, can be utilized to inventory virtually any of the resources in a forest (understory vegetation, soils, water, etc.).

As the book has developed over the last several years, we find that we are using it as a reference as well as a textbook. Some of the topics such as double sampling with point sampling and sampling with partial replacement have been available only in scattered journal articles or in more theoretically oriented textbooks. Inventory is a job which most forest resource managers will use repeatedly throughout their careers. This book should allow them to work confidently in forest inventory regardless of the specific inventory problem.

Barry D. Shiver
Bruce E. Borders

TABLE OF CONTENTS

INTRODUCTION

A forest inventory is a description of the quantity and quality of trees and other organisms that live in the forest and the characteristics of the land on which the forest grows. Examples of inventory objectives include estimation of volume or value of timber on a tract of land, number of deer per square mile, habitat quality for quail, presence of endangered plants or animals, amount of fuel present, number of miles of road, types of soil series, and almost any other characteristic that would be of interest to forest managers and planners. This book will focus on methods for conducting these and other types of inventories.

Why do foresters conduct inventories? The preceding list of example objectives gives some hints. When timber is bought or sold, both buyer and seller need a good estimate of the volume or value of timber present. A year after trees are planted, a regeneration inventory is often conducted to determine whether enough trees survived to classify the planting as a success. Management inventories are conducted to estimate stand density or volume and the information is then used to decide how the stand will be managed in the future. Inventories may be conducted to estimate growth and may then be the basis for management planning or lease fees. Similarly, wildlife inventories may be the source of information for hunting leases. Inventories to determine the presence or absence of threatened or endangered species may have a profound effect on future management. The key that links all of these different inventories is information. Inventories serve as the source of information for decision making. They have been, and will continue to be, a necessary activity for foresters.

Any forest landowner, including government agencies, private individuals, and corporations, must decide how to manage that land. Their objectives may differ greatly, but to make rational decisions they must all have information. How much timber or how many quail are present? If a specified level of harvest is implemented, is it sustainable? If not, what level is sustainable? Under various management regimes, what cash flows would be generated? All of these questions require information on what quantities of various resources are present and how fast they are increasing or decreasing. An inventory can provide this information.

Inventory in a retail business is an accounting of goods on hand. The process in a grocery store, for example, consists of listing the names of all items for sale in the store and counting the number of each item. This procedure is called a 100% inventory because every item in the store is counted. The entire inventory process takes place within the store, an area of at most several thousand square feet.

Contrast this business inventory to a forest inventory that routinely takes place over several hundred to several thousand acres. The items being inventoried (trees, animals, and so on) are biological organisms and are not identical. They must be individually measured rather than counted. A 1000-acre forest could easily contain 500,000 trees. A 100% inventory on such a tract is not economically or practically feasible.

The alternative to a 100% inventory is a sample. Sampling is the process of obtaining information by examining only a portion of the whole. It is certainly not a process unique to forestry. Probably the highest-profile samples are those referred to as polls, which are usually conducted prior to elections. The poll is actually a sample. Some voters are asked how they intend to vote, and the poll results reflect their answers. Marketing firms conduct samples to predict the population acceptance of new products. Sampling, then, is a process that affects all of us, directly or indirectly, every day.

As much as sampling is used, it may still cause uneasiness because information is collected on only a portion of the whole. What if the portion does not really look, act, or answer the way the whole would? We intuitively feel that the risk of becoming misinformed is much smaller from a 100% inventory than from a sample. In actuality, depending on factors that will be described for each technique throughout this book, sampling may provide quite accurate values from a very small portion of the whole. In addition, sampling may be more reliable than a 100% inventory since more time can be taken with a sample to make careful measurements. Because of time and financial limitations, sampling, rather than 100% inventories, will be a necessity in most forestry situations when inventory information is needed. The various structures of forests and stands to be inventoried, and different objectives for different inventories, led to the development of different sampling methods. The underlying objective of any forester, or anyone who must use information to make decisions, should be to choose the sampling method or combination of sampling methods that will result in the most efficient collection of reliable information.

Sampling methods are presented beginning in Chapter 3 with systematic and simple random sampling. Chapter 2 contains a review of statistics with which the reader should be familiar. Those readers with a good statistical background may wish to examine only the section on notation (2.8) in Chapter 2 before moving directly to Chapter 3. Chapter 4 introduces the reader to unequal probability sampling with point sampling. Chapter 5 discusses stratified sampling. Chapters 6 and 7 cover the use of auxiliary variables to aid in estimation. Ratio and regression estimation are presented in Chapter 6. Double sampling, a method underutilized in forestry, is the focus of discussion in Chapter 7. Chapter 8 discusses methods for sampling large acreages and includes a discussion of cluster sampling. Growth, both past and future, is useful for planning, and Chapter 9 presents different sampling and resulting estimation methods for estimating growth. There are sampling methods for use when the population to be inventoried is difficult to define; these methods are the focus of Chapter 10. Finally, Chapter 11 presents commonly used inventory methods for evaluating wildlife population sizes.

It would be convenient if there were one sampling method that was so flexible and so efficient that it could be used regardless of the forest type and inventory objective. Unfortunately, that is not the case in forest inventory. As each sampling method is covered, its advantages and disadvantages are discussed to provide insight into when and where that particular method should be used to provide efficient estimates. Objective methods for comparing different sampling designs are also presented.

A REVIEW OF NECESSARY STATISTICS AND NOTATION

Forest inventory involves the direct application of statistical methods. This chapter is a review of basic, necessary statistical methods.

2.1 SUMMATION NOTATION

Most forest inventory estimates are calculated by adding appropriate values (such as tree heights). A shorthand notation has been developed to indicate which operations must be carried out and which numbers should be summed. This notation is used throughout this book. Assume that y_1 is the tree height for tree 1, y_2 is the tree height for tree 2, and so on. Then $\sum_{i=1}^{n} y_i$ means sum up all of the tree heights beginning with tree 1 and ending with tree n. If there were a total of four trees, $\sum_{i=1}^{4} y_i = (y_1 + y_2 + y_3 + y_4)$. This summation notation can also be used to indicate other operations with a variable. For example, $\sum_{i=1}^{n} y_i^2$ indicates first to square each value and then to add them up. Again, if $n = 4$, $\sum_{i=1}^{4} y_i^2 = (y_1^2 + y_2^2 + y_3^2 + y_4^2)$.

Parentheses are sometimes used to change the order of the operations: $\left(\sum_{i=1}^{n} y_i\right)^2$ indicates first to sum up the values of y from 1 to n and then to square the sum.

We may sometimes have two variables, each associated with the same subscript. For example, y_i might be the height of tree i as before, and x_i might be the diameter of tree i. The notation $x_i y_i$ means multiply the diameter of tree i by the height of tree i. Summation notation may be used as shorthand to indicate various operations with the two variables. Let $n = 4$:

$$\sum_{i=1}^{4} x_i y_i = (x_1 y_1 + x_2 y_2 + x_3 y_3 + x_4 y_4)$$

$$\sum_{i=1}^{4} x_i \sum_{i=1}^{4} y_i = (x_1 + x_2 + x_3 + x_4)\,(y_1 + y_2 + y_3 + y_4)$$

Another common occurrence is to have two subscripts, such as i and j, on the same variable. For example, y_{ij} might represent the height on tree j in stand type i. Assume that there are two stand types ($i = 1, 2$) and four trees in each type ($j = 1, 2, 3, 4$). Summation notation would be used as follows to indicate these operations:

$$\sum_{i=1}^{2} \sum_{j=1}^{4} y_{ij} = (y_{11} + y_{12} + y_{13} + y_{14} + y_{21} + y_{22} + y_{23} + y_{24})$$

$$\sum_{i=1}^{2} \sum_{j=1}^{4} y_{ij}^2 = (y_{11}^2 + y_{12}^2 + y_{13}^2 + y_{14}^2 + y_{21}^2 + y_{22}^2 + y_{23}^2 + y_{24}^2)$$

$$\left(\sum_{i=1}^{2} \sum_{j=1}^{4} y_{ij}\right)^2 = (y_{11} + y_{12} + y_{13} + y_{14} + y_{21} + y_{22} + y_{23} + y_{24})^2$$

If there is another variable, x_{ij}, then summation notation could be used to denote

$$\sum_{i=1}^{2} \sum_{j=1}^{4} x_{ij} y_{ij} = x_{11} y_{11} + x_{12} y_{12} + x_{13} y_{13} + x_{14} y_{14} + x_{21} y_{21} + x_{22} y_{22} + x_{23} y_{23} + x_{24} y_{24}$$

Note that in all of these cases, the first, or outer, summation variable is set at its first value (1 in this case) and then the second, or inner, summation goes through its entire range (1 to 4 in this case) before the first summation moves to its next value.

EXAMPLE 2.1.1

Assume we have 2 variables x and y with the following values:

i	x_i	y_i
1	22	162
2	34	199
3	51	109
4	16	254
5	39	201

$$\begin{aligned}\sum_{i=1}^{5} x_i &= x_1 + x_2 + x_3 + x_4 + x_5 \\ &= 22 + 34 + 51 + 16 + 39 \\ &= 162\end{aligned}$$

$$\begin{aligned}\sum_{i=1}^{5} y_i &= y_1 + y_2 + y_3 + y_4 + y_5 \\ &= 162 + 199 + 109 + 254 + 201 \\ &= 925\end{aligned}$$

$$\begin{aligned}\sum_{i=1}^{5} x_i y_i &= x_1y_1 + x_2y_2 + x_3y_3 + x_4y_4 + x_5y_5 \\ &= 22(162) + 34(199) + 51(109) + 16(254) + 39(201) \\ &= 27{,}792\end{aligned}$$

$$\begin{aligned}\sum_{i=1}^{5} x_i^2 &= x_1^2 + x_2^2 + x_3^2 + x_4^2 + x_5^2 \\ &= (22)^2 + (34)^2 + (51)^2 + (16)^2 + (39)^2 \\ &= 6018\end{aligned}$$

$$\begin{aligned}\sum_{i=1}^{5} y_i^2 &= y_1^2 + y_2^2 + y_3^2 + y_4^2 + y_5^2 \\ &= (162)^2 + (199)^2 + (109)^2 + (254)^2 + (201)^2 \\ &= 182{,}643\end{aligned}$$

$$\begin{aligned}\left(\sum_{i=1}^{5} x_i\right)\left(\sum_{i=1}^{5} y_i\right) &= (x_1 + x_2 + x_3 + x_4 + x_5)\,(y_1 + y_2 + y_3 + y_4 + y_5) \\ &= (22 + 34 + 51 + 16 + 39)\,(162 + 199 + 109 + 254 + 201) \\ &= (162)\,(925) \\ &= 149{,}850\end{aligned}$$

$$\left(\sum_{i=1}^{5} x_i\right)^2 = (x_1 + x_2 + x_3 + x_4 + x_5)^2$$
$$= (22 + 34 + 51 + 16 + 39)^2$$
$$= (162)^2$$
$$= 26{,}244$$

$$\left(\sum_{i=1}^{5} y_i\right)^2 = (y_1 + y_2 + y_3 + y_4 + y_5)^2$$
$$= (162 + 199 + 109 + 254 + 201)^2$$
$$= (925)^2$$
$$= 855{,}625$$

2.2 BASIC SAMPLING DEFINITIONS

A *population* is a collection of elements about which information is desired. The *sample* is the portion of the population that is examined to make inferences about the population. The population and the sample should be defined using the same elements or units. Consider a 100-acre pine stand. The element or unit being measured might be an individual tree and the value being measured on each tree could be tree volume. The population would be all tree volumes in the 100-acre stand. With the population defined as individual tree volumes, sampling would consist of selecting individual trees and measuring them to obtain their volumes. Rather than consider the individual tree as the unit being measured, the 100-acre stand could theoretically be divided into 1000 plots, each 1⁄10 acre in size. The volume of all trees on each 1⁄10-acre plot could be summed to obtain a plot volume. The population would then consist of 1000 plot volumes and sampling would be conducted by selecting plots from the 1000 available and measuring trees to obtain plot volumes. In this situation the plot is the unit by which both the population and the sample are defined.

There are no limits to the size of a population. Population size is determined entirely by the collection of elements about which information is desired. If the average diameter of the seven trees in a backyard is desired, the diameters of those seven trees constitute a population. If average volume per acre of slash pine (*Pinus elliotti* Engelm.) plantations in the coastal plain of Georgia is desired, then the aggregate of volumes per acre of slash pine in that region define a population.

Defining the population in the same units as those to be selected in the sample facilitates both selecting units from the population for inclusion in the sample and projecting from the sample estimates to the entire population. If the sampling will consist of selecting and measuring individual trees, then the population is defined in terms of individual trees. If sampling will consist of selecting fixed-area plots and measuring plot characteristics, then the population is defined in terms of plots. The units in which the population is defined and that are available to be selected in the sample are called *sampling units.*

A *sampling frame* is a list of all the sampling units in the population from which the sample will be selected. The type of information needed about the population will usually dictate the units in which the population is defined. If some characteristic per unit area (such as volume per acre) is desired, it is sensible to define the population in units that represent area rather than individual trees. If, on the other hand, some characteristic per tree is required, it is sensible to define the population in units of individual trees. There will always be a sampling frame, but it may sometimes be difficult to specify. For example, if a population is defined as sweetgum (*Liquidambar styraciflua* L.) sprouts in a 10-acre clearcut, and the individual sweetgum sprout is defined as the sampling unit, then, for many stands where sweetgum is common, it is impossible to write down a sampling frame simply because of the size (number of sampling units) of the population. Similarly, a list of individual trees in a 100-acre harvest would be very difficult to obtain.

A *parameter* is a population characteristic. It is the value that would be obtained for the characteristic of the population of interest if every sampling unit in the population were measured. The average tons of biomass per acre, the proportion of seedlings infected with a fungus in a nursery, the total number of trees in a forest, and the variability among units in a population are examples of population parameters.

The general objective of any sample is to estimate one or more population parameters. The value of the parameter as estimated from the sample is referred to as the *sample estimate* or sometimes simply as the *estimate.* It is always the sampler's hope to obtain sample estimates that are close to the actual population parameter values. Such estimates are said to be *accurate.* In fact it is usually very difficult to determine whether or not an estimate is accurate because the population parameter is unknown.

A sample estimate of a population parameter is calculated using a *sample estimator* in conjunction with sample data obtained from the population of interest. A sample estimator is simply a mathematical formula that is used to condense or summarize the sample data into a single number, which is used as an estimate of a population parameter. For example, the most common estimator for a population mean, μ, is the simple arithmetic average, $\bar{y}$, given by the formula

$$\bar{y} = \frac{1}{n} \sum_{i=1}^{n} y_i$$

where:

y_i = unit value of the ith sampling unit

n = number of sampling units in the sample

Accuracy and precision refer to the sample estimator. This is so because once a sample is taken from a population and the sample estimator is used to calculate a sample estimate, it is almost 100% certain that the sample estimate is not equal to the parameter it is estimating. Although this fact is disconcerting, it is actually inconsequential as long as there is a very high probability of being very close to the true population value. For example, if ten 1/10-acre sample plots from a 10-acre stand of trees are measured and the average volume per acre represented by this sample is calculated, it seems intuitively reasonable that the estimate, based on only ten 1/10-acre plots, is not going to equal exactly the true average volume per acre in this 10-acre stand; again, only a portion of the whole stand is measured. If we accept the fact that a sample estimate will never equal the population parameter that it estimates, then a criterion is needed to determine how "good" the estimate is. The "goodness" of an estimate is defined and discussed in terms of the estimator that gives rise to the estimate.

Sample estimators are said to be *precise* if they produce sample estimates that cluster together tightly about their own average. That is, if many samples are drawn from a given population and a sample estimate is obtained for each sample using the sample estimator, then a precise estimator will lead to a tight cluster of sample estimates. It is useful to think of a target bull's-eye as a population parameter and individual shots at the target as sample estimates of the parameter. A *precise* shooter is one who can group shots closely together, as in Figures 2.2.1*a* or 2.2.1*b*. An imprecise shooter is one whose shots scatter all over the target with individual shots ranging relatively far from the center of the grouping, as in Figures 2.2.1*c* and 2.2.1*d*. An *accurate* shooter is defined as a shooter whose shots cluster relatively tight around the bull's-eye, as in Figure 2.2.1*b*. A shooter is said to have a bias if shots cluster around a point on the target other than the bull's-eye (Figures 2.2.1*a* and 2.2.1*d*). A shooter may be inaccurate because of

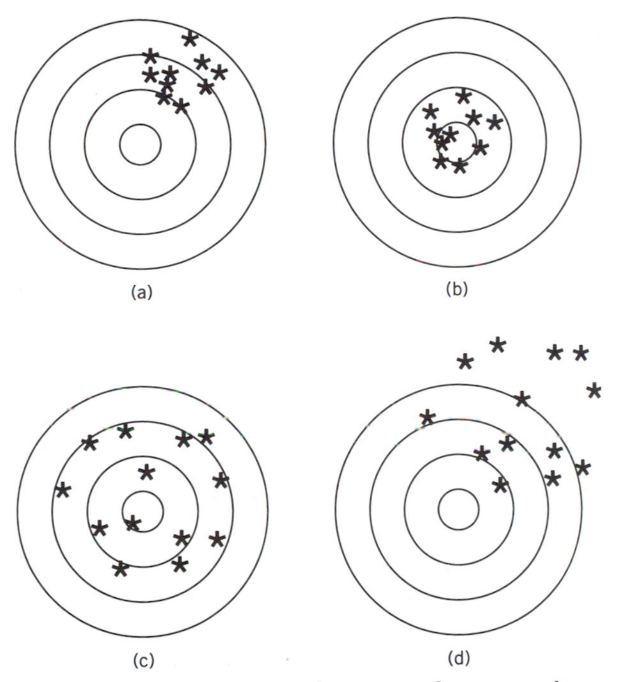

Figure 2.2.1 Precision and accuracy of a target shooter and a sample estimator. Assume that the target bull's-eye corresponds to the population parameter being estimated, and the individual shots are estimates of the parameter resulting from different samples drawn from the population under study. (a) Precise, biased. (b) Precise, unbiased (accurate). (c) Imprecise, unbiased. (d) Imprecise, biased.

imprecision (Figures 2.2.1*c* and 2.2.1*d*). Accuracy occurs only with both precision and unbiasedness (Figure 2.2.1*b*).

A direct correspondence exists between the precision and accuracy of a target shooter and the precision and accuracy of a sample estimator. Precise estimators produce tightly grouped estimates from sample to sample. Accurate estimators produce estimates that are tightly grouped about the true parameter (bull's-eye) from sample to sample. Biased estimators produce estimates around a value other than the true parameter value. Ideally, accurate estimators should be used. That is, estimators that produce sample estimates that cluster tightly around the population parameter being estimated are preferred. Most of the estimators used for the various sampling strategies discussed in the following chapters are accurate estimators. In statistical jargon, they are *unbiased* (that is, they cluster around the true value of the parameter being estimated) and have minimum variance (that is, their spread or cluster size is small compared with other estimators). Even though estimators with these desirable properties are used, there are other factors associated with sampling that will affect how close a specific estimate (obtained from a given sample) will be to the true population value. These factors are referred to as errors. Two major types of errors can be made.

Sampling errors are errors that occur because the sample units selected from the population are not representative of the population. This is the error instinctively feared when only a portion (sample) of the population of interest is measured. Assuming that the value of the population parameter was known, the sampling error for any one sample could be measured as the difference between the parameter value and the sample estimate (assuming no nonsampling errors were made). Three factors affect the sampling error: sample size, variability of the units in the population, and sampling method. It seems reasonable to expect that the larger the sample, the better is the probability that the sample could be representative of the population. If the entire population were sampled (a 100% inventory), there would be no sampling error. Similarly, if the units in the population differ from each other by large amounts (the variability between units is high), there is a smaller probability of obtaining a representative sample with any given sample size. Finally, some sampling methods can make selection of a representative sample a much higher probability. Stratified sampling, discussed in Chapter 5, is a sampling method that makes selecting a representative sample for a given sample size more probable.

It is possible to make errors that are not related to sampling. Not surprisingly, they are called *nonsampling errors.* These errors are due to mistakes in work. They can and do occur in measurements of 100% of the population units (complete enumeration) as well as samples. In fact, because of closer supervision and fewer measurements, sampling may result in fewer nonsampling errors than complete enumeration (100% inventories). If the mistakes are random occurrences such as writing down a wrong number, the resulting error is called a random nonsampling error. It is hoped that there will be as many low errors as high errors, and these will average out. The precision of the estimator will be decreased, but it should still be unbiased if it would have been unbiased without the mistakes. Nonrandom errors are errors that result from systematic error. Foresters measure the diameter of trees at 4.5 ft above ground level, but they seldom take the time to measure this height. If a forester is tall and systematically measures tree diameters above 4.5 ft, the result is a nonrandom nonsampling error. This type of error leads to estimator bias. The best way to decrease nonsampling errors is to train and educate field personnel.

2.3 MEAN

The mean is the arithmetic average. Two means will be discussed, a parameter and a sample estimator of the parameter. The population mean, designated μ, is the arithmetic average of all sampling units in the population:

$$\mu = \frac{\sum_{i=1}^{N} y_i}{N}$$

where:

μ = population mean

y_i = value of ith sampling unit

N = total number of all sampling units in the population

Another mean of interest is the arithmetic mean from a sample:

$$\bar{y} = \frac{\sum_{i=1}^{n} y_i}{n}$$

where:

$\bar{y}$ = sample mean

n = total number of sampling units in this particular sample

y_i = value of ith sampling unit

In general, $\bar{y}$ is a sample estimator of μ, the population parameter. For a particular sample of size n, the resulting value of $\bar{y}$ is the sample estimate. Note that there can be many different samples of the same sample size.

EXAMPLE 2.3.1

The following numbers represent the tree heights for all trees in a neighbor's backyard. If the average height of trees in her backyard is of interest, these five tree heights constitute a population. Of course, for a population of this size the heights of all trees in the population could be measured (a 100% inventory). However, if we decide to sample the population by measuring two tree heights, how many different samples are there, and what are the different estimators of μ?

The five tree heights are 37, 42, 55, 50, and 46 ft. There are 10 possible samples of size $n = 2$. The resulting samples and sample estimates of the mean are as follows:

$$37,42 \quad \bar{y} = \frac{37 + 42}{2} = 39.5$$

$$37,55 \quad \bar{y} = \frac{37 + 55}{2} = 46.0$$

$$37,50 \quad \bar{y} = \frac{37 + 50}{2} = 43.5$$

$$37,46 \quad \bar{y} = \frac{37 + 46}{2} = 41.5$$

$$42,55 \quad \bar{y} = \frac{42 + 55}{2} = 48.5$$

$$42,50 \quad \bar{y} = \frac{42 + 50}{2} = 46.0$$

$$42,46 \quad \bar{y} = \frac{42 + 46}{2} = 44.0$$

$$55,50 \quad \bar{y} = \frac{55 + 50}{2} = 52.5$$

$$55,46 \quad \bar{y} = \frac{55 + 46}{2} = 50.5$$

$$50,46 \quad \bar{y} = \frac{50 + 46}{2} = 48.0$$

The population mean μ is

$$\mu = \frac{37 + 42 + 55 + 50 + 46}{5} = 46.0$$

In this small population, two of the sample estimates actually were exactly the same as the population parameter. In a population of the size commonly encountered in forestry, the probability that a sample estimate will exactly equal the population parameter is essentially zero.

Is this estimator unbiased? Obviously, not all of the sample estimates are equal to the population mean, but note that the question refers to the estimator, $\bar{y}$, not the individual estimates. If the estimator is unbiased, then the average over all possible sample estimates should equal the population parameter. This would indicate that there is no tendency for sample estimates to cluster around a number other than the population mean. In most sampling situations, we cannot calculate all possible sample estimates, but in this small population it is possible. The average of the sample estimates is

$$\frac{39.5 + 46.0 + 43.5 + 41.5 + 48.5 + 46.0 + 44.0 + 52.5 + 50.5 + 48.0}{10}$$

$$= \frac{460}{10} = 46.0$$

Since $\mu = 46.0$, the estimator is an unbiased estimator.

2.4 VARIANCE

Virtually all biological populations exhibit variability. This means that not all unit values in the population are the same. For example, not all plot volumes in a stand will be the same, and not all tree diameters or heights will be the same. Just as a population will have a mean, μ, it will also have a variance, designated σ_y^2:

$$\sigma_y^2 = \sum_{i=1}^{N} \frac{(y_i - \mu)^2}{N}$$

If all of the values (y_i) in the population were the same, they would all equal μ. The difference in the numerator of σ_y^2 would then be zero. In biological populations this essentially never happens. The sample variance, an estimator of the population variance, is calculated as

$$S_y^2 = \sum_{i=1}^{n} \frac{(y_i - \bar{y})^2}{n-1} = \frac{\sum_{i=1}^{n} y_i^2 - \frac{\left(\sum_{i=1}^{n} y_i\right)^2}{n}}{n-1}$$

where:

$\bar{y}$ = arithmetic mean of y_i

n = sample size

Note that unlike the population mean and its estimator, there is a discrepancy between the population variance formula and the sample variance formula. In the sample variance, the denominator is $n - 1$. The 1 is subtracted because we had to estimate μ, in the numerator, with $\bar{y}$. In statistics, $n - 1$ is referred to as the degrees of freedom. Use of $n - 1$ makes S_y^2 an unbiased estimator of the population variance. The two expressions for S_y^2 in the equation are algebraically equivalent, but the one on the right is preferred for computations.

EXAMPLE 2.4.1

A sample of 10 tree diameters (y_i) was measured from a population of 100 trees. The measurements were as follows (in inches):

$$10,\ 9,\ 9,\ 10,\ 8,\ 9,\ 8,\ 7,\ 10,\ 9$$

$$\sum_{i=1}^{10} y_i = 10 + 9 + 9 + \cdots + 9 = 89$$

$$\sum_{i=1}^{10} y_i^2 = 10^2 + 9^2 + 9^2 + \cdots + 9^2 = 801$$

$$S_y^2 = \frac{801 - \frac{(89)^2}{10}}{9} = 0.988889 \text{ in.}^2$$

Note that the units associated with variance are square units (in Example 2.4.1, square inches). To return the units to inches, take the square root of the variance, $\sqrt{S_y^2} = S_y$. This is called the standard deviation among sampling units. In this example, $\sqrt{S_y^2} = \sqrt{0.98889} = 0.99443$ in. This number is a measure of how much the unit values (tree diameters in this case) of the sample vary from the mean. It will be used to estimate the dispersion of the unit values in the population about the true mean. The sample variance S_y^2 is the sample estimator of the population variance σ_y^2, and the sample standard deviation S_y is the sample estimator of the population standard deviation σ_y. Notice that it takes a sample of at least size $n = 2$ to calculate S_y^2; otherwise, $(n - 1)$ in the denominator of S_y^2 is 0, which is undefined.

2.5 STANDARD ERROR OF AN ESTIMATE AND CONFIDENCE INTERVALS

Refer back to Example 2.3.1. There were 10 possible estimates from a population of size 5 based on samples of size $n = 2$. It is possible to calculate the number of possible samples for any population size and sample size using the theory of combinations. C_n^N is notation for the combination of N things taken n at a time. The combination formula makes use of factorials. A factorial of any integer is that integer multiplied by all smaller integers down to 1. For example, $5! = 5 \times 4 \times 3 \times 2 \times 1$. Note, $0!$ is defined to be 1.

$$C_n^N = \frac{N!}{n!\,(N-n)!}$$

where:

N = number of sampling units in the population

n = number of sampling units in the sample

In Example 2.3.1, $N = 5$, $n = 2$, and

$$C_2^5 = \frac{5!}{2!(5-2)!} = \frac{5 \times 4 \times 3 \times 2 \times 1}{(2 \times 1)(3 \times 2 \times 1)}$$
$$= \frac{5 \times 4 \times 3!}{2 \times 3!} = \frac{5 \times 4}{2} = 10$$

Now consider a large population of $N = 100$ tree diameters (unit values). If, rather than sampling, a complete census of the 100 trees were taken, there would be only one possible value for the mean, the population mean, μ. Rather than measuring all 100 trees, what if a sample of size $n = 99$ were chosen? How many different samples of size 99 are there? There are ($C_{99}^{100} = 100!/(99!1!) = (100 \times 99!)/(1 \times 99!) =$) 100 different samples of size 99. This is intuitively easy to see; tree number 1 could be left out of the sample for one sample, tree number 2 for a second sample, and so on. Now, will the sample mean calculated for the different samples be the same? No; as demonstrated in Example 2.3.1, this rarely happens. The point is that the sample estimate of the population mean depends on the particular sample. In most inventories only one sample will be taken. If all possible samples of size 99 were taken and the sample mean for each sample were calculated, the variance and standard deviation of 100 sample mean values could be calculated. This standard deviation of means is given a special name; the standard error of the mean. It represents the variability of the different sample means if the population is repeatedly sampled. As such it represents the dispersion in estimates and it is therefore useful as an estimate of the sampling error.

Now consider taking a more reasonable 10% sample from this population of size 100. How many possible different samples are there?

$$C_{10}^{100} = \frac{100!}{10!\ 90!} = 1.731031 \times 10^{13}$$

Obviously, there is no way to take every possible sample of size 10 to calculate the standard error of these means. Think, though, about how this relationship should work. If all but one tree diameter is included, all of the calculated sample means for each sample of size 99 should be very close together, and the calculated standard error of the means should be small. With $n = 10$, however, many samples will have no trees in common. One sample will be for the 10 smallest trees. Another will be for the 10 largest trees. If the standard deviation (standard error) among these means were calculated, it should obviously be larger than the standard error among means when $n = 99$. There will be more variability among sample means based on the smaller sample size.

EXAMPLE 2.5.1

Calculate the standard error of the mean using the sample estimates with $n = 2$ given in Example 2.3.1.

$$\sigma_{\bar{y}}^2 = \frac{\sum_{i=1}^{m} \bar{y}_i^2 - \frac{\left(\sum_{i=1}^{m} \bar{y}_i\right)^2}{m}}{m}$$

where:

$\bar{y}_i$ = sample estimate of the mean for sample i

m = total number of sample estimates

$\sigma_{\bar{y}}^2$ = the variance of the means

The 10 means were 39.5, 46.0, 43.5, 41.5, 48.5, 46.0, 44.0, 52.5, 50.5, and 48.0.

$$\sum_{i=1}^{10} \bar{y}_i = 460$$

$$\sum_{i=1}^{10} \bar{y}_i^2 = 21{,}305.5$$

$$\sigma_{\bar{y}}^2 = \frac{21{,}305.5 - \frac{(460)^2}{10}}{10} = 14.55$$

The standard error is the standard deviation of means, so it is obtained by taking the square root of the variance of means.

$$\sigma_{\bar{y}} = 3.81$$

Now, what if the same population of five trees is sampled with $n = 4$? There should be $C_4^5 = \frac{5!}{4!1!} = \frac{5 \times 4!}{4!} = 5$ sample estimates:

$$37,42,55,50 \quad \bar{y} = \frac{37 + 42 + 55 + 50}{4} = 46.0$$

$$37,55,50,46 \quad \bar{y} = \frac{37 + 55 + 50 + 46}{4} = 47.0$$

$$37,42,50,46 \quad \bar{y} = \frac{37 + 42 + 50 + 46}{4} = 43.75$$

$$37,42,55,46 \quad \bar{y} = \frac{37 + 42 + 55 + 46}{4} = 45.0$$

$$42,55,50,46 \quad \bar{y} = \frac{42 + 55 + 50 + 46}{4} = 48.25$$

The variance of the mean is

$$\sigma_{\bar{y}}^2 = \frac{\sum_{i=1}^{m} \bar{y}_i^2 - \frac{\left(\sum_{i=1}^{m} \bar{y}_i\right)^2}{m}}{m}$$

as before, but now $m = 5$:

$$\sigma_{\bar{y}}^2 = \frac{10{,}592.125 - \frac{(230)^2}{5}}{5} = 2.425$$

$$\sigma_{\bar{y}} = 1.56$$

The variability among sample means if the population of five tree heights is repeatedly sampled with $n = 4$ is less than one-half the variability among sample means in repeated sampling when $n = 2$. Thus the anticipated trends holds—the larger the sample size, the less variability is expected among the possible sample estimates.

Variability among unit values is also important in how large the standard error of the mean is for a given sample size. In the 100-tree-diameter example, if 99 of the 100 trees had the same diameter and one was different, the standard deviation would be very small. Of the 100 samples of size $n = 99$, ninety-nine would have the same value and so the standard error would be small. By contrast, if each of the 100 trees had different diameters, the population variance would be higher. In repeated sampling, the variability of sample estimates would also be higher. The more variable the population, the larger the standard error would become for a given sample size. These concepts are shown graphically in Figure 2.5.1.

The concept of standard error makes sense only in repeated sampling since it is the standard deviation of different sample estimates. It takes a sample size of at least $n = 2$ to calculate a standard deviation. Likewise, it takes at least two sample means to calculate a standard error. As previously stated, in most forest inventory situations only one sample will be conducted. If this is the case, how can standard error be estimated, and if it can, what value is it to foresters?

Standard error can be estimated from only one sample through use of one of the most important theorems in statistics, the Central Limit Theorem (CLT). Among other things, the CLT states that for any population with finite mean μ and variance σ_y^2 (all populations in forest inventory would apply), the standard error can be estimated as $\sigma_y/\sqrt{n}$. With a reasonably large sample to estimate σ_y using S_y, the sample standard error is denoted $S_{\bar{y}}$ and can be estimated by $S_{\bar{y}} = S_y/\sqrt{n}$.

The CLT also states that the sample estimates of the means will follow a normal distribution with mean μ and standard deviation $\sigma_y/\sqrt{n}$. The normal distribution is mound shaped and symmetrical around the population mean (Figure 2.5.2). It is

Figure 2.5.1 General impact of population variability and sample size on spread of sample means in samples. Y_S refers to the smallest unit value in the population; Y_L is the largest unit value in the population. $\bar{Y}_S$ and $\bar{Y}_L$ are the smallest and largest sample estimates of μ, the true population mean, respectively.

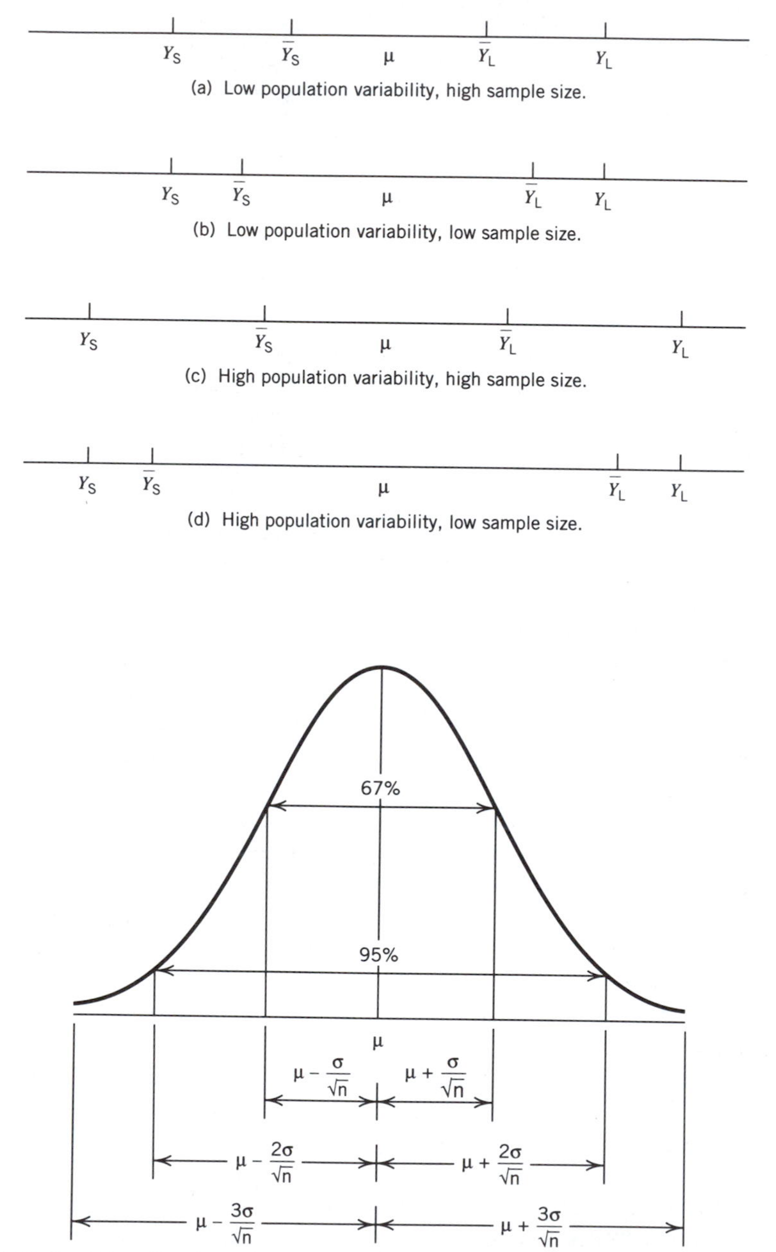

Figure 2.5.2 Distribution of sample means in repeated sampling of the same population.

important to emphasize that the population being sampled does not have to have a normal distribution. The population could have any distribution, even a distribution with more than one mound or one that begins higher and trends lower with no mound. The shape of the normal distribution describes the frequency of occurrence of the sample means based on different samples. The center of the normal distribution is the true population mean, μ. Since this is where the peak of the distribution occurs, the highest frequency of occurrence of sample means is around the true mean, μ. With increasing distance from μ in either direction, the frequency of occurrence decreases. The normal distribution has been widely studied, and it is well known that approximately 67% of the sample means lie within one standard error of the true mean, approximately 95% within two standard errors of the true mean, and approximately 99% within 2.6 standard errors of the true mean (Figure 2.5.2). Obviously, if only one sample is conducted and one sample mean is obtained, that particular sample mean could be very near the true mean or it could be two or three standard errors removed from the true mean.

This provides insight into why foresters should want to know the standard error. If it is known that 95% of sample means lie within two standard errors of the true mean and if the standard error can be estimated from a sample, then the interval in which the true mean should lie can be quantified. This interval is called a 95% confidence interval.

For samples of size $n > 30$, confidence intervals can be constructed as follows:

$$\bar{y} \pm Z\, S_{\bar{y}}$$

where Z is a value from the normal distribution and all other variables are as previously defined.

Values for Z vary depending on the probability level. For 95% confidence limits, $Z = 1.96$. This level of confidence is used often, and since 1.96 is very nearly 2, a 95% confidence interval can be approximated quickly by doubling the standard error and then adding that value and subtracting that value from the sample mean, $\bar{y}$. Throughout this book, 2 will be used to approximate the Z value for 95% confidence. For small samples ($n \leq 30$), a t distribution and t value apply rather than a normal distribution. Again, though, the t value for 95% is very near 2, and thus 2 is used as an approximation.

Assume that an inventory (sample) was conducted in a stand of trees with $n = 64$ and the average per acre dollar value was estimated to be \$1500 with a standard deviation of \$2000. Using the CLT, the standard error of the mean is estimated as $\$2000/\sqrt{64} = \$250$. An approximate 95% confidence interval for the true population mean is

$$\begin{aligned} &\bar{y} \pm Z\, S_{\bar{y}} \\ &\$1500 \pm 2(\$250) \\ &\$1500 \pm \$500 \\ &\$1000 \text{ to } \$2000 \end{aligned}$$

What does a confidence interval mean? A confidence interval has meaning only in a repeated sampling context. If a population is repeatedly sampled, 95% of all possible random samples will produce 95% confidence intervals that contain the true population mean. We will call these "good" samples. Five percent of all possible random samples will produce 95% confidence intervals that will not contain the true population mean. Since only one sample will be taken and only one confidence interval will be constructed, we can never be absolutely certain that the one confidence interval we construct contains the true mean. Since 95% of all confidence intervals constructed from different samples do contain the true mean, the true mean is probably in the interval. What would cause the true mean not to be in the interval? The answer is *sampling error.* If, by chance, all of the small values or all of the large values showed up in a particular sample, the confidence interval constructed could fall below or above the true population mean. This is not to suggest that sampling error occurs only if the confidence interval does not contain the true parameter value. In fact, sampling error is present in every sample since the chance of estimating the population value exactly is virtually zero. In most samples, however, the sampling error is small enough that the interval constructed does contain the true parameter value. In only a small percentage of samples will the true value not be in the confidence interval constructed.

EXAMPLE 2.5.2

Suppose we have a population of five sampling units. The values of the sampling units are

$$8, 10, 12, 14, 15$$

Since all sampling unit values in this population are known, the true mean (μ) per sampling unit can be calculated:

$$\mu = 11.8$$

For a population of size 5, there are only 10 possible random samples of size $n = 2$ which can be chosen. Below are listed each possible sample, its mean, its approximate lower 95% confidence limit (LCL $= \bar{y} - 2S_{\bar{y}}$), and its approximate upper 95% confidence limit (UCL $= \bar{y} + 2S_{\bar{y}}$):

Sample	Sample Unit Values	$\bar{y}$	LCL	UCL
1	8,10	9	7	11
2	8,12	10	6	14
3	8,14	11	5	17
4	8,15	11.5	4.5	18.5
5	10,12	11	9	13
6	10,14	12	8	16
7	10,15	12.5	7.5	17.5
8	12,14	13	11	15
9	12,15	13.5	10.5	16.5
10	14,15	14.5	13.5	15.5

Note that all samples produced a different sample estimate ($\bar{y}$) of the true population mean μ (recall $\mu = 11.8$). Further note that all confidence intervals except two, those for samples 1 and 10, contained the true mean value. Thus in hindsight we can say that samples 1 and 10 are "bad samples," that is, the sampling error is so large that they are not representative of the population. The bad sample proportion is 20% rather than 5% because the population is so small and because sample sizes less than about 30 are too small for the CLT to apply.

In practice, forest inventory populations tend to be much larger than the one in Example 2.5.2, and the true population parameters are never known (otherwise, we would not need to sample). Thus, unlike the example, we can never know when we will obtain a bad sample. When a bad sample occurs, it will not be obvious that anything is wrong. This fact must be accepted, but there is every reason to expect that the one sample taken is one of the many good samples that produce confidence intervals containing the true parameter. Note that the odds are very much in favor of obtaining a good sample.

Clearly there is no guarantee that our sample estimate is close to the population parameter. If no risk of error can be tolerated, then the only alternative is to conduct a 100% inventory. Adjusting the sample size can, however, affect the size of the confidence interval. As the sample size is increased from relatively low levels toward a 100% inventory, the standard error becomes smaller and the resulting confidence interval becomes more narrow. In the previous example, n was 64. Now let $n = 200$. The standard error is $\$2000/\sqrt{200} = \$141.43$. The 95% confidence interval is

$$\bar{y} \pm Z\, S_{\bar{y}}$$

$$\$1500 \pm 2(\$141.43)$$

$$\$1500 \pm \$282.86$$

$$\$1217.14 \text{ to } \$1782.86$$

If the sample estimate of the mean ($\bar{y}$) was chosen as the estimate of the true mean (μ), the maximum amount of error possible, assuming that the true mean is somewhere in the interval, is $2S_{\bar{y}}$ (in this example, \$282.86), one-half the width of the confidence interval. This value is sometimes called the *upper bound on the error of estimation* or simply the *bound.*

Remember that inventories are conducted to obtain information with which to make decisions. Assume that for the previous confidence interval example, a forestry procurement agent needs to estimate the average dollar value per acre within \$100 before risking an investment in the property. Assuming that the procurement agent is willing to accept the 5% chance that the confidence interval constructed does not contain the true value, the agent would still be unable to commit to the investment because the bound is \$282.86. This is far above the \$100 bound with which the procurement agent would be comfortable making his investment. With a bound so much wider than acceptable to the decision maker, the inventory information is worthless. The only alternative is to increase the sample size, thereby decreasing the standard error and the width of the bound. Evaluating the width of the confidence interval in light of the decision to be made with inventory estimates is an important reason to calculate a confidence interval.

The bound is sometimes considered the desired precision, and if it can be specified prior to inventory, it can be used to estimate how large the sample size will need to be to achieve this desired precision (a confidence interval with this half width). This procedure will be discussed for simple random sampling in Chapter 3 and for other sampling methods in the sample size section of the respective chapters.

Another way of expressing the bound is as a percentage of the parameter being estimated. That is, instead of specifying the bound in units such as cords, cubic feet, or dollars, we simply state that we would like our estimate to be within ±5%, ±10%, and so on. When expressed as a percentage, the bound is referred to as *allowable error* (AE). Sample sizes necessary to achieve desired bounds and allowable errors are calculated differently for different sampling methods. Formulas for calculating sample size will be given for the different methods in this book but all are derived from the fact that a bound is a half width of a confidence interval.

EXAMPLE 2.5.3

An inventory of a natural stand of loblolly pine was conducted, and the total volume of sawtimber was estimated to be 500,000 board feet with an associated standard error of 25,000 board feet.

1. An approximate 95% confidence interval for the board feet in this stand is

$$500{,}000 \pm 2(25{,}000)$$
$$450{,}000 \text{ bd ft to } 550{,}000 \text{ bd ft}$$

2. The upper bound on the error of estimation *(B)* is

$$B = 2(25{,}000) = 50{,}000 \text{ bd ft}$$

3. The realized allowable error (AE) (as a percentage of the estimate of the total tract board feet) is

$$\text{AE} = (100)\frac{50{,}000 \text{ bd ft}}{500{,}000 \text{ bd ft}} = 10\%$$

2.6 ESTIMATING TOTALS

In forest inventory, we are also concerned with estimating totals. Estimates of the population total (say, total tract volume or dollar value) and the standard error of the total are important estimates. To obtain an estimate of the tract total $(\hat{T})$ if the total number of sampling units and the sample mean per sampling unit are known, simply multiply the number of sampling units in the population by the sample mean. To obtain the standard error of the total ($S_{\hat{T}}$), multiply the standard error of the sample mean by the total number of sampling units.

All formulas presented in this review are for simple random sampling and are covered in greater detail in Chapter 3. Estimators for other sampling designs and estimation methods will be presented as those methods are discussed. This general method of expanding from a sampling unit to a total works for all sampling designs.

EXAMPLE 2.6.1

An inventory of a 55-acre loblolly pine stand was carried out by taking a random sample of 50 ⅕-acre sample plots. The merchantable cubic foot volume of chip-n-saw trees on each ⅕-acre sample plot was determined. The average volume per sample plot and its associated standard error are

$$\bar{y} = 510 \text{ ft}^3/\text{sampling unit}$$
$$S_{\bar{y}} = 100 \text{ ft}^3/\text{sampling unit}$$

1. How many ⅕-acre sampling units are there in the tract?

$$5 \text{ sampling units/acre} \times 55 \text{ acres} = 275 \text{ sampling units}$$

2. What is the estimate of the total cubic foot volume of chip-n-saw trees on this tract?

$$\hat{T} = 510 \text{ ft}^3/\text{sampling unit} \times 275 \text{ sampling units} = 140{,}250 \text{ ft}^3$$

3. What is the standard error of the total cubic foot volume of chip-n-saw trees on this tract?

$$S_{\hat{T}} = 100 \text{ ft}^3/\text{sampling unit} \times 275 \text{ sampling units} = 27{,}500 \text{ ft}^3$$

4. What is the approximate 95% confidence interval for the cubic foot volume of chip-n-saw trees on this tract?

$$\hat{T} \pm 2S_{\hat{T}}$$
$$140{,}250 \pm 2(27{,}500) = 85{,}250 \text{ ft}^3 \text{ to } 195{,}250 \text{ ft}^3$$

Note that this is a fairly wide confidence interval. To obtain a more precise estimate, a larger number of sample plots would be needed.

2.7 COEFFICIENT OF VARIATION

The coefficient of variation is the ratio of the standard deviation of the sampling units (S_y) to the mean, usually expressed as a percentage. If $\bar{y} = 5.3$ and $S_y = 3$, the coefficient of variation, CV, is (3/5.3)(100) = 56.3%.

The coefficient of variation puts variability on a relative basis (that is, the standard deviation relative to the mean). It is particularly useful where the variance is related to the size of the units. If we want to compare the variability in tree heights in a 20-year-old natural stand with those in a 4-year-old plantation, the data might look like this:

Natural Stand	Plantation
$\bar{y} = 40$ ft	$\bar{x} = 5.9$ ft
$S_y = 4.4$ ft	$S_x = 0.649$ ft

Obviously, the variability of the natural stand looks larger than the plantation, but actually both populations are equally variable relative to their means. Thus the coefficient of variation is often used when the variations of two or more populations are compared.

$$CV_y = \frac{4.4}{40}(100) = 11\% \qquad CV_x = \frac{0.649}{5.9}(100) = 11\%$$

2.8 NOTATION

The lack of a standard notation for describing sample and population means, totals, and variances for different sample designs makes it difficult to read and easily understand books written by different authors. This text will employ a notation that makes understanding sample estimators easy and eliminates as much confusion as possible. For any variable referred to as y (such as height, volume, or basal area) the following notation will be used:

$\bar{y}$ = sample mean per sampling unit

S_y^2 = sample variance among sampling units

S_y = sample standard deviation among sampling units, $\sqrt{S_y^2}$

$\hat{T}$ = sample estimate of population total (total tract volume)

$S_{\bar{y}}^2$ = variance of the sample mean ($\bar{y}$)

$S_{\hat{T}}^2$ = variance of the sample total ($\hat{T}$)

$S_{\bar{y}}$ = standard error of the mean ($\bar{y}$)

$S_{\hat{T}}$ = standard error of the total ($\hat{T}$)

When examining various sampling schemes, this text will use subscripts on the symbols defined above to indicate the sampling scheme. For example, the sample mean and total based on a stratified sample are denoted as follows:

$\bar{y}_{st}$ = sample mean per sampling unit from a stratified sample

$\hat{T}_{st}$ = sample estimate of the population total from a stratified sample

PROBLEMS FOR BETTER UNDERSTANDING

1. A random sample of ten 1⁄10 acre sample plots was obtained. The Scribner board foot volume of sawtimber trees for each plot was:

Plot	Volume (Scribner bd ft)
1	197
2	263
3	333
4	188
5	165
6	170
7	225
8	230
9	245
10	152

Let volume on a 1⁄10-acre plot be represented by the variable y_i.

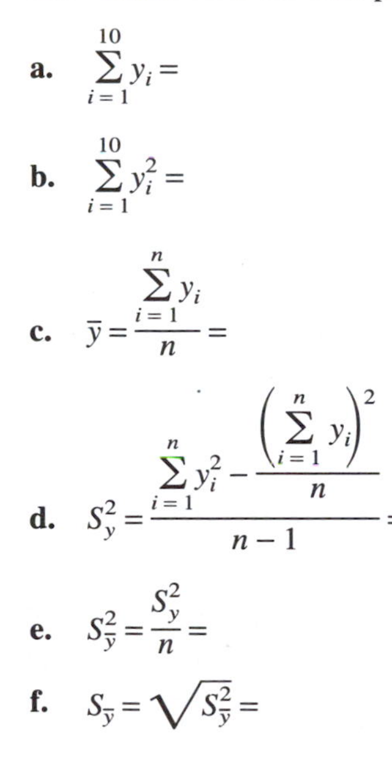

a. $\sum_{i=1}^{10} y_i =$

b. $\sum_{i=1}^{10} y_i^2 =$

c. $\bar{y} = \dfrac{\sum_{i=1}^{n} y_i}{n} =$

d. $S_y^2 = \dfrac{\sum_{i=1}^{n} y_i^2 - \dfrac{\left(\sum_{i=1}^{n} y_i\right)^2}{n}}{n-1} =$

e. $S_{\bar{y}}^2 = \dfrac{S_y^2}{n} =$

f. $S_{\bar{y}} = \sqrt{S_{\bar{y}}^2} =$

g. $CV = \frac{S_y}{\bar{y}}(100) =$

h. Discuss S_y^2, the variation among sampling units, and $S_{\bar{y}}^2$, the variation of the mean. What population parameters do these two sample statistics estimate?

2. Assume that the following data were collected:

Sample Unit	Volume (cords)
1	7
2	8
3	2
4	6
5	7
6	10
7	8
8	6
9	7
10	3

Let y_i = cords on sample unit i.

a. $\sum_{i=1}^{n} y_i =$

b. $\sum_{i=1}^{n} y_i^2 =$

c. $S_y^2 =$

d. $\bar{y} =$

e. $S_{\bar{y}} =$

f. CV =

3. Multiply the volume of each sampling unit in Problem 2 by 5. If these data were collected on ⅕-acre plots, this would serve to convert the sampling unit values (⅕-acre values) to per-acre values.

a. $\sum_{i=1}^{n} y_i =$

b. $\sum_{i=1}^{n} y_i^2 =$

c. $S_y^2 =$

d. $\bar{y} =$

e. $S_{\bar{y}} =$

f. $CV =$

g. How do the values calculated in Problem 3 compare with the corresponding quantities calculated in Problem 2?

4. The following data have been obtained for two variables on each of 12 sampling units.

Sampling Unit	y_i	x_i
1	73	30
2	50	20
3	128	60
4	170	80
5	87	40
6	108	50
7	135	60
8	69	30
9	148	70
10	132	60
11	127	50
12	62	20

Calculate the following quantities:

a. $\sum_{i=1}^{12} y_i =$

b. $\sum_{i=1}^{12} x_i =$

c. $\sum_{i=1}^{12} y_i^2 =$

d. $\sum_{i=1}^{12} x_i^2 =$

e. $\sum_{i=1}^{12} y_i x_i =$

f. $\left(\sum_{i=1}^{12} y_i\right)^2 =$

g. $\left(\sum_{i=1}^{12} x_i\right)^2 =$

h. $\left(\sum_{i=1}^{12} x_i\right)\left(\sum_{i=1}^{12} y_i\right) =$

i. $\bar{x} = \dfrac{\sum_{i=1}^{12} x_i}{12}$

j. $\bar{y} = \dfrac{\sum_{i=1}^{12} y_i}{12}$

5. Twenty-five 1/20-acre sample plots were measured for cubic foot volume of pulpwood-size trees. The data are as follows:

Plot	y_i (ft³/plot)
1	150
2	75
3	68
4	92
5	98
6	44
7	18
8	26
9	34
10	48
11	64
12	72
13	81
14	85
15	77
16	66
17	29
18	44
19	35
20	37
21	144
22	138
23	99
24	111
25	115

a. $\sum_{i=1}^{25} y_i =$ $\qquad \sum_{i=1}^{25} y_i^2 =$

b. Calculate the sample mean.

c. Calculate the variance among sample plots.

d. Calculate the variance of the mean and the standard error of the mean.

e. Calculate an approximate 95% confidence interval for the mean volume per plot.

f. What is the upper bound on the error of estimation?

g. Calculate the realized allowable error (AE).

h. Calculate the coefficient of variation (CV).

6. Explain what a 95% confidence interval means.

7. Define the following terms:

- **a.** Error of estimation
- **b.** Upper bound on the error of estimation
- **c.** Allowable error
- **d.** Coefficient of variation

8. Use a spreadsheet program or database management system to calculate the following quantities for a set of sample data containing measurements made on a variable y_i:

$$\sum_{i=1}^{n} y_i, \quad \sum_{i=1}^{n} y_i^2, \quad \bar{y}, \quad S_y^2, \quad S_{\bar{y}}, \quad \text{CV}, \quad \text{AE}$$

Test your program with data from Problems 1, 2, 4, and 5.

9. Explain the following terms:

- **a.** Sampling unit
- **b.** Sampling frame
- **c.** Population
- **d.** Sample
- **e.** Population parameter
- **f.** Sample estimator

10. Discuss the concepts of accuracy and precision in the context of sample estimators. What does repeated sampling have to do with these concepts?

11. Explain sampling and nonsampling errors.

12. What is the significance of the central limit theorem in forest sampling?

ELEMENTARY SAMPLING METHODS: SELECTIVE, SIMPLE RANDOM, AND SYSTEMATIC SAMPLING

3.1 SELECTIVE SAMPLING

Selective sampling was widely used in forestry before the advent of statistically sound sampling procedures. The method involved selecting (hence the name) areas that appeared to be representative of the average stand condition to the sampler (cruiser). Trees in the average areas were measured and stand characteristics (basal area per acre, volume per acre, and so on) desired were calculated for each representative area and finally averaged. This average was used to obtain tract characteristics. Obviously, the method was highly dependent on the skill of the cruiser. If the cruiser was very good at selecting average stand condition areas, the resulting estimates could be very good. If not, the estimates could be very poor. One important aspect of this sampling method is that no valid variance, and therefore no confidence interval, could be calculated. Since sampled areas were selected because they appeared to be average, their variability would necessarily be smaller than the true variability in the stand.

3.2 INTRODUCTION TO SIMPLE RANDOM SAMPLING

Simple random sampling (SRS) is the most basic probability sampling method. Sampling units are chosen from the population completely at random with no subjectivity allowed on the part of the cruiser. Estimators for SRS are unbiased and consistent, desirable statistical properties. SRS is the fundamental sample selection method for many other probability sampling procedures. Other probability sampling procedures are simply modifications to achieve better precision or greater economy.

By definition, a SRS is chosen such that every sample of size n sampling units has an equal probability of being selected. In Chapter 2 the number of different samples of size $n = 99$ that can possibly be selected from a population with $N = 100$ was determined to be 100. SRS from this population would be a sample in which every one of the 100 different samples of size 99 had an equal chance of being selected. This is accomplished by ensuring that every sampling unit has an equal probability of being selected throughout the selection process. With $N = 100$, defining the sampling frame and ensuring equal selection probability is relatively easy. A number could be assigned to each unit, the numbers 1 to 100 could be written on slips of paper and placed in a hat, and numbers could be drawn out one at a time until the sample size (in this case, $n = 99$) was reached. Unfortunately, in most forestry situations N is often much larger than 100. With individual trees as the sampling units, N may be over a million. Even using 1/10-acre plots, 100 acres will have $N = 1000$ such plots.

Selection of a SRS from a population requires the development of a frame (a list of all sampling units in the population). For timber stands this implies that aerial photographs, a map, or both are needed to establish the frame since the geographic location of each sampling unit must be known in order to visit and measure it. Only populations defined in terms of area can have a frame developed using maps or photos. For large areas, populations with sampling units defined as trees are very difficult to list. Assuming that the frame can be developed, the next order of business is to randomly select sampling units to be in the sample. This is usually carried out by selecting random numbers between one and the total number of sampling units in the population. For example, if the population of interest contains 5000 sampling units, we select random numbers between 1 and 5000. Random number selection can be carried out using random number generators available on some calculators and many computer software systems. Sample unit selection is usually carried out without replacement, which means that once a sampling unit is chosen, it may not be chosen again (if it is randomly selected again, simply ignore it and continue selecting additional sampling units).

Random selection of sampling units as described above is relatively painless and straightforward. In many applications SRS works very well. However, in inventorying tracts of timber several problems arise. First, the sampling units must be located on the ground. This can be a formidable problem. The usual procedure is to locate the sampling units chosen to be in the sample on an aerial photo or stand map and to establish a bearing and distance to the closest sampling unit from a known point of reference. All remaining sampling units are then located using an appropriate bearing and distance from the previous sampling unit. Obviously, establishing all of these bearings and distances using photos or maps can be fairly time-consuming. Locating the actual sampling units on the ground can also be very time-consuming, and it requires a high degree of accuracy in pacing and following compass bearings.

Another problem associated with random selection of sampling units from a stand of timber for inventory purposes is that there is a chance of obtaining a nonrepresentative sample. This may happen when the sampling units chosen at random clump together in one area of the tract. For example, assume that a 35-year-old shortleaf pine stand has approximately 60% of its area on land with a base-age 25 site index of 65 feet and the remaining 40% of its land with a base-age 25 site index of 50 feet. To obtain a truly representative sample, 60% of the sampling units should be placed on the site 65 area and 40% of the sampling units on the site 50 area. Unless the sample size is very large (that is, with a very high cost of inventory), there is little chance that the sample units selected will cover these two sites in the correct proportion. In samples where the sample proportions on the two sites are far from the population proportions, the sampling error will be very large, and the estimates ultimately obtained could be far from the true population parameters even if no measurement errors were made.

The problems associated with SRS in timber stand inventory applications led most foresters to abandon SRS in its purest form early on. Even so, it is worthwhile to become familiar with SRS selection procedures and estimators because it is a useful sampling design for many situations other than stand inventories. Furthermore, SRS forms the basis for other sampling methods, and SRS estimators are often used even though plot selection is by systematic sampling (line-plot and line-point cruising) (see Section 3.5).

3.3 SRS ESTIMATORS OF POPULATION MEANS AND TOTALS

In timber inventory the population parameters of greatest interest are usually the mean per sampling unit (or mean per unit area, acre or hectare) and the population total (total board foot volume in the tract, total dollar value of the tract, and so on). The sample estimators of these parameters and their associated variance estimators are as follows:

Sample Mean

$$\bar{y} = \frac{1}{n}\sum_{i=1}^{n} y_i \qquad (3.1)$$

Variance of Sample Mean

$$S_{\bar{y}}^2 = \frac{S_y^2}{n}\left(\frac{N-n}{N}\right) \qquad (3.2)$$

where:

$$S_y^2 = \frac{1}{n-1}\left[\sum_{i=1}^{n} y_i^2 - \frac{\left(\sum_{i=1}^{n} y_i\right)^2}{n}\right]$$

y_i = measured characteristic of interest on sampling unit i (such as plot volume or plot basal area)

n = number of sampling units in the sample (for example, number of sample plots)

N = number of sampling units (for example, plots) in the population

Note that the variance of the sample mean has two parts. The first part, S_y^2/n, is the sample variance among sampling units (S_y^2) (see Section 2.4) divided by the sample size, n. This is the standard error of the mean (see Section 2.5) squared. The second part of the estimator, $\frac{N-n}{N}$, is a modifier used on S_y^2/n. This modifier is called the finite population correction factor (fpc) and is sometimes written in its algebraically equivalent form $1-\frac{n}{N}$. This fpc will always be a number between 0 and 1. To understand the purpose of the fpc, first look at the most intensive sampling situation. If all sampling units in the population were measured (that is, $n = N$, a 100% sample), then the sample mean would be the population mean (that is, everything in the population was measured, so the true population mean is known). Therefore, the estimate of the population mean has no variability, and since the fpc equals zero, the variance of the sample mean, calculated using Eq. 3.2, is also zero. If Eq. 3.2 did not contain the fpc, the variance estimate of the mean would not be zero when all sampling units are measured, which would be illogical. As discussed in Section 2.5, it seems logical that if n is almost as big as N, the resulting means of different samples of size n will have less variability than they would if n were smaller relative to N. This is the desirable logical property that the fpc gives $S_{\bar{y}}^2$. For example, if $n = 95$ and $N = 100$, S_y^2/n is multiplied by a fpc of 0.05. If $n = 10$ and $N = 100$, S_y^2/n is multiplied by a fpc of 0.90. Frequently the fpc is ignored in variance of the mean calculations when the sampling fraction, $\frac{n}{N}$, is between 0.0 and 0.05 because the adjustment is small. In other words, when less than 5% of the population is sampled (that is, $n/N \leq 0.05$), the fpc is ignored.

EXAMPLE 3.3.1

A timber cruiser has obtained a simple random sample of 20 ⅒-acre circular sample plots. Scribner board foot volume of high-quality hardwoods was determined for each plot on the 15-acre tract. Sample plot volumes are as follows

Plot	Volume (bd ft)	Plot	Volume (bd ft)
1	1450	11	664
2	1225	12	1258
3	1379	13	1101
4	2015	14	1309
5	775	15	464
6	1123	16	777
7	1679	17	645
8	874	18	956
9	259	19	1204
10	995	20	1517

An estimate of the average Scribner board feet per plot may be calculated using Eq. 3.1. Let y_i be the Scribner board foot volume on plot i. Then

$$\sum_{i=1}^{20} y_i = 21{,}669$$

$$\bar{y} = \frac{\sum_{i=1}^{20} y_i}{20} = \frac{21{,}669}{20} = 1083.45 \text{ bd ft/plot}$$

The standard error of the mean per plot is obtained by first calculating the variance of this mean using Eq. 3.2 and then taking the square root. From Eq. 3.2

$$S_{\bar{y}}^2 = \frac{S_y^2}{n}\left(\frac{N-n}{N}\right)$$

N must be determined and S_y^2 (the variance among sampling units) must be calculated in order to use this equation. The tract is 15 acres in size; this implies that there are 150 1/10-acre sample plots in the population ($N = 150$). Calculate S_y^2 using the following equation:

$$S_y^2 = \frac{1}{n-1}\left[\sum_{i=1}^{n} y_i^2 - \frac{\left(\sum_{i=1}^{n} y_i\right)^2}{n}\right]$$

Now

$$n = 20 \text{ plots}$$

$$\sum_{i=1}^{20} y_i = 21{,}669 \text{ (bd ft)}$$

$$\sum_{i=1}^{20} y_i^2 = 26{,}915{,}801 \text{ (bd ft)}^2$$

Thus

$$\begin{aligned} S_y^2 &= \frac{1}{20-1}\left[26{,}915{,}801 - \frac{(21{,}669)^2}{20}\right] \\ &= \frac{1}{19}[3{,}438{,}522.95] \\ &= 180{,}974.89 \text{ (bd ft/plot)}^2 \end{aligned}$$

Note that the units of S_y^2 are the square of the original units; this will always be the case. Finally, calculate $S_{\bar{y}}^2$ as

$$S_{\bar{y}}^2 = \frac{180{,}974.89}{20}\left(\frac{150-20}{150}\right)$$
$$= 9048.74\ (0.867)$$
$$= 7845.26\ (\text{bd ft/plot})^2$$

The square root of $S_{\bar{y}}^2$ is the standard error of the mean $S_{\bar{y}}$:

$$S_{\bar{y}} = \sqrt{S_{\bar{y}}^2} = \sqrt{7845.26\ (\text{bd ft/plot})^2}$$
$$S_{\bar{y}} = 88.57\ (\text{bd ft/plot})$$

Note that the units associated with the standard error of the mean are the original units of each sampling unit (in this case, bd ft/plot).

After the mean per sampling unit and its associated variance and standard error are calculated, these estimates are used to obtain an estimate of the population total and its variance and standard error.

Sample Total

$$\hat{T} = N\bar{y} \tag{3.3}$$

Variance of Sample Total

$$S_{\hat{T}}^2 = N^2 S_{\bar{y}}^2 \tag{3.4}$$

where:

$\bar{y}$ = sample mean calculated using Eq. 3.1

$S_{\bar{y}}^2$ = variance of the sample mean calculated using Eq. 3.2

Recall that $\bar{y}$ is an estimate of the true mean per sampling unit. Thus it is logical to multiply by N, the total number of sampling units in the population, to obtain an estimate of the population total. Note that the variance of the mean is multiplied by N^2 to obtain the variance of $\hat{T}$. The standard error of $\hat{T}$, $S_{\hat{T}}$, is then calculated as

$$S_{\hat{T}} = \sqrt{S_{\hat{T}}^2} = \sqrt{N^2 S_{\bar{y}}^2} = NS_{\bar{y}}$$

As with the standard error of the mean, the standard error of the total has meaning only for repeated samples. It is a measure of how different the estimates of the total would be if the population were repeatedly sampled using a sample size of n.

EXAMPLE 3.3.2

An estimate of the total Scribner board foot volume of the 15-acre tract described in Example 3.3.1 is desired. Recall that

$$N = 150 \text{ plots}$$
$$\bar{y} = 1083.45 \text{ bd ft/plot}$$
$$S_{\bar{y}}^2 = 7845.26 \text{ (bd ft/plot)}^2$$

Thus the estimated total tract volume, $\hat{T}$, is

$$\hat{T} = 150\ (1083.45) = 162{,}517.5 \text{ bd ft}$$

The variance of $\hat{T}$ is

$$S_{\hat{T}}^2 = (150)^2\ (7845.26) = 176{,}518{,}350 \text{ (bd ft)}^2$$

and the standard error of $\hat{T}$, $S_{\hat{T}}$,is

$$S_{\hat{T}} = \sqrt{S_{\hat{T}}^2} = \sqrt{176{,}518{,}350} = 13{,}286.0 \text{ bd ft}$$

Note that the standard error of $\hat{T}$ could have been calculated without first calculating the variance of $\hat{T}$ by using the fact that

$$S_{\hat{T}} = NS_{\bar{y}}$$
$$S_{\hat{T}} = 150(88.57) = 13{,}286.0 \text{ bd ft}$$

It is useful to look at the relationship between S_y^2 and $S_{\hat{T}}^2$ as well as between $S_{\bar{y}}$ and $S_{\hat{T}}$. Recall that $\hat{T}$ is obtained by multiplying $\bar{y}$ by N. In statistical terminology, $\bar{y}$ is a random variabie because it can have different values, depending on which sampling units are included in a sample of size n. Conversely, N is a constant because for a given population it never changes regardless of which sampling units are included in the sample. A general rule in statistical methodology is that whenever a random variable is multiplied by a constant, the result is a new random variable with variance equal to the variance of the original random variable multiplied by the constant squared, and a standard error equal to the standard error of the original random variable multiplied by the constant. In the context of estimating a population total, T, we multiply $\bar{y}$ (a random variable) by N (a constant). Thus the variance of $\hat{T}$ is equal to the variance of $\bar{y}$, $S_{\bar{y}}^2$, multiplied by N^2, which results in Eq. 3.4. Furthermore, the standard error of $\hat{T}$ is equal to the standard error of $\bar{y}$, $S_{\bar{y}}$, multiplied by N.

This general relationship between a constant and a random variable is useful in obtaining per-acre estimates of basal area, volume, and so on, and also in converting units of volume to units of money.

EXAMPLE 3.3.3

Suppose an estimate of the mean Scribner board feet per acre for the tract described in Example 3.3.1 is desired. Recall that the average volume per 1⁄10-acre plot is

$$\bar{y}_{PLOT} = 1083.45 \text{ bd ft/plot}$$

with a standard error of

$$S_{\bar{y}_{PLOT}} = 88.57 \text{ bd ft/plot}$$

To obtain an estimate of the average volume per acre, multiply the average volume of ⅒-acre plots, $\bar{y}_{PLOT}$, by 10 (since there are conceptually ten ⅒-acre plots in one acre). Thus

$$\bar{y}_{ACRE} = \bar{y}_{PLOT}(10) = 10{,}834.5 \text{ bd ft/acre}$$

Now, since $\bar{y}_{PLOT}$ was multiplied by the constant 10, the standard error of the average volume per acre is obtained by multiplying the standard error of the average volume per plot by 10. Thus

$$S_{\bar{y}_{ACRE}} = S_{\bar{y}_{PLOT}}(10) = 88.57\,(10) = 885.7 \text{ bd ft/acre}$$

This principle can be used when expanding any estimate (random variable) by a constant.

EXAMPLE 3.3.4

An estimate of the total tract dollar value of sawtimber volume and its associated standard error for the tract described in Example 3.3.1 is needed. Assume that the current stumpage value for the hardwoods in this example is \$250/MBF (MBF = thousand board feet). From Example 3.3.2, the estimated total tract volume is

$$\hat{T}_{VOLUME} = 162{,}517.5 \text{ bd ft}$$

and the estimated standard error is

$$S_{\hat{T}_{VOLUME}} = 13{,}286.0 \text{ bd ft}$$

To obtain the dollar value of the tract, first convert the volume and estimated standard error into MBF by dividing by 1000 to obtain

$$162.5175 \text{ MBF}$$

with a standard error of 13.286 MBF.

The estimated total dollar value of this tract is then

$$\hat{T}_{VALUE} = 162.5175 \text{ MBF } (\$250/\text{MBF}) = \$40{,}629.38$$

with a standard error of

$$S_{\hat{T}_{\text{VALUE}}} = 13.286 \text{ MBF } (\$250/\text{MBF}) = \$3321.50$$

3.4 CONFIDENCE INTERVALS FOR SRS ESTIMATES OF POPULATION MEANS AND TOTALS

Recall from Section 2.5 that an approximate 95% confidence interval (CI) for the true population mean can be calculated with the following equation:

$$\bar{y} \pm 2S_{\bar{y}} \tag{3.5}$$

The lower confidence limit (LCL) is defined to be $\bar{y} - 2S_{\bar{y}}$ and the upper confidence limit (UCL) is defined as $\bar{y} + 2S_{\bar{y}}$. As previously discussed, the 95% confidence level means that in the context of repeatedly sampling from the same population, 95% of the possible random samples will produce a CI that contains the true population mean μ.

The general form of Eq. 3.5 is

Sample estimator ± 2 × (Standard error of the sample estimator)

This general form holds true for any sample estimator; for example, an approximate 95% CI for the true population total is

$$\hat{T} \pm 2(S_{\hat{T}}) \tag{3.6}$$

To obtain an exact 95% CI for either a population mean or total, replace the standard error multiplier of 2 with the value of a t random variable. The numerical value of a t random variable depends on the confidence level desired, as well as the sample size n. For a confidence level of 95% the value of t is usually a number close to 2. For very large sample sizes t will be about 1.96, for moderate sample sizes it will be about 2.08, and for very small sample sizes it may be as high as 2.21. Hence, 2 is used as a general approximation of t for a 95% confidence interval. It is possible to develop confidence intervals for any confidence level. That is, you may wish to use a 90% CI or a 70% CI or any other level you feel comfortable with. As the confidence level goes down, there is a larger probability of obtaining a bad sample, a sample that results in a confidence interval that does not contain the true parameter value (see Section 2.5). For example, at the 70% level of confidence, there is a 30% chance of obtaining a sample that will produce an interval that does not contain the true population parameter.

EXAMPLE 3.4.1

An approximate 95% CI for the total tract board foot volume for the tract described in Example 3.3.1 will be calculated. From Example 3.3.2,

$$\hat{T} = 162{,}517.5 \text{ bd ft}$$

$$S_{\hat{T}} = 13{,}286.0 \text{ bd ft}$$

Thus, using Eq. 3.6,

$$162{,}517.5 \pm 2(13{,}286.0) \text{ bd ft}$$
$$162{,}517.5 \pm 26{,}572 \text{ bd ft}$$
$$\text{LCL} = 135{,}945.5 \text{ bd ft}$$
$$\text{UCL} = 189{,}089.5 \text{ bd ft}$$

Based on this sample, it is estimated that there are between 135,945.5 and 189,089.5 board feet in this tract. Now, which value should be used to make decisions about this stand, the LCL of 135,945.5 bd ft or the UCL of 189,089.5 bd ft? Actually, the midpoint of the confidence interval *($\hat{T}$)* should be used to make decisions about this stand, because the true population total is equally likely to be any value between the LCL and UCL. Thus, by using $\hat{T}$ as the estimate, the maximum error from the true total volume of this tract is 26,572 bd ft (2 standard errors, assuming our sample is one of the 95% good samples). Conversely, if either the LCL or the UCL is used as the estimate, it could differ from the true total volume of this tract by as much as 53,144 bd ft (4 standard errors).

In light of the previous example, the utility of constructing a confidence interval in everyday application may be questioned because, as discussed earlier, the sample estimator is used as the estimate of the population parameter. In practice, the utility of a CI is in knowing the *half-width* of the confidence interval. The half-width of a CI is defined as

$$2 \times \text{Standard error of the sample estimator}$$

This is simply the value that is added and subtracted to the sample estimator to obtain the UCL and LCL. This is the largest amount of error from the true population parameter, assuming that a good sample is obtained. Consequently, this half-width of a confidence interval is often referred to as the upper bound on the error of estimation, denoted as B. The term *error of estimation* is used to indicate that the sample estimate is not the same as the population parameter it is estimating. Thus B is the most we can be away from the population parameter if we have obtained a good sample.

The decision maker utilizing the information from a stand inventory to make a decision concerning the stand must decide whether B is within an acceptable limit. In other words, will the decision be rendered useless if the estimate is off by more than B? If so, then the only course of action is to obtain additional sampling units (that is, increase the sample size) because this will add information to the sample and decrease B by decreasing the standard error of the estimate. Sample size requirements and the use of B in obtaining them are discussed in Section 3.6.

EXAMPLE 3.4.2

A confidence interval and an upper bound on the error of estimation *(B)* can be calculated for any estimate for which there is a standard error. Recall from Example 3.3.4 that the total value of the tract described in Example 3.3.1 was estimated as

$$\hat{T}_{\text{VALUE}} = \$40{,}629.38$$

with standard error

$$S_{\hat{T}_{\text{VALUE}}} = \$3321.50$$

and sample size $n = 20$ (from Example 3.3.1).

Thus the approximate 95% CI is

$$\$40{,}692.38 \pm 2(\$3321.50)$$
$$\$40{,}692.38 \pm \$6643.00$$
$$\text{LCL} = \$34{,}049.38$$
$$\text{UCL} = \$47{,}335.38$$

and the upper bound on the error of estimation *(B)* is

$$\text{B} = \$6643.00$$

If this is a good sample, the largest possible difference between the estimate $\hat{T} = \$40{,}629.38$ and the true population total value should be \$6643.00.

3.5 SYSTEMATIC SAMPLING

For obtaining inventories of individual stands of trees, the sampling method of choice is usually some type of systematic sample. The term *systematic* refers to the location (or choice) of sampling units in the population. In a systematic sample of a stand of trees, sampling units are located in a predictable, systematic pattern rather than being randomly located as in SRS. Usually the sampling units (plots) are laid out on a square or rectangular grid across the stand. For example, a timber cruiser may run several "lines" through the stand, each five chains apart. Along each line a sample plot may be established and measured every three chains. Thus the sample plots would be distributed across the stand on a 3×5 chain grid. These types of samples are usually referred to as *line-plot cruises.*

There are several advantages associated with systematic sampling. First, it eliminates the need to develop a frame prior to sampling (although the tract boundaries and topography should still be ascertained) because the systematic location of sample plots simply requires the cruiser to walk straight lines and install a sample plot at a constant interval. Secondly, complete coverage of the entire stand with sample plots is ensured, and there is no risk that most plots will clump into one area (as is possible with random location of plots), resulting in an unusually large sampling error. Finally, it is less time-consuming and more cost-efficient to install plots systematically rather than randomly.

There is one potential difficulty associated with systematic sampling. Since the sampling units are not selected randomly, it is not possible to estimate the variance of the sample. This is a bit difficult to explain without going into a great deal of statistical theory; however, we can circumvent the problem for most populations encountered in the practice of forest inventory. Scheaffer et al. (1990) show that SRS estimators of variance serve as valid estimates of the variance of systematic sampling estimators for all types of populations except for a "periodic" population. The SRS estimators presented in Section 3.3 are used for systematic sampling in this book.

In a periodic population the SRS variance estimators will underestimate the true variance of the population. Periodic populations do occur in practice, and those who use systematic sampling must be aware of them. For example, in southern pine plantations residual logging slash is often windrowed. These windrows are approximately the same distance apart. Trees growing near windrows often grow significantly faster than other trees in these stands because of, among other factors, increased nutrient availability from decaying organic matter. If a systematic sample is used in a windrowed area for which more plots fall in windrowed areas than is representative of the acreage in and around windrows, then an obvious sampling error that will lead to a biased estimate has occurred. Obviously, this could happen if sample lines are perpendicular to windrows and the interval between plots within lines coincides with the interval between windrows. If this happens, the estimated volume will overestimate the true volume because the sample does not look like the population (an excessive sampling error). Furthermore, the variance of the estimate will be underestimated owing to the periodic nature of the population and the coincident location of sample plots within the population. When systematic sampling is used in such populations, care must be taken to identify periodicities and to structure the sample to avoid the periodicity.

Operationally, layout of cruise lines for a line-plot cruise is typically a rectangular grid with cruise lines run perpendicular to the topography as much as possible. To accomplish this, a base line is established along one side of the property to be inventoried. If a 3×5 chain grid will be used, the forester begins at one corner of the property, walks $2\frac{1}{2}$ ($\frac{1}{2}$ of 5) chains along the base line and then $1\frac{1}{2}$ chains ($\frac{1}{2}$ of 3) perpendicular to the base line. At that point, the first plot center is located. From that point on, all plots are located by walking three chains along the compass line. At the end of the first line, the forester walks perpendicular to the compass line for five chains and begins laying out plots again three chains apart.

EXAMPLE 3.5.1

A systematic sample of a 50-acre natural shortleaf pine stand was taken (assume that there is no periodicity within the stand). A total of 65 $\frac{1}{20}$-acre circular sample plots were measured, and the merchantable cubic-foot volume of stems greater than 5 in. diameter at breast height to an outside bark top diameter of 2 in. was determined for each plot. Let y_i represent the volume of plot i. The following summarized plot data are available:

$$\sum_{i=1}^{65} y_i = 9668.75 \text{ ft}^3$$

$$\sum_{i=1}^{65} y_i^2 = 2{,}507{,}051.71 \ (\text{ft}^3)^2$$

$$n = 65$$

To estimate the total merchantable cubic-foot volume in this tract, SRS estimators are justified since there is no periodicity within the stand. The average volume per ¹⁄₂₀-acre plot is

$$\bar{y} = \frac{\sum_{i=1}^{65} y_i}{65} = \frac{9668.75 \text{ ft}^3}{65 \text{ plots}} = 148.75 \text{ ft}^3/\text{plot}$$

The variance of $\bar{y}$ is calculated using Eq. 3.2. To use this equation, first calculate S_y^2 (variance among sampling units) and N (the total number of sampling units in the tract):

$$S_y^2 = \frac{\left[\sum_{i=1}^{n} y_i^2 - \frac{\left(\sum_{i=1}^{n} y_i\right)^2}{n}\right]}{n-1}$$

$$S_y^2 = \frac{\left[2{,}507{,}051.71 - \frac{(9668.75)^2}{65}\right]}{64}$$
$$= 16{,}700.39294 \ (\text{ft}^3/\text{plot})^2$$

The tract is 50 acres, which implies that there are

$$N = 50(20) = 1000$$

¹⁄₂₀-acre plots in the tract. The variance of $\bar{y}$, determined using Eq. 3.2, is

$$S_{\bar{y}}^2 = \frac{S_y^2}{n}\left(\frac{N-n}{N}\right)$$
$$= \frac{16{,}700.39294}{65}\left(\frac{1000-65}{1000}\right)$$
$$= 256.92912 \ (0.935)$$
$$= 240.22873 \ (\text{ft}^3/\text{plot})^2$$

The standard error of $\bar{y}$ is then obtained by taking the square root of $S_{\bar{y}}^2$:

$$S_{\bar{y}} = \sqrt{S_{\bar{y}}^2} = \sqrt{240.22873} = 15.5 \text{ (ft}^3\text{/plot)}$$

In practice $S_{\bar{y}}$ is often calculated directly, without first calculating $S_{\bar{y}}^2$, because the standard error, used to calculate confidence intervals, is really the objective. For this tract, calculate $S_{\bar{y}}$ as

$$S_{\bar{y}} = \frac{S_y}{\sqrt{n}}\sqrt{\left(\frac{N-n}{N}\right)} = \frac{129.23}{\sqrt{65}}\sqrt{0.935}$$

$$S_{\bar{y}} = 15.5 \text{ (ft}^3\text{/plot)}$$

which is exactly the same as the previous calculation.

Now the estimate of the total tract volume is obtained using Eq. 3.3:

$$\begin{aligned}\hat{T} &= (1000 \text{ plots})\ (148.75 \text{ ft}^3\text{/plot}) \\ &= 148{,}750 \text{ ft}^3\end{aligned}$$

The variance of $\hat{T}$ is calculated with Eq. 3.4:

$$\begin{aligned}S_{\hat{T}}^2 &= N^2 S_{\bar{y}}^2 \\ &= (1000)^2\ (240.22873) \\ &= 240{,}228{,}730 \text{ (ft}^3)^2\end{aligned}$$

Upon taking the square root of this variance, obtain the standard error of $\hat{T}$ as

$$S_{\hat{T}} = \sqrt{S_{\hat{T}}^2} = \sqrt{240{,}228{,}370}$$

$$S_{\hat{T}} = 15{,}449.3 \text{ ft}^3$$

As for the mean per plot, $S_{\hat{T}}$ can be obtained directly using this formula:

$$S_{\hat{T}} = NS_{\bar{y}}$$

$$S_{\hat{T}} = 1000\ (15.5) = 15{,}500 \text{ ft}^3$$

The slight difference in the two calculated values is due to rounding errors.

A 95% CI for the total merchantable volume in this stand can be obtained, using Eq. 3.6, as follows:

$$\begin{gathered}\hat{T} \pm 2S_{\hat{T}} \\ 148{,}750 \pm 2(15{,}500) \\ 148{,}750 \pm 31{,}000 \\ \text{LCL} = 117{,}750 \text{ ft}^3 \\ \text{UCL} = 179{,}750 \text{ ft}^3\end{gathered}$$

Of course, the upper bound on the error of estimation *(B)* is

$$B = 31{,}000 \text{ ft}^3$$

If a smaller *B* is desired to make a decision concerning this stand, additional sample plots need to be measured (that is, *n* would have to be increased abᴄ ve 65).

3.6 SAMPLE SIZE REQUIREMENTS FOR A POPULATION MEAN AND TOTAL

Sample size needed for a forest inventory is often overlooked, but it is the one inventory adjustment that will have a direct impact on inventory cost and efficiency. Foresters who use a constant-percentage cruise (10% is popular) are probably more precise than they need to be on some inventories and not precise enough on others. Calculation of sample size requires use of some statistical terms, and this may be why it is not used more often in practice. It also requires an estimate of variability among sampling units *before* the full-scale inventory takes place.

To determine the number of sampling units that are required for a given inventory, the decision must be made as to how close to the true parameter the sample estimate must be. In other words, what upper bound *(B)* on the error of estimation (see Section 3.4 for a detailed discussion of *B*) can be tolerated with an expectation of making a rational decision based on the inventory estimate? This bound *(B)* must be specified prior to sampling and may be given in units of the characteristic measured (volume, basal area, and so on) or as a percentage of the value of the parameter to be estimated (for example, 5%, 10%, or 15% of the total tract volume). When *B* is specified as a percentage, it is called the *allowable error* (AE). The *B* or AE may be specified for either the population mean or total.

Recall from Section 3.4 that the upper bound on the error of estimation *(B)* is synonymous with the half-width of a confidence interval. For an approximate 95% confidence level, the confidence interval half-width or upper bound on the error of estimation for estimating a population mean is

$$B_M = 2S_{\bar{y}}$$

$$B_M = 2\frac{S_y}{\sqrt{n}}\sqrt{\frac{N-n}{n}}$$

where B_M is the upper bound on the error of estimation for the sample mean and all other variables are as previously defined.

Recall that 2 is used rather than 1.96 or a specific *t* value. This equality can be solved algebraically for *n*, the sample size, as follows:

$$\frac{B_M}{2S_y} = \frac{1}{\sqrt{n}}\sqrt{\frac{N-n}{n}}$$

Now square both sides of the equality and write the fpc as $1 - \frac{n}{N}$:

$$\frac{B_M^2}{4S_y^2} = \frac{1}{n}\left(\frac{N-n}{N}\right) = \frac{1}{n}\left(1 - \frac{n}{N}\right)$$

$$\frac{B_M^2}{4S_y^2} = \frac{1}{n} - \frac{1}{N}$$

$$\frac{B_M^2}{4S_y^2} + \frac{1}{N} = \frac{1}{n}$$

$$\frac{B_M^2 N + 4S_y^2}{4NS_y^2} = \frac{1}{n}$$

$$n = \frac{4NS_y^2}{B_M^2 N + 4S_y^2}$$

For a given population this formula can be used to determine the sample size that is required to meet a given upper bound on the error of estimation with a confidence level of approximately 95%. To use this relationship in practice, N, S_y^2, and B_M must be known. The population size N is easily obtained for a finite population when sampling units are fixed-area plots if the total area is known. The upper bound on the error of estimation, B_M, is chosen so that the resulting sample estimate will be useful to the decision maker. Obtaining a value for S_y^2 may be somewhat difficult prior to sampling the population of interest. This problem will be addressed later in this section. A similar sample size equation can also be obtained for estimating a population total by solving the following equation for n:

$$B_T = 2N\frac{S_y}{\sqrt{n}}\sqrt{\frac{N-n}{N}}$$

where B_T is the upper bound on the error of estimation for the population total and all other variables are as previously defined.

It is often more straightforward to specify the desired allowable error for a population mean or total than to specify the upper bound directly. For example, it is easier to envision that an estimate for the total tract volume should be within ±10% of the true total volume than to give the upper bound for the total tract volume in cubic feet or other units. To obtain a sample size equation that incorporates allowable error, a similar procedure to that outlined earlier is used. For example, for a sample mean,

$$B_M = 2\frac{S_y}{\sqrt{n}}\sqrt{\frac{N-n}{N}}$$

By definition, the allowable error for a sample mean is

$$\mathrm{AE} = \frac{B_M}{\bar{y}}(100)$$

Now, if both sides of the above relationship are multiplied by $\frac{100}{\bar{y}}$, the following relationship is obtained:

$$\frac{B_M}{\bar{y}}(100) = 2\frac{S_y}{\bar{y}}(100)\frac{1}{\sqrt{n}}\sqrt{\frac{N-n}{N}}$$

This relationship simplifies to

$$\mathrm{AE} = 2(\mathrm{CV})\frac{1}{\sqrt{n}}\sqrt{\frac{N-n}{N}}$$

where CV is the coefficient of variation expressed as a percentage (see Section 2.4) and all other variables are as previously defined.

This relationship can be solved for sample size, n, as follows:

$$\left(\frac{\mathrm{AE}}{2(\mathrm{CV})}\right)^2 = \frac{1}{n}\left(1-\frac{n}{N}\right) = \frac{1}{n} - \frac{1}{N}$$

$$\left(\frac{\mathrm{AE}}{2(\mathrm{CV})}\right)^2 + \frac{1}{N} = \frac{1}{n}$$

$$\frac{(\mathrm{AE})^2}{4(\mathrm{CV})^2} + \frac{1}{N} = \frac{1}{n}$$

$$\frac{N(\mathrm{AE})^2 + 4(\mathrm{CV})^2}{4N(\mathrm{CV})^2} = \frac{1}{n}$$

$$n = \frac{4N(\mathrm{CV})^2}{N(\mathrm{AE})^2 + 4(\mathrm{CV})^2}$$

The same formula results for estimating n for a population mean or total when using AE as the measure of the bound.

All the sample size equations derived previously are for simple random sampling but are also valid for systematic sampling (line-plot cruising) as long as periodicities in populations are avoided (see Section 3.5). Following are summarized sample size equations for the three situations described earlier.

Bound *(B)* Specified For Population Mean Per Sampling Unit in Units of the Characteristic of Interest (Finite Populations)

$$n = \frac{4NS_y^2}{B_M^2 N + 4S_y^2} \tag{3.7}$$

where:

n = estimated sample size

N = number of sampling units in the population

S_y^2 = variance among sampling units in the population of interest

B_M = desired bound on the mean per sampling unit

Bound *(B)* Specified For Population Total in Units of the Characteristic of Interest (Finite Populations)

$$n = \frac{NS_y^2}{\frac{B_T^2}{4N} + S_y^2} \tag{3.8}$$

where:

B_T is the desired bound on the population total
and all other variables are as defined above

Bound Specified as a Percentage [Allowable Error (AE)] of Either the Population Mean or Total (Finite Populations)

$$n = \frac{4N(\text{CV})^2}{(\text{AE})^2 N + 4(\text{CV})^2} \tag{3.9}$$

where:

AE = desired allowable error (percent)

CV = coefficient of variation among sampling units (percent) (see Section 2.7)

and all other variables are as defined above.

These equations are for finite populations. As a general rule, the population will be considered infinite whenever the sampling fraction *(n/N)* is less than 0.05. No population is truly infinite, but if the population is so large that sampling even 5% of it seems unlikely, simpler equations exist to estimate sample size and are presented as Eqs. 3.11 through 3.13.

To use any of the finite-population sample size equations, the population size *(N)* must be known and an estimate of the population variance (S_y^2) or coefficient of variation (CV) is necessary. This appears to be a catch-22 situation: S_y^2 or CV, normally calculated using sample information, must be known for the population of interest prior to sampling the population. There are several ways of solving this dilemma. First, if variability information has previously been obtained in populations similar to the one in question, it can be used to determine required sample size in the current population. The CV may actually be more stable than S_y^2 since it is on a percentage basis. If the population is fairly large and we have little or no previous experience in this type of population, a pilot survey can be useful. A pilot survey is essentially a small sample that is installed for the sole purpose of obtaining an estimate of the population variance. A third, less accurate, procedure that is sometimes used to obtain a quick estimate of the population variance makes use of the relationship between the sample range (R) and standard deviation (S_y). It can be shown from statistical theory that the range (R) (the difference between the largest and smallest values of the sampling units in the population) is approximately equal to four standard deviations among the sampling units (S_y). This can be expressed as follows:

$$R \cong 4S_y$$

This equation can be rearranged algebraically to obtain

$$S_y \cong \frac{R}{4} \tag{3.10}$$

Thus, if the largest and smallest values per sampling unit in the population of interest are estimated, S_y is approximated using Eq. 3.10.

EXAMPLE 3.6.1

An inventory is to be carried out for a 100-acre natural loblolly pine stand. The objective is to estimate the total tract pine sawtimber volume to within 25,000 bd ft ($B_T = 25{,}000$). From a reconnaissance of the tract, an experienced timber cruiser estimates that the pine board foot volume per acre ranges from a minimum of 500 bd ft to a maximum of 6000 bd ft. The stand will be cruised using a systematic sample with 1/10-acre plots. To estimate the required number of sample plots, the population size (N) must first be calculated and an estimate of S_y^2 [the variance among sampling units (plots)] must be obtained.

$$N = 100 \text{ acres} \times (10 \text{ plots/acre})$$
$$N = 1000 \text{ plots}$$

The range of per-acre board foot volumes is available. However, the sampling unit is 1/10 of an acre, so the per-acre values must be converted to 1/10-acre values.

$$\text{Minimum volume per } \frac{1}{10} \text{ acre} = \frac{500}{10} = 50 \text{ bd ft}$$

$$\text{Maximum volume per } \frac{1}{10} \text{ acre} = \frac{6000}{10} = 600 \text{ bd ft}$$

Thus

$$R \text{ (range)} = 600 - 50 = 550 \text{ bd ft}$$

$$S_y \cong \frac{550}{4} = 137.5 \text{ bd ft}$$

$$S_y^2 \cong (137.5)^2 = 18{,}906.25 \text{ (bd ft)}^2$$

Now Eq. 3.8 is used to determine the sample size required to meet the desired bound of 25,000 bd ft:

$$n = \frac{1000(18{,}906.25)}{\dfrac{(25{,}000)^2}{4(1000)} + 18{,}906.25}$$

$$n = \frac{18{,}906{,}250}{175{,}156.25}$$

$$n = 107.9 = 108$$

So in this example it requires at least 108 sample plots to estimate the total volume in this tract to within 25,000 bd ft. Always round n to the next highest full plot since partial plots will not be taken. In this example, n is 107.9, so round up: $n = 108$ plots (even if n had turned out to be 107.1, the resulting sample size would still be 108 plots).

EXAMPLE 3.6.2

A forest consultant has been hired to inventory a 65-acre mixed hardwood stand to determine the total board foot volume of sawtimber-size trees. The owner of the tract wants the estimate to be within 10% of the true tract total (AE = 10). The consultant will use a systematic sample of 1⁄10-acre sample plots (that is, a line-plot cruise). From previous experience in dealing with this type of stand, the consultant estimates that the coefficient of variation among 1⁄10-acre plots will be 90%. The population size N is

$$N = 65 \text{ acres} \times (10 \text{ plots/acre})$$

$$N = 650 \text{ plots}$$

Now, using Eq. 3.9, estimate n as follows:

$$n = \frac{4(650)(90)^2}{(10)^2(650) + 4(90)^2}$$

$$n = \frac{21{,}060{,}000}{97{,}400} = 216.2 \text{ plots}$$

Thus it will require at least 216.2 ¹⁄₁₀-acre plots to reach the desired AE of 10% in this tract, so the consultant must use at least 217 plots.

This is a very large number of sample plots for such a small tract. However, the tract is highly variable (CV = 90%), so it will require a very intensive sample to estimate the total volume to within 10%. At this point the consultant should discuss the situation with the landowner. To avoid such an intensive (and expensive) inventory the landowner may decide to be satisfied with a tract total estimate that is within 20% of the true total. If so, then the required sample size is

$$n = \frac{4(650)(90)^2}{(20)^2(650) + 4(90)^2}$$

$$n = \frac{21{,}060{,}000}{292{,}400} = 72.02 \text{ plots}$$

Thus, by allowing the estimate to be within 20% rather than 10% of the true total, the required sample size drops from 217 plots to 73 plots.

It must be understood that sample size equations simply provide an *estimate* of the sample size required to estimate population parameters within certain bounds. There is no guarantee that the population parameter of interest (mean or total) will be estimated with the desired precision, for the following reasons. First of all, the equations require an estimate of the sample variance. Several methods were given to estimate sample variance, but at best it is usually a crude estimate. Second, even if there were an exact measure of the population variance, there would still be a chance that the parameter of interest would not be estimated with the desired precision. This is a direct corollary of the concept of repeated sampling and the definition of confidence intervals as discussed in Section 2.5. In fact, as shown earlier, the sample size equations are simply algebraic equivalents to confidence interval half-widths. The 4 that appears in the sample size equations is simply the 2 from a confidence interval half-width raised to the second power. The sample size equations, Eqs. 3.7, 3.8, and 3.9, have implied confidence levels of approximately 95%. This means that if the population variance is known exactly and a sample size to meet some desired bound is determined as shown above, there is still a 5% chance of obtaining a sample that will not give an estimate of the parameter of interest within the desired bound.

Exact expressions of Eqs. 3.7, 3.8, and 3.9 would contain t^2 values in place of the 4. However, since the variance (or CV) used in sample size calculations is usually a crude estimate of the true population variance (or CV), 4 provides a good approximation of t^2 for most situations. However, those readers interested in working at a confidence level other than 95% should replace the 4's in the equations with the appropriate t^2 value.

Equations 3.7, 3.8, and 3.9 are for finite populations. In situations where the anticipated sampling fraction, $\frac{n}{N}$, is so small (0.05 or less) that the finite population correction (fpc) factor is 0.95 or higher, the adjustment from applying the fpc to the standard error is very small. In these situations, the following sample size equations for infinite populations can be used for the three situations discussed previously. Since these equations are easier to use, a good plan would be to use these infinite equations first. If the sample size obtained is more than 5%, the finite population equations can be used to zero in on the correct value. If the sample size is less than 5%, the infinite equation value can be used. Sample size values from finite population equations will always be smaller than those for infinite population equations.

Development of sample size equations for infinite populations is more simple than for finite populations because the standard error does not include the finite population correction factor. For a sample mean, B_M is

$$B_M = 2S_{\bar{y}} = 2\frac{S_y}{\sqrt{n}}$$

where all variables are as previously defined.

This equation is easily solved for n:

$$\frac{B_M^2}{4S_y^2} = \frac{1}{n}$$

$$n = \frac{4S_y^2}{B_M^2}$$

Sample size equations for the three situations described above for finite populations are given below for infinite populations.

Bound *(B)* Specified For Population Mean Per Sampling Unit in Units of the Characteristic of Interest (Infinite Population)

$$n = \frac{4S_y^2}{B_M^2} \tag{3.11}$$

where all variables are as previously defined.

Bound *(B)* Specified For Population Total in Units of the Characteristic of Interest

$$n = \frac{4N^2S_y^2}{B_T^2} \tag{3.12}$$

where all variables are as previously defined.

Bound Specified as a Percentage [Allowable Error (AE)] of Either the Population Mean or Total

$$n = \frac{4(\text{CV})^2}{(\text{AE})^2} \tag{3.13}$$

where all variables are as previously defined.

Equations 3.11, 3.12, and 3.13 are often used in place of 3.7, 3.8, and 3.9, respectively, because they are simpler, and if the sampling fraction n/N is fairly large, they will produce a conservative estimate of required sample size (that is, the estimated sample size will be larger than would be calculated using the finite population sample size formulas). Of course, if cost of sampling is a major consideration, this approach is not appropriate.

EXAMPLE 3.6.3

A forest manager is going to perform an inventory of a 250-acre Douglas fir stand for management purposes. The objective is to estimate the average Douglas fir basal area per acre within 10%. From previous experience the manager expects the CV to run about 45% for ⅕-acre plots. Cost is no object, so the manager assumes that the population is infinite. To estimate the number of ⅕-acre sample plots required for this stand, Eq. 3.13 is used:

$$n = \frac{4(45)^2}{(10^2)} = 81.0 \text{ plots}$$

The large reduction in sample size obtained in Example 3.6.2 by accepting an AE = 20% instead of 10% emphasizes the importance of a reasonable AE. The reduction in AE from increasing the sample size is not linear. Rather, it follows the form presented in Figure 3.6.1. There is a separate curve for different coefficients of variation (CV), but for every curve a unit increase in the sample size *(n)*, when *n* is very small, results in large decreases in AE. There is a point of diminishing returns, however, and afterward a unit increase in *n* provides very little reduction in AE. Foresters should be aware of this relationship. For stands that have high CVs (for example, 100%), it may be economically infeasible to put in enough plots to obtain an AE such as ±10%. It may be much more sensible either to be satisfied with a high AE or, if that is not acceptable, to forgo the inventory altogether.

Sometimes more than one characteristic for a stand is of interest. For example, in a given stand separate estimates of the volume of softwood sawtimber and the volume of hardwood sawtimber may be desired. In the field, sample data for softwood and hardwood should be kept separately so that separate estimates can be calculated. To determine the sample size needed to estimate both of these characteristics within their desired bounds, calculate the sample size for each characteristic separately. Then the

Figure 3.6.1 Relationship between sample size and allowable error for different coefficients of variation.

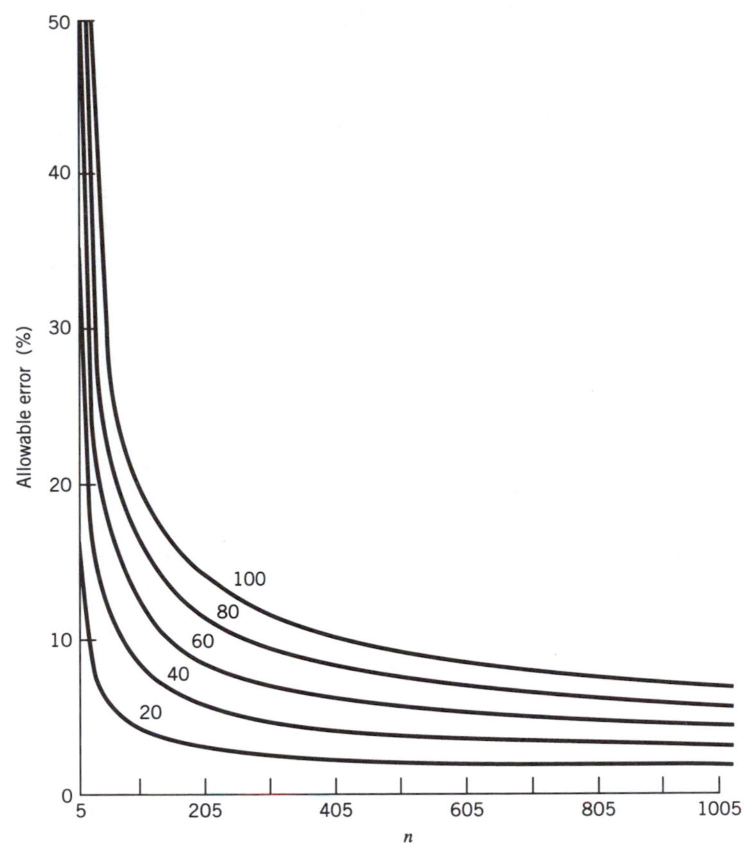

sample size used in the inventory will be the largest sample size—this will help ensure that the bound is met for the characteristic that requires the larger sample size and the bound will probably be more than met for the characteristic that requires the smaller sample size.

EXAMPLE 3.6.4

For the tract described in Example 3.6.3 the forest manager also wishes to estimate the average red alder basal area per acre within 15%. Based on previous experience, the manager expects the CV to run about 65% for ⅕-acre plots. As before, cost is no object, so the manager chooses to assume an infinite population. According to Eq. 3.13, the number of plots needed to estimate the red alder basal area to within 15% is

$$n = \frac{4(65)^2}{(15)^2} = 75$$

Since it will require 81 plots to reach the bound for the Douglas fir and 75 to reach the bound for the red alder, the manager will use 81 plots.

3.7 ESTIMATING POPULATION PROPORTIONS

To this point the estimation of population means and totals has been discussed using simple random or systematic sampling. A third population parameter that is often of interest is a population proportion. Some examples would be

The proportion of trees in a stand greater than 14 in. DBH

The proportion of trees in a stand infected with a given disease

The proportion of grade 1 sawlogs in a stand

The calculations involved in estimating a proportion and its associated variance and standard error depend on the type of sampling unit used in the inventory, either fixed-area plots or individual trees. When fixed-area sample plots are used to estimate a population proportion, a ratio estimator should be used. Ratio estimators are covered in Chapter 6.

Individual trees can be used as the sampling unit for estimating many characteristics of forest stands. Using Eq. 3.3 the total tract volume can be estimated by randomly or systematically sampling individual trees; however, it may be very difficult to know N–the total number of trees in the stand. Nevertheless, it could be done, and for some situations such as a marked timber sale, the number of trees composing the sale may be known. Similarly, the proportion of trees in the population with a certain characteristic can be estimated using the individual tree as the sampling unit. However, the problem arises as to what value to assign each sample tree when examining it for the desired characteristic. The solution to the problem is to assign the tree a value of 1 if it has the characteristic of interest and a value of 0 if it does not. Thus y_i, the value of sample unit i, can take on only two different values: 0 and 1. This type of variable falls into a class of variables known as discrete random variables (that is, it is either 0 or 1 and nothing else). Specifically, this variable is a binomial random variable. The main characteristic of this type of random variable is that it can have only one of two values (0 and 1). If success is defined to be the case for which the sampling unit has a desired characteristic, then the value of y_i will be 1. Conversely, if the sampling unit does not have the characteristic of interest, it is classified as a failure, and y_i is assigned a value of 0. For example, to estimate the proportion of trees in a stand that have one or more grade 1 sawlogs, define a success to be a tree with one or more grade 1 sawlogs and a failure to be a tree with no grade 1 sawlogs. Then, if n trees are randomly (or systematically) selected and examined for the presence of grade 1 sawlogs, an estimate of the proportion of trees with grade 1 sawlogs can be obtained.

The following equations are used to estimate a population proportion when each sampling unit is assigned either a 1 (success) or a 0 (failure):

$$\text{Let } y_i = \begin{matrix} 1 \text{ if success} \\ 0 \text{ if failure} \end{matrix}$$

$$\hat{P} = \frac{\sum_{i=1}^{n} y_i}{n} \tag{3.14}$$

$$S_{\hat{P}}^2 = \frac{\hat{P}(1-\hat{P})}{n-1}\left(\frac{N-n}{N}\right) \tag{3.15}$$

where $\hat{P}$ is the estimated value of the population proportion and all other variables are as previously defined.

It is easy to see why $\hat{P}$ provides an estimate of the proportion of the sampling units having the characteristic of interest. Since y_i has a value of 1 when a sampling unit has the desired characteristic and a value of 0 otherwise, the $\sum_{i=1}^{n} y_i$ is equal to the number of sampling units in the sample of size n that has the desired characteristic. Thus $\hat{P}$ is the proportion of sampling units sampled having the desired characteristic.

The variance equation for $\hat{P}$ is derived from the variance formula for a population mean (Eq. 3.2), which is

$$S_{\bar{y}}^2 = \frac{S_y^2}{n}\left(\frac{N-n}{n}\right)$$

Recall that

$$S_y^2 = \frac{\sum_{i=1}^{n} y_i^2 - \left[\frac{(\sum_{i=1}^{n} y_i)^2}{n}\right]}{n-1}$$

For a binomial random variable, y_i can take on only values of 0 and 1; thus $\sum_{i=1}^{n} y_i^2 = \sum_{i=1}^{n} y_i$. This leads to

$$S_y^2 = \frac{\sum_{i=1}^{n} y_i - \left[\frac{(\sum_{i=1}^{n} y_i)^2}{n}\right]}{n-1} = \frac{\sum_{i=1}^{n} y_i\left[1 - \frac{\sum_{i=1}^{n} y_i}{n}\right]}{n-1}$$

Substitution of this expression into Eq. 3.2 leads to the following expression:

$$S_{\hat{P}}^2 = \frac{\sum_{i=1}^{n} y_i \left[1 - \frac{\sum_{i=1}^{n} y_i}{n}\right]}{n(n-1)} \left(\frac{N-n}{N}\right)$$

which simplifies to

$$S_{\hat{P}}^2 = \frac{\hat{P}(1-\hat{P})}{n-1} \left(\frac{N-n}{N}\right)$$

when it is recognized that

$$\hat{P} = \frac{\sum_{i=1}^{n} y_i}{n}$$

EXAMPLE 3.7.1

A forester wishes to estimate the proportion of trees in a 17-year-old radiata pine plantation that are larger than 30 cm diameter at breast height (dbh). A systematic sample of every 50th tree resulted in a total sample size of $n = 328$ sample trees. A complete count of the trees, taken as the cruiser sampled, resulted in a total of 16,410 trees in the stand. The data obtained are summarized as follows:

Sample Tree	y_i
1	1
2	1
3	0
4	0
5	0
6	0
7	0
8	0
9	0
10	1
11	0
•	•
•	•
•	•
328	0
	$\sum_{i=1}^{328} y_i = 106$

Using Eqs. 3.14 and 3.15, the proportion of trees with a dbh greater than 30 cm and its associated standard error are estimated to be

$$\hat{P} = \frac{106}{328} = 0.3232$$

$$\begin{aligned} S_{\hat{P}}^2 &= \frac{(0.3232)(1 - 0.3232)}{327}\left(\frac{16{,}410 - 328}{16{,}410}\right) \\ &= 0.0006689\ (0.98) \\ &= 0.000655 \end{aligned}$$

Note that the fpc factor has a value of 0.98. Since this is higher than 0.95, the sampling fraction is less than 0.05 and it may be ignored. The resulting estimate of the variance of $\hat{P}$ is

$$S_{\hat{P}}^2 = 0.0006689$$

The standard error of $\hat{P}$ is then

$$S_{\hat{P}}^2 = \sqrt{S_{\hat{P}}^2} = 0.0259$$

Thus an approximate 95% CI for the proportion of trees in this stand with dbh greater than 30 cm is

$$\begin{gathered} \hat{P} \pm 2S_{\hat{P}} \\ 0.3232 \pm 2(0.0259) \\ 0.3232 \pm 0.0518 \\ \text{LCL} = 0.2714 \\ \text{UCL} = 0.3750 \end{gathered}$$

Thus between 27.14% and 37.50% of the trees in this stand have a dbh greater than 30 cm. The sample size, n, must be greater than 30 to calculate the confidence interval as shown.

When individual sampling units are assigned the values of 0 (failure) and 1 (success) as discussed previously, sample size required to estimate P within a certain bound is calculated using the following equations:

Finite Population

$$n = \frac{4N\hat{P}(1 - \hat{P})}{B^2N + 4\hat{P}(1 - \hat{P})} \tag{3.16}$$

Infinite Population

$$n = \frac{4\hat{P}(1 - \hat{P})}{B^2} \tag{3.17}$$

where B is the desired bound as a proportion ($0 < B < 1$) and all other variables are as previously defined.

Note that it may be difficult or impossible to use Eq. 3.16 with individual trees as the sampling unit since N must be known. For most situations in which individual trees are the sampling units, N will be so large that for all practical consideration the population will be infinite. Thus Eq. 3.17 will be used most often in forest inventory situations.

To use Eqs. 3.16 and 3.17, an estimate of P is required. Thus, just as for determining sample sizes for population means and totals, there is a catch-22 situation: An estimate of $\hat{P}$ is necessary before the sample size required to estimate $\hat{P}$ can be estimated. As previously discussed, prior experience can be used to come up with the initial estimate of $\hat{P}$, or a pilot inventory can be installed to estimate $\hat{P}$. There is one additional option in this situation. If there is no prior experience to draw from and no enthusiasm for conducting a pilot inventory, arbitrarily set $\hat{P}$ to 0.5. By doing this, both Eqs. 3.16 and 3.17 will produce the largest sample sizes possible. That is, for a given B, the maximum sample size produced by Eqs. 3.16 and 3.17 is when $\hat{P}$ is 0.5. Thus, when very little information is available about the population under consideration, if sample size is determined using $\hat{P} = 0.5$, the sample will be more than adequate to meet the desired bound *(B)* for any value of the population proportion.

EXAMPLE 3.7.2

A forest manager needs to know what proportion of the trees in a black cherry *(Prunus serotina)* stand have at least one clear log. He would like the estimate to be within 5% of the true proportion. From previous experience in this type of stand, he estimates $\hat{P}$ to be 0.3. To determine the required sample size, use Eq. 3.17 because no knowledge of N is available and N should be very large relative to the sample size to be taken. The forest manager wishes the estimate to be within 5% of the true proportion, which implies that the bound on the proportion will be $B = 0.05$. From Eq. 3.17,

$$n = \frac{4(0.3)(1-0.3)}{(0.05)^2} = 336 \text{ trees}$$

If the manager had no previous experience in this type of stand, he could have used Eq. 3.17 with $\hat{P}$ set to 0.5 to obtain

$$n = \frac{4(0.5)(1-0.5)}{(0.05)^2} = 400 \text{ trees}$$

Obviously, this sample size is more than adequate if $\hat{P}$ is actually 0.3 (which requires that $n = 336$ trees). The reader may wish to calculate n using Eq. 3.17 for any other value of $\hat{P}$ (between 0 and 1) to determine that setting $\hat{P} = 0.5$ yields the largest sample size possible for a given B.

3.8 SAMPLING UNITS AND TREE MEASUREMENTS

Usually in forest inventory the sampling unit is a fixed-area plot because the population parameters of interest are defined on a unit-area basis (such as volume/acre or basal area/acre). However, as shown in Section 3.7, the individual tree is defined as the sampling unit in some situations. Furthermore, some sampling designs implicitly assume the sampling unit to be the individual tree (as in 3P sampling—see Chapter 10). For the more elementary sampling methods, a sample design that uses the individual tree as the sampling unit will often be more time-consuming and thus more expensive to implement correctly.

Regardless of the sampling unit used in a given inventory, there are some basic individual tree measurements that are often obtained. These include diameter at breast height (dbh), total height, and (or) merchantable height. The dbh can be measured to the nearest 0.1 in. using a diameter tape or caliper. However, dbh is often tallied into 1- or 2-in.-wide dbh classes. The height measurement obtained in the woods is dictated by the volume (or weight) table that will be used to estimate tree volume (or weight). Some volume tables require total height in feet, whereas others require merchantable height to a given top diameter. Top diameter varies by product. Minimum top diameters may be 2 in. for pulpwood trees, whereas it may be 8 in. for veneer logs. Consequently, product determination for each tree must also be designated. Product determination is based on species, size, and quality of the trees. Total and merchantable tree heights are usually obtained using a hypsometer. Many times merchantable height is measured in units such as the number of logs (sawtimber trees) or number of pulpwood bolts (pulpwood trees). These types of heights are used when the volume table requires them as input.

Another tree measurement that may be needed is a measure of form. Form is used as an indication of how cylindrical the main stem of a tree is. Several form indexes have been developed and are used in various areas of the world. One of the more often-used measures of form in the United States is Girard form class. For detailed information on Girard form class and other individual tree measurements, consult a mensuration book such as *Forest Measurements* by Avery and Burkhart (1994) or *Forest Mensuration* by Husch et al. (1982).

3.9 SAMPLE PLOT SHAPE

Given that many forest inventories are and will continue to be carried out using fixed-area sample plots as sampling units, the question often arises as to the shape and size of sample plots.

Sample plots are usually square, rectangular, or round. For example, a ⅕-acre sample plot could be a square with 93.3-ft sides, a rectangle with various combinations of length and width (for example, 120 ft × 72.6 ft or 150 ft × 58.1 ft), or a circle with a radius of 52.66 ft. Much effort has been put forth to determine the optimum plot shape (that is, one that provides estimates with small variance) for various forest stand conditions in many parts of the world. However, any plot shape discussed earlier can be used with confidence if care is taken in determining which trees are in and out of the plot. Square and rectangular sample plots are relatively time-consuming to establish on the ground compared with circular plots. Furthermore, the amount of edge on a sample plot is a minimum for a circle. Since one of the potentially largest nonsampling errors in forest inventory is the incorrect omission or inclusion of trees near plot edges in sample plots, circular sample plots are often preferred over square or rectangular plots.

Plantations, especially those with very nearly equal spacing between rows, present real problems for foresters with regard to plot shape. One solution is to use rectangular plots with plot corners equidistant between rows and trees within rows. This plot shape ensures that the area in the plot represents the area on which the trees are growing. A smaller rectangle could enclose the same number of trees. Since it would be smaller, the trees per acre and volume per acre would be overestimated.

Circular plots can also be used in plantations with care. Plantations represent a periodic population so it is important that the distance between plots is not a multiple of the between-row spacing. Cruise lines should be perpendicular to the rows of trees. If, for example, the plot center always fell exactly between two rows, the radius could easily be such that outlying rows were either just in or just out of the plot. If the location of the plot center is varied, the circular plot should generally result in good estimates.

3.10 SAMPLE PLOT SIZE

Once the plot shape has been determined, the question of plot size arises. Clearly, it is more time-consuming and expensive to use a large plot size than a small plot size. However, it may not be so clear that the larger the plot size, the smaller is the variation among plots (that is, the smaller S_y^2). Think about the distribution of trees in a stand: In most stands of trees this distribution will vary from areas of high density (such as clumps of trees) to areas of very low density or complete voids (such as "holes" in the stand). If a very small plot size is used, some plots will fall in high-density clumps and some will fall in the holes. Thus the variation among these sample plots (S_y^2) will be very large. Conversely, if a relatively large plot size is used, high-density clumps and holes can fall in the same plot and average out over the plot. Thus the variation among sample plots (S_y^2) will be smaller. This is not to say that large plots should be used. Clearly, for the same expenditure of time or money it is possible to measure more small plots than large plots. Recall from Section 3.2 that the variance of a sample mean, $\bar{y}$, is

$$S_{\bar{y}}^2 = \frac{S_y^2}{n}\left(\frac{N-n}{N}\right)$$

If the fpc factor is 1,

$$S_{\bar{y}}^2 = \frac{S_y^2}{n}$$

The structure of $S_{\bar{y}}^2$ shows that the question of plot size is not intuitively obvious. If relatively large plots are used, S_y^2 will decrease, but the sample size n will be smaller for a given cost (in units of time or money). If small sample plots are used, S_y^2 will increase, but the sample size will be relatively large for a given cost. For an informed decision to be made about plot size, S_y^2 must be known for various plot sizes in the population of interest. Furthermore, cost (in units of time or money) per sampling unit must be known for the various plot sizes under consideration (this cost will include factors such as travel time between plots, plot establishment time, and plot measurement time).

A relatively straightforward and objective analysis for determining optimum plot size can be carried out as follows:

1. Calculate the number of sample plots required to meet a predefined bound on the mean volume per acre (n_1 for plot size 1, n_2 for plot size 2, and so on) using their respective sample variances or coefficients of variation.
2. Multiply each sample size by the appropriate cost (or relative cost) per sampling unit [C_1 is cost (or relative cost) of plot size 1, C_2 is cost (or relative cost) of plot size 2, and so on] to obtain the expected total cost (TC_i) for each plot size: $TC_1 = n_1C_1$ = the expected total cost for plot size 1, $TC_2 = n_2C_2$ = the expected total cost for plot size 2, and so on.
3. The optimal plot size is the one with the lowest total cost.

To carry out this analysis, the inventory person must have a great deal of prior information. That is, for each distinctly different stand type, estimates of S_y^2 and cost per sampling unit must be available for all plot sizes under consideration. Although not available to many foresters, data of this type are not very difficult or expensive to generate. Forest managers and consultants usually deal with many stands of the same basic structure (as regards species, density, age, and so on). Ideally, several stands of each structure should be identified. Then each stand should be inventoried (with a line-plot cruise) using the various plot sizes under consideration. If three plot sizes were of interest, each stand would be inventoried three times (once with each plot size). These multiple inventories of the same stand will provide estimates of S_y^2 and cost per sampling unit for each plot size in the stand structure of interest. The analysis described previously can then be carried out, and the optimal plot size identified for each stand structure can be considered. It is not necessary to carry out totally independent inventories, and all sample plots can be installed in one pass through the stand by overlaying the various plots on each plot center and recording sample data separately for each plot size. The added cost from these data-gathering inventories can be paid for many times over by more efficient sampling of these stand types in the future.

EXAMPLE 3.10.1

A forest consultant has obtained the following information about S_y^2 and cost per sample plot *(C)* for three circular plot sizes in two stands in a major stand type in her region:

Stand	Plot Size (Acres)	S_y^2 (ft^3 per acre)^2	C ($/plot)
1	1/20	4,100,000	11
1	1/10	650,000	18
1	1/5	475,000	32
2	1/20	4,500,000	10
2	1/10	720,000	17
2	1/5	495,000	32

Assume that the desired bound on the estimated volume per acre is

$$B = 200 \text{ ft}^3/\text{acre}$$

Now ignore the fpc in calculating sample size and use the sample size equation for infinite population size (Eq. 3.11) to determine n for each plot size in each stand:

Stand	Plot Size (Acres)	n (Sample Size)	TC = $n \times C$
1	1/20	410	4510
1	1/10	65	1170
1	1/5	48	1536
2	1/20	450	4500
2	1/10	72	1224
2	1/5	50	1600

Average the expected total cost (TC) for each plot size:

Plot Size (Acres)	TC ($)
1/20	4505
1/10	1197
1/5	1568

Based on this analysis, the 1/10-acre sample plot should be preferred in this stand type.

This analysis can also be carried out using the coefficient of variation (CV) as the measure of variation among plots. In this case the bound on the mean per acre or tract total would be given in a percentage as the allowable error (AE) (see Section 3.6). Since CV as a percentage removes the size contribution to variance, it may actually be the preferred measure of variability in examining plot size. Foresters will find that although CV varies widely across all stand types, it stays in a much smaller range within a stand type in a region. After a few months of keeping records, foresters will have a good feel for the range of CV for a given stand type in their area. For determining optimal plot size, it is ideal to use each sample plot size in the same stand (that is, multiple inventories of the same stand); however, it is not required. If, in a given region, there are many stands with the same basic structure, then an alternative, less ideal, approach to the problem is to inventory several stands having the same structure with the plot sizes under consideration (but only one plot size will be used in a given stand). This avoids having to inventory the same stand more than once, and thus the procedure may be more readily accepted by field foresters.

EXAMPLE 3.10.2

A district forester wishes to identify the optimal sample plot size for a major stand type in his region. To make an informed, objective decision he decides that he will use the next nine stands he cruises in this stand type to generate the data needed to make this decision. The first three will be inventoried with 1/20-acre plots, the next three with 1/10-acre plots, and the final three with 1/5-acre plots. After a six-month period, he finally completes his goal and has the following data:

Stand	Plot Size (Acres)	CV	C (\$/plot)
1	1/20	55	9
2	1/20	60	8
3	1/20	57	9
4	1/10	45	16
5	1/10	49	17
6	1/10	51	15
7	1/5	37	26
8	1/5	35	28
9	1/5	39	25

The allowable error used in this situation is 5%; thus

$$AE = 5$$

Now, ignoring the fpc in sample size calculation, use Eq. 3.13 to calculate the required sample size to meet this AE for each plot size in each stand. The expected total cost (TC) can then be calculated by multiplying sample size *(n)* by cost per plot *(C):*

Stand	Plot Size (Acres)	n	TC = $n \times C$
1	1/20	484	4356
2	1/20	576	4608
3	1/20	520	4680
4	1/10	324	5184
5	1/10	385	6545
6	1/10	417	6255
7	1/5	220	5720
8	1/5	196	5488
9	1/5	244	6100

Obtain the average expected total cost (TC) for each of these plot sizes for this stand type:

Plot Size (Acres)	TC ($)
1/20	4548
1/10	5995
1/5	5769

In this stand type the 1/20-acre sample plot has the lowest TC and is preferred.

The costs in these discussions assume that fixed costs are the same for different plot sizes and that optimal plot size can therefore be obtained by ranking variable costs. If fixed costs differ, they can easily be added to this general problem-solving framework. The important point is that a well-thought-out, organized approach to the problem is used to determine optimal plot size.

3.11 SAMPLE PLOT LOCATION

Choice of and subsequent location of sample plots in a simple random sample were discussed briefly in Section 3.2. Since systematic sampling is preferred in forest inventory (for reasons discussed in Section 3.5), the following discussion will concentrate on plot location and layout for systematic samples. This type of sampling is usually referred to as *line-plot sampling* when fixed-area sample plots are used as the sampling units. This name comes from the fact that parallel lines running perpendicular to the major topographic or drainage characteristics of the stand are used to lay out the sample plots. Each line is placed at a predefined interval, and then on each line a sample plot is established and measured on another predefined interval. A rectangular stand configuration is illustrated in Figure 3.11.1.

Figure 3.11.1 Typical layout of plots in a systematic line-plot sample of a timber stand. Lines are on an interval of distance x, and plots along a line are on an interval of distance y.

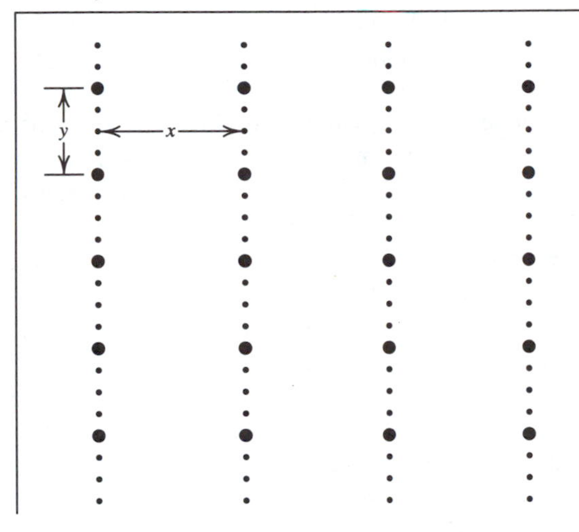

If sample size has been determined, the distance between lines and the distance between sample plots within a line that will yield the desired sample size must be determined. Of course, this assumes that the size of the tract is known. When the tract size is given in units of acres, it is convenient to define the line interval and plot interval in units of chains. Recall that a chain is 66 feet in length and that 10 square chains is equal to one acre.

The first decision to make for sample plot layout is whether the plots will be on a square grid. If a square grid is used, the line interval equals the plot interval. If a rectangular grid is used, should the line interval be greater than the plot interval or vice versa? In most instances rectangular grids are established by using a line interval greater than the plot interval in order to decrease walking time between plots. Choice of line and plot interval will be dictated by the required sample size, n. The choice of a square or rectangular grid should be made according to the structure of the stand to be inventoried. Ideally, sample plots should be located so that all stand conditions are represented in the sample. If aerial photos or topographic maps of the stand are available, it is a good idea to use a grid that will help to ensure that all stand conditions are represented. At a minimum, if the choice is made to use a rectangular grid with a line interval greater than the plot interval, then the lines should be perpendicular to the drainage patterns. The objective is to distribute the plots across the stand so that the proportion of sample plots falling in a given stand component is representative of the component.

EXAMPLE 3.11.1

A forester has determined that he will need to measure 65 $\frac{1}{20}$-acre sample plots to estimate the total volume of a 100-acre stand within his desired AE of 10%. He must determine how to distribute the plots on the ground. First he calculates the number of acres represented by each plot:

$$\frac{100 \text{ acres}}{65 \text{ plots}} = 1.54 \text{ acres/plot}$$

The stand is fairly irregular in shape with several low, wet areas, as depicted in Figure 3.11.2. If a square grid is used, the line and plot interval will be 3.9 chains (257.4 ft). This value is derived as follows: 1.54 acres = 15.4 square chains. To obtain square spacing each side must be $\sqrt{15.4} = 3.9$ chains.

To establish the first plot, the forester arbitrarily picks point A. Alternatively, he could draw a grid of 1000 ⅒-acre plots on the stand map, number each one, and randomly choose a starting plot. All subsequent plots would then be established relative to this randomly chosen one. This is a fairly time-consuming procedure and really is not any more or less valid than arbitrarily picking a starting point. Once point A is established, lines are run perpendicular to the contours installing a new plot every 3.9 chains. At the end of the first line, he offsets 3.9 chains to establish the next line. Plots are then established at 3.9 chain intervals within the new line. This is continued until all 65 plots are on the map. Of course, shape irregularities of the stand will be such that it will be nearly impossible to lay out exactly the required 65 sample plots. However, since the sample size, n, is simply an estimate based on an estimated variance, S_y^2, it should not be cause for concern if 63 or 67 plots result when 65 is the goal. The objective should be to lay out the plots such that they represent all conditions in the stand and to get as close as practically possible to the estimated required sample size.

If the stand conditions were found to be fairly uniform parallel to the drainage pattern based on study of aerial photos and a preliminary visit to the stand, the forester would then be justified in using a rectangular grid in which the line interval is greater

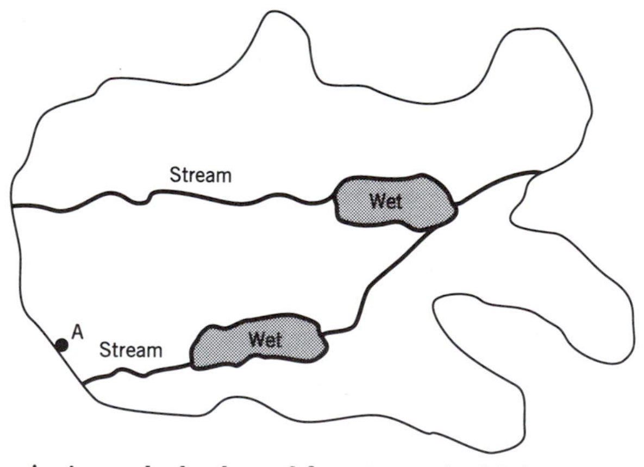

Figure 3.11.2 An irregularly shaped forest stand with low wet areas and streams flowing through it.

than the plot interval. For example, the forester may determine that he can place lines five chains apart without missing any major stand changes. This would dictate that plots within each line be on a 3.1-chain interval using the following calculations:

$$\frac{1.54 \text{ acres}}{\text{plot}} \times \frac{10 \text{ chains}^2}{\text{acre}} = \frac{15.4 \text{ chains}^2}{\text{plot}}$$

$$\text{Plot interval} = \frac{15.4 \text{ chains}^2/\text{plot}}{5 \text{ chains between lines}} = 3.1 \text{ chains within line}$$

Thus with this rectangular grid more plots will be installed along each line. This type of grid is desirable when stand conditions are expected to change more rapidly within lines than between lines. This situation usually occurs when lines run perpendicular to topographic and drainage patterns.

3.12 ESTIMATING ACREAGES

Frequently foresters must inventory tracts without having aerial photos, stand maps, or even an estimate of the acreage of the stand. To obtain an accurate estimate of total tract volume, a survey should be conducted to determine the acreage (a 100% sample of all trees in the tract could be done if the stand is relatively small, but this is usually not possible). If for one reason or another there is no way to obtain an accurate estimate of the tract acreage, then a systematic sample of plots can be used to obtain a rough estimate of the acreage. The procedure is simple:

1. Choose an appropriate grid (usually rectangular with lines running perpendicular to the drainage and for which the interval between lines is greater than the interval within lines).
2. Arbitrarily choose a starting point near one of the tract corners.
3. Install and measure fixed-area sample plots across the stand.

Needless to say, in this situation it is not possible to determine an estimated required sample size for meeting a predefined bound or allowable error. Upon completion of the sample, the tract acreage can be estimated by multiplying the total number of plots by the number of acres represented by each plot. For example, if a 5×3 chain grid were used, then each plot represents

$$5_{ch} \times 3_{ch} = \frac{15 \text{ chains}^2/\text{plot}}{10 \text{ chains}^2/\text{acre}} = \frac{1.5 \text{ acres}}{\text{plot}}$$

Of course, tract acreage estimated in this way is only an approximation. The more irregularly shaped the tract, the worse will be the approximation.

EXAMPLE 3.12.1

A forester has been hired to inventory a forest stand. There are no aerial photos or maps with which to obtain an estimate of tract area. After a visit to the tract, the drainage pattern is ascertained and the appropriate line bearing is established. The forester decides to use a line-plot cruise with lines spaced 150 m apart and plots within lines spaced at 100 m. On completion of the cruise, 60 plots were measured. What is the best estimate of the stand area in hectares (1 ha = 10,000 m^2)?

Each plot represents

$$\frac{150_m \times 100 \text{ m}}{10{,}000 \text{ m}^2/\text{ha}} = \frac{1.5 \text{ ha}}{\text{plot}}$$

Total stand area is

$$\frac{1.5 \text{ ha}}{\text{plot}} \times 60 \text{ plots} = 90 \text{ ha}$$

All calculations of means and totals can now be carried out as previously described using this estimated stand area.

A slight variation of the procedure just described has been devised for inventorying stands in the absence of area estimates. The procedure is as follows:

1. Choose the line and plot intervals as previously described—calculate the area each plot represents.
2. Divide the plot area by the area represented by each plot and multiply by 100—this is the percent cruise.
3. Obtain an estimate of the total volume (or basal area or value) and its associated standard error on the n sample plots.
4. Multiply the total and its associated standard error obtained in step 3 by 100 divided by the percent cruise to obtain the total tract estimate and its associated standard error.

This may seem different from the previous procedure, but in fact the procedures are equivalent and will produce the same estimates.

EXAMPLE 3.12.2

A forester must inventory a tract to determine the total cubic-foot volume of hardwood pulpwood. There are no maps, photos, or acreage estimates for the tract. From previous experience the forester believes that he can obtain a fairly accurate estimate by using 1/10-acre plots on a 2 chain × 5 chain grid. Thus each plot will represent

$$\frac{2\text{ ch} \times 5\text{ ch}}{\text{plot}} \div \frac{10\text{ ch}^2}{\text{acre}} = \frac{1\text{ acre}}{\text{plot}}$$

Now the percent cruise is

$$\frac{1/10\text{ acre/plot}}{1\text{ acre/plot}} = 0.1(100) = 10\%$$

A total of $n = 53$ sample plots were measured, and the following data are available:

Plot	y_i = Volume (ft^3)
1	25
2	42
•	•
•	•
•	•
•	•
53	51

$$\sum_{i=1}^{53} y_i = 2438\text{ ft}^3$$

$$\sum_{i=1}^{53} y_i^2 = 115{,}528\ (\text{ft}^3)^2$$

First calculate the average volume per plot:

$$\bar{y} = \frac{2438\text{ ft}^2}{53\text{ plots}} = 46\text{ ft}^3/\text{plot}$$

Now the variance of $\bar{y}$ is calculated using Eq. 3.2 without the fpc (N is unknown):

$$S_{\bar{y}}^2 = \frac{S_y^2}{n}$$

$$S_y^2 = \frac{1}{52}\left(115{,}528 - \frac{2438^2}{53}\right) = 65\ (\text{ft}^3)^2$$

$$S_{\bar{y}}^2 = \frac{65}{53} = 1.2264\ (\text{ft}^3/\text{plot})^2$$

The standard error of $\bar{y}$ is

$$S_{\bar{y}} = \sqrt{1.2264} = 1.1074 \text{ ft}^3/\text{plot}$$

The total volume on the 53 sample plots $(\hat{T})$ is then obtained by using the formula for a total (Eq. 3.3) with N set to 53:

$$\hat{T} = 53(46) = 2438 \text{ ft}^3$$

The standard error of $\hat{T}$ is then

$$S_{\hat{T}} = 1.1074\ (53) = 58.6922$$

Now to obtain the total tract volume multiply $\hat{T}$ by 100 divided by the percent cruise:

$$\hat{T} = 2438\left(\frac{100}{10}\right) = 24{,}380 \text{ ft}^3$$

The standard error of $\hat{T}$ is then

$$S_{\hat{T}} = \left(\frac{100}{10}\right)(58.6922) = 586.9 \text{ ft}^3$$

Of course, the tract acreage could have been estimated as follows: Each plot represents 1 acre and 53 plots were installed; thus the tract acreage is estimated to be 53 acres. With this information the tract total can be estimated using estimators from Section 3.2. Verify that the same estimates will result using this method. (Note: Be sure not to use the fpc since it was not used in this example.)

Clearly, it is possible to obtain tract estimates without using maps or photos to determine tract acreage. However, as previously stated, both methods described for doing this can have relatively large errors associated with them. Consequently, these methods should be used only when it is impossible to estimate stand acreage using more accurate methods.

Global positioning system (GPS) technology is now used routinely by many foresters to calculate acreages. Compared to the method described in Section 3.12, GPS acreages are very accurate. In addition, calculation requires simply walking the perimeter of the stand obtaining a GPS coordinate intermittently.

3.13 STAND VOIDS

Some sample plots may fall on roads, in ponds, on power line easements, and so on. The question then arises as to whether or not to measure a plot if it falls in such areas. If the plot falls in one of these types of stand voids, there will be no trees measured;

thus these plots are referred to as *no-tally* plots. Inventory foresters often question the utility of no-tally plots and choose to move these plots out of stand voids and back into the stand. This is the *wrong* solution to the problem. To arrive at the appropriate solution to the problem, one simple question must be answered: Has the stand void been (or will it be) counted as part of the stand acreage?

For example, if there is a 150-ft-wide powerline easement running through the stand, has the acreage in this easement been counted toward the total stand acreage? Whenever the answer to this question is "Yes, the stand void has been included in the total stand acreage," any plots falling in these voids are legitimate sample plots and should be recorded as no-tally plots (that is, the plot characteristic is zero). Not doing so will result in overestimates of tract totals and underestimates of the associated standard errors.

When the answer to the question posed above is "No, the stand void has not been included in the total stand acreage," the following procedure is used. When installing a line-plot sample (or, for that matter, a simple random sample), the stand voids are simply disregarded altogether. Plots are not allowed to fall in the voids because the voids are not part of the population—they have not been counted in the stand acreage. Thus, when a line-plot sample is installed, do not move the sample plots falling in the voids; simply disregard any acreage that has been removed from the tract acreage. This means that in practice, when you are installing plots three chains apart along a line and you have just moved one chain from the previous plot and have run into a stand void (such as a road, pond, or easement), you move across the void without counting the distance and then continue another two chains once you reenter the stand on the other side of the void.

Thus the predefined sample grid is maintained. This ensures that only the population included in the acreage estimate is sampled. In situations where there are no maps, photos, or acreage estimates, there will undoubtedly be legitimate no-tally plots. It is important that legitimate no-tally plots be included since these plots have a large impact on the estimate of the mean and the variance.

3.14 STAND EDGE

It is well known among field foresters that trees growing on the edge of stands grow differently from trees within the stand if the surrounding area is nonforest or a different forest type. This is due to many factors, but primarily to the fact that edge trees experience less intertree competition than trees within the stand.

In a line-plot sample in the field, a sample plot will often straddle the edge of the stand. There are a couple of legitimate solutions to the problem, as well as a questionable solution. The questionable solution, practiced by many field inventory personnel, is to move a sample plot away from the stand edge so that it falls entirely within the stand. This solution can lead to relatively large sampling errors if the stand in question has a large proportion of its area in edge (as in a long narrow tract). The problem is that not enough edge trees are included in the sample; they are underrepresented. Of course, when edge is not a large proportion of the tract area, the sampling error will be relatively small but still present.

One appropriate way to handle this problem is to establish the sampling unit exactly where it falls on the stand edge. Of course, only a portion of the sample plot will actually be within the stand. The area of the plot falling within the stand must be determined and recorded along with the sample tree information. Determining this partial plot area can be very time-consuming and complex (especially for circular sample plots). Furthermore, the calculations needed to estimate the population total and mean also become more complex for sampling units of various sizes. The calculations needed to obtain a valid estimate of a population mean or total in this situation make use of a ratio estimator (Chapter 6). Because of the increased field time and more complex calculations involved, this option is usually not preferred.

A variation of this method is the use of half-plots. In this method a plot of half the usual size is installed exactly on the stand edge. Trees in this half-plot are then tallied, and plot characteristics are calculated as usual and then doubled so that the half-plot represents a whole plot.

Another procedure for dealing with plots falling on the stand edge is known as the mirage method. The mirage method (Schmid-Haus, 1969) was developed for use with circular sample plots. The procedure is relatively simple to apply in the field and the calculations involved in working up the sample data are the same as for any simple random or systematic sample. Assume that circular plots of a given area (that is, a given radius) are used and a plot center falls near the stand edge so that the entire plot does not lie within the stand (Figure 3.14.1). The problem is that the plot radius, y, is larger than the distance between the plot center and the stand edge, x. The mirage method can be implemented as follows:

1. Establish the plot exactly where the plot center falls and measure and record all trees falling in the plot that are inside the stand.
2. Measure or pace the distance, x, from the plot center to the stand edge along the line used to establish plots.
3. Continue on the same line and pace this same distance x from the stand edge into the area outside the stand.
4. From this point, establish a plot using the plot radius y and measure and record all trees falling in this "plot" that are inside the stand.

Thus some trees near the stand edge are tallied twice on the same plot. Geometrically, the mirage method creates a full plot by folding the plot over on itself, as illustrated in

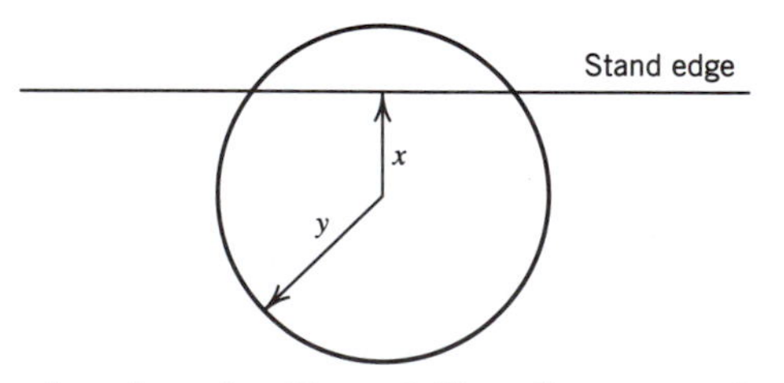

Figure 3.14.1 Circular plot of radius y falling distance x from the stand edge.

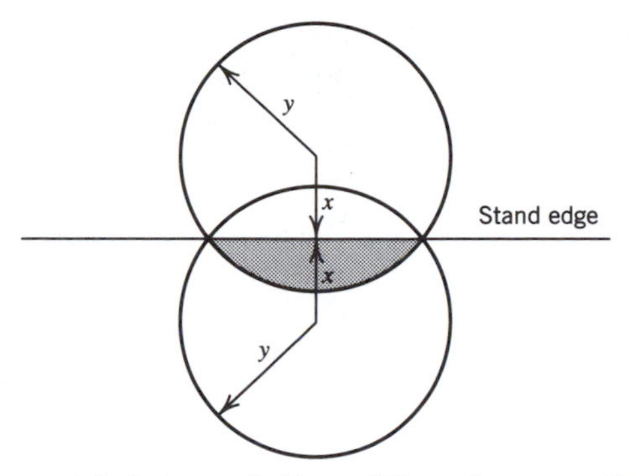

Figure 3.14.2 Geometric interpretation of the mirage method. Trees falling in the shaded region will be tallied twice.

Figure 3.14.2. This procedure may seem a bit strange since some trees are recorded twice on the same plot. However, the procedure produces unbiased estimates of stand characteristics and ensures that trees on the stand edge are represented in the correct proportion (Gregoire, 1982).

3.15 STAND AND STOCK TABLES

A stand table presents the number of trees (frequency) by diameter at breast height (dbh) classes, height classes (total or merchantable), and species or species groups on a unit-area basis. The information obtained in the woods while cruising timber is the type of information needed to create a stand table. This stand table information can be recorded separately for each sample plot (or point) (discussed in Chapter 4), or it can be recorded without regard to plot identity. However, we recommend that all forest inventory information always be recorded separately by sample plot (or point) so that variability information can be calculated.

A stock table presents tree volume and/or weight by dbh classes, height classes, and species or species groups on a unit-area basis. The stock table is obtained from the stand table with volume (weight) tables or equations.

Procedures for development of the stock table are dependent on the type of information available in the stand table. Differences are related mainly to the height measurements obtained in the woods. If heights of all sample trees are measured or estimated, then a standard volume or weight equation can be used. If no height measurements are obtained in the woods, then a local volume or weight equation will be required. If a subset of heights is obtained in the woods, then a local volume or weight equation can be derived using a standard volume or weight equation. This method requires either development of a regression equation to predict height from diameter or volume from basal area or a large sample of heights in each diameter class from which average heights by diameter class can be calculated.

The following example illustrates how to obtain a stock table from a stand table using standard volume equations. Derivation of local volume equations is not covered here. Interested readers are referred to Husch et al. (1982) and Avery and Burkhart (1994).

EXAMPLE 3.15.1

The following tally was obtained from a ⅒-acre sample plot in a loblolly pine plantation:

dbh (in.)	Average Total Height (ft)	Number of Trees
8	47	2
9	51	3
10	54	7
11	58	6
12	64	7
13	68	4
14	73	2

The following volume equation is available for use:

$$V = 0.00432\ D^{1.953}\ H^{0.897}$$

where:

V = total stem volume (ft^3)

D = dbh (in.)

H = total height (ft)

The first step in the development of the stand and stock table is to estimate the volume per tree for each dbh class. For example, for the 8-in. dbh class,

$$D = 8 \text{ in.}$$

$$H = 47 \text{ ft}$$

$$V = 0.00432(8)^{1.953}\ (47)^{0.897} = 7.93 \text{ ft}^3$$

Then, since a stand table is defined on a per-acre basis and each tree on a ⅒-acre plot represents 10 trees per acre, the number of trees tallied is multiplied by 10. Thus, from the plot tally given above, the following stand table is obtained:

dbh (in.)	Average Total Height (ft)	Number of Trees/Acre	Volume/Tree
8	47	20	7.93
9	51	30	10.74
10	54	70	13.88
11	58	60	17.83
12	64	70	23.08
13	68	40	28.50
14	73	20	35.10

Next multiply the number of trees per acre by volume per tree for each dbh class to obtain the volume per dbh class.

dbh (in.)	Average Total Height (ft)	Number of Trees/Acre	Volume/ Tree (ft^3)	Volume/ Class (ft^3)
8	47	20	7.93	158.6
9	51	30	10.74	322.2
10	54	70	13.88	971.6
11	58	60	17.83	1069.8
12	64	70	23.08	1615.6
13	68	40	28.50	1140.0
14	73	20	35.10	702.0
		310		5979.8

Volume per acre represented on the sample plot is easily obtained by summing volume per class over all dbh classes. For this example the volume per acre represented by the plot is 5979.8 ft^3.

REFERENCES

Avery, T. E., and H. E. Burkhart. 1994. *Forest measurements*. McGraw-Hill, New York.

Gregoire, T. G. 1982. The unbiasedness of the mirage correction procedure for boundary overlap. *For. Sci.* 28:504–508.

Husch, B., C. I. Miller, and T. W. Beers. 1982. *Forest mensuration*. 3rd ed. Wiley, New York.

Scheaffer, R. L., W. Mendenhall, and L. Ott. 1990. *Elementary survey sampling*. PWS-KENT, Boston.

Schmid-Haus, P. 1969. Stichproben am Waldrond (Sampling at the edge of the forest). *Milt Schweiz Anst Forest Versuchswes* 43(3):234–303.

PROBLEMS FOR BETTER UNDERSTANDING

1. You have been hired to inventory a 25-acre tract of longleaf pine. You took a systematic sample of 19 1/10-acre fixed-radius plots. Cubic foot volume per plot was

Plot	Volume (ft^3)	Plot	Volume (ft^3)
1	32.7	11	34.4
2	49.8	12	47.8
3	62.3	13	56.9
4	41.3	14	51.4
5	37.9	15	63.4
6	75.9	16	71.1
7	59.4	17	69.3
8	39.4	18	38.6
9	64.9	19	44.4
10	71.3		

   a. Obtain an estimate of the mean volume per acre on this tract.

   b. Obtain an approximate 95% confidence interval for your estimate in part a.

   c. Obtain an estimate of the total tract volume.

   d. Obtain an approximate 95% confidence interval for your estimate in part c.

   e. Explain what a confidence interval means so that a layman can understand. (Do *not* say that we are 95% confident that the true value lies in the interval.)

2. Suppose that the stumpage value for the tract described in Problem 1 is $0.65/$ft^3$.

   a. Calculate the average dollar value per acre in this stand.

   b. What is the approximate 95% confidence interval for your estimate in part a?

   c. Calculate the total dollar value for this tract.

   d. What is the approximate 95% confidence interval for your estimate in part c?

3. A natural stand of mixed conifers located in west central Oregon was inventoried using 1/5-acre circular plots. On each plot measurements were made and international 1/4-in. board feet of merchantable conifer volume was determined. A total of 93 plots were obtained from the 144-acre stand. Let y_i be the volume on plot i; the sum and sum of squared plot volumes are

$$\sum_{i=1}^{93} y_i = 116{,}246$$

$$\sum_{i=1}^{93} y_i^2 = 180{,}667{,}300$$

a. Calculate an estimate of the total board foot volume on this tract.

b. Calculate the standard error of the estimate obtained in part a.

c. Calculate an approximate 95% confidence interval for the estimate obtained in part a.

d. What is the coefficient of variation in this stand?

e. Assume that the stumpage value of the timber in this stand is $265 per thousand board feet (MBF). Calculate the total dollar value of the timber in this stand.

f. Calculate an approximate 95% confidence interval for the estimate obtained in part e.

4. An inventory of a mixed pine hardwood stand in the Appalachian mountains of central Virginia was carried out. On each 1/10-acre plot measurements were made so that per-acre basal area of pine and basal area of hardwood could be determined. Let y_i be the pine basal area on plot i and x_i be the hardwood basal area on plot i. A total of 17 plots were measured in the 30-acre stand; the data are as follows:

Plot	y_i (ft²/plot)	x_i (ft²/plot)
1	4.2	3.6
2	5.1	2.8
3	6.9	2.2
4	3.8	4.2
5	7.5	3.1
6	8.0	4.1
7	2.5	2.9
8	2.0	3.0
9	3.4	4.2
10	6.2	5.9
11	7.7	6.1
12	5.4	6.5
13	2.7	1.9
14	2.4	2.5
15	6.1	4.6
16	5.3	2.7
17	4.8	3.3

a. Calculate the per-acre estimate of pine basal area.

b. Calculate the per-acre estimate of hardwood basal area.

c. Obtain approximate 95% confidence intervals for the estimates obtained in parts a and b.

d. Calculate the per-acre estimate of total basal area per acre (pine and hardwood) and obtain an approximate 95% confidence interval for this estimate.

5. You have been given the opportunity to estimate the total cordwood volume of a 200-acre slash pine stand located in northwest Florida. You have decided to use ⅒-acre sample plots. Based on a pilot cruise you estimate the standard deviation among ⅒-acre sample plots to be $S_y = 1.3$ cords. How many plots must be used in order to estimate the total volume with an upper bound on the error of estimation of 300 cords?

6. A 225-acre 55-year-old second growth Douglas fir stand is to be inventoried. One-fifth-acre sample plots will be used. From previous experience in similar stands we know that the coefficient of variation will run about 65%. How many sample plots are required to obtain an estimate of the total tract volume with an allowable error of 10%?

7. A random sample of 225 trees was taken from a 38-acre mixed conifer stand in Idaho. Each tree was examined and classified as sawtimber or nonsawtimber. The tree was given a value of 1 if it was a sawtimber tree and a value of 0 if it was not. A total of 99 trees were classified as sawtimber.

a. What type of random variable takes on values of 1 and 0 only?

b. Obtain an estimate of the proportion of sawtimber trees in the stand.

c. Estimate the variance of the proportion obtained in part b (Hint: Since N is unknown, use infinite population formulas).

d. Obtain an approximate 95% confidence interval for the proportion obtained in part b.

8. Refer to Problem 5. Determine the systematic sampling grid (in chains) needed to install the approximate number of plots required to meet the desired bound.

a. Assume a square grid.

b. Assume a rectangular grid with sample lines twice as far apart as sample plots within lines.

9. A consulting forester working in the Inland Empire of the northwestern United States is undertaking a small study to determine which size of fixed-area sample plot should be used to cruise natural mixed conifer stands between 70 and 90 years old. Three stands meeting these criteria were each cruised using ⅒-, ⅕-, and ¼-acre sample plots. The coefficient of variation and average cost per plot for each stand-plot size combination are as follows:

Stand	Plot Size (Acres)	CV (%)	Cost ($/plot)
1	⅒	75	16
1	⅕	60	24
1	¼	53	29
2	⅒	79	18
2	⅕	63	27

Stand	Plot Size (Acres)	CV (%)	Cost ($/plot)
2	1/4	57	31
3	1/10	85	14
3	1/5	64	22
3	1/4	55	26

Use an allowable error of 10% and determine which plot size should be preferred. Note: Use the infinite population size formulas.

10. Use Eq. 3.13 to create a table of required sample sizes for coefficients of variation of 20%, 40%, 60%, 80%, and 100% and allowable errors of 5%, 10%, 15%, 20%, 25%, and 30%. (Be sure to round n to the next highest number of whole plots.)

11. Use the data created in Problem 10 and plot sample size versus allowable error for each coefficient of variation. Using your graphs, determine the allowable error that seems reasonable for each coefficient of variation. (Consider reduction in AE per increase in number of plots.)

12. Derive the sample size formula for estimating a population total within a bound of B_T. Assume a finite population and work at an approximate 95% confidence level.

13. Show that the sample size formula for population means and totals are identical when the upper bound on the error of estimation (B_u and B_T) are given as allowable error (assume infinite population size).

14. Design a data sheet for carrying out a line-plot cruise for a stand type in your area. Be sure to design it so that the data can be kept separate by sample plot. Include space for appropriate individual tree measurements.

CHAPTER 4

HORIZONTAL POINT SAMPLING

Point sampling is a sampling method unique to forestry. The method was developed by Walter Bitterlich (1947), an Austrian forester. It was introduced to American foresters and popularized by Lewis R. Grosenbaugh (1952, 1957, 1958, 1967). Point sampling has been the subject of many papers in the forestry literature and has been called variable plot sampling, plotless sampling, angle count sampling, prism cruising, angle gauge sampling, and Bitterlich sampling. The method was quickly recognized by many foresters as an efficient sampling method.

This chapter will include some background on why and how point sampling works, a description of how to conduct a point sample, point sampling estimators, and suggestions on modifications to point sampling to increase sampling efficiency. Finally, a discussion of plot sampling versus point sampling and how those comparisons should be made is included.

4.1 SAMPLING WITH PROBABILITY PROPORTIONAL TO SIZE

All of the sampling methods discussed in this book up to this chapter would collectively be called equal-probability sampling methods. With simple random sampling or systematic sampling, the size of the sampling units did not affect the probability of being selected for the sample. Point sampling is an unequal-probability-selection sampling method. The larger sampling units (trees) have a higher probability of selection so that point sampling is called a *probability-proportional-to-size* sampling method. The probability of selection is proportional to tree basal area. Other probability-proportional-to-size sampling methods will be discussed in Section 8.6 and in Chapter 10.

What is the rationale behind giving one sampling unit a higher probability of selection in the sample than another? Larger trees have more volume and typically more value than smaller trees. The inventory objectives often include estimation of volume or value or both. Intuitively, if the sample can be constructed so as to include a higher proportion of higher-volume and higher-value trees, less time would be spent on smaller trees and the sampling method should be more efficient. This is, in fact, the case.

Bitterlich suggested the use of an angle to select sample trees. An arbitrary and constant angle is projected from a random point in the forest. The forester conducting the inventory sights at breast height on every tree visible as he or she rotates through 360 degrees around the point. Three possibilities exist (Figure 4.1.1) for each tree within viewing distance. If the tree is larger than the projected angle, the tree is a tally tree. If the tree is smaller than the projected angle, the tree is not selected as a sample tree. In situations where the angle is tangent to both sides of the tree, the tree is a borderline tree. More measurements, detailed later, are necessary to determine whether a borderline tree is a sample tree. Since the two sides of any projected angle diverge as the distance from the point increases, it is difficult for small trees to qualify as sample trees unless they are near the point. Larger trees can be much further from the point and still qualify as sample trees. Because they qualify as sample trees over a greater distance, larger trees have a higher probability of being selected than do smaller trees. The exact probabilities will be calculated later in this chapter.

It would seem that if smaller trees are discriminated against in the selection process, this sampling method would be biased and lead to overestimates of volume, value, and the like. In actuality, the bias toward large trees occurs only in the selection process. During the cruise workup the large trees account for fewer trees per acre than do the small trees, as discussed in Section 4.5. This effectively reverses the bias in the selection process, and the result is an unbiased estimator.

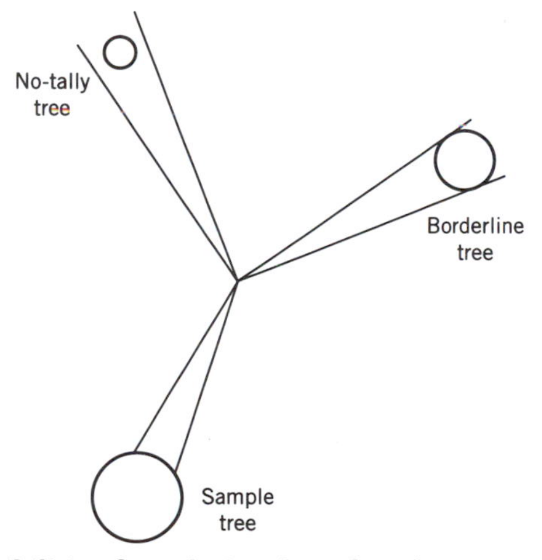

Figure 4.1.1 Possibilities for relationship of angle to tree size in point sampling.

4.2 PROJECTING THE ANGLE

Anything that can be used to project an angle will work for conducting a point sample. Foresters have used coins or their thumbs held at arm's length to project an angle, the apex of which is in their eye. These are just two crude examples of angle gauges. Most commonly, angle gauges are small pieces of metal mounted on a wooden rod. Commercially made angle gauges, which are patterns cut into metal at the appropriate width, are available. With any angle gauge the tree is viewed as in Figure 4.1.1, and if the tree is larger than the projected angle, the tree is a sample (tally) tree.

Another commonly used instrument for projecting angles is the wedge prism, which was introduced by Bruce (1955). This is a ground and calibrated prism that bends light at a specific angle. Unlike an angle gauge, the apex of the angle is in the prism rather than in the eye of the cruiser. When viewed through a prism, the trunk of the tree appears to be offset (Figure 4.2.1). When the two images overlap each other, the tree is a sample (tally) tree.

A third instrument for projecting angles is the relascope, developed by Bitterlich for point sampling. The relascope projects a choice of several different angles and automatically corrects for slope. The instrument will also determine upper stem diameters and tree heights. The relascope is held up to the eye and the tree is viewed through a sight on the instrument, which means that the eye should remain over the point as trees are viewed. This sighting mechanism is less effective for viewing trees on cloudy days and in dense, shaded stands.

All of these instruments for projecting angles require that the apex of the angle be kept over the point. In the case of angle gauges and relascopes, this requires the forester to keep his or her eye over the point while rotating through 360 degrees to view all trees. With the prism, the instrument must be kept over the point as trees are viewed.

Figure 4.2.1 Images visible through a wedge prism for (*a*) tally (sample), (*b*) borderline, and (*c*) no-tally trees for point sampling.

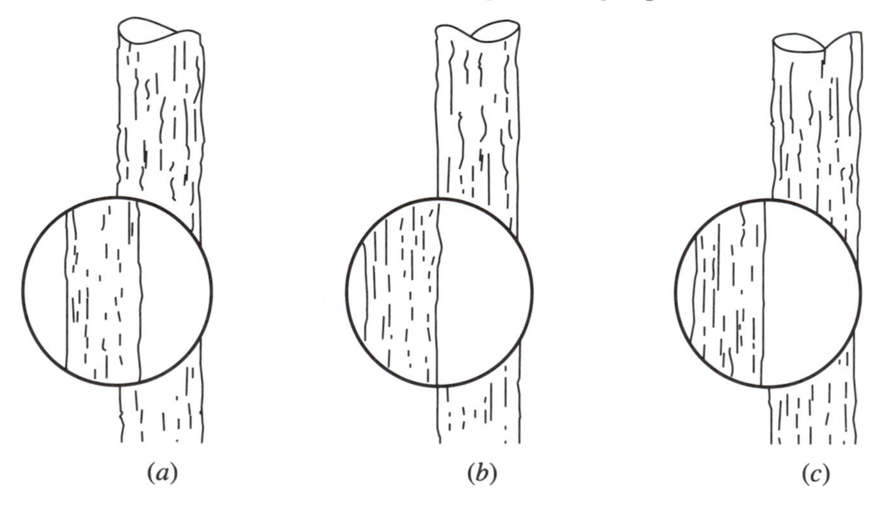

Point sampling as discussed in this chapter is horizontal point sampling. Related sampling methods such as vertical point sampling, horizontal line sampling, and vertical line sampling are discussed by Husch et al. (1982). Horizontal point sampling is by far the most popular of the four methods.

4.3 IMAGINARY ZONES

To compare point sampling with more traditional fixed-radius plot sampling, it is helpful to consider a tree in the borderline condition. In the borderline condition, the tree is the maximum distance *(R)* that it can be from the point and still be considered a sample tree. Figure 4.3.1 shows the relationship between the dbh *(D)* in inches and this critical distance *(R)* in feet. Note that if *R* increases (the point is further from the center of the tree), the sides of the projected angle diverge and the tree will no longer be a sample tree. The dashed line represents an imaginary circle of radius *R* particular to this projected angle and this tree size. If the tree is moved further from the point, the point will fall outside the imaginary circle. Conversely, if the tree is nearer the point, the point will fall inside the imaginary circle and the tree will be a sample tree. When a tree is in the borderline condition, the ratio of the diameter of the tree to the critical distance (both in units of feet) is a constant, *k*.

$$k = \frac{D}{12R} \tag{4.1}$$

Figure 4.3.1 Relationship between the dbh *(D)* in inches and the critical distance *(R)* in feet for a borderline tree.

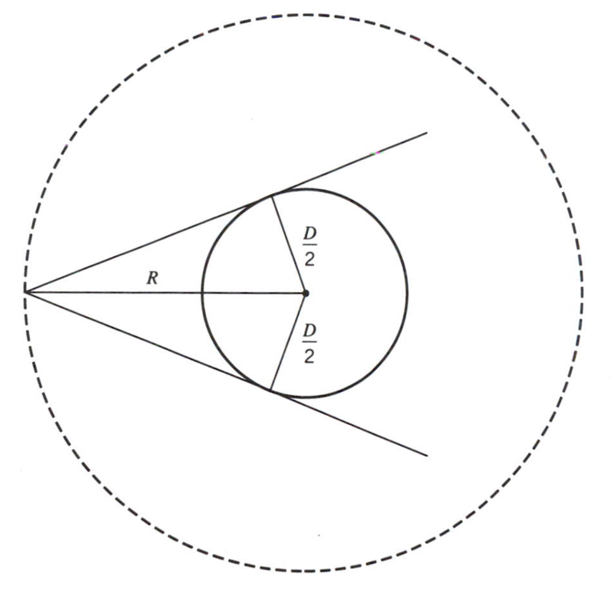

If D increases, R will also have to increase to keep the tree in the borderline condition. Again, this means that larger trees have larger imaginary zones. A point dropped at random on a tract has a higher probability of falling inside a large zone than inside a smaller one. Beers and Miller (1964) present a detailed discussion of imaginary zones.

If the projected angle changes, then k changes. Narrower projected angles result in more trees selected as sample trees. Larger angles result in fewer trees selected.

The critical distance, R, can be calculated for any tree diameter, D, given that k is known. Since $k = D/12R$, $R = D/12k$. Substituting 1 for D results in the number of feet R increases for each inch of dbh. This value is commonly called the plot radius factor (PRF).

Conversely, the constant, k, can easily be calculated once a projected angle is given by the following method:

> Move whatever distance away from a tree is necessary to put the tree in the borderline condition. Measure R to the tree pith in feet and D in inches and calculate k by Eq. 4.1.

A flat target may also be used to calibrate prisms or angle gauges with a slightly different methodology, as described by Husch et al. (1982).

4.4 PROBABILITY OF SELECTION

If simple random sampling is used, the probability of a tree on a 1/10-acre plot being selected on a per-acre basis is equal to the plot area divided by the area of an acre:

$$P(\text{selection}) = \frac{4356 \text{ ft}^2}{43{,}560 \text{ ft}^2} = \frac{1}{10}$$

This probability applies regardless of tree size. Trees with a dbh of 4 in. and a dbh of 10 in. have the same probability of selection.

Similarly, the probability of selection for a tree on a point sample is equal to its imaginary zone area divided by the area of an acre:

$$P(\text{selection}) = \frac{\text{Zone area}}{43{,}560 \text{ ft}^2}$$

$$= \frac{\pi R^2}{43{,}560 \text{ ft}^2}$$

Since $R = D/12k$,

$$= \frac{\pi\left(\frac{D}{12k}\right)^2}{43{,}560 \text{ ft}^2}$$

Multiply by 1, defined as 4/4:

$$= \frac{4}{43{,}560 \text{ ft}^2} \times \frac{\pi D^2}{4(144)}$$

$$= \frac{1}{10{,}890k^2} \times \frac{\pi D^2}{576}$$

$$= \frac{1}{10{,}890k^2} \times 0.005454D^2$$

The basal area of a tree (BA) can be determined from the area of a circle with the assumption that trees are circular:

$$A = \pi r^2$$

$$\text{BA} = \pi \left(\frac{D}{2}\right)^2$$

Since D is in inches, divide by 12 to obtain BA in ft^2:

$$\text{BA} = \pi \left(\frac{\text{D}}{12 \times 2}\right)^2$$

$$\text{BA} = \frac{\pi D^2}{576}$$

$$\text{BA} = 0.005454D^2$$

So

$$P(\text{selection}) = \frac{1}{10{,}890k^2} \times \text{BA} = \frac{\text{BA}}{10{,}890k^2}$$

Since $1/10{,}890k^2$ is a constant, the probability of selection is simply a constant times BA, and therefore the probability of selection is proportional to the basal area of a tree. This means that the imaginary zone around each tree is proportional to its basal area.

4.5 EXPANSION FACTOR AND TREES PER ACRE

The expansion factor used to express plot information on a per-acre basis is calculated as the inverse of the probability of selection. As previously calculated, for a 1/10-acre plot the probability of selection is 1/10 for all trees regardless of size. The expansion factor

Table 4.5.1 Commonly used basal area factors (BAFs) and their associated k values and PRF values

BAF	k	PRF
5	0.0214	3.889
10	0.0303	2.750
15	0.0372	2.245
20	0.0429	1.944
30	0.0526	1.588
40	0.0606	1.375
50	0.0676	1.230
60	0.0741	1.123

is then $\frac{1}{1/10} = 10$. This means that any tree on a 1⁄10-acre plot represents 10 trees per acre regardless of whether that tree is a 4-in. tree, a 10-in. tree, or a 20-in. tree.

For a point sample, each different tree size has a unique expansion factor since the probability of selection is proportional to basal area. The expansion factor is still the inverse of the selection probability. Since $P(\text{selection}) = \text{BA}/10{,}890k^2$, the expansion factor is $10{,}890k^2/\text{BA}$. Since $10{,}890k^2$ is a constant for any selected prism with value k, it is calculated just once and is called the basal area factor (BAF). As for fixed-radius plots, the expansion factor is actually the trees per acre (TPA) represented by one sample tree. With this notation, TPA = BAF/BA. Many foresters refer to prisms and angle gauges by their basal area factor rather than by the size of the angle projected or the k value. Thus it is common to hear about 10 factor prisms or angle gauges. Commonly used basal area factors, their associated k values, and their associated plot radius factors (PRFs) are presented in Table 4.5.1.

For a BAF = 10 prism, the following TPA values would be calculated for trees of different dbh sizes:

dbh	TPA = BAF/BA
4	114.59
5	73.34
6	50.93
7	37.42
8	28.65
9	22.64
10	18.34
11	15.15
12	12.73

It may be bothersome to have different TPA values for different dbh values, but this is consistent with the probability of selection. For a BAF = 10, the $k = 0.0303$, and from Table 4.5.1 the PRF = 2.75. Operationally, this means that $R = D \times 2.75$. For a 4-in.

tree, $R = 11$ ft. For an 8-in. tree, $R = 22$ ft. For trees of these two sizes, the area of imaginary zones can be calculated using the formula for the area of a circle:

$$A = \pi R^2$$
$$A_4 = \pi(11)^2 = 380.13 \text{ ft}^2$$
$$A_8 = \pi(22)^2 = 1520.53 \text{ ft}^2$$

The imaginary zone area of an 8-in. tree is exactly four times as large as the zone area of a 4-in. tree. This means that an 8-in. tree is four times more likely to be included in the sample than a 4-in. tree. Notice that one 4-in. tree represents 114.6 trees per acre, whereas one 8-in. tree represents only 28.7 trees per acre, ¼ as many. Intuitively, this also is reasonable. If the zone of a 4-in. tree is very small, it is unlikely that one will be included in the sample. If a 4-in. tree shows up in the sample, the implication is that there must be many of them on the tract for one to be located close enough to the random point to be a sample tree. The number of trees per acre represented should therefore be high compared to larger trees with larger zones. The TPA are sometimes called tree factors since they are the number of trees per acre represented by one tree of their respective sizes.

4.6 CALCULATING VOLUME PER ACRE

With fixed-radius plot sampling, it is possible to calculate volume per plot by summing the volumes of the individual trees present on the plot. It is not possible to calculate plot volumes for point sampling because points have no area. Since it is possible to calculate number of trees per acre represented by one sample tree, all inventory statistics for point sampling are calculated on a per-acre basis.

The method for calculating volume per acre for fixed-radius plots is to multiply the volume per tree by the expansion factor (trees per acre represented by one sample tree). Since all trees in that situation represent the same number of trees per acre, the expansion to an acre basis is often done after the volumes of trees on the plot are summed. For point sampling, the expansion to an acre basis must be done on a per-tree or at least per-size class basis because of differences in TPA, as shown in Eq. 4.2:

$$\text{VAC}_i = V_i \times \frac{\text{BAF}}{\text{BA}_i} = V_i \times \text{TPA} \tag{4.2}$$

where:

$\text{VAC}_i = \frac{\text{volume}}{\text{acre}}$ represented by tree i

$V_i = \frac{\text{volume}}{\text{tree}}$ for tree i

BA_i = basal area per acre for tree i

An example for trees of two different sizes is given below, assuming BAF = 10.

(1) dbh	BA	(2) $TPA = \frac{BAF}{BA}$	(3) $V = \frac{Volume}{Tree}$	(4) = (2) × (3) $VAC = \frac{Volume}{Acre}$
5	0.1364	73.31	2.0	146.62
10	0.5454	18.34	10.0	183.40

Column 4 represents the volume per acre represented by one tree with a diameter of the size in column 1. The sum of the volumes per acre represented by all of the sample trees at a point is an estimate of volume per acre at that point. The volume per acre represented by one sample tree (VAC) is sometimes called a volume factor.

4.7 CALCULATING BASAL AREA PER ACRE

The same logic that was used to calculate volume per acre should be used to calculate basal area per acre represented by one sample tree. That is,

$$BAC = BA_i \times TPA$$

where BAC is the basal area per acre represented by one sample tree. But TPA = BAF/BA_i. When substituted into the BAC equation, the BA_i terms cancel and BAC = BAF. This shows that regardless of the size of the tree, all trees represent the same amount of basal area per acre and that amount is equal to the basal area factor of the prism or angle gauge.

A constant BAF for all trees regardless of size is an artifact of the sampling process. Point sampling is sampling with probability proportional to basal area. Once the sample trees are selected and the data are being processed, TPA reverses the effects of selecting with probability proportional to size. The resulting calculation means that every tree represents the same amount of basal area per acre.

There is a real advantage to the fact that every tree represents the same amount of basal area per acre. Since basal area per acre represented by a sample tree does not vary with tree size, there is no reason to measure trees to obtain an estimate of basal area per acre. All that is required is a tree count using an angle gauge or prism. If there are 10 sample trees tallied at a point and the BAF = 5, the estimate of basal area per acre at the point is $10 \times 5 = 50$ ft^2. Basal area is the only characteristic that can be obtained without tree measurements. Both trees per acre and volume per acre require a diameter measurement for tree basal area (BA_i) calculation (see Section 4.5 and Eq. 4.2).

4.8 FIELD PROCEDURES

In theory, points should be placed on the ground at random just as plots should be placed at random for simple random sampling. For all of the reasons discussed in Chapter 3 regarding plot sampling, the common practice in point sampling is to locate points systematically.

Once a point is selected, the forester rotates through 360 degrees and views every tree at breast height with a prism or angle gauge to determine whether the point is in a tree's imaginary zone (a sample tree), out of the imaginary zone (not a sample tree), or borderline. If a tree appears to be borderline, the dbh of the tree should be measured. The critical distance, R, should be calculated as $D \times \text{PRF}$. A tape should be pulled from the point to the center of the tree and that horizontal distance compared with R. If the horizontal distance is greater than R, the tree is not a sample tree; otherwise, the tree is a sample tree. Table 4.8.1 lists critical distances for commonly used BAF values and tree sizes.

Iles and Fall (1988) conducted research to determine whether professional cruisers can evaluate the correct status of borderline trees without taping to them. They found that borderline trees account for 4% to 6% of the trees counted in a cruise and that professional cruisers guessed the status of individual trees incorrectly only 25% of the

Table 4.8.1 Critical distances (ft) for commonly used prism factors and various dbh values

Dbh (in.)	5	10	20	40
4	15.56	11.00	7.78	5.50
5	19.45	13.75	9.72	6.88
6	23.33	16.50	11.67	8.25
7	27.22	19.25	13.61	9.63
8	31.11	22.00	15.56	11.00
9	35.00	24.75	17.50	12.38
10	38.89	27.50	19.45	13.75
11	42.78	30.25	21.39	15.13
12	46.67	33.00	23.33	16.50
13	50.56	35.75	25.28	17.88
14	54.45	38.50	27.22	19.25
15	58.34	41.25	29.17	20.63
16	62.23	44.00	31.11	22.00
17	66.11	46.75	33.06	23.38
18	70.00	49.50	35.00	24.75
19	73.89	52.25	36.95	26.13
20	77.78	55.00	38.89	27.50
21	81.67	57.75	40.84	28.88
22	85.56	60.50	42.78	30.25
23	89.45	63.25	44.72	31.63
24	93.34	66.00	46.67	33.00
25	97.23	68.75	48.61	34.38
26	101.12	71.50	50.56	35.75
27	105.01	74.25	52.50	37.13
28	108.89	77.00	54.45	38.50
29	112.78	79.75	56.36	39.88
30	116.67	82.50	58.34	41.25

time. These errors tended to cancel out. Temporary workers (not professional cruisers) accounted for only 5% of the data in the study, but for 30% of the noncancellable errors. They concluded that measuring to determine the status of borderline trees was the preferred practice even for professional cruisers since such trees were a small proportion of the population anyway. In addition, the proportion that were judged to be sample trees would have to be visited to measure dbh as part of the inventory process anyway.

Once the sample trees are selected, all measurements necessary to satisfy objectives of the inventory should be made on the trees. If only basal area per acre is needed, a tree count is all that is required. For volume or weight calculation, dbh and one or more height measurements may be needed to use the applicable standard volume or weight equations to obtain V_i.

4.9 BOUNDARY OR EDGE EFFECT BIAS

Trees growing near a boundary of the stand or property may have imaginary zones that are partially off the property of interest. This makes their probabilities of selection smaller than they should be as calculated from their basal areas. The result is a bias in the estimates produced by point sampling. There have been numerous attempts to solve this problem. Beers (1966) developed a direct weighing approach with weights depending on the proportion of the zone, centered at the point rather than the tree, inside the forest area. Obviously, evaluating proportions of circles in the field is difficult. Schmid-Haus (1969) proposed a method called the mirage method, which works for edge effect bias of both fixed-radius and point samples. The method was discussed for fixed-radius plots in Chapter 3 and was described in English by Beers (1977) and evaluated for bias by Gregoire (1982). For point sampling, the cruiser would first count and measure all sample trees on the forest area. The cruiser would then establish a second point outside the forest along the same cruise line moving the same distance outside the property boundary as the distance from the first point to the boundary. The cruiser then looks back at the forest area and counts and measures any trees that are sample trees. Under this method, some trees may be tallied twice. This method may not always be possible to use because of the inability to continue along the cruise line across the boundary line, but it is very easy to apply in the field otherwise.

Foresters worry about edge effect bias especially for small tracts that are long and narrow. The concern may not be justified (Fowler and Arvenitis, 1981), especially for larger basal area factors. Larger BAFs lead to smaller imaginary zones, which decreases the problem. For large forest areas, the bias is theoretically present but negligible, since edge trees represent such a small proportion of the total population.

4.10 SLOPE CORRECTION

The theory for point sampling assumes a horizontal line of sight between the point and breast height on potential sample trees. In areas where the average slope is less than 10%, errors from slope are likely negligible. There have been many methods presented to account for varying slopes. The procedure presented here was recommended by Husch et al. (1982).

Bruce (1955) noted that by rotating a prism in the plane perpendicular to the line of sight through an angle equal to the slope of the line of sight, the proper slope adjustment would be made. To do this in practice, look across the top of the prism or angle gauge along the slope to breast height on the tree in question. Turn the gauge or prism back to the normal position for viewing the tree, but maintain the slope angle just established. Sight the tree normally and determine whether it is in (a sample tree) or out. The Purdue point sampling block (Beers and Miller, 1964) was designed to facilitate this procedure and to improve precision. This rotation does closely achieve the desired correction, but it must be considered a rough estimate since the rotated prism views a slightly different dbh. The following tape-check procedure more accurately determines the status of questionable trees:

1. If a tree appears in with an unrotated prism, it is in (it is a sample tree).
2. If a tree is slightly out or borderline with an unrotated prism, rotate the prism perpendicular to the line of sight and at the same angle as the slope from eye to breast height on the tree, and make the determination of in or out.
3. If the status of the tree is still in question after rotation, measure the tree dbh, determine the critical distance, *R*, and then modify the critical distance as follows:

$$\mathrm{MCD} = \sqrt{1 + \left(\frac{\mathrm{SL}}{100}\right)^2} \times R \tag{4.3}$$

where:

MCD = modified critical distance

SL = slope angle in percent

Compare the MCD with the distance from the point to the center of the tree along the slope. If the distance along the slope is less than the MCD, the tree is in and is a sample tree.

As an example of a MCD, consider a prism with BAF = 10 and a 10-in. dbh tree along a 15% slope. Then

$$\mathrm{MCD} = \sqrt{1 + \left(\frac{15}{100}\right)^2} \times R$$

$$\mathrm{R} = 2.75 \times 10 = 27.5$$

$$\mathrm{MCD} = 1.0111874 \times 27.5 = 27.8$$

The value of the modified critical distance is very near the value of *R*, which is why average slopes of less than 10% can be ignored.

One strategy for coping with steep slopes is to increase the basal area factor used. The effect is to decrease the critical distance for any given dbh with the result that in trees tend to be closer to the point. Another way of dealing with slope is to use a relascope rather than an angle gauge or wedge prism. The relascope automatically adjusts for slope.

4.11 CHOICE OF BASAL AREA FACTOR

The choice of basal area factor in point sampling is analogous to choice of plot size for fixed-radius plot sampling. The choice is based on two principal considerations (Wensel et al. 1980), visibility and approximate average number of sample trees desired at a point.

Of the two, visibility may be an overriding factor requiring a higher BAF than would be chosen given the average number of sample trees per point desired. For a 16-in. tree, the critical distance will be $16 \times 2.75 = 44$ ft for BAF = 10. For BAF = 20, the critical distance will decrease to $16 \times 1.94 = 31.1$ ft. The difference can mean more efficient cruising in areas with thick brush. Iles and Fall (1988) suggest choosing a prism so that the largest trees in the area will be close enough to be seen through the brush, even if the average tree count per point drops to only 3 to 5.

The study by Iles and Fall (1988) indicated that a large source of bias was trees not noticed by the cruiser. They also noted that the incidence of this error increased when the average number of trees per point was more than 10. The basal area factor of choice in the southern United States has been 10. For basal areas of over 100 ft^2/acre, a BAF of 10 will result in more than 10 sample trees per point. Dilworth and Bell (1984) propose an average tree count of 4 to 8 per point, whereas Beers and Miller (1964) recommend an average of 7 per point. All of these recommendations would dictate a higher basal area factor than 10 for many tracts in the southern United States and elsewhere. Wiant et al. (1984), working on Appalachian hardwood inventories, found that BAF = 5 and BAF = 10 resulted in serious underestimation of sawtimber volume. They recommend BAF = 20 or BAF = 40 for sawtimber inventory in the eastern United States. They also quote other studies where small BAF values have resulted in serious underestimation of volume (Zeide and Troxell 1979; Clutter, 1957; Husch, 1955; Solomon, 1975). Wensel et al. (1980) suggest estimating BAF as follows:

$$\text{BAF} = \frac{\text{Estimated stand basal area per acre}}{\text{Desired tree count per point}}$$

It is important to realize, however, that as BAF increases and the number of sample trees per point decrease, the variance between points increases. The effect of this increased variance is to require more sample points to achieve a desired allowable error (see Section 4.18). A compromise must be achieved between a BAF large enough for accurate work and yet small enough to give reasonable variance.

Using different BAF values for different strata in a stratified sample may make for more efficient cruises. In that case, the strata should be worked up separately and resulting estimates should be combined, as described in Chapter 5.

It is not good practice to change basal area factors from point to point within a stand or stratum in order to always obtain the desired tree count. This practice, called the constant tally rule, may be a more efficient field procedure, but it results in biased estimates from having both tree count and basal area factor as random variables (Wensel et al., 1980; Schreuder et al., 1981; Iles and Wilson, 1988). This is typically done as follows: The cruiser starts with a large basal area factor and makes a tree count at a point. There is a designated desired number of sample trees per point, and if the tree count is less than the desired number, the next smaller BAF is used. This process continues until the required number of trees is achieved. The process will always select the largest basal area factor that will produce the desired tree count. Iles and Wilson (1988) provide the following explanation:

> Consider, however, only the points which have too few trees. We have landed in a relatively sparse "hole" in the stand. When we double the plot size we not only double the area, but move outward into the more dense part of the stand. We would therefore more than double the tree count. Switching our prism when too few trees are found will therefore give a positive bias.
>
> What happens when we have too many trees? We have landed in a "clump" in the stand. When we reduce the plot size, the plot is likely to shrink into the clump. Although the plot size is reduced by half, it will be in an even denser part of the stand, so the tree count will not be reduced enough. Switching prisms when we find too many trees will therefore give a positive bias also.

The best advice is to carefully select a prism factor for a tract or a stratum within a tract and use it throughout. There will be some points with more than the desired number of sample trees. There will be some points with no sample trees. These are legitimate points, and a zero tally should be entered. Zero-tally points are certainly inexpensive to establish, and they provide information on the variability in the stand.

4.12 STAND AND STOCK TABLES WITH POINT SAMPLING

A stand and stock table can be generated for every point in a point sampling inventory. The method of construction depends primarily on the level at which data is recorded. With the data recorders in use by many foresters today, individual tree dbh values may be kept to the nearest 0.1 in. if the tree was measured with a dbh tape. Example 4.12.1 demonstrates calculation of a stand and stock table at a single point utilizing measured tree data.

EXAMPLE 4.12.1

A forester inventoried a stand using a basal area factor 20 prism ($k = \sqrt{20/10{,}890} = 0.042855$). The IN trees, or sample trees, at a single point are shown below along with their volumes *(V)* in column 3.

(1) Sample Tree	(2) dbh (in.)	(3) $V(\text{ft}^3)$	(4) Basal Area (BA)	(5) = BAF/(4) TPA (BAF/BA)	(6) = (3) × (5) Volume per Acre (VAC)
1	11.4	20.6	0.7088	28.2	580.9
2	10.4	15.1	0.5899	33.9	511.9
3	13.0	29.1	0.9218	21.7	631.5
4	9.4	8.3	0.4819	41.5	344.5
5	10.8	16.2	0.6362	31.4	513.5
	Totals			156.7	2582.3

The point data are worked up exactly as presented in this chapter. The volume in column 3 was obtained from a volume table entered using dbh and height. The basal area (column 4) was obtained from dbh as $0.005454D^2$. The trees per acre represented by one sample tree of this size was obtained using BAF/BA. Finally, volume per acre was obtained using Eq. 4.2. The tables indicate 157 stems per acre and volume of 2582.3 ft^3/acre represented at this point. Here is a stand and stock table by 1-in. dbh classes retaining all information:

dbh	Trees/Acre	Vol/Acre
9	41.5	344.5
10	33.9	511.9
11	59.9	1094.4
13	21.7	631.5
	157.0	2582.3

The stand and stock table was obtained by combining the information in the individual tree table for sample trees 1 and 5, which are both in the 11-in. dbh class.

Other methods of obtaining stand and stock tables would produce slightly different results. The method in Example 4.12.1 is most precise since it uses individual tree diameter measurements rather than diameter class midpoints to calculate TPAs. If data are being processed by a computer, the extra calculations are probably worthwhile for the extra precision gained. When working up cruises by hand, many foresters would place all trees in a dbh class at the diameter class midpoint, calculate the TPA and volume per tree for the midpoint only, and then multiply the volume per acre by the number of trees on the point in that class.

EXAMPLE 4.12.2

A forester examined all visible trees at a point using a 10 factor angle gauge. Fourteen trees were in and were tallied into diameter classes as follows:

Diameter Class	Frequency (Tally)
6	2
7	2
8	4
9	3
10	2

Since the actual measured diameters are not available and may not have even been made, the forester has no alternative but to use the diameter class midpoint as the diameter value to use in obtaining per-acre values from the point tally. The volumes per tree below (column 5) were obtained from a local volume equation. The workup to a per-acre basis and stand and stock table follow:

(1) Diameter Class	(2) Tally	(3) TPA = (BAF/BA)	(4) = (2) × (3) Trees per Acre	(5) Volume per Tree (*V*)	(6) = (4) × (5) Volume per Acre (VAC)
6	2	50.93	101.86	3.2	326.0
7	2	37.42	74.84	5.1	381.7
8	4	28.65	114.60	7.5	859.5
9	3	22.64	67.92	9.7	658.8
10	2	18.34	36.68	11.8	432.8
Totals			395.40		2658.8

Note that column 3 contains the number of trees per acre represented by one sample tree. Column 4 contains the trees per acre represented in each dbh class at this point and is obtained by multiplying column 3 by the tree tally for each dbh class.

4.13 POINT SAMPLE ESTIMATORS

Once a point sample is conducted, the average values, variances, and standard errors are easily calculated if the data are kept separate by point. The following equations should be used where Y could be volume per acre, basal area per acre, trees per acre, or some other characteristic of interest:

$$Y_i = \sum_{j=1}^{m_i} \mathrm{BAF} \frac{Y_{ij}}{\mathrm{BA}_{ij}}$$

where:

Y_i = per acre estimate of Y at point i ($i = 1, 2, \ldots, n$)

BAF = basal area factor

BA_{ij} = basal area of tree j on point i

m_i = number of sample trees on point i

Y_{ij} = volume, basal area, and so on for tree j on point i

The expression following the summation is Eq. 4.2 if Y_{ij} is volume per tree. Over all n points, the average value of Y per acre is

$$\bar{Y}_{\mathrm{ps}} = \frac{1}{n} \sum_{i=1}^{n} Y_i \tag{4.5}$$

The variance of Y among points is

$$S^2_{Y\text{ps}} = \frac{\sum_{i=1}^{n} Y_i^2 - \frac{\left(\sum_{i=1}^{n} Y_i\right)^2}{n}}{n-1} \tag{4.6}$$

The variance of $\overline{Y}_{\text{ps}}$ is

$$S^2_{\overline{Y}\text{ps}} = \frac{S^2_{Y\text{ps}}}{n} \tag{4.7}$$

and the standard error of $\overline{Y}_{\text{ps}}$ is

$$S_{\overline{Y}\text{ps}} = \frac{S_{Y\text{ps}}}{\sqrt{n}} \tag{4.8}$$

where all symbols are as previously defined.

These equations are the same as simple random sampling equations. The subscript ps is used to denote that this is a point sample. They are simple because we accounted for the unequal probability sample selection by using differential TPAs for different tree sizes. Estimates of the tract total are easily obtained by multiplying $\overline{Y}_{\text{ps}}$ by the tract area in acres:

$$\hat{T}_{Y_{\text{ps}}} = \overline{Y}_{\text{ps}} \times A$$
$$S_{\hat{T}_{\text{ps}}} = A \times S_{Y_{\text{ps}}}$$

where:

A = tract area in acres

$\hat{T}_{Y\text{ps}}$ = tract total value of Y

$\overline{Y}_{\text{ps}}$ = per acre average value of Y

$S_{\hat{T}_{\text{ps}}}$ = tract total standard error

$S_{\overline{Y}_{\text{ps}}}$ = per acre standard error of $\overline{Y}$

Note that A is used to expand to a tract total basis because N is infinite for a point sample.

EXAMPLE 4.13.1

A forester placed 20 points in a stand and worked up the volume per acre for each point as in Example 4.12.2. The results were as follows:

Point	Vol/Acre (ft^3)	Point	Vol/Acre (ft^3)
1	1004.6	11	860.6
2	820.7	12	915.0
3	770.3	13	1052.1
4	960.5	14	1187.5
5	1117.5	15	734.4
6	1207.6	16	1322.6
7	933.3	17	929.0
8	615.2	18	691.9
9	1422.8	19	1105.1
10	1217.4	20	1302.6

If Y_i = volume per acre at point i (that is, $Y_1 = 1004.6$, $Y_2 = 820.7$, and so on),

$$\sum_{i=1}^{20} Y_i = 20{,}170.7 \qquad \text{and} \qquad \sum_{i=1}^{20} Y_i^2 = 21{,}305{,}060.05$$

Using the preceding equations, average volume per acre is calculated as

$$\overline{Y}_{\text{ps}} = \frac{1}{n}\sum_{i=1}^{20} Y_i = \frac{20{,}170.7}{20} = 1008.535 \text{ ft}^3$$

The variance among points is calculated as

$$S^2_{Y_{\text{ps}}} = \frac{\sum_{i=1}^{20} Y_i^2 - \frac{\left(\sum_{i=1}^{20} Y_i\right)^2}{n}}{n-1} = \frac{21{,}305{,}060.05 - \frac{(20{,}170.7)^2}{20}}{19} = 50{,}642.26947 \ (\text{ft}^3/\text{acre})^2$$

The variance of the mean per acre is calculated as

$$S^2_{\overline{Y}_{\text{ps}}} = \frac{S^2_{Y_{\text{ps}}}}{n} = \frac{50{,}642.26947}{20} = 2532.113473 \ (\text{ft}^3/\text{acre})^2$$

The standard error of the mean per acre is $\sqrt{2532.1134773} = 50.32$ ft^3. An approximate 95% confidence interval for the mean volume per acre is calculated as $1008.535 \pm 2(50.32)$:

$$\text{LCL} = 907.89 \text{ ft}^3$$
$$\text{UCL} = 1109.18 \text{ ft}^3$$

If these points were taken from a 35-acre tract, total tract volume would be calculated as

$$\hat{T}_{Y_{ps}} = \overline{Y}_{ps} \times A$$
$$\hat{T}_{Y_{ps}} = 1008.535 \times 35 = 35{,}298.7 \text{ ft}^3$$

The standard error of the tract total is calculated as

$$S_{\hat{T}_{ps}} = A \times S_{\overline{Y}_{ps}} = 35 \times 50.32 = 1761.2 \text{ ft}^3$$

An approximate 95% confidence interval for the tract total volume is calculated as 35,298.7 ± (2)(1761.2):

$$\text{LCL} = 31{,}776.3 \text{ ft}^3$$
$$\text{UCL} = 38{,}821.1 \text{ ft}^3$$

4.14 CUMULATIVE TALLY

Some foresters do not keep tallies separate by points. They tally for all points on one tally card and merely keep up with the total number of points. By doing so, they eliminate the possibility of calculating variances, standard errors, and confidence intervals. This seems a high price to pay when it could be avoided by simply keeping inventory data separate by point and processing those data separately by point. When inventory data were processed by hand, the argument that separate estimates for each point were too labor intensive was more viable, but now most cruises are processed by computer. For foresters who wish to work up their inventories without variance, standard error, and confidence interval calculations, Example 4.14.1 details the calculations.

EXAMPLE 4.14.1

A forester cruised a 40-acre tract of timber with a 10 factor prism and obtained the following data over 40 points:

(1) Diameter Class	(2) Tract Tally	(3) TPA (BAF/BA)	(4) Volume per Tree	(5) = (2) × (3) × (4) Volume on 40 Acres	(6) = (5)/40 Volume per Acre (VAC)
6	46	50.93	3.2	7,496.9	187.4
7	72	37.42	5.1	13,740.6	343.5
8	133	28.65	7.5	28,578.4	714.5
9	126	22.64	9.7	27,670.6	691.8
10	62	18.33	11.8	13,410.2	335.3
11	21	15.15	13.7	4,358.7	109.0
Totals				95,255.4	2381.5

The volume per acre by diameter class (column 6) can be obtained by dividing column 5 values by 40 since 40 points were placed on the tract. Likewise, trees per acre, to complete the stand and stock table, can be obtained by multiplying columns 2 and 3 and dividing by 40 (the number of acres). To obtain the total tract value, the forester multiplies total volume per acre (2381.5) by the number of acres.

4.15 VOLUME BASAL AREA RATIOS (VBARS)

A slight modification to the cruise workup presented earlier involves the use of volume/basal area ratios (VBARs) or weight/basal area ratios (WBARs). The advantage associated with using VBARs or WBARs is that the laborious calculations involving volume calculations and tree basal area calculations are done only once and then printed in a table. This greatly reduces the amount of calculations necessary to obtain a point sampling estimate.

Table 4.15.1 contains sawtimber wood and bark green weight (lb) for natural loblolly pine in the Georgia Piedmont. This is simply an individual tree weight table. A table of WBARs can easily be calculated from this weight table by dividing each cell by the basal area associated with the diameter class (Table 4.15.2).

Take a 14-in., 2-log tree with a weight of 1394 lb in the sawlog portion of the tree. The basal area of a 14-in. tree is $0.005454 \times 14^2 = 1.0690$. The WBAR is $\frac{1394}{1.0690} = 1304.0$, which is very near the value in Table 14.15.2 (the slight difference is

Table 4.15.1 Sawtimber wood and bark green weights for natural loblolly pine in the Georgia Piedmont

	Logs						
Dbh	**1**	**1½**	**2**	**2½**	**3**	**3½**	**4**
10	406	581	750	916	1078		
12	508	813	1050	1281	1508	1732	1952
14	755	1080	1394	1702	2003	2300	2593
16	965	1381	1783	2176	2562	2941	3316
18	1199	1715	2215	2703	3183	3654	4119
20	1456	2083	2690	3282	3864	4437	5001
22	1736	2482	3206	3912	4605	5288	5961
24	2037	2914	3763	4592	5408	6207	6997
26	2361	3376	4360	5321	6264	7193	8108
28	2706	3870	4998	6100	7180	8244	9294
30	3072	4394	5675	6926	8153	9361	10553

Table 4.15.2 Sawtimber weight basal area ratio (WBAR) table for natural loblolly pine sawtimber in the Georgia Piedmont (rounded to nearest integer)

Dbh	1	1½	2	2½	3	3½	4
10	745	1065	1376	1679	1977		
12	724	1035	1337	1631	1920	2205	2486
14	706	1010	1305	1592	1874	2152	2426
16	691	989	1277	1559	1835	2107	2375
18	679	971	1254	1530	1801	2068	2331
20	667	955	1233	1505	1771	2034	2293
22	657	940	1214	1482	1745	2003	2258
24	648	927	1198	1462	1721	1976	2227
26	640	916	1183	1443	1699	1951	2199
28	633	905	1169	1426	1679	1928	2174
30	626	895	1156	1411	1661	1907	2150

due to rounding error). Let R_i be the sum of the VBARs or WBARs on point i. Then

$$\bar{Y}_{\text{ps}} = \frac{\text{BAF}\sum_{i=1}^{n} R_i}{n} \tag{4.9}$$

where:

$\bar{Y}_{\text{ps}}$ = average volume or weight per acre

n = number of points

BAF = basal area factor

If the WBARs or VBARs are kept separate by point, it is possible to estimate the average volume and calculate a variance, standard error, and confidence interval. Let R_i be the sum of the VBARs or WBARs on point i. The variance is then

$$S^2_{Y_{\text{ps}}} = \text{BAF}^2 \left[\frac{\sum_{i=1}^{n} R_i^2 - \frac{\left(\sum_{i=1}^{n} R_i\right)^2}{n}}{n-1} \right] \tag{4.10}$$

The standard error is

$$S_{\bar{Y}_{\text{ps}}} = \frac{S_{Y_{\text{ps}}}}{\sqrt{n}} \tag{4.11}$$

EXAMPLE 4.15.1

A cruise was conducted using a BAF = 10 prism in a natural loblolly pine stand in the Georgia Piedmont. The following tree measurements were made on the points:

Point	Number of Sample Trees	dbh (Logs)
1	8	10(1), 12(1), 12(1.5), 12(1.5), 14(2), 14(2), 14(2), 14(3)
2	9	12(1), 12(1), 12(1.5), 12(2), 12(2), 12(2), 12(2.5), 12(2.5), 14(2.5)
3	7	10(1), 12(2), 12(2), 12(2), 14(2.5), 14(2.5), 14(3)
4	5	14(2.5), 14(3), 16(2.5), 18(3), 20(4)
5	12	10(1.5), 12(2), 12(2), 12(2), 12(2), 12(2.5), 12(2.5), 12(2.5), 14(2.5), 14(2.5), 14(2.5), 14(2.5)
6	10	12(1), 12(1.5), 12(2), 12(2), 12(2.5), 12(2.5), 14(2), 14(2), 14(2.5), 16(2.5)
7	7	12(1.5), 12(2), 12(2.5), 12(2.5), 14(2.5), 14(3), 16(2.5)
8	7	12(1), 12(1.5), 12(2), 12(2.5), 14(2), 14(2.5), 16(2)
9	7	12(1.5), 12(2.5), 14(2), 14(2.5), 16(2), 18(3), 18(3.5)
10	7	12(2), 12(2.5), 14(2), 14(2.5), 14(2.5), 14(3), 14(3)
Total	79	

We will use the WBAR table for natural loblolly pine (Table 4.15.2) to estimate average weight (lb) per acre.

We will do this problem in two ways. First of all, we will calculate a WBAR for each tree and find a sum of WBARs for each point:

Point	WBARs
1	745, 724, 1035, 1035, 1305, 1305, 1305, 1874
2	724, 724, 1035, 1337, 1337, 1337, 1631, 1631, 1592
3	745, 1337, 1337, 1337, 1592, 1592, 1874
4	1592, 1874, 1559, 1801, 2293
5	1065, 1337, 1337, 1337, 1337, 1631, 1631, 1631, 1592, 1592, 1592, 1592
6	724, 1035, 1337, 1337, 1631, 1631, 1305, 1305, 1592, 1559
7	1035, 1337, 1631, 1631, 1592, 1874, 1559
8	724, 1035, 1337, 1631, 1305, 1592, 1277
9	1035, 1631, 1305, 1592, 1277, 1801, 2068
10	1337, 1631, 1305, 1592, 1592, 1874, 1874

The sum of WBARs by point results in

Point	$R_i = \Sigma$WBARs
1	9,328
2	11,348
3	9,814
4	9,119
5	17,674
6	13,456
7	10,659
8	8,901
9	10,709
10	11,205
Total	112,213

Using Eq. 4.9,

$$\bar{Y}_{ps} = \frac{\text{BAF} \sum_{i=1}^{n} R_i}{n}$$

$$\bar{Y}_{ps} = \frac{10(112{,}213)}{10} = 112{,}213 \text{ lb}$$

From Eq. 4.10 the variance is

$$S^2_{Y_{ps}} = \text{BAF}\left[\frac{\sum_{i=1}^{n} R_i^2 - \frac{\left(\sum_{i=1}^{n} R_i\right)^2}{n}}{n-1}\right]$$

$$S^2_{Y_{ps}} = 10\left[\frac{1{,}321{,}770{,}445 - \frac{(112{,}213)^2}{10}}{9}\right]$$

$$S^2_{Y_{ps}} = 10\,(6{,}954{,}967.556)$$

$$S^2_{\bar{Y}_{ps}} = \frac{S^2_{Y_{ps}}}{n} = \frac{10\,(6{,}954{,}967.556)}{10} = 6{,}954{,}967.556$$

From Eq. 4.11 the standard error of the mean is

$$S_{\bar{Y}_{ps}} = 2637.23 \text{ lb}$$

As noted earlier, foresters sometimes make a cumulative tally rather than keep a separate tally by point. This practice removes any possibility of calculating a variance, standard error, and confidence interval, but it should result in the same estimate for the mean. The cumulative tally from this same sample would look like this:

	Logs						
Dbh	**1**	**1½**	**2**	**2½**	**3**	**3½**	**4**
10	2	1					
12	5	7	15	12			
14			8	14	6		
16			2	3			
18					2	1	
20							1

Again, we utilize Table 14.15.2 for WBARs. The sum of the weight/basal area ratios over all points would be

$$\begin{aligned}&2(745) + 1(1065) + 5(724) + 7(1035) + 15(1337) + 12(1631)\\&+ 8(1305) + 14(1592) + 6(1874) + 2(1277) + 3(1559) + 2(1801)\\&+ 1(2068) + 1(2293) = 112{,}213\end{aligned}$$

Now, using Eq. 4.9,

$$\bar{Y}_{\text{ps}} = \frac{\sum_{i=1}^{n} R_i}{n} \times \text{BAF} = \frac{112{,}213}{10} \times (10) = 112{,}213 \text{ lb}$$

No variance can be calculated since the tally was cumulative. Note, however, that the volume per acre is the same regardless of which way the WBARs are used.

4.16 VOLUME FACTORS

It is good to use the same BAF within a stand or stratum. For this reason, some foresters develop a volume factor table by multiplying the VBAR or WBAR values by the BAF. Notice that this is the outcome of the numerator of Eq. 4.9 and is equivalent to Eq. 4.2. The outcome is a table of values that represents the contribution to volume or weight per acre from the tally of one tree of the size that occupies any particular cell in the table. Making such a table is simple when a VBAR or WBAR table exists: Take each entry in the VBAR or WBAR table and multiply by the BAF. Separate tables can be made for commonly used BAF values. Table 4.16.1 was obtained by multiplying Table 4.15.2 by BAF = 10. Weight factor tables with BAF = 5, 20, and 40 could be constructed by multiplying each cell value in Table 14.15.2 by 5, 20, and 40, respectively.

In summary, to construct a volume or weight factor table from any applicable volume or weight equation, obtain the tree volume or weight from the volume or weight equation and divide this value by the basal area of the tree (obtained as a function of dbh). This produces the VBAR or WBAR, which is then multiplied by the BAF of the prism or angle gauge being used to produce the volume or weight factor to be entered into the table.

Working up a cruise with a volume or weight factor requires very few calculations. Simply add up the volume or weight factors for each tally tree at a point to obtain volume or weight per acre for that point. For cumulative tally, add up the volume or weight factors of all trees tallied and divide by the number of points to obtain volume or weight per acre.

Table 4.16.1 Table of weight factors for the sawtimber portion of natural loblolly pine trees in the Georgia Piedmont using a BAF = 10 prism

Dbh	1	1½	2	2½	3	3½	4
10	7,450	10,650	13,760	16,790	19,770		
12	7,240	10,350	13,370	16,310	19,200	22,050	24,860
14	7,060	10,100	13,050	15,920	18,740	21,520	24,260
16	6,910	9,890	12,770	15,590	18,350	21,070	23,750
18	6,790	9,710	12,540	15,300	18,010	20,680	23,310
20	6,670	9,550	12,330	15,050	17,710	20,340	22,930
22	6,570	9,400	12,140	14,820	17,450	20,030	22,580
24	6,480	9,270	11,980	14,620	17,210	19,760	22,270
26	6,400	9,160	11,830	14,430	16,990	19,510	21,990
28	6,330	9,050	11,690	14,260	16,790	19,280	21,740
30	6,260	8,950	11,560	14,110	16,610	19,070	21,500

EXAMPLE 4.16.1

Take the cumulative tally from Example 4.15.1 and obtain the average weight per acre using the weight factors in Table 4.16.1. Using the tally presented in Example 4.15.1, we have two trees in the 10-in., 1 log class, which, according to Table 4.16.1, each have a weight factor of 7450. To obtain the average weight, add all of the weight factors and divide by the number of points (10).

$$\begin{aligned}\bar{Y} = \tfrac{1}{10}[&2(7450) + 10{,}650 + 5(7240) + 7(10{,}350) + 15(13{,}370)\\ &+ 12(16{,}310) + 8(13{,}050) + 14(15{,}920) + 6(18{,}740)\\ &+ 2(12{,}770) + 3(15{,}590) + 2(18{,}010) + 20{,}680 + 22{,}930]\end{aligned}$$

$$\bar{Y} = \tfrac{1}{10}(1{,}122{,}130) = 112{,}213 \text{ lb}$$

Volume and weight factors have been published for different species (Wiant and Wingerd, 1981), but as demonstrated here, tables can easily be constructed from any volume or weight table or equation.

4.17 *POINT SAMPLING BY TREE HEIGHT*

A major advantage of point sampling is that basal area per acre estimates may be obtained without measuring tree diameters. With minor adjustments to the way volumes and weight of point samples are calculated, these stand characteristics can also be estimated without measuring tree diameters.

Examine Table 14.15.2 or 14.16.1, tables of WBARs and weight factors. Notice that large changes in WBAR or weight factors result from changing height classes, whereas the change across dbh classes is relatively small. This is particularly clear considering that the range in dbh values in a particular stand is seldom from 10 to 30. In even-aged stands the diameter distribution could be expected to be one-half that range or less. This observation has led some cruisers to average out VBARs or WBARs (or the factors) within a height class so that the only important variable to obtain from a sample tree is height or height class (in the case of calling logs for sawtimber). Dbh tallies are omitted and the resulting loss in accuracy is small.

For a special class of volume equations called *constant form factor volume equations*, the VBARs are constant within height classes across dbh classes. Constant form factor volume equations have the form

$$V = b_1 D^2 H$$

where:

V = individual tree volume

D = dbh

H = height

The VBAR for such a volume equation would take the form

$$\text{VBAR} = \frac{V}{\text{BA}} = \frac{b_1 D^2 H}{0.005454 D^2} = \frac{b_1 H}{0.005454} = \frac{b_1}{0.005454}(H)$$

Thus, for any constant form factor volume or weight equation, removing dbh from the tally is as easy as taking the value given for b_1 and dividing by 0.005454. In this situation average volume or weight per acre ($\overline{Y}$) is calculated by

$$\overline{Y} = \frac{(b_1/0.005454)\,(SH) \times \text{BAF}}{n} \tag{4.12}$$

where:

SH = the sum of all cumulative heights on the point

n = number of sample points

EXAMPLE 4.17.1

Wiant and Wingerd (1981) present an equation for total dry weight of northern red oak as $W = 0.113166D^2H$, a constant form factor equation, where D = dbh in inches and H = total height in feet. Since $W = 0.113166D^2H$,

$$\text{WBAR} = \frac{0.113166 D^2 H}{0.005454 D^2} = 20.75H$$

This means that the dry weight accumulates 20.75 lb per square foot of basal area for each increment of height in feet.

Assume that on a particular point the only sample trees using a BAF = 20 prism were three northern red oaks with total heights of 67, 78, and 82 ft. The estimate of dry weight per acre for northern red oak at that point is obtained by

$$Y_i = 20.75(67 + 78 + 82) \times \text{BAF}$$
$$Y_i = 20.75(227)(20)$$
$$Y_i = 94{,}205 \text{ lb}$$

where Y_i is weight per acre represented by trees at this point. To obtain an average weight per acre, this procedure would be followed on every point to obtain weight per acre at each point. Estimates of weight per acre, variances, and standard errors would then be obtained using Eqs. 4.9, 4.10, and 4.11. Alternatively, to obtain an average per-acre weight, accumulate heights of northern red oak across all points and use Eq. 4.12 where $\frac{b_1}{0.005454} = 20.75$ and SH is the sum of all northern red oak heights.

This procedure is particularly useful for estimating volume or weights where the volume or weight equation requires height classes such as 16-ft logs or 8-ft pulpwood sticks or veneer bolts. Since these values are often estimated by eye, the cruise proceeds very quickly. The only dbh values measured are those required to determine the status of borderline trees. Heights are accumulated as number of logs or bolts without regard to the dbh of trees.

4.18 SAMPLE SIZES FOR POINT SAMPLING

In theory, point sampling always occurs on an infinite population. Since a point has no area, there can be an infinite number of points in even the smallest stand. The equations necessary to obtain a given bound on the error of estimation with a specified degree of confidence using point sampling are identical to the SRS sample size formulas for infinite populations presented in Chapter 3:

$$\text{Mean:} \quad n = \frac{4S^2_{Y_{ps}}}{B^2_A} \quad \text{or} \quad n = \frac{4(\text{CV})^2}{(\text{AE\%})^2}$$

$$\text{Total:} \quad n = \frac{4S^2_{Y_{ps}}A^2}{B^2_T} \quad \text{or} \quad n = \frac{4(\text{CV})^2}{(\text{AE\%})^2}$$

where:

n = sample size = number of points needed

4 = an approximate z^2 value for 95% confidence

$S^2_{Y_{ps}}$ = variance between points (per-acre basis)

B_A = desired bound (per-acre basis)

B_T = desired bound (total tract basis)

A = number of acres in tract

AE% = allowable error in percent

CV = coefficient of variation in percent

It is important to remember that $S^2_{Y_{ps}}$ and CV are dependent not only on the variability of the tract but also on the BAF. It is not valid to determine CV using one BAF prism for sample size calculations and then to switch to another BAF for the inventory.

EXAMPLE 4.18.1

A forester did a preliminary cruise using a 10 factor prism on a tract and calculated a coefficient of variation (CV) of 60%. If an allowable error of ±15% with 95% confidence is desired, how many points should he use in an inventory of the property?

$$n = \frac{4(\text{CV})^2}{(\text{AE\%})^2} = \frac{4(60)^2}{(15)^2} = 64 \text{ sample points}$$

Note that these sample size equations are based on the assumption that there is an infinite number of points in even the smallest of areas. However, for smaller tracts (less than 200 acres), these equations will lead to excessive sample size requirements. For example, if a 25-acre stand has a coefficient of variation of 85% and we wish to estimate the total tract volume within 10% with approximately 95% confidence,

$$n = \frac{4(85)^2}{(10)^2} = 289 \text{ points}$$

Thus, according to this result, we would measure 289 points in a 25-acre stand. Clearly, this is not desirable or realistic. There is no clear and straightforward solution to this problem.

One way to deal with this situation is to use the finite population sample size formulas given in Chapter 3 (Eqs. 3.7, 3.8, and 3.9). These formulas can be used if N (population size) is known. To determine an approximate N, use a plot size such as 0.1 or 0.2 acres, but be sure to use the estimate of variation (CV or S^2_Y) that is based on points. Of course, choice of plot size will have a large impact on the sample size obtained. Some foresters have suggested using a plot size equal to the imaginary zone area of the average tree. For example, for the 25-acre stand with a CV of 85%, suppose the quadratic mean diameter tree (the tree of average basal area) was 12 in. If the basal area factor is 10, the plot size would be

$$\pi\left(\frac{66}{2}\right)^2 = 3421.19 \text{ ft}^2$$

which is approximately 0.079 acres. Thus

$$N = \frac{25}{0.079} = 316.5 = 317$$

Now, using Eq. 3.9,

$$n = \frac{4(317)(85)^2}{(10)^2(317) + 4(85)^2} = \frac{9{,}161{,}300}{60{,}600}$$

$$n = 152$$

This is still a rather large number of points for this small tract. However, a coefficient of variation of 85% indicates a large amount of variability in the stand. Furthermore, this procedure does not rest on underlying theory; it is an ad hoc method.

Clearly, estimating the number of points needed to meet a predefined bound on the error of estimation or allowable error for smaller tracts is not straightforward. Once again, common sense and experience will prove useful in this task.

4.19 COMPARISON OF POINT AND PLOT SAMPLING

There has been considerable debate over the relative merits of point sampling versus various fixed-radius plot sampling methods. Unfortunately, some of these comparisons have been done on a point-versus-plot basis as if the costs for each were the same. Except in the case of very small fixed-area plots, points will usually have higher variance between sampling units because fewer trees are measured. As a result, on any comparison of equal sample sizes the relative efficiency of plots to points will usually result in plots being favored. If, however, the variances are used in sample size formulas and the number of points and plots necessary to obtain a given bound, B, are calculated, relative costs to establish an average point and plot can be used to determine which is best for a given situation. A reasonable way to make the comparison is to look at the relative costs of conducting an inventory with both methods to achieve the same bound (Example 4.19.1). Obviously, this will work only on areas large enough to provide valid results from the point sampling sample size formulas.

EXAMPLE 4.19.1

Suppose an area is to be cruised and preliminary work has been done; several ⅒-acre plots have been established over the area. A 10 factor prism was also used at each plot center. Variability in volume per acre between sampling units was calculated for each method as follows:

$$S^2_{\text{point}} = 56.25 \text{ cords}^2$$
$$S^2_{\text{plot}} = 25.00 \text{ cords}^2$$

To obtain a bound on the error of estimation of 1.5 cords with approximately 95% confidence for the volume per acre, we will need

$$n_{\text{point}} = \frac{4S_Y^2}{B^2} = \frac{4(56.25)}{2.25} = 100$$

$$n_{\text{plot}} = \frac{4S_Y^2}{B^2} = \frac{4(25)}{2.25} = 44.44 \quad \text{(use 45)}$$

If it costs twice as much to establish a 1⁄10-acre plot as a point on average, plots are the better method because the relative efficiency (*RE*)

$$RE = \frac{n_{\text{point}} \times C_{\text{point}}}{n_{\text{plot}} \times C_{\text{plot}}} = \frac{100(1)}{45(2)} = 1.11 > 1$$

If it costs three times as much to establish a 1⁄10-acre plot as a point on average, the point sampling method is the better method because

$$RE = \frac{100(1)}{45(3)} < 1$$

REFERENCES

Beers, T. W. 1966. The direct correction for boundary-line slop-over in horizontal point sampling. *Purdue Univ. Agric. Exp. Stn. Res. Prog. Rep.* No. 224.

Beers, T. W. 1977. Practical correction of boundary overlap. *South. J. Appl. For.* 1(1):16–18.

Beers, T. W., and C. I. Miller. 1964. Point sampling: Research results, theory and applications. *Purdue Univ. Agric. Exp. Stn. Res. Bulletin No.* 786.

Bitterlich, W. 1947. Die Winkelzahlmessing (Measurement of basal area per hectare by means of angle measurement). *Allg. Forest. Holzwirtsch, Ztg.* 58:94–96.

Bruce, D. 1955. A new way to look at trees. *J. Forestry* 53:163–167.

Clutter, J. L. 1957. The effect of stand conditions and angle size on plotless cruising basal area estimates in loblolly pine. Unpublished master's thesis, Duke University, Durham, NC.

Dilworth, J. R., and J. F. Bell. 1984. *Variable probability sampling.* Oregon State University Bookstores, Corvallis.

Fowler, G. W., and L. G. Arvenitis. 1981. Aspects of statistical bias due to the forest edge: Horizontal point sampling. *Can. J. For. Res.* 11:334–341.

Gregoire, T. G. 1982. The unbiasedness of the mirage correction procedure for boundary overlap. *For. Sci.* 28:504–508.

Grosenbaugh, L. R. 1952. Plotless timber estimates—New, fast, easy. *J. Forestry* 50:32–37.

Grosenbaugh, L. R. 1958. Point-sampling and line-sampling: Probability theory, geometric implications, synthesis. *U.S. For. Serv. South. For. Exp. Stn. Occas. Pap.* No. 160.

Grosenbaugh, L. R. 1967. The gains from sample tree selection with unequal probabilities. *J. Forestry* 65:203–206.

Grosenbaugh, L. R., and W. S. Stover. 1957. Point-sampling compared with plot-sampling in southeast Texas. *For. Sci.* 3:2–14.

Husch, B. 1955. Results of an investigation of the variable plot method of cruising. *J. Forestry* 53:570–574.

Husch, B., C. I. Miller, and T. W. Beers. 1982. Forest mensuration. 3rd edition. Wiley, New York.

Iles, K., and M. Fall. 1988. Can an angle gauge really evaluate "borderline trees" accurately in variable plot sampling? *Can. J. For. Res.* 18:774–781.

Iles, K., and W. H. Wilson. 1988. Changing angle gauges in variable plot sampling: Is there bias under ordinary conditions? *Can. J. For. Res.* 18:768–773.

Schmid-Haus, P. 1969. Stichproben am Waldrond (Sampling at the edge of the forest). *Milt Schweiz Anst Forest Versuchswes* 45(3):234–303.

Solomon, D. S. 1975. A test of point sampling in northern hardwoods. *U.S. Dept. Agric. Forest Serv. Res.* Note NE-215.

Wensel, L. C., J. Levitan, and K. Barber. 1980. Selection of basal area factor in point sampling. *J. Forestry* 78:83–84.

Wiant, H. V., Jr., and D. E. Wingerd. 1981. Biomass factors for point sampling in Appalachian hardwoods. *J. Forestry* 79:221–222.

Wiant, H. V., Jr., D. O. Yandle, and R. Andreas. 1984. Is BAF 10 a good choice for point sampling? *North. J. Appl. For.* 2:23–24.

Zeide, B., and J. K. Troxell. 1979. Selection of the proper metric basal area factor for Appalachian mixed hardwoods. W. E. Frayer, ed., *Forest Resource Inventory Workshop Proceeding*, Colorado State University, Fort Collins, CO, pp. 261–269.

PROBLEMS FOR BETTER UNDERSTANDING

1. Calculate the basal area in square feet for trees with the following dbh (in.) values:

$$\text{dbh} = 12.3,\ 14.7,\ 10.9,\ 11.6,\ 8.3,\ 5.1,\ 4.2,\ 16.7,\ 21.8,\ 19.7.$$

2. Calculate the expansion factor (TPA) associated with each tree dbh given in Problem 1 for basal area factors of 5, 10, and 20. Explain what a TPA represents.
3. Recall that for a basal area factor of 10 the imaginary zone radius *(R)* for a tree of a given dbh is

$$R = 2.75 \times \text{dbh}$$

Create a table of imaginary zone radii for dbh values of 4 to 25 in. Note that these radii are referred to as limiting distances. What value would a table like this be in carrying out a point sample?

4. For a basal area factor of 20 the imaginary zone radius *(R)* for a tree of a given dbh is

$$R = 1.94 \times \text{dbh}$$

Create a table of limiting distances for dbh values of 4 to 25 in. for a BAF = 20.

5. Use the local volume table (Table 4.A.1, page 114) to estimate the volume per acre represented by the following sample of trees obtained at a single point using a 10 factor prism.

Sample Tree	dbh (in.)
1	13.2
2	12.7
3	9.3
4	14.6
5	8.1
6	13.9
7	12.5
8	4.9
9	14.1

6. Use the local volume table (Table 4.A.1, page 114) to estimate the volume per acre represented by the following tally of trees obtained at a single point using a 5 factor prism.

dbh Class	Tally
8	3
9	4
10	5
11	6
12	4

7. Refer to the data in Problems 5 and 6. Estimate the trees per acre and basal area represented at each of these two points.

8. Set up a spreadsheet that will work up estimates of trees per acre, basal area per acre, and volume per acre represented by a sample of trees at a single point. Be sure to make the spreadsheet general enough so that it will work up individual trees (as in Problem 5) or tree tallies by dbh class (as in Problem 6) for any basal area factor. Test your program with data from Problems 5 and 6.

9. Twenty-five 20 factor prism points were installed in a 32-acre slash pine stand. The per-acre board foot volume (Scribner) on each point is as follows:

Point	Volume (Bd Ft/Acre)	Point	Volume (Bd Ft/Acre)
1	3200	14	1650
2	2500	15	1350
3	800	16	1200
4	4500	17	700
5	1200	18	2950
6	2650	19	3000
7	2700	20	2550
8	1150	21	2750
9	1350	22	2800
10	1600	23	950
11	1900	24	1500
12	2150	25	1900
13	4700		

a. Estimate the average board foot volume per acre in this stand.

b. Obtain an approximate 95% confidence interval for the estimate of average board foot volume per acre.

c. Estimate the total board foot volume in the tract.

d. Obtain an approximate 95% confidence interval for the tract volume.

e. What is the coefficient of variation for these data?

f. Assume that stumpage for this tract is valued at $275/MBF (thousand board feet). Estimate the total dollar value of the timber on this tract.

g. Obtain an approximate 95% confidence interval for the estimate in part f.

10. Suppose there are five trees located near a point at which you are carrying out a 10 factor prism cruise that are questionable as to whether they should be included in the sample. You, as an informed point sampler, measure the distance from the point to the center of each tree and measure their dbh as well. The following information is obtained:

Tree	DBH	Distance (ft)
1	12.3	35.2
2	8.7	19.3
3	14.6	36.9
4	13.9	39.3
5	16.8	46.2

Which trees should be included at the point?

11. Suppose thirty-five 20 factor prism points were installed and measured in a 50-acre mixed pine hardwood stand. The merchantable pine stems were tallied at each point by 1-in. dbh classes and 10-ft total height classes resulting in the following information.

	Height (ft)			
	40	50	60	70
dbh (in.)	Trees Tallied			
7	15	7		
8	12	20	6	
9		17	35	
10		22	45	
11		10	17	3
12		5	23	8
13		4	15	6
14			12	9

Use the standard volume table for southern pine given in Table 4.A.2 (page 115) and obtain an estimate of the total cubic foot volume in this 50-acre tract. Also obtain an estimate of the total number of trees, total basal area on the tract, and the average cubic foot volume per acre.

12. Use the standard volume table for southern pine given in Table 4.A.2 (page 115) and construct a VBAR table. Use the tally in Problem 11 along with your VBAR table and obtain an estimate of average cubic foot volume per acre. Compare your results with the answer from Problem 11.

13. Construct a volume factor table using the same volume table as in Problem 11. Use the volume factor table and the tally in Problem 11 to estimate average cubic foot volume per acre. Compare your answer with your answers from Problems 11 and 12.

14. Use the volume factor table introduced in Problem 13. Average the volume factors within a height class to obtain a table with height alone as an input variable. Again, work up the cruise in Problem 11, but use your height accumulation table. Obtain volume per acre and compare with your answers to Problems 11, 12, and 13.

15. A cruise is to be carried out in a 250-acre natural pine hardwood stand. An estimate of high-quality hardwood volume is desired with an allowable error of 10%. Based on a small pilot survey the coefficient of variation is estimated to be 75% for 10 factor prism points. Determine the number of points required to meet the allowable error of 10%.

16. Refer to Problem 15. If the cruise is carried out with the number of points calculated, will the final estimate of volume be guaranteed to be within the desired allowable error of 10%? Why or why not?

Table 4.A.1 Local volume table for southern pine

dbh (in.)	Volume (ft^3)
4	1.6
5	2.8
6	4.7
7	6.3
8	9.4
9	11.8
10	16.3
11	20.4
12	25.8
13	31.2
14	36.1
15	41.4

Table 4.A.2 Standard volume table for southern pine

dbh (in)	Total Height (ft) 15	20	25	30	35	40	45	50	55	60	65	70	75	80	85
2	0.20	0.25	0.30	0.36	0.41	0.46	0.50	0.55							
3	0.44	0.56	0.68	0.79	0.91	1.02	1.13	1.23	1.34						
4	0.78	0.99	1.20	1.41	1.61	1.80	1.99	2.18	2.37	2.55					
5		1.55	1.87	2.19	2.50	2.81	3.11	3.40	3.69	3.98	4.26	4.54			
6		2.22	2.69	3.15	3.59	4.03	4.46	4.88	5.30	5.71	6.12	6.52			
7			3.65	4.27	4.88	5.47	6.06	6.63	7.20	7.76	8.31	8.86	9.40		
8			4.76	5.57	6.36	7.14	7.90	8.64	9.38	10.11	10.83	11.54	12.25	12.95	
9				7.04	8.04	9.01	9.98	10.92	11.85	12.77	13.69	14.59	15.48	16.36	
10				8.68	9.91	11.11	12.30	13.46	14.61	15.75	16.87	17.98	19.08	20.17	
11						13.43	14.86	16.27	17.66	19.03	20.38	21.72	23.05	24.37	25.67
12								19.33	20.99	22.62	24.23	25.82	27.40	28.96	30.51
13								22.44	24.13	26.51	28.40	30.27	32.12	33.95	35.77
14										30.71	32.90	35.06	37.21	39.33	41.44
15										35.22	37.73	40.21	42.67	45.10	47.52

CHAPTER 5

STRATIFIED RANDOM SAMPLING

Randomly or systematically locating plots or points over the entire area to be inventoried is an efficient sampling method only if the area is relatively uniform. For foresters, this generally means that the trees in the forested area are all about the same in terms of age, species, site quality, and so on. If the area is not homogeneous, then stratified sampling can be a much more efficient sampling scheme. Stratified sampling consists of dividing the population (area) into subpopulations called *strata* that are relatively homogeneous and then sampling each stratum separately. Foresters commonly use stand types (plantation versus natural), age, product class, site quality, species composition, topographic position, and the like to define stratum boundaries. Stratified sampling will typically yield population estimates that have smaller standard errors than if the area had been sampled as part of one large cruise with the same sample size. An important advantage of stratified sampling is that it yields separate estimates for each stratum as well as an overall estimate for the whole population.

Once the decision is made to stratify the population, a stratified random sample is obtained by taking a simple random sample within each stratum. More often than not, systematic samples are used within each stratum; when this is the case the procedure is called *stratified systematic sampling*. As discussed in Section 3.5, random sampling estimators can be used for systematically located plots unless a periodicity is known to exist in the strata. When such a periodicity exists, plot layout should be modified to avoid the periodicity (see Section 3.5). The remainder of this chapter will apply to both stratified random and stratified systematic sampling; both methods are referred to as stratified sampling.

There are potential disadvantages associated with stratified sampling. First, each sampling unit must be assigned to one and only one stratum. In situations where the strata are well defined, this may be very easy (as in plantations versus natural stands); in other situations this may be very difficult. For example, three strata might be defined as follows:

Conifers (conifers > 80%)

Hardwoods (hardwoods > 80%)

Mixed conifer-hardwood (20% < conifers < 80%)

Aerial photos or previous inventory information may be used to assign each sample unit to one of these strata prior to sampling. However, the sampling units may be poststratified; that is, sampling units may be assigned to strata after sampling (this is discussed in more detail in Section 5.11). A second disadvantage of stratified sampling is that each stratum size must be known to obtain sample estimates of population parameters and their associated variance or standard error. In many situations this will not be a problem; however, in some situations it can be quite difficult to determine stratum size. But this is not unique to stratified sampling because, as discussed in Section 3.7, it is sometimes difficult to determine the size of a population that is not stratified.

5.1 STRATIFIED SAMPLING NOTATION AND STRATUM ESTIMATES

Define:

L = number of strata into which the population will be divided

N_h = number of sampling units in stratum h

N = number of sampling units in entire population; $N = \sum_{h=1}^{L} N_h$

n_h = number of sampling units from stratum h included in the sample

n = total number of sampling units from all strata included in the sample;

$n = \sum_{h=1}^{L} n_h$

$y_{h,i}$ = an observed value of the variable y on sampling unit i in stratum h

The sample mean for stratum h is denoted $\bar{y}_h$:

$$\bar{y}_h = \frac{1}{n_h} \sum_{i=1}^{n_h} y_{h,i} \tag{5.1}$$

The variance of the sample mean for stratum h is denoted $S^2_{\bar{y}_h}$:

$$S^2_{\bar{y}_h} = \frac{S^2_{y_h}}{n_h}\left(\frac{N_h - n_h}{N_h}\right) \tag{5.2}$$

where:

$S^2_{y_h}$ = sample variance among sampling units within stratum h

$$S^2_{y_h} = \frac{1}{n_h - 1}\left[\sum_{i=1}^{n_h} y^2_{h,i} - \frac{\left(\sum_{i=1}^{n_h} y_{h,i}\right)^2}{n_h}\right] \tag{5.3}$$

and all else is as defined earlier.

The sample total for stratum h is denoted $\hat{T}_h$:

$$\hat{T}_h = N_h\bar{y}_h \tag{5.4}$$

The variance of the sample total for stratum h is denoted $S^2_{\hat{T}_h}$

$$S^2_{\hat{T}_h} = (N_h)^2 S^2_{\bar{y}_h} \tag{5.5}$$

The equations for the stratum mean ($\bar{y}_h$), stratum variance among sampling units ($S^2_{y_h}$), and variance of the stratum mean ($S^2_{\bar{y}_h}$) look a bit different from equations for simple random sampling, but for a given stratum they are exactly the same. In the stratified sampling equations presented, an additional subscript, h, has been added to denote the stratum the plot is in. For example, if stratum 1 is plantation pine, then the sample mean for plantation pine is denoted $\bar{y}_1$, the variance among sampling units in this stratum is denoted $S^2_{y_1}$, and the variance of the mean for the plantation pine stratum is denoted $S^2_{\bar{y}_1}$. If a total of 67 1⁄10-acre plots was measured in the plantation pine stratum, individual plot values are denoted as follows:

$y_{1,1}$

$y_{1,2}$

$y_{1,3}$

$y_{1,4}$

•

•

•

$y_{1,67}$

Note that the first number in the subscript denotes the stratum the plot is in and the second number denotes the plot number within the stratum. The sample size in stratum 1 is denoted n_1 and is 67. If a second stratum is defined as natural hardwood-pine, it may be denoted as stratum 2. If 54 ⅒-acre sample plots were measured in stratum 2, their values would be denoted as follows:

$y_{2,1}$
$y_{2,2}$
$y_{2,3}$
$y_{2,4}$
•
•
•
$y_{2,54}$

The sample mean, sample variance among sampling units, and sample variance of the mean for stratum 2 are denoted as $\bar{y}_2$, $S^2_{y_2}$, and $S^2_{\bar{y}_2}$, respectively. The sample size in stratum 2 is denoted $n_2 = 54$.

It should be clear that the calculations involved in estimating a population mean and its associated variance are identical to those for nonstratified simple random or systematic sampling. This also holds for calculating a stratum total ($\hat{T}_h$) and its associated variance ($S^2_{\hat{T}_h}$). Thus, when sample plots are kept separately by stratum, individual stratum means and totals as well as associated variances are calculated the same way as for sample plots taken from a nonstratified population.

EXAMPLE 5.1.1

A forested area was divided into two strata. Stratum 1 is a 72-acre, 55-year-old Douglas fir stand, and stratum 2 is a 50-acre, all-aged natural mixed conifer-hardwood stand. A systematic sample of 65 ⅕-acre plots was taken in stratum 1 and a systematic sample of 75 ⅕-acre plots was taken in stratum 2. On each plot the merchantable cubic-foot volume of conifers was determined. The following data summaries are available for each stratum:

Stratum 1	**Stratum 2**
$n_1 = 65$	$n_2 = 75$
$\sum_{i=1}^{65} y_{1,i} = 50{,}186$	$\sum_{i=1}^{75} y_{2,i} = 80{,}494$
$\sum_{i=1}^{65} y^2_{1,i} = 41{,}792{,}128$	$\sum_{i=1}^{75} y^2_{2,i} = 92{,}733{,}290$

(a) Estimate the total cubic foot volume and its standard error for stratum 1.

Use Eqs. 5.4 and 5.5. These equations require that we first estimate the stratum mean per sampling unit and its variance using Eqs. 5.1 and 5.2. Thus

$$\bar{y}_1 = \frac{1}{65}(50{,}186) = 772.1 \text{ ft}^3\text{/plot}$$

Now estimate the variance among plots in stratum 1.

$$S_{y_1}^2 = \frac{1}{64}\left[41{,}792{,}128 - \frac{(50{,}186)^2}{65}\right] = 47{,}560.99 \text{ (ft}^3)^2$$

To calculate the variance of the mean for stratum 1, first calculate the size of stratum 1, N_1 (the total number of ⅕-acre plots in stratum 1). Obviously, this is

$$N_1 = 72 \text{ acres} \times (5 \text{ plots/acre}) = 360 \text{ plots}$$

Now,

$$S_{\bar{y}_1}^2 = \frac{47{,}560.99}{65}\left(\frac{360-65}{360}\right) = 599.59 \text{ (ft}^3)^2$$

Next use Eqs. 5.4 and 5.5 to estimate the total merchantable volume in stratum 1 and its variance:

$$\hat{T}_1 = 360(772.1) = 277{,}956 \text{ ft}^3$$
$$S_{\hat{T}_1}^2 = (360)^2(599.59) = 77{,}706{,}864 \text{ (ft}^3)^2$$

The standard error of the total, $S_{\hat{T}_1}$, is

$$S_{\hat{T}_1} = \sqrt{S_{\hat{T}_1}^2} = 8815 \text{ ft}^3$$

An approximate 95% confidence interval for the total merchantable volume in stratum 1 is then

$$\hat{T}_1 \pm 2S_{\hat{T}_1}$$
$$277{,}956 \pm 2(8815)$$
$$\text{LCL} = 260{,}326 \text{ ft}^3$$
$$\text{UCL} = 295{,}586 \text{ ft}^3$$

Thus, if we have obtained a good sample from stratum 1, the total cubic-foot merchantable volume should fall somewhere between 260,326 ft^3 and 295,586 ft^3.

(b) Estimate the total cubic-foot volume and its standard error for stratum 2.

The same procedure as for stratum 1 is followed:

$$\bar{y}_2 = \frac{1}{75}(80{,}494) = \frac{1073.3 \text{ ft}^3}{\text{plot}}$$

$$S_{y_2}^2 = \frac{1}{74}\left[92{,}733{,}290 - \frac{(80{,}494)^2}{75}\right] = 85{,}714 \text{ (ft}^3)^2$$

$$N_2 = 50 \text{ acres} \times (5 \text{ plots/acre}) = 250 \text{ plots}$$

$$S_{\bar{y}_2}^2 = \frac{85{,}714}{75}\left(\frac{250 - 75}{250}\right) = 800 \text{ (ft}^3)^2$$

$$\hat{T}_2 = 250\,(1073.3) = 268{,}325 \text{ ft}^3$$

$$S_{\hat{T}_2}^2 = (250)^2(800) = 50{,}000{,}000 \text{ (ft}^3)^2$$

$$S_{\hat{T}_2} = \sqrt{S_{\hat{T}_2}^2} = 7071 \text{ ft}^3$$

The approximate 95% confidence interval is

$$\text{LCL} = 254{,}183 \text{ ft}^3$$
$$\text{UCL} = 282{,}467 \text{ ft}^3$$

From this example, it should be clear that obtaining individual stratum estimates is no different than for simple random or systematic sampling.

If everything involved in estimating stratum means and totals is the same as for nonstratified sampling why should stratified sampling be considered separately from nonstratified sampling? The answer is that the estimates from the different strata can be combined to obtain overall population estimates of the mean and total. Stratified estimates of the population mean and total will have smaller variance than nonstratified estimates if the strata were defined such that variance within strata is less than variation among strata. The practical implication of this is that stratified sampling will lead to more precise (smaller standard error) estimates of population parameters than nonstratified simple random or systematic sampling for a given number of sample plots or points (that is, for the same costs). Conversely, stratified sampling will produce an estimate as precise as simple random or systematic sampling using fewer sample plots or points (that is, for a lower cost the same accuracy can be obtained using stratified sampling).

5.2 COMBINING STRATUM ESTIMATES TO OBTAIN STRATIFIED SAMPLING ESTIMATES

Once estimates of individual stratum parameters (mean, total, and so on) have been calculated, estimates of the overall population parameters can be calculated. For example, the total merchantable pine volume in each of three strata may have been calculated, and now an estimate of the total merchantable pine volume for all three strata combined is desired. The following notation and equations will be used.

The sample mean for the entire population, denoted $\bar{y}_{ST}$, is

$$\bar{y}_{ST} = \sum_{h=1}^{L} \frac{N_h}{N} \bar{y}_h = \frac{1}{N} \sum_{h=1}^{L} N_h \bar{y}_h \tag{5.6}$$

Variance of the overall sample estimate of the population mean, denoted $S^2_{\bar{y}_{ST}}$, is

$$S^2_{\bar{y}_{ST}} = \sum_{h=1}^{L} \left(\frac{N_h}{N}\right)^2 S^2_{\bar{y}_h} \tag{5.7}$$

The sample total for the entire population, denoted $\hat{T}_{ST}$, is

$$\hat{T}_{ST} = N\bar{y}_{ST} = N\left(\frac{1}{N} \sum_{h=1}^{L} N_h \bar{y}_h\right) = \sum_{h=1}^{L} \hat{T}_h \tag{5.8}$$

Variance of the overall sample estimate of the population total, denoted $S^2_{\hat{T}_{ST}}$, is

$$S^2_{\hat{T}_{ST}} = N^2 S^2_{\bar{y}_{ST}} = \sum_{h=1}^{L} N_h^2 S^2_{\bar{y}_h} = \sum_{h=1}^{L} S^2_{\hat{T}_h} \tag{5.9}$$

Note that the sample estimates given each have an ST subscript. This subscript is used to denote that these are sample estimates based on a stratified sample. Close inspection of Eq. 5.6 for the stratified sample mean reveals that it is simply the weighted average of the individual stratum means, $\bar{y}_h$. The weights used are the stratum sizes, which implies that a large stratum will have a greater influence on the overall population mean than will a smaller stratum. Similarly, the variance of the overall population mean (Eq. 5.7) is a weighted average of individual stratum variances. Once the overall population sample mean, $\bar{y}_{ST}$, is obtained, multiply by N to get an estimate of the overall population total, $\hat{T}_{ST}$ (Eq. 5.8). Another way to obtain $\hat{T}_{ST}$ is to add estimates of all individual stratum totals, $\hat{T}_h$ (Eq. 5.8). Finally, note that the variance of the overall population total is obtained by adding together the variance of each individual stratum total (Eq. 5.9).

EXAMPLE 5.2.1

We wish to obtain an estimate of the average merchantable cubic-foot conifer volume as well as the total tract volume for the 122-acre tract described in Example 5.1.1. As always, the variance for each one of these estimates will also be calculated. Recall that this population was divided into two strata, one a 72-acre Douglas fir plantation and one a 50-acre mixed conifer-hardwood natural stand.

The overall population mean is calculated using Eq. 5.6:

$$\bar{y}_{\text{ST}} = \frac{1}{N} \sum_{h=1}^{L} N_h \bar{y}_h$$

Note that N, the population size, is the sum of the stratum sizes (N_h) and in this example is

$$N = N_1 + N_2 = 360 + 250 = 610 \text{ plots}$$

$$\bar{y}_{\text{ST}} = \frac{1}{610}[360(772.1) + 250(1073.3)]$$

$$= 895.5 \text{ ft}^3$$

Now calculate the variance of $\bar{y}_{\text{ST}}$ using Eq. 5.7:

$$S^2_{\bar{y}_{\text{ST}}} = \left(\frac{360}{610}\right)^2 599.59 + \left(\frac{250}{610}\right)^2 800$$

$$= 343.2 \text{ (ft}^3)^2$$

The total tract volume is calculated using Eq. 5.8:

$$\hat{T}_{\text{ST}} = N\bar{y}_{\text{ST}} = 610(895.5) = 546{,}255 \text{ ft}^3$$

or

$$\hat{T}_{\text{ST}} = \sum_{h=1}^{2} \hat{T}_h = 277{,}956 + 268{,}325 = 546{,}281 \text{ ft}^3$$

(Note that the difference in these two estimates is due to rounding.) The variance of the total tract volume is calculated using Eq. 5.9:

$$S^2_{\hat{T}_{\text{ST}}} = \sum_{h=1}^{L} S^2_{\hat{T}_h} = 77{,}706{,}864 + 50{,}000{,}000$$

$$= 127{,}706{,}864 \text{ (ft}^3)^2$$

Now obtain the standard error of the tract volume $S_{\hat{T}_{ST}}$ by taking the square root of $S^2_{\hat{T}_{ST}}$:

$$S_{\hat{T}_{ST}} = \sqrt{127{,}706{,}864} = 11{,}301 \text{ ft}^3$$

An approximate 95% confidence interval for the total tract volume is (using 546,255 as $\hat{T}_{ST}$)

$$\hat{T}_{ST} \pm 2S_{\hat{T}_{ST}}$$
$$546{,}255 \text{ ft}^3 \pm 2(11{,}301 \text{ ft}^3)$$
$$\text{LCL} = 523{,}653 \text{ ft}^3$$
$$\text{UCL} = 568{,}857 \text{ ft}^3$$

It should now be clear that obtaining overall population estimates of means and totals is relatively simple and straightforward.

In Examples 5.1.1 and 5.2.1 the population of interest was divided into two strata, and in each stratum the merchantable cubic-foot volume of conifers was obtained. It is logical to combine the stratum estimates into an overall estimate of the total tract volume in this case because both strata were measured for the same characteristic (that is, merchantable volume of conifers). However, strata are often measured for different characteristics. For example a relatively large tract of timber may be broken down into the following three strata based on stand type:

Stratum	**Stand Type**
1	Hardwood bottom
2	Mixed hardwood-pine
3	Pine plantation

In this situation combining volume estimates from the three strata doesn't make much sense because each stratum is made up of completely different species or products that are illogical to combine. However, volume may be converted to dollar value in each stratum and then all calculations can be carried out in terms of dollars rather than volume units. Then combining stratum estimates of dollar value into an overall dollar value for the entire tract is logical. For a given sample size stratified sampling in this situation will lead to a more precise estimate of the total tract value than if each stratum were inventoried independently of one another.

EXAMPLE 5.2.2

A stratified sample was carried out on a 350-acre tract. Three strata were defined:

Stratum	Acreage	Products
1. Hardwood bottom	75	Hardwood sawtimber
2. Mixed hardwood-pine	150	Hardwood sawtimber Pine sawtimber
3. Pine plantation	125	Pine pulpwood Pine chip-and-saw

Obviously, these strata are very different and the products available in each are also quite different and will probably be measured in different volume units (board feet versus cubic feet or cords). A total of 250 1/10-acre sample plots were measured: 54 in stratum 1, 107 in stratum 2, and 89 in stratum 3. All plots were measured for the appropriate characteristics so that appropriate volumes and subsequently dollar values could be determined. Estimates of total dollar value and associated standard errors are as follows:

Stratum	Sample Plots	Total Value $\hat{T}_h$ (\$)	Standard Error $S_{\hat{T}_h}$ (\$)
1. Hardwood Bottom	54	22,400	1400
2. Mixed Hardwood-Pine	107	48,000	3000
3. Pine Plantation	89	122,000	4500

Note that to determine dollar value per stratum and associated standard errors, the dollar value for each sample plot (on a per-plot or per-acre basis) in each stratum must be determined. For example, in the mixed hardwood-pine stand a given sample plot may have the following per-acre values:

Hardwood sawtimber	850 board feet/acre (Doyle)
Pine sawtimber	1275 board feet/acre (Scribner)

Given that stumpage values are

\$225/MBF (Doyle)	Hardwood
\$175/MBF (Scribner)	Pine

the dollar value/acre assigned to this plot is

Hardwood	\$191.25
Pine	\$223.12
Total	\$414.37

When the dollar value for each sample plot in each stratum is determined, stratum estimates (dollars) and associated standard errors (in dollars) are calculated using Eqs. 5.1 through 5.5. Note that in these equations, $y_{h,i}$ represents the dollar value of plot i in stratum h rather than a characteristic such as cubic foot volume or board foot volume. Once stratum value and standard errors are determined, the tract value and standard error are easily obtained using Eqs. 5.6 through 5.9. In this example the estimated total dollar value and associated standard error for each of the three strata are given. Equation 5.8 is used to obtain an estimate of the total dollar value for the entire 350-acre tract.

$$\hat{T}_{\mathrm{ST}} = \sum_{h=1}^{L} \hat{T}_h$$

Thus

$$\begin{aligned}\hat{T}_{\mathrm{ST}} &= \hat{T}_1 + \hat{T}_2 + \hat{T}_3\\ &= \$22{,}400 + \$48{,}000 + \$122{,}000\\ &= \$192{,}400\end{aligned}$$

The variance of $\hat{T}_{\mathrm{ST}}$ (Eq. 5.9) is the sum of the variances for the individual stratum. Thus

$$\begin{aligned}S^2_{\hat{T}_{\mathrm{ST}}} &= S^2_{\hat{T}_1} + S^2_{\hat{T}_2} + S^2_{\hat{T}_3}\\ &= (\$1400)^2 + (\$3000)^2 + (\$4500)^2\\ &= 31{,}210{,}000(\text{dollars})^2\end{aligned}$$

The standard error of the total value is then calculated by taking the square root of this variance:

$$S_{\hat{T}_{\mathrm{ST}}} = \$5587$$

Now an approximate 95% confidence interval is calculated as

$$\hat{T}_{\mathrm{ST}} \pm 2S_{\hat{T}_{\mathrm{ST}}}$$

$$\$192{,}400 \pm 2(\$5587)$$

$$\mathrm{LCL} = \$181{,}226$$

$$\mathrm{UCL} = \$203{,}574$$

5.3 COMBINING STRATUM ESTIMATES BASED ON POINT SAMPLING

When individual strata are inventoried using point sampling, estimates are obtained somewhat differently than just shown. Close examination of Eqs. 5.6 through 5.9 shows that stratum sizes (number of plots per stratum), N_h, must be known in order to obtain estimates. Obviously, points have no area associated with them and thus there are an infinite number of possible points in any given stratum. The question now becomes what values should be used as the size of the strata. The answer is that stratum area (in acres) is used as N_h and the entire tract area (in acres) as N.

EXAMPLE 5.3.1

A stratified sample was carried out for a 275-acre tract. Three strata were identified and point sampling was used in each to determine the merchantable cubic-foot volume of conifers. Below, stratum size (in acres), estimated average merchantable cubic-foot volume per acre ($\bar{y}_h$), and associated standard errors ($S_{\bar{y}_h}$) are given:

Stratum	Acreage	$\bar{y}_h$ (ft^3)	$S_{\bar{y}_h}$ (ft^3)
Valley bottom	100	2450	125
East-facing slope	125	2120	75
Ridge line	50	1475	175

To obtain an estimate of the merchantable volume of conifers for the entire tract, first use Eq. 5.4 for each stratum using the stratum acreage as N_h:

$$\hat{T}_1 = N_1\bar{y}_1 = 100(2450) = 245{,}000 \text{ ft}^3$$
$$\hat{T}_2 = N_2\bar{y}_2 = 125(2120) = 265{,}000 \text{ ft}^3$$
$$\hat{T}_3 = N_3\bar{y}_3 = 50(1475) = 73{,}750 \text{ ft}^3$$

Next the variance for each stratum total is calculated using Eq. 5.5 with the stratum acreage as N_h:

$$S^2_{\hat{T}_1} = (N_1)^2 S^2_{\bar{y}_1} = (100)^2(125)^2 = 156{,}250{,}000 \text{ (ft}^3)^2$$

$$S^2_{\hat{T}_2} = (N_2)^2 S^2_{\bar{y}_2} = (125)^2(75)^2 = 87{,}890{,}625 \text{ (ft}^3)^2$$

$$S^2_{\hat{T}_3} = (N_3)^2 S^2_{\bar{y}_3} = (50)^2(175)^2 = 76{,}562{,}500 \text{ (ft}^3)^2$$

The standard error for each stratum total is easily obtained by taking the square root of the stratum variance:

$$S^2_{\hat{T}_1} = 12{,}500 \text{ ft}^3$$

$$S^2_{\hat{T}_2} = 9375 \text{ ft}^3$$

$$S^2_{\hat{T}_3} = 8750 \text{ ft}^3$$

Now the total tract merchantable volume is obtained using Eq. 5.8:

$$\hat{T}_{ST} = \sum_{h=1}^{3} \hat{T}_h = 245{,}000 + 265{,}000 + 73{,}750$$
$$= 583{,}750 \text{ ft}^3$$

The variance of this estimate is obtained with Eq. 5.9:

$$S^2_{\hat{T}_{ST}} = \sum_{h=1}^{3} S^2_{\hat{T}_h}$$
$$= 156{,}250{,}000 + 87{,}890{,}625 + 76{,}562{,}500$$
$$= 320{,}703{,}125 \text{ (ft}^3)^2$$

Now the standard error of $\hat{T}_{ST}$ is the square root of the variance of $\hat{T}_{ST}$:

$$S_{\hat{T}_{ST}} = 17{,}908 \text{ ft}^3$$

An approximate 95% confidence interval is

$$\hat{T}_{ST} \pm 2(S_{\hat{T}_{ST}})$$
$$583{,}750 \pm 2(17{,}908)$$
$$\text{LCL} = 547{,}934 \text{ ft}^3$$
$$\text{UCL} = 619{,}566 \text{ ft}^3$$

5.4 SAMPLE SIZE REQUIREMENTS

As for simple random or systematic sampling, it is prudent to determine the number of sampling units required to meet a predefined bound or allowable error for stratified sampling. However, for stratified sampling, sample size determination is complicated by the fact that various strata have been identified. These strata may differ considerably in size as well as in the inherent variability among sampling units. Once sample size for a given stratified population is determined, the number of sampling units allocated to each stratum must be determined. Such sample size allocation among the strata may be dependent on individual stratum size and variability, as well as the cost of sampling in the stratum.

Following are sample size equations for two of the three situations described in Chapter 3 for estimating sample sizes for nonstratified simple random or systematic samples:

I. Bound specified for population mean per sampling unit in units of the characteristic of interest.

II. Bound specified for population total in units of the characteristic of interest.

Sample size equations that use allowable error (AE) as input are not given because information required to use resulting equations render them difficult to use in practice. Note that there are equations for both finite and infinite population size. Recall that the population is usually assumed to be infinite when the sampling fraction (n/N) is less than 0.05.

The finite population sample size equations for the two situations listed above are as follows:

I. Bound (approximate 95% confidence level) specified for population mean per sampling unit in units of the characteristic of interest:

$$n = \frac{\sum_{h=1}^{L} \frac{N_h^2 S_{y_h}^2}{W_h}}{\frac{N^2 B_M^2}{4} + \sum_{h=1}^{L} N_h S_{y_h}^2} \tag{5.10}$$

where:

n = estimated sample size

N = number of sampling units in the population = $\sum_{h=1}^{L} N_h$

N_h = number of sampling units in stratum h

L = number of strata into which the population is divided

$S_{y_h}^2$ = sample variance among sampling units within stratum h

B_M = desired bound on the overall population mean per sampling unit

W_h = proportion of sample size allocated to stratum h ($0 < W_h < 1$); calculation of W_h is discussed below

II. Bound (approximate 95% confidence level) specified for population total in units of the characteristic of interest:

$$n = \frac{\sum_{h=1}^{L} \frac{N_h^2 S_{y_h}^2}{W_h}}{\frac{B_T^2}{4} + \sum_{h=1}^{L} N_h S_{y_h}^2} \tag{5.11}$$

where:

B_T = desired bound on the overall population total
and all other variables are defined as before.

If the stratum sizes are assumed to be infinite, that is, sampling fractions $\left(\frac{n_h}{N_h}\right)$ are expected to be less than .05 for all strata, then the following sample size equations can be used for the two situations just discussed.

I.
$$n = \frac{4 \sum_{h=1}^{L} \frac{N_h^2 S_{y_h}^2}{W_h}}{B_M^2 N^2} \tag{5.12}$$

where all variables are as defined earlier.

II.
$$n = \frac{4 \sum_{h=1}^{L} \frac{N_h^2 S_{y_h}^2}{W_h}}{B_T^2} \tag{5.13}$$

where all variables are as defined earlier.

Note that in Eqs. 5.10 through 5.13 the proportion of the sample allocated to each individual stratum must be known (that is, we must know the W_h values). The proportion of the sample allocated to stratum h (W_h) is

$$W_h = \frac{n_h}{n}$$

This implies that the number of sampling units allocated to stratum h (n_h) is

$$n_h = W_h n \tag{5.14}$$

EXAMPLE 5.4.1

Assume that we want to estimate the total tract volume with a bound of 14,000 ft^3 for the tract described in Example 5.2.1. For this tract the following information is known:

Stratum	N_h	$S_{y_h}^2$
1	360	47,560.99
2	250	85,714.00
	$N = 610$	

Since the bound is given for the total tract volume, Eq. 5.11 is used. To use Eq. 5.11, W_1 and W_2, the proportion of the sample allocated to each stratum, must be determined. There are several ways to allocate the sampling units among the strata; however, for this example W_1 and W_2 are arbitrarily set to 0.5. Note that $W_1 + W_2 = 1$.

In general it must be true that

$$\sum_{h=1}^{L} W_h = 1$$

To determine n first calculate the numerator of Eq. 5.11:

$$\sum_{h=1}^{L} \frac{N_h^2 S_{y_h}^2}{W_h} = \frac{(360)^2(47{,}560.99)}{0.5} + \frac{(250)^2(85{,}714.00)}{0.5}$$
$$= 2.304205 \times 10^{10}$$

Next calculate the two components of the denominator:

$$\frac{B_T^2}{4} = \frac{(14{,}000)^2}{4} = 49{,}000{,}000$$

$$\sum_{h=1}^{L} N_h^2 S_{y_h}^2 = 360(47{,}560.99) + 250(85{,}714.00)$$
$$= 38{,}550{,}456.4$$

Now put everything together in Eq. 5.11 to obtain

$$n = \frac{2.304205 \times 10^{10}}{49{,}000{,}000 + 38{,}550{,}456.4} = 263.2 \text{ plots}$$

As always, round this number up to $n = 264$ plots. Finally, to determine the number of sampling units to allocate to each stratum, use Eq. 5.14 (recall that $W_1 = W_2 = 0.5$):

$$n_1 = 0.5(264) = 132$$
$$n_2 = 0.5(264) = 132$$

Thus, to obtain an estimate of the total tract volume with an upper bound on the error of estimation of 14,000 ft^3, approximately 132 plots should be measured in each stratum.

The results of the previous example would have been different if sample plots had been allocated among strata differently. In fact, the choice of an equal proportion allocated to each stratum is usually very inefficient and may lead to larger sample sizes than are required with other more well-thought-out sample allocation strategies.

EXAMPLE 5.4.2

Consider the tract described in Example 5.4.1. Estimate the required sample size, n, using Eq. 5.13 (bound specified for the population total in units of the characteristic of interest for infinite populations) for a bound of $B_T = 14{,}000$ ft^3. Use $W_1 = W_2 = 0.5$. The numerator of Eq. 5.13 is

$$4\sum_{h=1}^{L}\frac{N_h^2 S_{y_h}^2}{W_h} = 4\left[\frac{(360)^2(47{,}560.99)}{0.5} + \frac{(250)^2(85{,}714.00)}{0.5}\right]$$
$$= 9.216823 \times 10^{10}$$

The denominator is

$$B_T^2 = (14{,}000)^2 = 196{,}000{,}000$$

Thus

$$n = \frac{9.216823 + 10^{10}}{196{,}000{,}000} = 470.2$$

Use $n = 471$ plots.

Then from Eq. 5.16,

$$n_1 = n_2 = 0.5(471) = 235.5$$

Use $n_1 = n_2 = 236$ plots.

This example illustrates the fact that the infinite sample size equations produce larger sample size estimates than finite sample size equations. Consequently, it is important to use the finite sampling equations when one or more of the sampling fractions, $\frac{n_h}{N_h}$, will be greater than 0.05.

As previously stated and illustrated, strata within a population usually vary in size and variability among the sampling units within the stratum. Additionally, the cost of measuring a sample plot or point may vary among strata. A major advantage of stratified sampling is that sample plots or points can be allocated to the various strata based on stratum size, variability, and cost of sampling.

If the sampling effort is appropriately allocated among the strata, the following statements will be true:

1. Stratified sampling will produce a more precise estimate of the population parameter of interest (mean or total) than nonstratified sampling for a given sample size (or cost).
2. Stratified sampling will produce an estimate of the population parameter of interest as precise as nonstratified sampling while using a smaller overall sample size (that is, for lower cost).

Thus, if strata are defined well and sampling units are allocated among the strata appropriately, more information about the population will be obtained than would be by using the same effort in a nonstratified sample. Further, and maybe more importantly, overall sampling effort (and consequently costs) can be reduced if strata are defined well and sampling units are allocated among strata appropriately.

5.5 PROPORTIONAL ALLOCATION

This is the most basic and easily implemented sample allocation strategy. Proportional allocation allocates sample plots or points among strata in direct proportion to the size of the strata. Thus larger strata will have larger numbers of sample plots or points than smaller strata. The proportion of plots allocated to a given stratum is

$$W_h = \frac{N_h}{N} \tag{5.15}$$

When Eqs. 5.14 and 5.15 are used in conjunction with any of the sample size equations (5.10 through 5.13), total sample size, n, as well as the number of sample plots allocated to each stratum (n_h) can be determined.

EXAMPLE 5.5.1

Refer to Example 5.4.1. Assume we still desire to have a bound on the total tract volume of 14,000 ft^3, but now proportional allocation will be used to allocate the sample units. Recall the following:

Stratum	N_h	$S^2_{y_h}$	$W_h = \frac{N_h}{N}$
1	360	47,560.99	0.59016
2	250	85,714.00	0.40984
	$N = 610$		

Use Eq. 5.11 with the preceding values as input. The numerator of Eq. 5.11 is

$$\sum_{h=1}^{L} \frac{N_h^2 S^2_{y_h}}{W_h} = \frac{(360)^2(47{,}560.99)}{(0.59016)} + \frac{(250)^2(85{,}714.00)}{(0.40984)}$$
$$= 2.351572 \times 10^{10}$$

Note that the components in the denominator of Eq. 5.11 do not change from our previous calculations in Example 5.4.1. Thus

$$\frac{B_T^2}{4} = 49{,}000{,}000$$

$$\sum_{h=1}^{L} N_h S^2_{y_h} = 38{,}550{,}456.4$$

Then

$$n = \frac{2.351572 \times 10^{10}}{49{,}000{,}000 + 38{,}550{,}456.4} = 268.6 \text{ plots}$$

Use $n = 269$ plots. To determine the number of sample plots allocated to each stratum using Eq. 5.15,

$$n_1 = 0.59016\ (269) = 158.8$$

$$n_2 = 0.40984\ (269) = 110.2$$

Approximately 159 plots in stratum 1 and 111 plots in stratum 2 will be used.

Note that proportional allocation does not allow for differences in variability among strata. In fact, the underlying assumption of proportional allocation is that the variability among sampling units is the same for all strata. If there is reason to believe that the variation among sampling units is different and estimates of individual stratum variation are available, then sample plots should be allocated using Neyman allocation.

5.6 NEYMAN ALLOCATION

If there is reason to believe that variability among plots within individual strata is quite different from stratum to stratum, then these differences should be taken into account in allocating the sample. It makes sense that more sampling units should be used in a stratum with high variability among sampling units and fewer in a stratum with relatively low variability among sampling units. Neyman allocation takes into account differences in stratum variability as well as stratum size in sample allocation. The equation for W_h is

$$W_h = \frac{N_h S_{y_h}}{\sum_{h=1}^{L} N_h S_{y_h}} \tag{5.16}$$

where all variables are as previously defined.

For a given population the denominator of Eq. 5.16 is a constant. Clearly then, W_h increases (that is, the number of plots or points allocated to stratum h increases) when either stratum size, N_h, or stratum variability, S_{y_h}, increases.

EXAMPLE 5.6.1

Refer to Example 5.4.1. An estimate of the total tract volume with a bound of 14,000 ft^3 is desired. Recall the following:

Stratum	N_h	$S^2_{y_h}$
1	360	47,560.99
2	250	85,714.00
	$N = 610$	

First calculate the W_h values using Eq. 5.16 for Neyman allocation:

$$W_1 = \frac{360\sqrt{47{,}560.99}}{360\sqrt{47{,}560.99} + 250\sqrt{85{,}714.00}}$$

$$= \frac{78{,}510.53624}{78{,}510.53624 + 73{,}192.38348}$$

$$= \frac{78{,}510.53624}{151{,}702.9197}$$

$$= 0.5175$$

$$W_2 = \frac{250\sqrt{85{,}714.00}}{151{,}702.9197}$$

$$= 0.4825$$

The numerator of Eq. 5.11 is

$$\sum_{h=1}^{L} \frac{N_h^2 S^2_{y_h}}{W_h} = \frac{(360)^2(47{,}560.99)}{(0.5175)} + \frac{(250)^2(85{,}714.00)}{(0.4825)}$$
$$= 2.301377 \times 10^{10}$$

Both quantities in the denominator of Eq. 5.11 were calculated in Example 5.4.1. They are

$$\frac{B_T^2}{4} = 49{,}000{,}000$$

$$\sum_{h=1}^{L} N_h S^2_{y_h} = 38{,}550{,}456.4$$

Thus

$$n = \frac{2.301377 \times 10^{10}}{49{,}000{,}000 + 38{,}550{,}456.4} = 262.9$$

Use $n = 263$ plots. The number of plots allocated to each stratum is obtained from Eq. 5.14 as

$$n_1 = 0.5175(263) = 136.1$$
$$n_2 = 0.4825(263) = 126.9$$

Use $n_1 = 137$ plots and $n_2 = 127$ plots.

It is instructive to look at the results for sample size requirements obtained using $W_1 = W_2 = 0.5$ with results of proportional and Neyman allocation. In the examples just given, the total sample size required for each allocation scheme was as follows:

Allocation Scheme	**Total Required Sample Size (n)**
$W_1 = W_2 = 0.5$	264
Proportional	269
Neyman	263

Neyman allocation resulted in the smallest sample size (although the difference is essentially of no consequence). However, among these three allocation schemes Neyman allocation will almost always result in the smallest overall sample size. Proportional allocation will usually result in a smaller total sample size than allocating the same number of units to each stratum (that is, $W_1 = W_2 = 0.5$). However, this was not true for these examples because $W_1 = W_2 = 0.5$ is closer to the Neyman allocation of $W_1 = 0.5175$ and $W_2 = 0.4825$ than is the proportional allocation $W_1 = 0.59016$ and $W_2 = 0.40984$. Consequently, it is difficult to make generalizations as to whether proportional allocation is preferable to equal number of sample plots in each stratum. The answer depends on the relationship between stratum size and stratum variability. In the example above, the smaller stratum (2) had greater variability than the larger stratum (1). However, if the smaller stratum has variability less than or equal to the larger stratum, proportional allocation will lead to a smaller total sample size (usually quite a bit smaller than equal allocation). Thus, if information about stratum size is available and there is no reason to believe that variability is different among strata, then proportional allocation is preferred to equal allocation (that is, $W_1 = W_2 = \cdots = W_L$). If information about stratum size and stratum variability is known to differ among strata, then Neyman allocation is preferred to both proportional and equal allocation. Consequently, equal allocation is almost never employed in practice.

EXAMPLE 5.6.2

A 375-acre population has been divided into three strata. The volume of merchantable pine timber is the characteristic being measured on the $\frac{1}{10}$-acre sample plots. From previous experience the following information is available for each stratum:

Stratum	N_h (1/10-Acre Plots)	$S^2_{y_h}$
1. Pine plantation	1500	1175
2. Natural pine stand	1000	575
3. Hardwood bottom	1250	1850
	$N = 3750$	

If an equal number of plots is allocated to each stratum, then

$$W_1 = W_2 = W_3 = 1/3 = 0.333\overline{3}$$

Assume we want to estimate the merchantable pine volume of the 375-acre tract to within 7500 ft^3 (that is, $B_T = 7500$). Equation 5.11 should be used to calculate n. The numerator of Eq. 5.11 is

$$\sum_{h=1}^{L} \frac{N_n^2 S_{y_h}^2}{W_h} = \frac{(1500)^2(1175)}{0.3333} + \frac{(1000)^2(575)}{0.3333} + \frac{(1250)^2(1850)}{0.3333}$$

$$= 1.832812 \times 10^{10}$$

Next calculate the two components of the denominator of Eq. 5.11:

$$\frac{B_T^2}{4} = \frac{(7500)^2}{4} = 14{,}062{,}500$$

$$\sum_{h=1}^{L} N_h S_{y_h}^2 = (1500)(1175) + (1000)(575) + (1250)(1850)$$

$$= 4{,}650{,}000$$

$$D = \text{denominator} = 14{,}062{,}500 + 4{,}650{,}000$$

$$D = 18{,}712{,}500$$

Now

$$n = \frac{1.832812 \times 10^{10}}{18{,}712{,}500} = 979.5$$

Use $n = 980$ 1/10-acre plots.

Thus, using Eq. 5.14,

$$n_1 = n_2 = n_3 = 980\ (0.333\overline{3}) = 326.7$$

Use $n_1 = n_2 = n_3 = 327$ plots.

Next use proportional allocation in lieu of equal allocation:

$$W_1 = \frac{1500}{3750} = 0.4000$$

$$W_2 = \frac{1000}{3750} = 0.2667$$

$$W_3 = \frac{1250}{3750} = 0.3333$$

Use Eq. 5.11 to calculate n. The denominator of Eq. 5.11 does not change; as shown earlier, it is

$$D = 18{,}712{,}500$$

Now the numerator is

$$\sum_{h=1}^{L} \frac{N_h^2 S_{y_h}^2}{W_h} = \frac{(1500)^2(1175)}{0.4000} + \frac{(1000)^2(575)}{0.2667} + \frac{(1250)^2(1850)}{0.3333}$$
$$= 1.743809 \times 10^{10}$$

Thus, using proportional allocation,

$$n = \frac{1.743809 \times 10^{10}}{18{,}712{,}500} = 931.9$$

Use $n = 932$ ⅒-acre plots.

Equation 5.14 yields

$$n_1 = 932(0.4) = 372.8$$
$$n_2 = 932(0.2667) = 248.6$$
$$n_3 = 932(0.3333) = 310.6$$

Use $n_1 = 373$, $n_2 = 249$, and $n_3 = 311$.

Finally, use Neyman allocation. Recall that Eq. 5.16 is used for this.

$$W_h = \frac{N_h S_{y_h}}{\sum_{h=1}^{L} N_h S_{y_h}}$$

The denominator is

$$\sum_{h=1}^{L} N_h S_{y_h} = 1500\sqrt{1175} + 1000\sqrt{575} + 1250\sqrt{1850}$$
$$= 129{,}161.1001$$

Then

$$W_1 = \frac{1500\sqrt{1175}}{129{,}161.1001} = 0.39809$$

$$W_2 = \frac{1000\sqrt{575}}{129{,}161.1001} = 0.18565$$

$$W_3 = \frac{1250\sqrt{1850}}{129{,}161.1001} = 0.41626$$

To calculate n, use Eq. 5.11. As shown previously, the denominator of Eq. 5.11 is

$$D = 18{,}712{,}500$$

The numerator is calculated as

$$\sum_{h=1}^{L} \frac{N_h^2 S_{y_h}^2}{W_h} = \frac{(1500)^2(1175)}{0.39809} + \frac{(1000)^2(575)}{0.18565} + \frac{(1250)^2(1850)}{0.41626}$$
$$= 1.668258 \times 10^{10}$$

Thus, using Neyman allocation,

$$n = \frac{1.668258 \times 10^{10}}{18{,}712{,}500} = 891.52$$

Use $n = 892$ 1/10-acre plots.

Finally, stratum sample sizes using Neyman allocation are

$$n_1 = 892\ (0.39809) = 355.1$$
$$n_2 = 892\ (0.18565) = 165.6$$
$$n_3 = 892\ (0.41626) = 371.3$$

So use $n_1 = 356$, $n_2 = 166$, and $n_3 = 372$.
Here is a summary of the three allocation methods:

Allocation Method	n	n_1	n_2	n_3
Equal	980	327	327	327
Proportional	932	373	249	311
Neyman	892	356	166	372

In this example; allocating proportional to stratum size rather than equally reduces overall sample size by 48 plots. Note, as expected, that the largest stratum receives the largest number of sample plots. Required sample size is reduced further by allocating using Neyman allocation. In fact, by using Neyman allocation, the overall sample size was reduced by an additional 40 plots. Note that fewer plots were allocated to stratum 2 (natural pine) using Neyman allocation since this is the least variable stratum ($S_{y_2}^2 = 575$). Conversely, a larger number of plots is allocated to stratum 3, the most variable stratum ($S_{y_3}^2 = 1850$), in Neyman allocation. The sample size allocated to stratum 1 was about the same for Neyman and proportional allocation since stratum 1 variability was close to the average variability of the three strata ($S_{y_1}^2 = 1175$).

The preceding example illustrates the most important advantage of stratified sampling. The same level of precision can be obtained using a smaller number of sample plots by allocating the sample in a prudent fashion (proportional to stratum size and/or stratum variability). Of course, stratum variability estimates must be available prior to field data collection. This information can be obtained from a pilot survey or from previous experience in similar tracts (see the discussion in Section 3.6).

5.7 OPTIMAL ALLOCATION

More often than not, cost of sampling is a major consideration in the determination of the sample size to use for a forest inventory. In certain situations cost of sampling a given size of plot may vary among strata. For example, it may take twice as long to establish and measure a ⅒-acre plot in a 23-year-old pine plantation with thick underbrush than it does in a relatively open 85-year-old natural pine stand. The difference in time is due not only to the differences in underbrush but also to the fact that the old natural stand will have fewer trees to measure than the pine plantation. Of course, time is highly correlated with cost, so the "cost" of a plot in the plantation could arbitrarily be set to 2 and the "cost" of a plot in the natural stand to 1. When costs are known to vary among strata and there is a limited budget, the number of "expensive" plots should be kept to a minimum while still meeting the desired bound on the population parameter of interest (total tract volume and so on). To accomplish this the allocation scheme referred to as *optimal allocation* is used. The proportion of sample plots allocated to a given stratum using optimal allocation is

$$W_h = \frac{N_h S_{y_h} / \sqrt{C_h}}{\sum_{h=1}^{L} N_h S_{y_h} / \sqrt{C_h}} \tag{5.17}$$

where:

C_h = cost (or relative cost) of a sample unit in stratum h
and all else is as defined earlier.

For a given population the denominator of this equation will be a constant. Thus it should be clear that for optimal allocation the proportion of plots allocated to stratum h will

1. Increase as stratum size (N_h) increases.
2. Increase as stratum variability (S_{y_h}) increases.
3. Decrease as stratum cost (C_h) increases.

EXAMPLE 5.7.1

Refer to Example 5.6.2. We will now assume that we have relative cost information for measuring a sample plot in each of the three strata. It takes twice as long to install a plot in the pine plantation as in the natural pine stand, but only three-fourths as long to install a plot in the hardwood bottom as in the natural pine stand. We will assume that time is directly proportional to cost. Thus the following information is available for each stratum:

Stratum	N_h	$S^2_{y_h}$	Relative Cost
1. Pine plantation	1500	1175	2
2. Natural pine stand	1000	575	1
3. Hardwood bottom	1250	1850	¾
	$N = 3750$		

The proportion allocated to each stratum is calculated using Eq. 5.17. The denominator of Eq. 5.17 for this example is

$$\sum_{h=1}^{L} \frac{N_h S_{y_h}}{\sqrt{C_h}} = \frac{1500\sqrt{1175}}{\sqrt{2}} + \frac{1000\sqrt{575}}{\sqrt{1}} + \frac{1250\sqrt{1850}}{\sqrt{3/4}}$$
$$= 122{,}418.6917$$

Now

$$W_1 = \frac{1500\sqrt{1175}/\sqrt{2}}{122{,}418.6917} = 0.29699$$

$$W_2 = \frac{1000\sqrt{575}/\sqrt{1}}{122{,}418.6917} = 0.19588$$

$$W_3 = \frac{1250\sqrt{1850}/\sqrt{3/4}}{122{,}418.6917} = 0.50713$$

As before, the desired bound on the total tract volume will be 7500 ft^3 (BT = 7500). To determine n, Eq. 5.11 is used. From Example 5.6.2 the denominator for Eq. 5.11 is

$$D = 18{,}712{,}500$$

The numerator is calculated as

$$\sum_{h=1}^{L} \frac{N_h^2 S_{y_h}^2}{W_h} = \frac{(1500)^2(1175)}{0.29699} + \frac{(1000)^2(575)}{0.19588} + \frac{(1250)^2(1850)}{0.50713}$$
$$= 1.753725 \times 10^{10}$$

The total required sample size using optimal allocation is

$$n = \frac{1.753725 \times 10^{10}}{18{,}712{,}500} = 937.2$$

Use $n = 938$ ⅒-acre plots.

The sample is then allocated among the stratum as

$$n_1 = 938(0.29699) = 278.9$$
$$n_2 = 938(0.19588) = 183.7$$
$$n_3 = 938(0.50713) = 475.7$$

Use $n_1 = 279$, $n_2 = 184$, and $n_3 = 476$.

Note that the total sample size required using optimal allocation is 938 plots. This is greater than required sample sizes for both proportional ($n = 932$ plots) and Neyman allocation ($n = 892$ plots). However, if the relative cost information is correct, it will cost less to install the plots according to the optimal allocation scheme than the other allocation schemes. This is easily seen by calculating the total relative cost for each stratum for each allocation scheme. The total relative cost is the number of plots allocated to the stratum multiplied by the relative cost per plot:

	Total Relative Cost		
Stratum	**Proportional**	**Neyman**	**Optimal**
Pine plantation	746	712	558
Natural pine stand	249	166	184
Hardwood bottom	233	279	357
Total	1228	1157	1099

Note that the same bound on the total tract volume will be met using any of the allocation methods. This bound will be met for least cost using the optimal allocation scheme described earlier.

A great deal of prior information is required for optimal allocation. In most situations it will not be possible to have such detailed information about plot costs and stratum variances. However, when this information is available it can be put to good use in an optimal allocation scheme.

5.8 ESTIMATING POPULATION PROPORTIONS WITH STRATIFIED SAMPLING

As discussed in Section 3.7, an estimate of a population proportion, such as the proportion of trees in a stand that have a disease, may be of interest. Calculation of a sample estimate of the population proportion and its standard error is dependent on the sampling unit being used. Ratio estimators of population proportions should be used when the sampling unit is a fixed-area plot or a point. These situations are covered in detail in Chapter 6. Estimators for a population proportion are presented here for individual tree sampling units.

A binomial random variable for each sample tree in each stratum must be defined when the individual tree is the sampling unit (see Section 3.7). For example, we can define

$$y_{h,i} = \begin{Bmatrix} 1 \text{ success} \\ 0 \text{ failure} \end{Bmatrix}$$

which means that tree i in stratum h is assigned a value of 1 if it has the characteristic of interest or a value of 0 if it does not have the characteristic. Assume that sample tree number 12 in stratum 2 has the characteristic of interest (say it has a disease). In the notation described above,

$$y_{2,12} = 1$$

The estimator of the proportion of trees in stratum h having a characteristic of interest is

$$\hat{P}_h = \frac{\sum_{i=1}^{n_h} y_{h,i}}{n_h} \tag{5.18}$$

and its variance is

$$S^2_{\hat{P}_h} = \frac{\hat{P}_h(1 - \hat{P}_h)}{n_h - 1}\left(\frac{N_h - n_h}{N_h}\right) \tag{5.19}$$

where all variables are as previously defined.

It should be clear that these equations are identical to the equations for nonstratified sampling for a population proportion that were presented in Section 3.7. The only difference is the addition of the h subscript, which is simply a bookkeeping tool used to identify the stratum for which the estimates apply.

EXAMPLE 5.8.1

A 110-acre forested area in the north central United States was divided into two strata. Stratum 1 is a 60-acre, 38-year-old red pine plantation and stratum 2 is a 50-acre, all-aged natural hardwood pine stand. A systematic sample of every 50th merchantable tree was taken in each stratum and it was noted whether or not the tree was larger than 12 in. dbh. That is,

$$y_{h,i} = \begin{Bmatrix} 1 \text{ if tree dbh} > 12 \text{ in.} \\ 0 \text{ otherwise} \end{Bmatrix}$$

A total of 352 trees was sampled in stratum 1 ($n_1 = 352$) and a total of 369 trees was sampled in stratum 2 ($n_2 = 369$). The following data summary is available:

Stratum 1	**Stratum 2**
$n_1 = 352$	$n_2 = 369$
$\sum_{i=1}^{352} y_{1,i} = 151$	$\sum_{i=1}^{369} y_{2,i} = 199$

(a) Estimate the proportion of trees in stratum 1 with dbh > 12 in. and calculate its standard error.

$$\hat{P}_1 = \frac{\sum_{i=1}^{n_1} y_{1,i}}{n_1} = \frac{151}{352} = 0.429$$

$$S^2_{\hat{P}_1} = \frac{\hat{P}_1(1 - \hat{P}_1)}{n_1 - 1}\left(\frac{N_1 - n_1}{N_1}\right)$$

Note that N_1, the total number of trees in stratum 1, is unknown. However, it can be estimated. Every 50th tree the cruiser walked by was sampled; thus, if no trees were overlooked, then N_1 should be

$$N_1 = n_1(50) = 352(50) = 17{,}600 \text{ trees}$$

Note that the sampling fraction in stratum 1 is

$$\frac{n_1}{N_1} = \frac{352}{17{,}600} = 0.02$$

which is less than 0.05. Thus ignore the finite population correction factor

$$\left(\frac{N_h - n_h}{N_h}\right)$$

and calculate the variance of $\hat{P}_1$ as

$$S^2_{\hat{P}_1} = \frac{\hat{P}_1(1-\hat{P}_1)}{n_1 - 1} = \frac{0.429(1-0.429)}{352-1}$$

$$S^2_{\hat{P}_1} = 0.00069789$$

The standard error of $\hat{P}_1$ is

$$S_{\hat{P}_1} = \sqrt{S^2_{\hat{P}_1}} = \sqrt{0.00069789} = 0.0264$$

Thus an approximate 95% confidence interval for the proportion of trees larger than 12 in. dbh in stratum 1 is

$$0.429 \pm 2(0.0264)$$
$$\text{LCL} = 0.376$$
$$\text{UCL} = 0.482$$

To report the results in terms of a percentage, multiply the proportion by 100. Thus 42.9% of the trees in stratum 1 have a dbh larger than 12 in. The approximate 95% confidence interval for this percentage is

$$\text{LCL} = 37.6\%$$
$$\text{UCL} = 48.2\%$$

(b) Estimate the proportion of trees in stratum 2 with dbh > 12 in. and calculate its standard error.

Follow the same procedure as for stratum 1.

$$\hat{P}_2 = \frac{199}{369} = 0.539$$

$$S^2_{\hat{P}_2} = \frac{0.539(1-0.539)}{369-1} = 0.00067521$$

Note that again the finite population correction factor is ignored:

$$S_{\hat{P}_2} = 0.0260$$

An approximate 95% confidence interval for $\hat{P}_2$ is

$$0.539 \pm 2(0.0260)$$
$$\text{LCL} = 0.487$$
$$\text{UCL} = 0.591$$

Thus there is approximately 95% confidence that between 48.7% and 59.1% of the trees in stratum 2 have a dbh > 12 in.

5.9 COMBINING STRATUM ESTIMATES OF POPULATION PROPORTIONS

To obtain an estimate of a population proportion across all strata, individual stratum estimates must be combined just as for a population mean or total. The sample estimate of the overall population proportion is

$$\hat{P}_{ST} = \sum_{h=1}^{L} \frac{N_h \hat{P}_h}{N} = \frac{1}{N} \sum_{h=1}^{L} N_h \hat{P}_h \tag{5.20}$$

The variance of $\hat{P}_{ST}$ is

$$S^2_{\hat{P}_{ST}} = \frac{1}{N^2} \sum_{h=1}^{L} N_h^2 S^2_{\hat{P}_h} \tag{5.21}$$

Of course, the standard error of $\hat{P}_{ST}$, $S_{\hat{P}_{ST}}$, is obtained by taking the square root of Eq. 5.21.

EXAMPLE 5.9.1

Assume we wish to obtain an estimate of the proportion of trees with dbh > 12 in. in the 110-acre stand described in Example 5.5.1. Recall that this stand was stratified into a 60-acre red pine plantation and 50-acre all-aged natural hardwood pine stand. Use Eq. 5.20 to obtain the estimate. Note that N_1 and N_2 are needed to use this equation.

Using the logic presented above, N_1 is estimated by noting that every 50th tree was sampled and that a total of 352 trees were actually sampled in stratum 1. Thus

$$N_1 = 50(n_1) = 50(352) = 17{,}600 \text{ trees}$$

Similarly, for stratum 2,

$$N_2 = 50(n_2) = 50(369) = 18{,}450 \text{ trees}$$

Thus

$$N = N_1 + N_2 = 17{,}600 + 18{,}450 = 36{,}050 \text{ trees}$$

Now estimate $\hat{P}_{ST}$ as

$$\hat{P}_{ST} = \frac{1}{36{,}050}[17{,}600\ (0.429) + 18{,}450\ (0.539)]$$
$$= 0.485$$

The variance of $\hat{P}_{ST}$ is obtained using Eq. 5.21

$$S^2_{\hat{P}_{ST}} = \frac{1}{(36{,}050)^2} = [(17{,}600)^2(0.00069789) + (18{,}450)^2(0.0067521)]$$
$$S^2_{\hat{P}_{ST}} = 0.00193$$

The standard error of $\hat{P}_{ST}$ is

$$S_{\hat{P}_{ST}} = \sqrt{0.00193} = 0.0440$$

An approximate 95% confidence interval for $\hat{P}_{ST}$ is

$$0.485 \pm 2(0.0440)$$
$$\text{LCL} = 0.397$$
$$\text{UCL} = 0.573$$

So with approximate 95% confidence the percentage of trees with dbh greater than 12 in. on this 110-acre area is estimated to be between 39.7% and 57.3%.

5.10 SAMPLE SIZE REQUIREMENTS

In the estimation of a population proportion, the following equation can be used to obtain an estimate of the number of sampling units required to meet a given bound on the error of estimation.

$$n = \frac{\sum_{h=1}^{L} \frac{N_h^2 \hat{P}_h(1 - \hat{P}_h)}{W_h}}{\frac{N^2 B_P^2}{4} + \sum_{h=1}^{L} N_h \hat{P}_h(1 - \hat{P}_h)} \tag{5.22}$$

where:

W_h = proportion of sample size allocated to stratum h $(0 < W_h < 1)$

B_P = desired bound on the overall population proportion

and all other variables are as defined previously.

This is the same sample size equation used for a population mean (Eq. 5.10) with $S_{y_h}^2$ replaced by $\hat{P}_h(1 - \hat{P}_h)$. To use this equation the W_h values must first be determined. The W_h values can be determined using optimal allocation, Neyman allocation, or proportional allocation:

Optimal Allocation

$$W_h = \frac{N_h\sqrt{\hat{P}_h(1 - \hat{P}_h)/C_h}}{\sum_{h=1}^{L} N_h\sqrt{\hat{P}_h(1 - \hat{P}_h)/C_h}} \tag{5.23}$$

Neyman Allocation

$$W_h = \frac{N_h\sqrt{\hat{P}_h(1 - \hat{P}_h)}}{\sum_{h=1}^{L} N_h\sqrt{\hat{P}_h(1 - \hat{P}_h)}} \tag{5.24}$$

Proportional Allocation

$$W_h = \frac{N_h}{N} \tag{5.25}$$

where:

C_h = cost per sampling unit in stratum h
and all else is as defined earlier.

If the population is so large that the sample size will be less than 5% of the population, the following formula may be used to estimate the number of sampling units required:

$$n = \frac{4\sum_{h=1}^{L}\frac{N_h^2\hat{P}_h(1 - \hat{P}_h)}{W_h}}{B_P^2N^2}$$

For a detailed discussion of optimal, Neyman, and proportional allocation schemes, see Sections 5.5, 5.6, and 5.7. To use the equations just given to determine sample size requirements, a great deal of information is needed. Previous estimates of the stratum proportions ($\hat{P}_h$) are needed for optimal and Neyman allocation. Number of sampling units per stratum (N_h) as well as the total number of sampling units in the population are required for all three allocation schemes. Estimates of the stratum proportions may be obtained from a pilot survey or previous experience. If no information can be obtained concerning the $\hat{P}_h$ values, then they can all be set to 0.5 to obtain a conservative estimate of the required sample size (see Section 3.7). This still leaves the problem of determining the N_h values. When the sampling units are fixed-area plots, the problem is trivial. However, when sampling units are individual trees, determining the N_h values with any reliability may be impossible. In certain situations estimates of the average number of trees per unit area may be available for each stratum. For example, survival counts in pine plantations will yield such information.

5.11 POSTSTRATIFICATION OF THE SAMPLE

Sometimes a large tract of timber is inventoried as a single entity, and then, after field data collection is complete, sample plots are placed in two or more strata. This is known as poststratification.

For example, a large tract of timber may be composed of several distinct species types with relatively large differences in the amount of standing volume in each. A given species type is dispersed throughout the tract in a noncontiguous fashion. Acreage estimates of each species type are available from aerial photographs. However, it is not practical to lay out a sampling plan for each of the separate species types because of their noncontiguous nature. Thus the inventory forester opts to use a systematic sample on a predetermined grid across the entire stand. The field crews then obtain necessary measurements on each sample plot and place them into one of the predefined species groups (strata). Thus the number of plots measured within a given stratum is not known until after the inventory is complete.

The fact that the number of plots falling in a given stratum is unknown until after the sample is taken complicates estimation of the variance and standard error for estimates of the population mean ($\bar{y}_{ST}$), total ($\hat{T}_{ST}$), and proportion ($\hat{P}_{ST}$). The variance and standard error for these estimators increases when using poststratification instead of prestratification. However, the increase is usually very small and when n, the total sample size, as well as n_h, individual stratum sample sizes, are large, the increase in the variance is negligible. Thus new formulas for calculating the variance of the estimates for poststratification are not presented. When poststratification is used as just described, calculate the estimate and associated standard error as previously discussed. However, be aware that the calculated standard error will slightly underestimate the true standard error.

Poststratification as described here implies that relatively good estimates of strata sizes, N_h, are known prior to sampling (that is, from aerial photos) or can be estimated relatively accurately during the course of field data collection (that is, type mapping). When stratum sizes cannot be determined, they can be estimated with a procedure known as *double sampling*. For most inventory situations this will not be necessary. However, inventorying very large acreages for which little information is available may require estimating stratum sizes using double sampling. Refer to Section 7.9 for more detailed information on double sampling for stratification.

PROBLEMS FOR BETTER UNDERSTANDING

1. List the major advantages of stratified sampling.
2. List potential disadvantages associated with stratified sampling.
3. What is the proper way to define strata to help ensure that the advantages of stratification are realized?
4. A population has been divided into three strata. The acreages of each strata are as follows:

Stratum	Acreage
1	125
2	190
3	50

Fixed-area plot sampling with 1⁄10-acre plots will be used. Determine N_1, N_2, N_3, and N for this population.

5. Refer to Problem 4. Assume the following additional data are available:

Stratum	n_h	$\bar{y}_h$	S_y^2
1	35	275	24,000
2	52	312	32,000
3	13	178	18,000

   a. Calculate an estimate of the variance for each stratum mean (use fpc's).
   b. Estimate the total volume in each stratum.
   c. Calculate the variance of each stratum total estimated in part b.

6. Refer to Problems 4 and 5.
   a. Calculate approximate 95% confidence intervals for the total volume in each stratum.
   b. Estimate the total volume for the entire population.
   c. Calculate the variance of the estimate obtained in part b.
   d. Calculate an approximate 95% confidence interval for the total tract volume obtained in part b.

7. Three sample allocation schemes, proportional, Neyman, and optimal, were presented and discussed. Explain how the number of sampling units allocated to a particular stratum changes as
   a. Stratum size increases.

b. Stratum variability increases.

c. Cost per sampling unit within a stratum increases.

8. The following table contains the results of a stratified sample in three timber types. The sample was conducted using ⅕-acre fixed-radius plots in all strata.

Timber Type	Size (Acres)	Average Plot Volume (Cords)	Variances	n_h	Value ($/cord)
1	200	2.0	2.70	30	10
2	300	0.5	0.05	20	30
3	500	4.0	12.50	50	20
				100	

a. Estimate total volume in each timber type.

b. Find the standard error of the total volume estimate in each type. Ignore all fpc's.

c. Estimate total value in each timber type.

d. Find the standard error of the total value estimate in each timber type. Ignore all fpc's.

e. Estimate total tract value. Place an approximate 95% confidence interval around the total value estimate.

f. What sample size would be necessary to estimate total value with a bound of $50,000 using proportional allocation with approximately 95% confidence?

9. A forest property consists of three distinct timber types. Cecil Swag has been hired to cruise the property and to provide estimates of volume. Cecil decides to allocate his sample plots proportionally among the three types. The following volumes were obtained from his ⅕-acre plots:

Type I—70 Acres Volume (Cords/Plot)		Type II—20 Acres Volume (Cords/Plot)	Type III—10 Acres Volume (Cords/Plot)
7	10	13	4
9	6	16	4
12	4	11	9
6	7	9	0
6	6	14	7
5	7	14	SUM = 24
8	8	12	
6	8	15	

Type I—70 Acres Volume (Cords/Plot)		Type II—20 Acres Volume (Cords/Plot)	Type III—10 Acres Volume (Cords/Plot)
11	9	12	
10	13	12	
6	7	SUM = 128	
3	7		
7	8		
8	9		
9	3		
9	5		
9	6		
	7		
	SUM = 261		

a. Find the total volume in each type and calculate the standard error of the estimates.

b. Find the total volume for the tract as a whole and calculate the standard error of the estimate.

c. If Cecil had decided to use Neyman allocation, how many of his 50 plots would have been placed in each of the three strata?

d. How many sample plots should Cecil use to obtain a desired bound on the error of estimation of the total of 150 using proportional allocation (assume approximately 95% confidence)?

e. How many of the plots (from d) should be placed in each stratum?

f. If cord stumpage for the three types is worth \$5, \$15, and \$10 per cord, respectively, find the value of the timber on the property and its standard error.

10. A stratified random sample was obtained from a population of 80 sampling units using four strata. The strata sizes, sample sizes, observed stratum means, and observed stratum variances are shown in the following table. Estimate the population mean and calculate the variance of the estimate.

Stratum	Stratum Size	Number of Samples	$\bar{y}_h$	$S^2_{y_h}$
1	16	8	15	16
2	16	6	5	6
3	24	4	20	12
4	24	8	10	8

11. A receiving facility for an integrated forest products concern receives tree-length logs. Some logs are large enough to contain sawtimber, whereas others can be used only as pulpwood. For the past year the company has kept records to gain information on the input to the facility. Logs were received from four different logging areas. The following information was collected for each area:

- The total number of tree-length logs was determined.
- For 50 randomly selected logs from each logging area, cubic-foot volumes were determined.
- Each of the 50 sample logs from each area was classified as to whether or not it contained sawtimber material.

The data are summarized in the following table:

	Logging Area			
	I	**II**	**III**	**IV**
Total number of logs processed	5,164	6,840	3,122	9,446
Number of sample logs:				
with sawtimber	31	38	26	15
without sawtimber	19	12	24	35
ΣY_i				
with sawtimber	1,184.20	1,713.80	947.44	467.10
without sawtimber	124.07	99.00	141.84	168.71
	1,308.27	1,812.80	1,089.28	635.81
ΣY_i^2				
with sawtimber	48,236.44	82,102.38	36,899.71	15,665.49
without sawtimber	850.68	885.50	930.27	932.13
	49,087.12	82,987.88	37,829.98	16,597.62

where Y_i = the cubic foot volume for the *i*th log.

a. Estimate the total cubic-foot volume of logs processed by the receiving facility. Determine the standard error of this estimate.

b. Estimate the total cubic-foot volume of logs containing sawtimber that were processed by the receiving facility. Determine the standard error of this estimate.

c. Estimate the number of logs containing sawtimber that were processed by the receiving facility. Determine the standard error of this estimate.

During the coming year the facility will be processing logs from the same four logging areas. The cost of measuring a log is the same for all four areas. The desired standard error for total cubic-foot volume processed is 5000 ft^3. Assume that the number of logs processed in the coming year for a particular area will be equal to the number processed last year.

d. With Neyman allocation of the sample, how many logs should be measured from each of the four areas?

e. If it is required that the same number of logs be measured from each area, what total sample size will be required?

12. A major use of wood in tropical countries is as fuel, and plantations are often established with this goal in mind. Growth rates of up to 40 cubic meters per hectare per year or more are possible with the right species/site combination. In 1980 an African country took advantage of a foreign aid grant to establish a 3000-hectare woodlot. It was unsure of the best species to plant on the site so it planted three. Seven years later it decided to inventory the woodlot. It had resources to establish 150 temporary sample plots of 1/10-hectare each. Results of that inventory are summarized in the following table:

Species	Hectares	Sample Mean (m^3)	Sample Variance	Sample Size
Eucalyptus saligna	2000	14	312.5	50
Grevillea robusta	800	29	612.5	50
Cassia siamea	200	10	50.0	50

a. Estimate the total amount of wood growing in the woodlot. Place an approximate 95% confidence interval on your estimate.

b. Criticize the allocation of sampling units. How would you have allocated sample units to the three species with no prior knowledge of the variability within each species. Make the allocation.

c. If Neyman allocation were used, which of the three species would certainly gain in number of sample units over the number it would have using proportional allocation? Why? Do *not* actually do the allocation.

13. A proportionally allocated stratified random sample is to be obtained from a population of 100 elements using three strata.

What total sample size should be used to obtain a bound on the error of estimation of the mean equal to 2.0 with approximately 95% confidence if the strata sizes and variances are those shown in the following table:

Stratum	Stratum Size	Estimated Stratum Variance
1	50	22
2	30	10
3	20	30
	100	

14. A forester confronted with the problem of obtaining an overall estimate of total volume in a forested area of 110 hectares decided to divide the area into three homogenous units based on information from aerial photographs. The forester then conducted a simple random sample in each unit. Information on unit size, numbers of sample plots, average volume per unit, and sample variances per unit are shown in the following table:

Unit	Size Hectares	Number of ⅕-Hectare Plots	Average Volume	Sample Variance
1	40	8	5	5
2	50	10	2	1
3	20	6	3	2

a. What is the best estimate of total forest volume and its standard error? Ignore the fpc.

b. Cost of inventory does not vary much by units, but size and variability appear to be important. If he uses the sizes and variances shown, how many plots would be necessary to obtain a standard error of the total volume of 150?

c. How should the plots in part b be distributed among the three units?

15. An inventory was carried out to determine the volume of merchantable pine volume on a 10,000-acre tract. The tract was divided into three strata:

1. Upland pine
2. Upland pine-hardwood
3. Bottom and pine-hardwood

Merchantable pine pulpwood volumes were measured on a number of randomly located ⅕-acre plots in each of the three strata. The data obtained are shown below with the volumes expressed as cords per acre. Estimate the average volume per acre and the total tract volume, and determine the standard error associated with each of these estimates. The acreages and numbers of plots measured to the three strata were as follows:

Stratum	Acreage	Number of Plots
1	6002	21
2	2794	9
3	1204	14

Plot Data

Stratum 1	Stratum 2	Stratum 3
13.4	3.4	1.5
10.3	4.5	2.0
9.3	5.2	4.5
11.7	4.0	0.4

Stratum 1	Stratum 2	Stratum 3
13.0	5.5	3.4
9.7	4.2	4.0
11.3	4.9	0.5
12.3	5.2	3.7
10.1	7.2	4.4
13.2		0.3
11.3		1.2
14.5		2.9
11.4		2.9
13.0		2.1
10.5		
12.0		
16.2		
14.2		
8.6		
11.0		
15.0		

CHAPTER 6

RATIO AND REGRESSION ESTIMATORS

To this point several sampling designs have been introduced: simple random or systematic sampling with fixed-area plots or points and stratified random or systematic sampling with fixed-area plots or points. This chapter introduces two new sample estimators (ratio and regression estimators) that may be used in conjunction with any of the sampling designs discussed. Although these estimators are not unique to a particular sampling design, the structure of the estimators changes for stratified and nonstratified sampling designs. Only nonstratified sampling designs will be discussed here. Those readers interested in using ratio or regression estimators for a stratified sample are referred to Cochran (1977) and DeVries (1986).

6.1 AUXILIARY VARIABLES

For all sampling designs considered so far, the assumption is that the variable of interest is measured on each and every sampling unit in the sample. For example, to determine the total board foot volume of grade 1 hardwood sawlogs in a stand, each sample plot or point is measured for the information necessary to determine the board foot volume of grade 1 hardwood sawlogs per plot or point. Ratio and regression estimators make use of an auxiliary variable that is measured on each sampling unit in addition to the variable of interest. For example, in addition to determining the board foot volume of grade 1 hardwood sawlogs discussed earlier, the basal area of hardwood trees that contain grade 1 sawlogs may also be determined. This basal area measurement is the auxiliary variable (that is, it is auxiliary to the variable of interest). The utility of such a procedure may not be clear since additional measurements may be required on each sampling unit and this obviously translates directly to extra costs. However, if the auxiliary variable is highly correlated with the variable of interest, this extra effort will often result in a more precise (that is, less variable) estimate of the population parameter of interest. Furthermore, there are certain situations in which a population ratio is the parameter of interest and this dictates that a ratio estimator be used. Also, some sampling situations arise for which it is desired to estimate a population total for the variable of interest without knowledge of the population size (N). Clearly, this negates the use of the previous population total estimators, which all require knowledge of N. In these situations the problem may be formulated such that a ratio estimator will lead to an estimate of the population total without knowledge of the population size N.

6.2 RATIO ESTIMATORS

When a ratio estimator is used, population parameters for the variable of interest (y) as well as the auxiliary variable must be defined. The auxiliary variable is referred to as x. The population parameters associated with x and y are

T_x = population total of the auxiliary variable

μ_x = population mean of the auxiliary variable

T_y = population total of the variable of interest

μ_y = population mean of the variable of interest

A new population parameter that may be of interest is the ratio defined as

$$R = \frac{\mu_y}{\mu_x} = \frac{\mathrm{T}_y}{\mathrm{T}_x} = \frac{N\mu_y}{N\mu_x} \tag{6.1}$$

The meaning of this ratio depends on the definition of y and x. For example, if y is defined to be the height of a tree (ft) and x is the dbh of the tree (in.), then R is feet of height per inch of dbh. If y is merchantable volume per plot of all merchantable trees and x is basal area per plot of all merchantable trees, then R is the amount of volume per unit of basal area for the merchantable trees. The ratio R may be used to quantify growth. Define y to be volume per acre today and x to be volume per acre five years ago. Then the ratio, R, is the proportionate increase (growth) in volume over the five-year period. There are many other situations in which R may prove useful in forest inventory.

Ratio estimators are used to obtain estimates of R, μ_y, and T_y. The estimators are, respectively,

$$\hat{R} = \frac{\bar{y}}{\bar{x}} = \frac{\frac{1}{n}\sum_{i=1}^{n} y_i}{\frac{1}{n}\sum_{i=1}^{n} x_i} = \frac{\sum_{i=1}^{n} y_i}{\sum_{i=1}^{n} x_i} \tag{6.2}$$

$$\bar{y}_R = \frac{\bar{y}}{\bar{x}} \mu_x = \hat{R}\mu_x \tag{6.3}$$

$$\hat{T}_R = \hat{R}T_x \tag{6.4}$$

where n is the number of sampling units on which both y and x are measured, and all else is as defined earlier. Note that Eq. 6.3 requires that μ_x be known and Eq. 6.4 requires that T_x must be known. That is, in order to use Eqs. 6.3 and 6.4 to obtain estimates of μ_y and T_y, μ_x and T_x must be known. Clearly, this may present a problem in many forest inventory situations. However, if the auxiliary variable is defined wisely so that μ_x and T_x will be known, the estimators in Eqs. 6.3 and 6.4 can be very precise (that is, they can have small variance compared with nonratio estimators discussed in Chapters 3 and 4).

Examination of the equation for estimating the mean value of y (Eq. 6.3) provides some insight into the logic of ratio estimators. If the sample of size n leads to a value of $\bar{x}$ that is identical to the true mean of x, μ_x, then μ_x and $\bar{x}$ cancel with one another and the ratio estimator of the mean of y is simply $\bar{y}$ (the usual simple random sampling estimator). If $\bar{x}$ is less than μ_x, then the sample taken resulted in an underestimate of μ_x. If x and y are highly correlated, the implication is that $\bar{y}$ is probably underestimating μ_y. The ratio estimator will modify $\bar{y}$ by the ratio $\mu_x/\bar{x}$, which in this case will be greater than 1 (since $\bar{x}$ is underestimating μ_x). Thus the simple random sampling estimate of the mean, $\bar{y}$, is increased by the ratio $\mu_x/\bar{x}$. In situations when $\bar{x}$ is greater than μ_x, the reverse process takes place and $\bar{y}$ is adjusted downward.

Here are variances of estimators presented in Eqs. 6.2, 6.3, and 6.4, respectively:

$$S_{\hat{R}}^2 = \frac{1}{\mu_x^2} \frac{S_u^2}{n} \left(\frac{N-n}{N}\right) \tag{6.5}$$

where

$$S_u^2 = \frac{\sum_{i=1}^{n} y_i^2 + \hat{R}^2 \sum_{i=1}^{n} x_i^2 - 2\hat{R} \sum_{i=1}^{n} x_i y_i}{n-1}$$

N = number of sampling units in the population
and all else is as defined previously.

$$S_{\bar{y}_R}^2 = \frac{S_u^2}{n} \left(\frac{N-n}{N}\right) \tag{6.6}$$

$$S_{\hat{T}_R}^2 = T_x^2 \frac{1}{\mu_x^2} \frac{S_u^2}{n} \left(\frac{N-n}{N}\right) \tag{6.7}$$

where all is as defined previously.

S_u^2 quantifies variation in the relationship (correlation) between x and y. When x and y are highly correlated with one another in a linear fashion, the variances of the

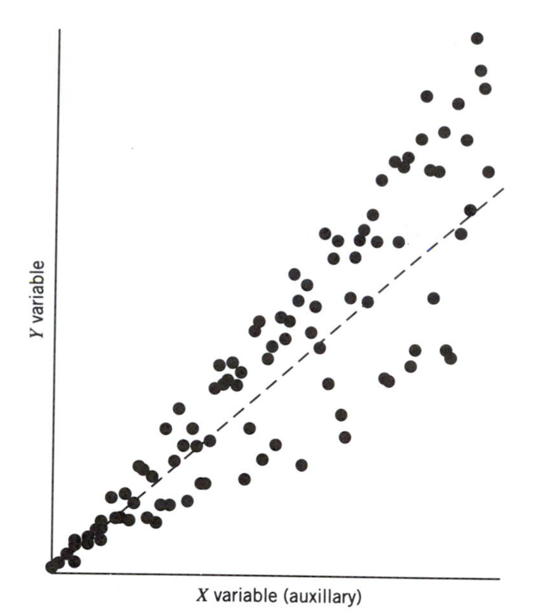

Figure 6.2.1 Ideal relationship between x and y for ratio estimators.

estimators $\hat{R}$, $\bar{y}_R$, and $\hat{T}_R$ are smaller than the corresponding nonratio estimators. It should be mentioned that $\hat{R}$ is an unbiased estimator of R if and only if the relationship between x and y is linear and goes through the (0,0) point on x–y axes (Figure 6.2.1) (see Section 2.2 for a discussion of bias) and the variation in y increases as x increases. However, this does not mean that these estimators are useless when the relationship is not linear from the origin. It can be shown that as long as the relationship between x and y is linear (not necessarily starting at the origin), the amount of bias is negligible as long as the sample size is large ($n > 30$).

For those not well versed in statistical methods, the previous discussion may be a bit confusing. The bottom line is that ratio estimators are good estimators, and if the auxiliary variable, x, is defined such that it is highly correlated with y, and x is relatively inexpensive to measure, then it is possible to obtain estimates that are more precise than nonratio estimators for less cost.

EXAMPLE 6.2.1

A forester needs to obtain an estimate of the proportion of the total basal area of pine that is in trees with dbh > 9.5 in. in a 53-acre mixed pine-hardwood stand in the Piedmont of Alabama. A total of 35 1/10-acre sample plots were installed on a three-chain-by-five-chain grid. On each plot all trees were measured for dbh. The total basal area on each plot is denoted as the x variable and the basal area of trees with dbh > 9.5 in. is denoted as the y variable. The following summarized data are available:

$$\sum_{i=1}^{35} x_i = 292 \qquad \sum_{i=1}^{35} y_i = 112$$

$$\sum_{i=1}^{35} x_i^2 = 2698 \qquad \sum_{i=1}^{35} y_i^2 = 468$$

$$\sum_{i=1}^{35} x_i y_i = 1085$$

To obtain an estimate of the proportion of the total basal area in trees with dbh > 9.5 in., use Eq. 6.2:

$$\hat{R} = \frac{\sum_{i=1}^{n} y_i}{\sum_{i=1}^{n} x_i} = \frac{112}{292}$$

$$\hat{R} = 0.384$$

Thus, on a percentage basis, approximately 38.4% of the total basal area in this stand is in trees with dbh > 9.5 in. The variance of this estimate is calculated using Eq. 6.5. Note that μ_x appears in Eq. 6.5. This is the true mean basal area of pines per 1⁄10-acre sample plot. Obviously, this parameter is not known since all 1⁄10-acre sample plots in this stand have not been measured. Thus the best estimate of it, which is $\bar{x}$, will be used:

$$\bar{x} = \frac{\sum_{i=1}^{n} x_i}{n} = \frac{292}{35} = 8.34286 \text{ (ft}^2\text{/plot)}$$

Next calculate S_u^2 using the following equation:

$$S_u^2 = \frac{\sum_{i=1}^{n} y_i^2 + \hat{R}^2 \sum_{i=1}^{n} x_i^2 - 2\hat{R} \sum_{i=1}^{n} x_i y_i}{n-1}$$

$$= \frac{468 + (0.384)^2(2698) - 2(0.384)(1085)}{34}$$

$$= 0.957538$$

As always, determine N, the number of sample plots in the stand, by multiplying the stand acreage by the number of plots per acre:

$$N = 10 \times 53 = 530 \text{ plots}$$

Now use Eq. 6.5:

$$S_{\hat{R}}^2 = \frac{1}{(8.34286)^2} \frac{0.957538}{35} \left(\frac{530 - 35}{530} \right)$$

$$S_{\hat{R}}^2 = 0.0003671$$

The standard error of $\hat{R}$ is obtained as the square root of $S_{\hat{R}}^2$:

$$S_{\hat{R}} = \sqrt{S_{\hat{R}}^2} = 0.01916$$

Now an approximate 95% confidence interval for $\hat{R}$ is

$$\hat{R} \pm 2S_{\hat{R}}$$
$$0.384 \pm 2(0.01916)$$
$$0.384 \pm 0.038$$
$$\text{LCL} = 0.346$$
$$\text{UCL} = 0.422$$

Thus there is approximately 95% confidence that between 34.6% and 42.2% of the total pine basal area is in trees with dbh > 9.5 in.

Example 6.2.1 illustrated how a population proportion (that is, proportion of total basal area comprised of trees > 9.5 in. dbh) can be estimated using a ratio estimator. This procedure differs from the procedure for estimating a population proportion discussed in Section 3.7. The difference is related to the definition of the sampling unit. In section 3.7 the sampling unit was defined as the individual tree. In example 6.2.1 the sampling unit was a fixed area plot containing many trees. Since, in example 6.2.1, the estimate of interest was an individual tree characteristic (dbh > 9.5 in.), but the sampling unit was a fixed area plot, the ratio estimator should be used. This procedure is further illustrated and discussed in example 6.2.2.

EXAMPLE 6.2.2

Suppose a forester is interested in estimating the proportion of trees in a European Larch (*Larix decidua,* Mill) stand that has larch canker (*Dusyscypha willkommii* [Hart.]). Ten ⅕-acre sample plots were systematically sampled from a 20-acre European Larch stand. On each plot the total number of trees was counted and the total number of trees with larch canker was determined. Define x_i as the total number of trees on plot i and y_i as the number of trees on the plot infected with larch canker. The data are as follows:

Plot	x_i	y_i
1	35	24
2	18	12
3	42	31
4	25	17
5	16	4
6	29	17
7	34	28
8	21	15
9	28	14
10	39	28

First calculate the following sums:

$$\sum_{i=1}^{10} x_i = 287 \qquad \sum_{i=1}^{10} y_i = 190$$

$$\sum_{i=1}^{10} x_i^2 = 8937 \qquad \sum_{i=1}^{10} y_i^2 = 4264$$

$$\sum_{i=1}^{10} x_i y_i = 6091$$

Now, with x_i and y_i as defined earlier, the ratio estimator $\hat{R}$ provides an estimate of the proportion of trees in the stand with larch canker:

$$\hat{R} = \frac{\sum_{i=1}^{10} y_i}{\sum_{i=1}^{10} x_i} = \frac{190}{287} = 0.66$$

Use equation 6.5 to get $S_{\hat{R}}^2$. First we must calculate S_u^2 as

$$S_u^2 = \frac{4264 + (0.66)^2(8937) - 2(0.66)(6091)}{9}$$

$$S_u^2 = \frac{116.8372}{9} = 12.9819$$

Next

$$N = 20 \text{ acres} \times 5 \text{ plots/acre} = 100 \text{ plots}$$

Note μ_x (true average number of trees per plot) is unknown so we will use $\bar{x}$ in its place

$$\bar{x} = 28.7$$

Thus

$$S_{\hat{R}}^2 = \frac{1}{(28.7)^2} \frac{12.9819}{10} \left(\frac{100 - 10}{100}\right) = 0.0014185$$

$$S_{\hat{R}} = \sqrt{S_{\hat{R}}^2} = 0.038$$

An approximate 95% confidence interval for the proportion of trees with larch canker is

$$\text{LCL} = 0.66 - 2(0.038) = 0.58$$
$$\text{UCL} = 0.66 + 2(0.038) = 0.74$$

So we can say we have approximately 95% confidence that between 58% and 74% of the trees in this stand have larch canker infections.

A question that may come to mind is why not calculate the proportion of infected trees on each plot (P_i) and then use simple random sampling formulas to get the average infection and its standard error. This is easily done as follows:

Plot	P_i
1	0.69
2	0.67
3	0.74
4	0.68
5	0.25
6	0.59
7	0.82
8	0.71
9	0.50
10	0.72

Use equation 3.14 as follows

$$\hat{P} = \frac{\sum_{i=1}^{10} P_i}{n} = 0.64$$

Next

$$S_P^2 = \frac{1}{n-1}\left[\sum_{i=1}^{10} P_i^2 - \frac{\left(\sum_{i=1}^{10} P_i\right)^2}{n}\right] = 0.02587$$

Use equation 3.15 to get

$$S_{\hat{P}}^2 = \frac{S_P^2}{n}\left(\frac{N-n}{n}\right) = \frac{0.02587}{10}\left(\frac{100-10}{100}\right) = 0.00233$$

$$S_{\hat{P}} = \sqrt{S_{\hat{P}}^2} = 0.048$$

An approximate 95% confidence interval is

$$\text{LCL} = 0.64 - 2(0.048) = 0.54$$
$$\text{UCL} = 0.64 + 2(0.048) = 0.74$$

The problem with working up the proportion of infected trees in this fashion has to do with the fact that infection is an individual tree characteristic and not a unit area value such as volume per acre. Some sample plots will have a larger number of trees than others and the non-ratio estimator approach does not account for this. Using the ratio estimator approach described earlier allows for a different number of trees on each plot. This ratio estimator approach can be shown to be synonymous with single stage cluster sampling that is discussed in section 8.2.

Use your imagination to identify various uses for this ratio. For example, the proportion of grade 1 sawlogs in a stand may be of interest. This is easily estimated by defining y_i to be the number of grade 1 sawlogs on the sample plot and x_i to be the total number of sawlogs on the sample plot. The procedure illustrated in Example 6.2.1 can then be followed to obtain the estimate and its associated standard error.

EXAMPLE 6.2.3

A district forester wants to obtain an estimate of the total merchantable volume in a 45-acre stand. The forester has in her employ a very experienced timber cruiser who has the ability to obtain very good estimates of standing volume by simply walking through the stand and "eyeballing" it. The district forester is fairly confident in this experienced cruiser's estimates but wants to have a more objective estimate than simply an eyeball estimate. She decides to carry out the following type of cruise to go along with the overall eyeball estimate. In addition to the eyeball estimate of the stand volume, the cruiser will install 30 ⅒-acre sample plots laid out on a three-chain-by-four-chain grid across the stand. On each plot, the cruiser will take appropriate sample tree measurements required to calculate the desired volume estimate (y_i). In addition, he will estimate the board-foot volume of the plot by the eyeball method (x_i).

The following data were obtained:

y_i (Measured Plot Volume in bd ft)	x_i (Eyeballed Plot Volume in bd ft)
340	320
375	360
405	410
200	195
180	180
228	215
392	365
375	370
348	330
369	320
450	475
425	400
410	420
305	300
160	150
140	130
225	215
248	230
100	75
175	150
160	140
130	130
152	140
169	160
175	170
190	200
185	175
165	185
295	275
268	250

The eyeball estimate of the total stand volume is T_x (that is, the true guessed stand volume based on the cruiser's extensive experience).

$$T_x = 120{,}000 \text{ bd ft}$$

$$\sum_{i=1}^{30} x_i = 7435 \qquad \sum_{i=1}^{30} y_i = 7739$$

$$\sum_{i=1}^{30} x_i^2 = 2{,}170{,}425 \qquad \sum_{i=1}^{30} y_i^2 = 2{,}319{,}581$$

$$\sum_{i=1}^{30} x_i y_i = 2{,}240{,}230$$

Note that since x_i is the eyeballed volume on sample plot i, μ_x is the true eyeballed volume per 1/10-acre sample plot. T_x and N are known; thus

$$\mu_x = \frac{T_x}{N} = \frac{120{,}000}{450} = 266.67 \text{ bd ft}$$

Equation 6.4 is used to estimate the total volume on the tract. Recall that Eq. 6.4 is

$$\hat{T}_R = \hat{R} T_x$$

$$\hat{R} = \frac{\sum_{i=1}^{n} y_i}{\sum_{i=1}^{n} x_i} = \frac{7739}{7435} = 1.04088769$$

Thus

$$\begin{aligned}\hat{T}_R &= 1.04088769\ (120{,}000)\\ &= 124{,}906.5 \text{ bd ft}\end{aligned}$$

The variance of $\hat{T}_R$ is obtained using Eq. 6.7:

$$S_{\hat{T}_R}^2 = T_x^2 \frac{1}{\mu_x^2} \frac{S_u^2}{n} \left(\frac{N-n}{N} \right)$$

First calculate S_u^2 as follows:

$$\begin{aligned}S_u^2 &= \frac{2{,}319{,}581 + (1.04088769)^2(2{,}170{,}425) - 2(1.04088769)(2{,}240{,}230)}{29}\\ &= \frac{7466.192}{29} = 257.4548966\end{aligned}$$

Then

$$S_{\hat{T}_R}^2 = (120{,}000)^2 \frac{1}{(266.67)^2} \frac{257.4548966}{30} \left(\frac{450 - 30}{450}\right)$$

$$= 1{,}621{,}925.3 \text{ (bd ft)}^2$$

Now the standard error of $\hat{T}_R$ is obtained by taking the square root of the variance:

$$S_{\hat{T}_R} = \sqrt{S_{\hat{T}_R}^2} = 1273.5 \text{ bd ft}$$

An approximate 95% confidence interval for the total tract board foot volume is

$$\hat{T}_R \pm 2S_{\hat{T}_R}$$
$$124{,}906.5 \pm 2(1273.5)$$
$$\text{LCL} = 122{,}359.4 \text{ bd ft}$$
$$\text{UCL} = 127{,}453.6 \text{ bd ft}$$

Example 6.2.3 should be examined more closely. The ratio estimator used the ratio of measured plot volumes to guessed plot volumes to adjust the eyeball estimate of total volume. The ratio of measured volumes to guessed volumes was greater than 1, which indicates that the experienced forester was consistently underestimating the plot volumes. Thus the logical thing to do is to adjust the eyeball estimate of total volume upward, which is exactly what the ratio estimator did (the eyeball estimate was adjusted upward to 124,906.5 bd ft). The underlying assumption is that if the forester consistently underestimates plot volumes, she also underestimated the total tract volume.

Here is the next question: Why not disregard the eyeballed volume estimates altogether and use the measured plot volumes, as is done with the traditional simple random sampling (or systematic sampling) estimate of the total. If this is done, the following estimate of the total volume is obtained:

$$\bar{y} = \frac{\sum_{i=1}^{n} y_i}{n} = \frac{7739}{30} = 257.966667 \text{ bd ft}$$

$$\hat{T} = N\bar{y} = 450(257.966667)$$

$$\hat{T} = 116{,}085 \text{ bd ft}$$

The variance of this estimate is obtained using Eq. 3.4:

$$S_{\hat{T}}^2 = N^2 S_{\bar{y}}^2$$

$$S_{\bar{y}}^2 = \frac{S_y^2}{n}\left(\frac{N-n}{N}\right)$$

$$S_y^2 = \frac{\sum_{i=1}^{n} y_i^2 - \left(\sum_{i=1}^{n} y_i\right)^2}{n-1}$$

$$= \frac{2{,}319{,}581 - \frac{(7739)^2}{30}}{29} = 11{,}144.03334$$

$$S_{\bar{y}}^2 = \frac{11{,}144.03334}{30}\left(\frac{450-30}{450}\right) = 346.70326$$

$$S_{\hat{T}}^2 = (450)^2(346.70326)$$

$$= 70{,}207{,}410.05 \text{ (bd ft)}^2$$

Now the standard error is

$$S_{\hat{T}} = \sqrt{S_{\hat{T}}^2} = 8379 \text{ bd ft}$$

An approximate 95% confidence interval for the total is

$$116{,}085 \pm 2(8379)$$

$$\text{LCL} = 99{,}327 \text{ bd ft}$$

$$\text{UCL} = 132{,}843 \text{ bd ft}$$

Clearly, this nonratio estimate is much more variable than the ratio estimate. The reason is that the measured volumes were highly correlated with the eyeballed volumes. Thus the additional information available from the experienced forester is of great value in reducing uncertainty about the tract volume. Obtaining the same level of precision with a nonratio estimator would require measuring many more sample plots.

In certain sampling situations, it may be impossible to determine the population size N (the number of sampling units in the population). Thus it would be impossible to use the usual simple random sampling (or systematic sampling) estimator for the total (Eq. 3.3) since it requires knowledge of N. It may be possible to formulate the problem and estimate the population total using a ratio estimator in some of these situations.

EXAMPLE 6.2.4

A pulp mill manager desires to estimate the dry weight of wood for a certain number of truckloads of 5-ft pulpwood bolts entering the mill every week. One way the estimates could be obtained would be to randomly or systematically select a certain number of bolts for measurement. These bolts would then be debarked and dried and the mean dry weight of this sample of bolts could be calculated. Then using this average dry weight along with the total number of bolts on the truckload, N, the total truckload dry weight of wood could be estimated using Eq. 3.3:

$$\hat{T} = N\bar{y}$$

The problem is that the number of 5-ft bolts on a 40-ft trailer is large, and obtaining this count is time-consuming. Furthermore, the bolts selected to be debarked, dried, and weighed may not be representative of the average bolt size on the load. To avoid these and other potential problems in the sampling scheme just described, the following scheme, which utilizes a ratio estimator, can be used to obtain a more precise estimate with less effort.

First define the following variables:

x_i = green weight (wood and bark) of pulpwood bolt i
y_i = dry weight (wood only) of pulpwood bolt i
T_x = green weight (wood and bark) of the entire load of pulpwood bolts
T_y = dry weight (wood only) of the entire load of pulpwood bolts

The following sampling scheme will be used:

1. Determine T_x by taking the difference between the weight of the truck loaded and unloaded (a procedure that is usually followed at most mills).
2. Randomly or systematically select a sample of n bolts and weigh each to obtain x_i (green weight of wood and bark).
3. Debark and dry the n bolts in the sample and weigh each to obtain y_i (dry weight of wood only).
4. Use a ratio estimator to estimate the total dry weight of wood on the load.

Assume that a sample of $n = 30$ bolts was taken from a sample load. The following summarized data are available:

$$\sum_{i=1}^{30} x_i = 3316 \qquad \sum_{i=1}^{30} y_i = 1802$$

$$\sum_{i=1}^{30} x_i^2 = 392{,}440 \qquad \sum_{i=1}^{30} y_i^2 = 118{,}360$$

$$\sum_{i=1}^{10} x_i y_i = 214{,}738$$

The total green weight (including bark) of all bolts on the load was

$$T_x = 24{,}225 \text{ lb}$$

First calculate $\hat{R}$, the ratio of dry weight of wood only to green weight of wood and bark:

$$\hat{R} = \frac{\sum_{i=1}^{30} y_i}{\sum_{i=1}^{30} x_i} = \frac{1802}{3316} = 0.5434258$$

Now using Eq. 6.4 estimate $\hat{T}_R$, the total dry weight of wood of the entire truckload of pulpwood bolts. Recall that

$$\begin{aligned}\hat{T}_R &= \hat{R}T_x \\ &= 0.5434258\ (24{,}225) \\ &= 13{,}164.5 \text{ lb}\end{aligned}$$

Think about how this estimate was obtained. First the ratio of dry weight of wood to green weight of wood and bark was estimated by sampling 30 bolts. Next this ratio was multiplied by the total green weight of wood and bark to obtain an estimate of the total dry weight of wood on the truck. It was not necessary to know the total number of logs on the load as is required for a traditional simple random sampling (or systematic sampling) estimate of the total. The key point is that information that is always available from mill scale houses is used along with a ratio estimator to obtain the estimate of interest.

The variance of this estimate is obtained using Eq. 6.7:

$$S^2_{\hat{T}_R} = T_x^2 \frac{1}{\mu_x^2} \frac{S_u^2}{n} \left(\frac{N-n}{N}\right)$$

Note that N is unknown; thus it is assumed that it is sufficiently large that the finite population correction factor can be ignored. Furthermore, μ_x is also unknown, so $\bar{x}$ is used in its place. Now

$$\bar{x} = \frac{3316}{30} = 110.5\overline{3}$$

First

$$S_u^2 = \frac{118{,}360 + (0.5434258)^2(392{,}440) - 2(0.5434258)(214{,}738)}{29}$$

$$S_u^2 = 29.784324$$

Thus

$$S_{\hat{T}_R}^2 = (24{,}225)^2 \frac{1}{(110.5\bar{3})^2} \frac{29.784324}{30}$$
$$= 47{,}687.82667 \text{ (lb)}^2$$

The standard error of $\hat{T}_R$ is

$$S_{\hat{T}_R} = \sqrt{S_{\hat{T}_R}^2} = 218.4 \text{ lb}$$

An approximate 95% confidence interval for $\hat{T}_R$, the dry weight of wood of the entire truckload, is

$$\hat{T}_R \pm 2S_{\hat{T}_R}$$
$$13{,}164.5 \pm 2(218.4)$$
$$\text{LCL} = 12{,}727.7 \text{ lb}$$
$$\text{UCL} = 13{,}601.3 \text{ lb}$$

Clearly, this is a very precise estimate. The variation in the estimate is very small because the total truckload green weight of wood and bark was used to obtain the estimate. As should be expected, there is a very strong correlation (relationship) between dry weight of wood only and green weight of wood and bark.

Another application of a ratio estimator in forest inventory is estimating stand parameters for data obtained with a strip cruise. A strip cruise is usually carried out by randomly or systematically measuring strips of forest area that are perpendicular to contours of the land, as depicted in Figure 6.2.2. All trees in the target population in each strip are measured. An estimate of the total volume is usually obtained by multiplying the sum of the volume in all strips by the following expansion factor:

$$\frac{\text{Stand area}}{\text{Total strip area}}$$

If all strips have the same area, the variance of the estimated stand parameter (volume, value, and so on) can be calculated using simple random sampling equations by assuming each strip is a sampling unit. However, in most real-world applications

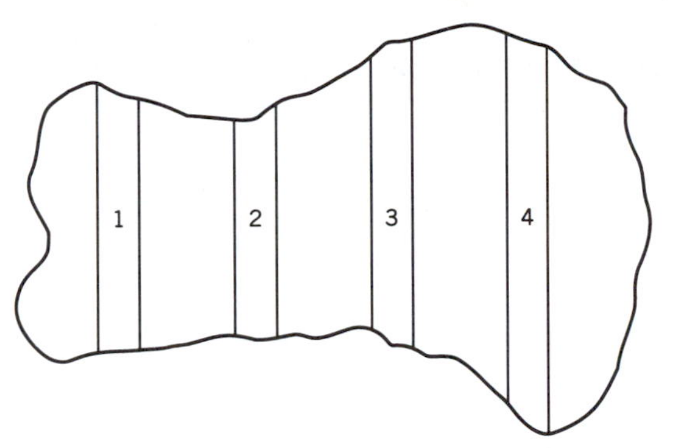

Figure 6.2.2 Strip cruise layout for a stand in which four strips are identifiable.

of strip cruising, the strips vary in length and, hence, area. This presents a problem in estimating means and totals as well as variances associated with these estimates. This problem can be overcome by formulating the strip sample problem using a ratio estimator.

EXAMPLE 6.2.5

Suppose 10 one-chain-wide (66-ft) sample strips are taken from a mixed hardwood stand in the Appalachian mountains of the southeastern United States that has been marked for a selective cut. The strips were chosen systematically and laid out perpendicular to the major contour of the land. All marked trees in each strip were measured for Scribner board feet. The following information is available for each strip:

Strip	**Volume (bd ft)**	**Area (Acres)**
1	5650	2.5
2	4400	1.8
3	6250	3.2
4	6400	2.7
5	4375	2.1
6	3500	1.8
7	2900	1.1
8	1600	0.8
9	5950	2.6
10	7130	2.9

Define volume per strip as the variable of interest, y_i, and strip area as the auxiliary variable, x_i. Suppose T_x, the total stand area, was determined to be 73 acres using an aerial photograph or a stand map. N, the total number of one-chain-wide strips in the stand is determined by dividing the width of the stand by 66 ft (one chain) and rounding to the closest whole number. This stand is 2315 ft wide, so

$$N = \frac{2315}{66} = 35.1\text{, or 35 strips}$$

Now use Eq. 6.4 to obtain an estimate of the total stand volume. Recall that this formula is

$$\hat{T}_R = \hat{R}T_x$$

First calculate the following sums:

$$\sum_{i=1}^{10} x_i = 21.5 \qquad \sum_{i=1}^{10} y_i = 48{,}155$$

$$\sum_{i=1}^{10} x_i^2 = 51.69 \qquad \sum_{i=1}^{10} y_i^2 = 259{,}905{,}025$$

$$\sum_{i=1}^{10} x_i y_i = 115{,}429.5$$

Then

$$\hat{R} = \frac{\sum_{i=1}^{10} y_i}{\sum_{i=1}^{10} x_i} = \frac{48{,}155}{21.5} = 2239.76744 \text{ bd ft/acre}$$

Note that the units for $\hat{R}$ are board feet per acre. Now it should be obvious that the total stand volume can be obtained by multiplying by the total stand acreage, T_x. This is exactly what the equation for the ratio estimate of the total does:

$$\begin{aligned}\hat{T}_R &= 2239.76744(73)\\ &= 163{,}503 \text{ bd ft}\end{aligned}$$

Next the variance of this estimate is obtained using Eq. 6.7:

$$S_{\hat{T}_R}^2 = T_x^2 \frac{1}{\mu_x^2} \frac{S_u^2}{n} \left(\frac{N-n}{N}\right)$$

Since T_x and N are both known, μ_x, the true average area per strip, can be determined as follows:

$$\mu_x = \frac{T_x}{N} = \frac{73}{35} = 2.085714 \text{ acres}$$

First

$$S_u^2 = \frac{259{,}905{,}025 + (2239.76744)^2(51.69) - 2(2239.76744)(115{,}429.5)}{9}$$
$$= 237{,}827.3556$$

Then

$$S_{\hat{T}_R}^2 = (73)^2 \frac{1}{(2.085714)^2} \frac{237{,}827.3556}{10} \left(\frac{35-10}{35}\right)$$
$$= 20{,}809{,}899.32 \text{ (bd ft)}^2$$

The standard error of $\hat{T}_R$ is

$$S_{\hat{T}_R} = \sqrt{S_{\hat{T}_R}^2} = 4561.8 \text{ bd ft}$$

An approximate 95% confidence interval for $\hat{T}_R$ is

$$\hat{T}_R \pm 2S_{\hat{T}_R}$$
$$163{,}503 \pm 2(4561.8)$$
$$\text{LCL} = 154{,}379.4 \text{ bd ft}$$
$$\text{UCL} = 172{,}626.6 \text{ bd ft}$$

The volume per strip, y_i, and the area per strip, x_i, are highly correlated, and y_i should be zero when x_i is zero, which indicates that the relationship between x_i and y_i begins at the origin on an x–y coordinate system. Thus the ratio estimator is unbiased and more precise than the nonratio estimator of total tract volume.

Recall that the simple random sampling (systematic sampling) estimator of the total tract volume is Eq. 3.3 with variance given by Eq. 3.4. For this tract, if each strip is treated as a sampling unit,

$$\bar{y} = \frac{\sum_{i=1}^{n} y_i}{n} = \frac{48{,}155}{10} = 4815.5 \text{ bd ft/strip}$$

$$\hat{T} = N\bar{y} = 35\ (4815.5) = 168{,}542.5 \text{ bd ft}$$

The variance of $\hat{T}$ is

$$S_{\hat{T}}^2 = N^2 S_{\bar{y}}^2$$

$$S_{\bar{y}}^2 = \frac{S_y^2}{n}\left(\frac{N-n}{N}\right)$$

$$S_y^2 = \frac{\sum_{i=1}^{n} y_i^2 - \frac{\left(\sum_{i=1}^{n} y_i\right)^2}{n}}{n-1}$$

$$= \frac{259{,}905{,}025 - \frac{(48{,}155)^2}{10}}{9}$$

$$= 3{,}112{,}735.833$$

Now

$$S_{\bar{y}}^2 = \frac{3{,}112{,}735.833}{10}\left(\frac{35-10}{35}\right)$$

$$S_{\bar{y}}^2 = 222{,}338.2738$$

Thus

$$S_{\hat{T}}^2 = (35)^2(222{,}338.2738)$$

$$= 272{,}364{,}385.4$$

The standard error of $\hat{T}$ is

$$S_{\hat{T}} = \sqrt{S_{\hat{T}}^2} = 16{,}503.5 \text{ bd ft}$$

This standard error is approximately 3.5 times larger than the standard error of the ratio estimate of the total tract volume. This increased variation is due to the fact that in addition to the inherent variation of the stand, there is variation in volume per strip (sampling unit) that is due solely to variation in strip area. The ratio estimator allows for this added variation, whereas the simple random sampling estimator does not.

6.3 SAMPLE SIZE REQUIREMENTS FOR RATIO ESTIMATORS

When a ratio estimator is used in conjunction with simple random or systematic sampling, determining the number of sampling units required to meet a desired bound on the error of estimation is relatively straightforward. Recall from Chapter 3 that the bound we use is the half-width of an approximate 95% confidence interval. When a population ratio, R, is estimated with a ratio estimator, $\hat{R}$, this bound is

$$B_R = 2S_{\hat{R}}$$

Substitution for $S_{\hat{R}}$ (the square root of Eq. 6.5) gives

$$B_R = 2\frac{1}{\mu_x}\frac{S_u}{\sqrt{n}}\sqrt{\frac{N-n}{N}}$$

This equation is easily solved for n as follows:

$$\frac{B_R^2\mu_x^2}{4S_u^2} = \frac{1}{n}\left(\frac{N-n}{N}\right)$$

$$\frac{B_R^2\mu_x^2 N + 4S_u^2}{4S_u^2 N} = \frac{1}{n}$$

$$n = \frac{4S_u^2 N}{B_R^2\mu_x^2 N + 4S_u^2} \tag{6.8}$$

where all variables are as previously defined.

Note that S_u^2, μ_x^2, and N must be known to use Eq. 6.8. If the ratio estimator is used because N is unknown, then required sample sizes can not be determined. However, if N is assumed to be large enough so that the finite population correction factor can be ignored, then

$$B_R = 2\frac{1}{\mu_x}\frac{S_u}{\sqrt{n}}$$

and

$$n = \frac{4S_u^2}{B_R^2\mu_x^2} \tag{6.9}$$

where all variables are as previously defined.

Regardless of whether N is known, S_u^2 and μ_x must be estimated from previous experience or from a pilot sample (see Section 3.6).

When a ratio estimator is used to estimate a population mean, the following sample size formulas should be used:

Finite Populations

$$n = \frac{4S_u^2 N}{B_M^2 N + 4S_u^2} \tag{6.10}$$

Infinite Populations

$$n = \frac{4S_u^2}{B_M^2} \tag{6.11}$$

where

B_M = desired upper bound on the population mean, μ_y and all other variables are as previously defined.

When a ratio estimator is used to estimate a population total, the following sample size formulas should be used:

Finite Populations

$$n = \frac{4N^2 S_u^2}{B_T^2 + 4NS_u^2} \tag{6.12}$$

Infinite Populations

$$n = \frac{4N^2 S_u^2}{B_T^2} \tag{6.13}$$

where

B_T = desired upper bound on the population total, T_y and all other variables are as previously defined.

EXAMPLE 6.3.1

Refer to Example 6.2.3. Suppose that we wanted to estimate the total tract volume within 1250 bd ft. How many sample plots would be required to achieve this bound? Use Eq. 6.12 since this is a population total for a finite population estimated with a ratio estimator. For the tract we have

$$S_u^2 = 257.45$$
$$N = 450$$
$$B_T = 1250$$

Now

$$n = \frac{4(450)^2(257.45)}{(1250)^2 + 4(450)(257.45)}$$

$$n = 102.9 \text{ plots}$$

Use 103 plots.

Thus, an additional 73 plots must be obtained to reduce the bound from 2547 bd ft to 1250 bd ft.

As discussed previously, there are many potential applications of ratio estimators in forest inventory. Several applications have been illustrated here. We hope that, as foresters become more aware of them, ratio estimators will find more utility in forest inventory.

6.4 REGRESSION ESTIMATION

A regression estimator uses highly correlated auxiliary information to obtain more precise estimates of the variable of interest. However, a regression estimator should be used when the relationship between the variable of interest, y_i, and the auxiliary variable, x_i, is linear but not necessarily passing through the origin of the x–y coordinate system, as illustrated in Figure 6.4.1. Note that the regression estimator is a biased estimator, but the bias will be negligible when the relationship between x and y is linear. The population mean and total can be estimated using a regression estimator. A population

Figure 6.4.1 Type of relationship for which a regression estimator is appropriate.

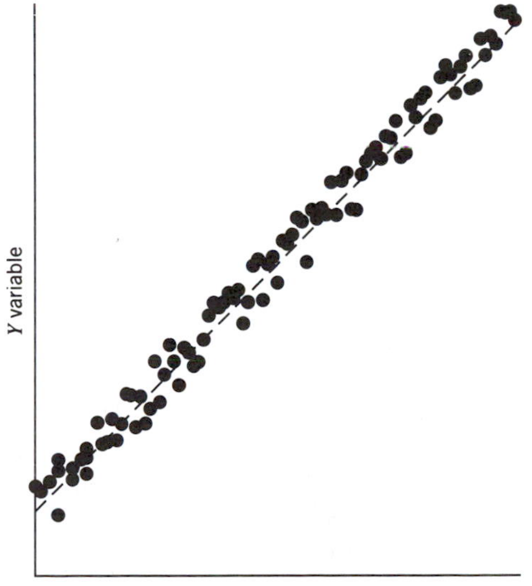

ratio cannot be estimated with a regression estimator; the ratio estimator must be used for this purpose. The regression estimator for a population mean of the variable of interest, y_i, when both y_i and the auxiliary variable, x_i, are measured on each sampling unit is

$$\bar{y}_{\mathrm{LR}} = \bar{y} + b(\mu_x - \bar{x}) \tag{6.14}$$

where

$\bar{y}$ = the sample mean of the y_i values measured on each sampling unit

$\bar{x}$ = the sample mean of the x_i values measured on each sampling unit

μ_x = the true population mean of the x_i values

b = the slope of the straight-line relationship between y_i and x_i and is calculated as

$$b = \frac{\sum_{i=1}^{n} x_i y_i - \dfrac{\left(\sum_{i=1}^{n} x_i\right)\left(\sum_{i=1}^{n} y_i\right)}{n}}{\sum_{i=1}^{n} x_i^2 - \dfrac{\left(\sum_{i=1}^{n} x_i\right)^2}{n}} \tag{6.15}$$

The regression estimate of the population total for the variable of interest is

$$\hat{T}_{\mathrm{LR}} = N\bar{y}_{\mathrm{LR}} \tag{6.16}$$

where all variables are as previously defined.

Note that the subscript on the estimators above is LR, which stands for linear regression. Those readers familiar with simple linear regression will recognize b as the slope coefficient from a simple linear regression of y on x. For those not familiar with simple linear regression, b quantifies the linear relationship between y_i and x_i. Note that it is possible to use multiple linear regression estimators; however, these are beyond the scope of this discussion. Readers interested in more in-depth discussions of regression estimators are referred to Cochran (1977). When y_i and x_i are highly correlated and the relationship does not pass through the origin, a regression estimator will provide a more precise estimate of a population total or mean than simple random sampling (systematic sampling) estimators. However, note that just as for ratio estimators, regression estimators require knowledge of μ_x, the true population mean per sampling unit for the auxiliary variable. Thus some thought must be put into potential applications of regression estimators in forest inventory.

The variance of $\bar{y}_{\mathrm{LR}}$ is

$$S^2_{\bar{y}_{\mathrm{LR}}} = \frac{S^2_{y \cdot x}}{n}\left(\frac{N-n}{N}\right) \tag{6.17}$$

where

$$S^2_{y \cdot x} = \frac{\left\{\sum_{i=1}^{n} y_i^2 - \frac{\left(\sum_{i=1}^{n} y_i\right)^2}{n}\right\} - b^2\left\{\sum_{i=1}^{n} x_i^2 - \frac{\left(\sum_{i=1}^{n} x_i\right)^2}{n}\right\}}{n-2} \tag{6.18}$$

and all else is as previously defined.

Note that $S^2_{y \cdot x}$ estimates the variation in y (the variable of interest) that is not "explained" by knowing x. The variance of $\hat{T}_{\mathrm{LR}}$ is

$$S^2_{\hat{T}_{LR}} = N^2 S^2_{\bar{y}_{\mathrm{LR}}} \tag{6.19}$$

where all variables are as previously defined.

EXAMPLE 6.4.1

A forester is marking a stand of trees for a selective cut. Every tree that is marked is measured for dbh. On a sample of the marked trees, measurements are taken to determine the Scribner board foot volume. A total of 500 trees are marked and a sample of 35 are measured for board foot volume. The following data are available for the 35 volume sample trees:

dbh (in.)	*x* BA (ft^2)	*y* Vol (bd ft)
12.3	0.825	75
13.4	0.979	94
18.6	1.887	244
16.7	1.521	185
15.3	1.277	136
17.2	1.614	246
21.1	2.428	304
12.5	0.852	61
23.2	2.936	374
14.2	1.100	119
19.5	2.074	290
20.2	2.226	295
17.3	1.632	215

dbh (in.)	x BA (ft^2)	y Vol (bd ft)
14.4	1.131	114
15.6	1.327	157
15.8	1.362	136
13.2	0.950	107
13.9	1.054	114
17.5	1.670	184
18.5	1.867	209
19.5	2.074	240
20.2	2.226	270
21.0	2.405	358
22.0	2.640	398
24.5	3.274	484
16.2	1.431	159
16.8	1.539	185
17.7	1.709	215
19.1	1.990	240
19.8	2.138	281
11.1	0.672	49
12.5	0.852	85
14.4	1.131	130
14.8	1.195	150
15.2	1.260	160

Note that dbh in inches is converted to basal area in square feet by multiplying dbh squared by 0.005454. The variable of interest, y, is the Scribner board foot volume and the auxiliary variable, x, is the basal area. The population of interest is all marked trees. Thus the true mean basal area per marked tree, μ_x, is known since all trees in the population were measured for dbh (that is, basal area). For this stand μ_x, average basal area per marked tree, was found to be

$$\mu_x = 1.525 \text{ ft}^2$$

Now the regression estimator will be used to obtain an estimate of the mean board foot volume per tree using Eq. 6.14. First calculate b using Eq. 6.15. The sums and sums of squares for the 35 sample trees are

$$\sum_{i=1}^{35} x_i = 57.248 \qquad \sum_{i=1}^{35} y_i = 7063$$

$$\sum_{i=1}^{35} x_i^2 = 107.373 \qquad \sum_{i=1}^{35} y_i^2 = 1{,}781{,}123$$

$$\sum_{i=1}^{35} x_i y_i = 13{,}722{,}673$$

Thus

$$b = \frac{13{,}722.673 - \dfrac{(57.248)(7063)}{35}}{107.373 - \dfrac{(57.248)^2}{35}}$$

$$= \frac{2170.0266}{13.7348} = 157.994$$

Now

$$\bar{y} = \frac{7063}{35} = 201.8$$

$$\bar{x} = \frac{57.248}{35} = 1.636$$

Then using Eq. 6.14 the linear regression estimate of the average volume per tree is

$$\begin{aligned} \bar{y}_{\mathrm{LR}} &= 201.8 + 157.994(1.525 - 1.636) \\ &= 184.3 \text{ bd ft/tree} \end{aligned}$$

The total board foot volume of the 500 marked trees is calculated using Eq. 6.16:

$$\hat{T}_{\mathrm{LR}} = N\bar{y}_{\mathrm{LR}}$$

$$\hat{T}_{\mathrm{LR}} = 500(184.3) = 92{,}150 \text{ bd ft}$$

Next calculate the variance of the estimate. First calculate the variance of $\bar{y}_{\mathrm{LR}}$ using Eq. 6.17:

$$S^2_{\bar{y}_{\mathrm{LR}}} = \frac{S^2_{y \cdot x}}{n}\left(\frac{N-n}{N}\right)$$

where

$$S^2_{y \cdot x} = \frac{\left(\sum_{i=1}^{n} y_i^2 - \dfrac{\left(\sum_{i=1}^{n} y_i\right)^2}{n}\right) - b^2\left(\sum_{i=1}^{n} x_i^2 - \dfrac{\left(\sum_{i=1}^{n} x_i\right)^2}{n}\right)}{n-2}$$

Thus

$$S_{y \cdot x}^2 = \frac{\left(1{,}781{,}123 - \dfrac{(7063)^2}{35}\right) - (157.994)^2\left(107.373 - \dfrac{(57.248)^2}{35}\right)}{33}$$

$$= \frac{12{,}957.6}{33} = 392.6454$$

Then

$$S_{\bar{y}_{\text{LR}}}^2 = \frac{392.6545}{35}\left(\frac{500 - 35}{500}\right)$$
$$= 10.433391$$

Finally, the variance of $\hat{T}_{\text{LR}}$ is obtained using Eq. 6.19:

$$S_{\hat{T}_{\text{LR}}}^2 = N^2 S_{\bar{y}_{\text{LR}}}^2$$
$$= (500)^2\ (10.433391)$$
$$= 2{,}608{,}347.75\ (\text{bd ft})^2$$

The standard error of $\hat{T}_{\text{LR}}$, the board foot volume of marked trees, is

$$S_{\hat{T}_{\text{LR}}} = \sqrt{S_{\hat{T}_{\text{LR}}}^2} = \sqrt{2{,}608{,}347.75}$$
$$= 1615.0 \text{ bd ft}$$

An approximate 95% confidence interval for the total board foot volume is

$$92{,}150 \pm 2(1615)$$
$$\text{LCL} = 88{,}920 \text{ bd ft}$$
$$\text{UCL} = 95{,}380 \text{ bd ft}$$

For comparison, total board foot volume and the associated variance of the 500 marked trees will be calculated using the 35 trees measured for board foot volume with the simple random sampling formulas from Chapter 3. Recall that the sample mean $\bar{y}$ is

$$\bar{y} = \frac{\sum_{i=1}^{35} y_i}{n} = \frac{7063}{35} = 201.8 \text{ bd ft/tree}$$

Then

$$\hat{T} = N\bar{y} = 500\ (201.8) = 100{,}900 \text{ bd ft}$$

The variance of $\bar{y}$ (Eq. 3.2) is

$$S_{\bar{y}}^2 = \frac{S_y^2}{n}\left(\frac{N-n}{N}\right)$$

$$S_y^2 = \frac{\sum_{i=1}^{35} y_i^2 - \frac{\left(\sum_{i=1}^{35} y_i\right)^2}{n}}{n-1} = \frac{1{,}781{,}123 - \frac{(7063)^2}{35}}{34}$$

$$= 10{,}464.98824$$

$$S_{\bar{y}}^2 = \frac{10{,}464.98824}{35}\left(\frac{500-35}{500}\right) = 278.06969$$

The variance of $\hat{T}$ (Eq. 3.4) is

$$S_{\hat{T}}^2 = N^2 S_{\bar{y}}^2$$

$$= (500)^2\,(278.06969) = 69{,}517{,}421.88\ (\text{bd ft})^2$$

The standard error of $\hat{T}$ is

$$S_{\hat{T}} = \sqrt{S_{\hat{T}}^2} = 8337.7 \text{ bd ft}$$

The approximate 95% confidence interval is

$$100{,}900 \pm 2(8337.7)$$

$$\text{LCL} = 84{,}224.6 \text{ bd ft}$$

$$\text{UCL} = 117{,}575.4 \text{ bd ft}$$

Clearly, the regression estimator is much more precise than the nonregression estimator in this example. The increase in precision is attributed to the information obtained by measuring all trees for the auxiliary variable (basal area) and the strong relationship between tree volume and basal area.

As with the ratio estimator, it is informative to look at the relationship between $\bar{y}_{\text{LR}}$ (the regression estimate of average volume per tree) and $\bar{y}$ (the simple random sample estimate of average volume per tree) for Example 6.4.1. The simple random sample estimate, $\bar{y}$, was "adjusted" down from 201.8 to 184.3 bd ft/tree. The adjustment was downward since the sample of 35 trees that were measured for both volume and basal area produced a sample estimate of average basal area per tree

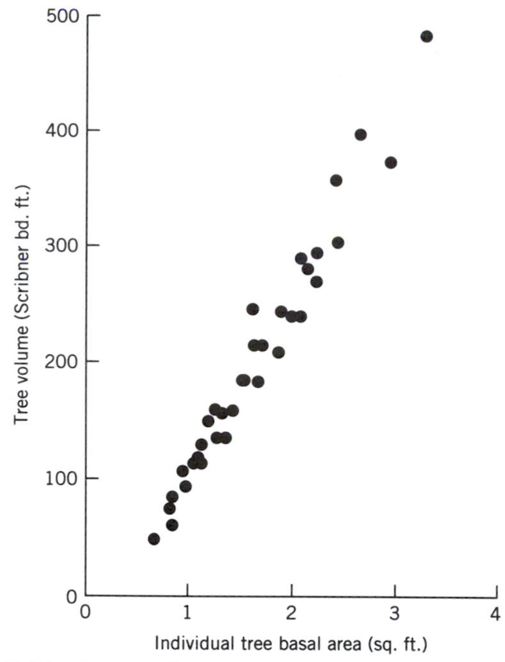

Figure 6.4.2 Individual tree volume versus individual tree basal area for sample data from Example 6.4.1.

($\bar{x} = 1.636$ ft^2/tree) that overestimated the true population average basal area per tree ($\mu_x = 1.525$ ft^2/tree). The logic is that since the sample of 35 trees overestimated the true average basal area per tree, the sample most likely has resulted in an overestimate of the true average board foot volume per tree. Clearly, this will be true since basal area and volume per tree are highly correlated in a linear fashion (Figure 6.4.2).

Obviously, regression estimators can be very precise. However, their use in forest inventory is limited to situations for which the true population mean of the auxiliary variable is known. As discussed earlier, this same limitation applies to ratio estimators. In Chapter 7 a sampling procedure called double sampling, which utilizes ratio and regression estimators, is introduced. However, in double sampling it is not necessary to know population parameters for the auxiliary variable. Thus double sampling is an efficient sampling procedure that has great utility in many forest inventory situations.

REFERENCES

Cochran, W. G. 1977. *Sampling techniques.* 3rd ed. Wiley, New York.

DeVries, P. G. 1986. *Sampling theory for forest inventory.* Springer-Verlag, New York.

PROBLEMS FOR BETTER UNDERSTANDING

1. Explain how an auxiliary variable is different from the variable of interest.
2. Think of five situations for which a ratio estimator would be useful in forest resource sampling. Define the auxiliary variable, x, and the variable of interest, y, for each situation.
3. Assume per-acre basal area for a red pine plantation was determined to be 90 ft^2 in 1984. In 1994 the average basal area per acre was 135 ft^2. Estimate the percent basal area growth from 1984 to 1994 using a ratio estimator.
4. What assumptions are the following estimators based on?
   a. Ratio estimator
   b. Regression estimator
5. A sample of size $n = 10$ was taken from a population of size $N = 400$. The variable of interest, y, and an auxiliary variable, x, were determined for each of the sample plots. The total of the auxiliary variable is known to be 24,800. The following summarized data are available:

$$\sum_{i=1}^{10} y_i = 22{,}405 \qquad \sum_{i=1}^{10} y_i^2 = 51{,}449{,}525$$

$$\sum_{i=1}^{10} x_i = 681 \qquad \sum_{i=1}^{10} x_i^2 = 47{,}553$$

$$\sum_{i=1}^{10} x_i y_i = 1{,}561{,}600$$

   a. Estimate the total, T_y, using a ratio estimator.
   b. Estimate the total, T_y, using a traditional random sampling estimator.
   c. How do the estimates in parts a and b compare? What was the result of using the ratio estimator? Why did it adjust the nonratio estimate in the direction that it did?
6. Refer to Problem 5.
   a. Calculate the variance of the traditional random sampling estimate of T_y.
   b. Calculate the variance of the ratio estimate of T_y.
   c. How do the variances in parts a and b compare? Which estimate of T_y should be preferred in this case? Why?
7. Again, refer to Problem 5.
   a. Estimate the total, T_y, using a regression estimator.
   b. Calculate the variance of the estimate obtained in part a.
8. Thirty trees were randomly sampled from a red pine stand. The stand is 10 acres and has a total of 6800 trees, and the average basal area per acre is known to be

160 ft^2. Diameter at breast height (D) and cubic foot volume (V) was determined for each tree and is shown below:

D (in.)	V (ft^3)	D (in.)	V (ft^3)
5.7	19.5	5.4	17.5
3.8	6.5	6.1	25.3
6.9	30.9	7.3	38.4
8.4	49.4	6.6	25.7
10.2	72.8	6.3	23.0
3.6	5.3	5.9	21.6
5.2	14.9	5.8	21.1
6.4	25.4	6.5	30.0
7.0	32.8	6.6	28.8
6.3	25.8	7.1	33.8
6.7	29.2	5.8	20.9
6.8	31.4	6.1	23.8
7.2	37.3	5.1	15.1
9.1	58.0	4.9	12.5
11.0	90.8	5.7	17.9

a. Calculate the basal area (square feet) for each tree.

b. Plot V versus basal area.

c. Based on the plot in part b above, determine what estimator should be used to estimate total tract volume.

9. Refer to Problem 8. Estimate the total volume in the stand and an upper bound on the error of estimation using a ratio estimator. (*Hint:* Use tract information to calculate the true mean basal area per tree.)

10. Refer to Problem 8. Estimate the total volume in the stand and an upper bound on the error of estimation using a regression estimator.

11. To estimate the dry weight of pulpwood logs (without bark) on a 40-ft truckload, 10 logs were randomly selected. Each log was weighed green with bark and then was debarked, dried, and weighed again. The following data are available:

Log	Green Weight o.b. (lb)	Dry Weight i.b. (lb)
1	50	25
2	125	85
3	75	45
4	150	60
5	100	50
6	200	110

Log	Green Weight o.b. (lb)	Dry Weight i.b. (lb)
7	150	100
8	100	40
9	50	30
10	75	40

There was a total of 230 logs on the truck with a total green weight o.b. of 33,000 lb.

a. Define the variable of interest and the auxiliary variable so that a ratio estimator can be used to estimate the total dry weight of pulpwood inside bark.

b. Use a ratio estimator to estimate the total dry weight of pulpwood inside bark.

c. Obtain the upper bound on the error of estimation for the estimate obtained in part b.

12. Refer to Problem 11.

a. Use a regression estimator to estimate the total dry weight of pulpwood inside bark.

b. Obtain the upper bound on the error of estimation for the estimate obtained in part a.

13. Eight strips, each 50 feet wide, were laid out in a systematic fashion in a 65-acre natural loblolly pine stand. All merchantable trees in each strip were tallied and cubic-foot volume was determined for each. The following summarized information is available:

Strip	Volume (ft^3)	Area (Acres)
1	3983	1.6
2	1763	0.8
3	2254	1.2
4	6471	2.5
5	5310	2.1
6	1012	0.6
7	1273	0.5
8	2131	1.1

It was determined that a total of 42 strips, each 50 feet wide, could fit across the width of the stand.

a. Use a ratio estimator to estimate the total cubic-foot volume on the 65-acre tract.

b. Calculate an upper bound on the error of estimation for the estimate obtained in part a.

14. Derive sample size formulas for estimating a population mean with a ratio estimator for both finite and infinite populations.

CHAPTER 7

DOUBLE SAMPLING OR TWO-PHASE SAMPLING

The two estimation methods in Chapter 6, ratio and regression estimation, required knowledge of the population mean or total of the auxiliary variable (x) to estimate the mean or total of the variable of interest. In Chapter 5 the estimators used for stratified sampling required knowledge of stratum sizes. Use of standard volume or weight equations requires input values for dbh and height for every tree sampled. For these and other similar situations in forestry where more complete and detailed knowledge than is usually available is required, double sampling can be very efficient.

In the first phase of a double sample, inventory resources are spent on obtaining reliable values for a variable needed for estimation, but not the variable of interest. For the ratio and regression estimators in Chapter 6, the first phase of a double sample would estimate the auxiliary variable mean or total. For stratified sampling, the first phase of a double sample would estimate the proportion of the property in each stratum.

The first phase may actually use up a majority of the resources in a double sample even though the variable of interest is not measured. Why would this type of sampling design work efficiently? For ratio and regression estimators, a high correlation coefficient between the auxiliary variable (x) and the variable of interest (y) is necessary for double sampling, as it was for regular ratio and regression estimation. If the collection of information on the x variable is faster and less expensive than collection of information on the y variable, then a two-phase sampling design should be considered. Double sampling for stratification may represent the only opportunity to use stratified sampling and can result in much more precise estimators than nonstratified systematic sampling, especially over large areas.

Procedures for deciding whether double sampling should be used are presented later in this chapter, but in general double sampling should be used only when the gain in precision from use of double sampling more than offsets the loss in precision from reducing the size of the sample on which only the variable of interest (y) is measured. The reduction in sample size is necessitated by the resources spent on the first-phase sample.

Double sampling with point sampling is presented as an efficient sampling scheme where the x variable is basal area per acre and the y variable is volume or weight per acre. Of course, basal area per acre is obtained quickly with point sampling by merely counting trees.

There is no reason why even more complex sampling designs such as three- or four-phase sampling could not be used, but double sampling is used much more often then these multiphase sampling schemes. This chapter will discuss some uses of double sampling in forestry, beginning with a discussion of double sampling with ratio and regression estimation.

7.1 NOTATION FOR DOUBLE SAMPLING REGRESSION AND RATIO ESTIMATORS

The notation for double sampling is slightly different from that for the designs previously described because the estimates for the auxiliary variable mean or total from the larger (first-phase) sample must be distinct from the auxiliary variable estimate in the smaller (second-phase) sample. The distinction is made by using a prime (′) as a superscript on variables with values determined by the first-phase sample. The following notation is used for double sampling:

n' = sample size for the first-phase (large) sample
$\bar{x}'$ = mean of auxiliary variable from the first-phase sample
n = sample size for second-phase sample on which both x and y are measured
$\bar{x}$ = mean of auxiliary variable from second-phase sample
$\bar{y}$ = mean of variable of interest from second-phase sample

7.2 REGRESSION ESTIMATORS FOR THE POPULATION MEAN AND TOTAL

The estimation process for double sampling with regression is identical to the process for regular regression estimation. The only difference is that $\bar{x}'$ is substituted in the estimator in place of μ_x. The resulting equation is

$$\bar{y}_{\text{dslr}} = \bar{y} + b(\bar{x}' - \bar{x}) \tag{7.1}$$

where b = slope of the regression of y on x:

$$b = \frac{\sum_{i=1}^{n} x_i y_i - \frac{\left(\sum_{i=1}^{n} x_i\right)\left(\sum_{i=1}^{n} y_i\right)}{n}}{\sum_{i=1}^{n} x_i^2 - \frac{\left(\sum_{i=1}^{n} x_i\right)^2}{n}} \tag{7.2}$$

and all other variables are as defined earlier. The subscript, dslr, denotes double sampling with linear regression. The logic for the equation is similar to regular regression estimation. The correlation coefficient between x and y is high so that if $\bar{x}$ overestimates μ_x, then $\bar{y}$ probably also overestimates μ_y. In the absence of knowledge about the population mean of the x's, $\bar{x}'$ is considered to be the best estimate available for μ_x because it comes from a larger sample than does $\bar{x}$. As a result, if $\bar{x}'$ and $\bar{x}$ do not match perfectly, then the estimate for $\bar{y}$ is adjusted since the two are highly correlated. The amount of the adjustment is not the absolute difference in the auxiliary variable means, however. Rather, it is the difference multiplied by b, the least-squares estimate of the amount that y changes for a one-unit change in x.

The population total can be estimated using the following equation:

$$\hat{T}_{\text{dslr}} = N\bar{y}_{\text{dslr}} \tag{7.3}$$

where all variables are as defined earlier.

EXAMPLE 7.2.1

A 250-acre pine stand is to be inventoried. The forester in charge of the job decided that he would use double sampling. He installs 100 ⅒-acre plots in a systematic fashion (line-plot cruise). On all 100 plots he measures the dbh of all "in" trees (that is, he can calculate basal area on each ⅒-acre plot). On 10% of the plots (10 plots in this case) he measures diameters and heights of all trees so that he can calculate plot merchantable volumes. The data are as follows:

Average basal area of all 100 ⅒-acre plots = 8.7 ft^2

For the 10 height-measured plots, the data are as follows:

Plot	Basal Area (ft^2)	Merchantable Volume (ft^3)
8	8.5	40
18	8.3	37

Plot	Basal Area (ft^2)	Merchantable Volume (ft^3)
28	9.3	42
38	9.7	45
48	10.0	49
58	8.7	41
68	8.2	37
78	7.5	35
88	10.2	50
98	9.4	43

The variable of interest *(y)* is merchantable volume. Basal area is the auxiliary variable *(x)*.

$$n' = 100 \qquad n = 10 \qquad \overline{x}' = 8.7$$

$$\sum_{i=1}^{10} x_i = 89.8 \qquad \sum_{i=1}^{10} y_i = 419$$

$$\sum_{i=1}^{10} x_i^2 = 813.30 \qquad \sum_{i=1}^{10} y_i^2 = 17{,}783$$

$$\sum_{i=1}^{10} x_i y_i = 3801$$

To estimate the mean volume per plot, use Eq. 7.1:

$$\overline{y}_{\text{dslr}} = \overline{y} + b\,(\overline{x}' - \overline{x})$$

First estimate b using Eq. 7.2:

$$b = \frac{\sum_{i=1}^{n} x_i y_i - \frac{\left(\sum_{i=1}^{n} x_i\right)\left(\sum_{i=1}^{n} y_i\right)}{n}}{\sum_{i=1}^{n} x_i^2 - \frac{\left(\sum_{i=1}^{n} x_i\right)^2}{n}} = \frac{3801 - \frac{(89.8)\,(419)}{10}}{813.30 - \frac{(89.8)^2}{10}} = \frac{38.38}{6.896}$$

$$b = 5.56$$

Thus

$$\overline{y}_{\text{dslr}} = 41.9 + 5.56\,(8.7 - 8.98) = 40.3 \text{ ft}^3/\text{plot}$$

This is the estimate of the average volume on a per-sampling-unit (1/10-acre-plot) basis. To get average volume per acre ($\bar{y}_A$), multiply by 10 to obtain

$$\bar{y}_A = 10 \times 40.3 = 403 \text{ ft}^3$$

Note that this estimate is lower than the SRS estimate ($\bar{y} = 41.9$, or 419 ft^3/acre). Also note that $\bar{x}$ was larger than $\bar{x}'$. Since $\bar{x}'$ is the best estimate of μ_x, $\bar{x}$ probably overestimates μ_x. Since x and y are highly correlated, $\bar{y}$ probably also overestimates μ_y. Therefore the adjustment is down and is made automatically by the double sampling estimator.

There are two general methods for taking the two samples in a double sample. The second-phase (small) sample can be a subsample of the first-phase (larger) sample, or the second-phase sample can be taken independently of the first-phase sample. In most forestry situations the second phase will probably be a subsample of the first phase. Theoretically the difference is important because the variance formulas are different for dependent and independent second-phase samples. As DeVries (1986) notes, however, if sample sizes are large, the same formula can be used for both situations. He recommends the following formula for the estimated variance:

$$S^2_{\bar{y}_{\text{dslr}}} = \frac{S_y^2}{n}\left(1 - \left(\frac{n' - n}{n'}\right)\rho^2\right) \tag{7.4}$$

This equation consists of an adjustment to the simple random sampling variance, S_y^2:

$$S_y^2 = \frac{\sum_{i=1}^{n} y_i^2 = \frac{\left(\sum_{i=1}^{n} y_i\right)^2}{n}}{n - 1}$$

and

$$\rho = \frac{\sum_{i=1}^{n} x_i y_i - \frac{\left(\sum_{i=1}^{n} x_i\right)\left(\sum_{i=1}^{n} y_i\right)}{n}}{\sqrt{\sum_{i=1}^{n} x_i^2 - \frac{\left(\sum_{i=1}^{n} x_i\right)^2}{n}}\sqrt{\sum_{i=1}^{n} y_i^2 - \frac{\left(\sum_{i=1}^{n} y_i\right)^2}{n}}} = \frac{SS_{xy}}{\sqrt{SS_x}\sqrt{SS_y}} \tag{7.5}$$

and all variables are as defined previously.

The correlation coefficient, ρ, gives an indication of how much information about y is available by knowing x. If $\rho = 1$, then knowledge of x gives exact knowledge of y. If $\rho = 0$, then knowledge of x gives absolutely no knowledge about y. If $\rho = -1$, then knowledge of x again gives complete knowledge of the value of y, but the negative sign indicates that the relationship is inverse. In other words, a high value of x would indicate a low value of y and vice versa. With S_y^2 and ρ calculated, obtaining a value for the variance of the mean for double sampling with regression ($S_{\bar{y}_{dslr}}^2$) is simple. The variance of the estimate of the total obtained with Eq. 7.3 is

$$S_{\hat{T}_{dslr}}^2 = N^2 S_{\bar{y}_{dslr}}^2 \tag{7.6}$$

EXAMPLE 7.2.2

Now calculate the variance of the estimate obtained in Example 7.2.1. First calculate S_y^2:

$$S_y^2 = \frac{17{,}783 - \dfrac{(419)^2}{10}}{9} = \frac{226.9}{9} = 25.211$$

Next calculate ρ using Eq. 7.5. Note that the numerator of Eq. 7.5 is exactly the same as the numerator of Eq. 7.2, which for this example was 38.38. Thus

$$\rho = \frac{38.38}{\sqrt{813.3 - \dfrac{(89.8)^2}{10}}\sqrt{17{,}783 - \dfrac{(419)^2}{10}}}$$
$$= 0.97$$

Now obtain the variance of the mean using Eq. 7.4:

$$S_{\bar{y}_{dslr}}^2 = \frac{S_y^2}{n}\left(1 - \left(\frac{n' - n}{n'}\right)\rho^2\right)$$
$$= \frac{25.211}{10}\left(1 - \left(\frac{100 - 10}{100}\right)(0.97)^2\right)$$
$$= 0.3862$$

As always the standard error of the mean is calculated by taking the square root of the variance of the mean:

$$S_{\bar{y}_{dslr}} = \sqrt{S_{\bar{y}_{dslr}}^2} = \sqrt{0.3862} = 0.62$$

For this example, an approximate 95% confidence interval for the mean is

$$\bar{y}_{\text{dslr}} \pm 2S_{\bar{y}_{\text{dslr}}}$$
$$40.3 \pm 2(0.62)$$
$$\text{LCL} = 39.06 \text{ ft}^3/\text{plot}$$
$$\text{UCL} = 41.54 \text{ ft}^3/\text{plot}$$

To convert to a per-acre basis from the per-sampling-unit basis, simply multiply the estimate and standard error by the expansion factor of 10 (plots are 1/10 acre).

$$\bar{y}_{\text{Acre}} = 40.3(10) = 403 \text{ ft}^3/\text{acre}$$
$$\text{LCL} = 390.6 \text{ ft}^3/\text{acre}$$
$$\text{UCL} = 415.4 \text{ ft}^3/\text{acre}$$

Total tract volume can be estimated using Eq. 7.3:

$$\hat{T}_{\text{dslr}} = N\bar{y}_{\text{dslr}}$$

Recall that the stand is 250 acres, so

$$N = 250 \times 10 = 2500 \text{ plots}$$

Thus

$$\hat{T}_{\text{dslr}} = 2500 \times 40.3 = 100{,}750 \text{ ft}^3$$

The total tract volume could also have been obtained by multiplying the per-acre estimate of volume by the stand acreage, which results in the same estimate:

$$\hat{T}_{\text{dslr}} = 403 \times 250 = 100{,}750 \text{ ft}^3$$

The variance of the total tract volume is obtained using Eq. 7.6:

$$\begin{aligned} S^2_{\hat{T}_{\text{dslr}}} &= N^2 S^2_{\bar{y}_{\text{dslr}}} \\ &= (2500)^2 (0.3862) \\ &= 2{,}413{,}750 \end{aligned}$$

The standard error of the total is calculated as

$$S_{\hat{T}_{\text{dslr}}} = \sqrt{2{,}413{,}750} = 1553.6 \text{ ft}^3$$

An approximate 95% interval for this tract total is

$$\hat{T}_{\text{dslr}} \pm 2S_{\hat{T}_{\text{dslr}}}$$
$$100{,}750 \pm 2(1553.6)$$
$$\text{LCL} = 97{,}643 \text{ ft}^3$$
$$\text{UCL} = 103{,}857 \text{ ft}^3$$

7.3 RATIO ESTIMATES FOR THE POPULATION MEAN AND TOTAL

As in ratio estimation, double sampling with ratio estimation is useful when the relationship between x and y is linear through the origin and when the variance of the y's is proportional to the x's (that is, as values for x become larger, so does the variability in values for y). The notation for double sampling with ratio estimation is the same as for double sampling with regression, and the sampling methods are the same. The only difference is in the estimation process. The mean value of y on a per-sampling-unit basis is estimated by

$$\bar{y}_{\text{dsr}} = \hat{R}\bar{x}' \tag{7.7}$$

where:

$$\hat{R} = \frac{\bar{y}}{\bar{x}}$$

and all other variables are as defined previously.

The estimate for the population total is

$$\hat{T}_{\text{dsr}} = N\bar{y}_{\text{dsr}} \tag{7.8}$$

where all variables are as defined previously. The subscript, dsr, denotes double sampling with ratio estimation.

Again, the logic for this estimator is that x and y are highly correlated, and if $\bar{x}$ overestimates $\bar{x}'$, then $\bar{y}$ probably overestimates the true population mean per sampling unit. As such, $\bar{y}$ is adjusted downward by $\bar{x}'/\bar{x}$, which will be < 1 since $\bar{x} > \bar{x}'$. A similar adjustment upward is made if $\bar{x} < \bar{x}'$. No adjustment will be made if $\bar{x} = \bar{x}'$.

As with double sampling with regression estimation, the method is efficient only if the correlation coefficient is high and if it is less time-consuming and less costly to obtain information on x than on y.

EXAMPLE 7.3.1

In order to assess the relative size of each year's seed crop, a forest geneticist noted the relationship between numbers of pine cones per acre and general size of the seed crop. Every spring she needs an estimate of the number of cones per acre to estimate the size of the crop for the fall. It is impossible to count all the cones in a stand. However, there is a good relationship between the crown area of a tree and the number of cones that the tree will produce. The geneticist has worked out a sampling scheme in which she takes $\frac{1}{20}$-acre plots. On most of the plots she measures crown radii. On a small subset she measures crown radii and counts cones. For a particular year and 50-acre stand her sample data are as follows:

Plot	Sum of Crown Area Per Plot (Acres)	Total Number of Cones/Plot
1	0.0325	
2	0.0472	
3	0.0380	
4	0.0264	
5	0.0372	722
6	0.0455	
7	0.0145	
8	0.0247	
9	0.0300	
10	0.0410	801
11	0.0391	
12	0.0425	
13	0.0270	
14	0.0118	
15	0.0184	390
16	0.0220	
17	0.0352	
18	0.0387	
19	0.0444	
20	0.0261	510
21	0.0199	
22	0.0192	
23	0.0235	
24	0.0288	
25	0.0270	545
26	0.0341	
27	0.0175	
28	0.0411	
29	0.0333	
30	0.0462	919
31	0.0345	
32	0.0347	
33	0.0405	
34	0.0385	

Plot	Sum of Crown Area Per Plot (Acres)	Total Number of Cones/Plot
35	0.0350	731
36	0.0322	
37	0.0291	
38	0.0287	
39	0.0331	
40	0.0382	694
41	0.0185	
42	0.0272	
43	0.0345	
44	0.0435	
45	0.0480	880
46	0.0362	
47	0.0366	
48	0.0415	
49	0.0334	
50	0.0311	592

$$\sum_{i=1}^{50} x_i = 1.6278 \qquad \bar{x}' = 0.0325560$$

$$\sum_{i=1}^{10} x_i = 0.3482 \qquad \bar{x} = 0.03482$$

$$\sum_{i=1}^{10} y_i = 6784 \qquad \bar{y} = 678.40$$

A ratio estimator will give an estimate of the average number of cones per 1⁄20-acre plot.

$$\bar{y}_{\text{dsr}} = \frac{\bar{y}}{\bar{x}}\bar{x}' = \hat{R}\bar{x}' = \frac{678.40}{0.03482}(0.0325560) = 19483.06\ (0.0325560)$$

$$\bar{y}_{\text{dsr}} = 634.29$$

On a per-acre basis, there should be an average of

$$634.29 \times 20 = 12{,}685.8 \text{ cones}$$

How good is this estimate? Calculate the standard error of the estimate to find out. This is double sampling in which the second phase is a subset of the first phase. Therefore the phases are dependent. The equation for the variance of the mean for this sample design has been derived by DeVries (1986).

$$S^2_{\bar{y}_{\text{dsr}}} = \frac{k}{n} + \frac{l}{n'} + m \tag{7.9}$$

where:

$$k = S_y^2 + \hat{R}^2 S_{x'}^2 - 2\hat{R}S_{xy}$$

$$l = 2\hat{R}S_{xy} - \hat{R}^2 S_{x'}^2$$

$$m = -\left(\frac{S_y^2}{N}\right)$$

$$S_{x'}^2 = \frac{\sum_{i=1}^{n'} x'^2 - \frac{\left(\sum_{i=1}^{n'} x'\right)^2}{n'}}{n' - 1} \tag{7.10}$$

$$S_{xy} = \frac{\sum_{i=1}^{n} x_i y_i - \frac{\left(\sum_{i=1}^{n} x_i\right)\left(\sum_{i=1}^{n} y_i\right)}{n}}{n - 1} = \frac{SS_{xy}}{n - 1} \tag{7.11}$$

and all other variables are as defined previously.

The variance of the population total from a double sample with a ratio estimator is calculated as

$$S_{\hat{T}_{\text{dsr}}}^2 = N^2 S_{\bar{y}_{\text{dsr}}}^2 \tag{7.12}$$

where all variables are as defined previously.

EXAMPLE 7.3.2

Calculate the variance of the estimate obtained in Example 7.3.1. Recall the following:

$$n' = 50 \qquad \sum_{i=1}^{50} x_i = 1.6278$$

$$n = 10 \qquad \sum_{i=1}^{10} x_i = 0.3482 \qquad \sum_{i=1}^{10} y_i = 6784$$

$$\hat{R} = \frac{\bar{y}}{\bar{x}} = 19{,}483.06$$

The following sums of squares and cross products are needed:

$$\sum_{i=1}^{10} y_i^2 = 4{,}857{,}532$$

$$\sum_{i=1}^{50} x_i^2 = 0.0569002$$

$$\sum_{i=1}^{10} y_i x_i = 250.1062$$

First calculate $S_{x'}^2$ using Eq. 7.10:

$$S_{x'}^2 = \frac{0.0569002 - \dfrac{(1.6278)^2}{50}}{49} = 0.0000797$$

Next obtain S_{xy}, the sample covariance, using Eq. 7.11:

$$S_{xy} = \frac{250.1062 - \dfrac{(0.3482)(6784)}{10}}{9} = 1.5430356$$

Now S_y^2 is

$$S_y^2 = \frac{4{,}857{,}532 - \dfrac{(6784)^2}{10}}{9} = 28{,}362.93$$

With the values calculated

$$k = S_y^2 + \hat{R}^2 S_{x'}^2 - 2\hat{R}S_{xy}$$
$$k = 28{,}362.93 + (19{,}483.06)^2\,(0.0000797) - 2(19{,}483.06)\,(1.5430356)$$
$$k = -\,1509.8871$$

and l is

$$\begin{aligned} l &= 2\hat{R}S_{xy} - \hat{R}^2 S_{x'}^2 \\ &= 2(19{,}483.06)\,(1.5430356) - (19{,}483.06)^2\,(0.0000797) \\ &= 29{,}872.8171 \end{aligned}$$

Finally, m is

$$m = -\left(\frac{S_y^2}{N}\right)$$

$$= -\left(\frac{28{,}362.93}{1000}\right) = -28.36$$

So using Eq. 7.9 the variance of the mean is

$$S_{\bar{y}_{\text{dsr}}}^2 = \frac{-1509.8871}{10} + \frac{29{,}872.8171}{50} - 28.36$$
$$= 418.1076$$

The standard error is

$$S_{\bar{y}_{\text{dsr}}} = \sqrt{418.1076} = 20.4 \text{ cones/plot}$$

An approximate 95% confidence interval for the mean number of cones per plot is

$$\bar{y}_{\text{dsr}} \pm 2S_{\bar{y}_{\text{dsr}}}$$
$$718.94 \pm 2(20.4)$$
$$\text{LCL} = 678$$
$$\text{UCL} = 760$$

7.4 RATIO ESTIMATION IN DOUBLE SAMPLING WITH INDEPENDENT PHASES

In most forestry situations the second-phase sample will be a subset of the first-phase sample (that is, the phases will be dependent). Occasionally, however, it may be impossible to have the second phase be a subset of the first phase. In this situation, the double sampling with ratio estimation procedure may still be used, but the variance equation changes to recognize that the two phases are independent. The variance equation for a sample mean estimated for double sampling with ratio estimation with two independent phases is (DeVries, 1986)

$$S_{\bar{y}_{\text{dsri}}}^2 = \left(\frac{N-n}{N}\right)\left(\frac{S_y^2 + \hat{R}^2 S_{xp}^2 - 2\hat{R}S_{xy}}{n} + \frac{\hat{R}^2 S_{xp}^2}{n'}\right) \tag{7.13}$$

where:

$$S_{xp}^2 = \frac{\left[\left(\sum_{i=1}^{n'} x_i^2 - \frac{\left(\sum_{i=1}^{n'} x_i\right)^2}{n'}\right) + \left(\sum_{i=1}^{n} x_i^2 - \frac{\left(\sum_{i=1}^{n} x_i\right)^2}{n}\right)\right]}{n' + n - 2} \tag{7.14}$$

and all other variables are as defined previously.

Of course, the variance for the ratio estimate of a population total obtained from a double sample with two independent samples is

$$S_{\hat{T}_{\text{dsri}}}^2 = N^2 S_{\bar{y}_{\text{dsri}}}^2 \tag{7.15}$$

where all variables are as defined previously.

EXAMPLE 7.4.1

A forester wanted an estimate of total outside bark volume for a 100-acre stand. He cruised the stand in his usual manner, ocularly estimating all diameters and a subsample of heights on 1⁄10-acre plots. Rather than measuring to borderline trees to determine whether they were on the plot or off, he paced to them. Data for his cruise (50 plots) were as follows:

Plot	Volume (ft^3)	Plot	Volume (ft^3)	Plot	Volume (ft^3)
1	101.5	18	137.6	35	103.2
2	146.8	19	57.9	36	77.2
3	141.8	20	93.6	37	95.4
4	111.5	21	115.3	38	122.7
5	131.5	22	66.0	39	102.1
6	113.1	23	125.0	40	131.4
7	121.4	24	131.8	41	127.8
8	112.9	25	121.4	42	120.5
9	70.9	26	131.4	43	137.1
10	94.3	27	108.7	44	127.4
11	155.4	28	111.6	45	119.2
12	121.7	29	133.1	46	116.7
13	143.4	30	125.5	47	120.8
14	93.7	31	113.8	48	134.5
15	126.8	32	86.1	49	83.1
16	145.0	33	80.0	50	108.0
17	135.6	34	86.9		

When the forester returned to the office and worked up his cruise, he felt uneasy about the results. He felt that his visual estimate was very different from what his figures were telling him. He decided to go back to the stand again and put in ocular plots as before, but also to carefully measure trees on the same plots to see if there was a difference. He marked 20 plot centers with flagging and visually estimated diameters, heights, and "in" trees as before. Then he went back to the flagged centers and actually measured the trees and distances. Results were as follows:

Plot	Estimated Volume (ft^3)	Measured Volume (ft^3)	Plot	Estimated Volume (ft^3)	Measured Volume (ft^3)
51	87.9	96.7	61	96.7	107.3
52	146.6	158.6	62	135.2	143.3
53	81.4	94.4	63	119.1	129.8
54	136.5	142.4	64	138.3	151.1
55	78.2	98.5	65	110.0	117.8
56	139.4	151.9	66	132.8	141.2
57	135.1	133.2	67	131.8	146.3
58	126.9	135.3	68	79.7	91.7
59	82.2	91.2	69	78.2	87.3
60	123.1	132.3	70	96.4	108.0

This is a double sample with independent sampling phases. To estimate the volume using ratio estimation for this sample, the following summary data are needed:

$$n' = 50 \qquad n = 20$$

$$N = 1000\ \tfrac{1}{10}\text{-acre plots}$$

Let

$$x_i = \text{estimated volume on plot } i$$

$$y_i = \text{measured volume on plot } i$$

To estimate the mean volume per plot, use Eq. 7.7:

$$\bar{y}_{\text{dsr}} = \hat{R}\bar{x}'$$

where:

$$\hat{R} = \frac{\bar{y}}{\bar{x}}$$

$\bar{x}'$ = mean of the first-phase (large) sample

$$\bar{y} = \frac{\sum_{i=51}^{70} y_i}{20} = \frac{2458.30}{20} = 122.9 \text{ ft}^3/\text{plot} = \text{average measured volume}$$

$$\bar{x} = \frac{\sum_{i=51}^{70} x_i}{20} = \frac{2255.5}{20} = 112.775 \text{ ft}^3/\text{plot} = \text{average estimated volume on plots where volume was also measured}$$

$$\hat{R} = \frac{122.9}{112.775} = 1.08978054 = \text{ratio of average measured volume to average estimated volume on those plots where both estimated and measured volumes were taken}$$

$$\bar{x}' = \frac{\sum_{i=1}^{50} x_i}{50} = \frac{5720.10}{50} = 114.40 \text{ ft}^3/\text{plot} = \text{average estimated volume on plots where volume only was estimated}$$

So

$$\bar{y}_{\text{dsr}} = (1.08978054)\,(114.40) = 124.7 \text{ ft}^3/\text{plot}$$

Calculate the variance of this estimate using Eq. 7.13 since the phases are independent. First calculate S_{xy}, S_y^2, and S_{xp}^2 using the following sums and sums of squares:

$$\sum_{i=51}^{70} y_i = 2458.30 \qquad \sum_{i=51}^{70} y_i^2 = 312{,}978.47$$

$$\sum_{i=51}^{70} x_i = 2255.5 \qquad \sum_{i=51}^{70} x_i^2 = 266{,}098.85$$

$$\sum_{i=51}^{70} x_i y_i = 288{,}342$$

$$\sum_{i=1}^{50} x_i = 5720.10 \qquad \sum_{i=1}^{50} x_i^2 = 678{,}839.35$$

Now

$$S_y^2 = \frac{\sum_{i=51}^{70} y_i^2 - \frac{\left(\sum_{i=51}^{70} y_i\right)^2}{n}}{n-1} = \frac{312{,}978.47 - \frac{(2458.30)^2}{20}}{19}$$

$$S_y^2 = 569.29$$

$$S_{xy} = \frac{\sum_{i=51}^{70} x_i y_i - \frac{\left(\sum_{i=51}^{70} x_i\right)\left(\sum_{i=51}^{70} y_i\right)}{n}}{n-1} = \frac{288{,}342 - \frac{(2255.5)(2458.3)}{20}}{19}$$

$$S_{xy} = 584.59$$

The pooled variance S_{xp}^2 is obtained using Eq. 7.14:

$$S_{xp}^2 = \frac{\left[\left(\sum_{i=1}^{50} x_i^2 - \frac{\left(\sum_{i=1}^{50} x_i\right)^2}{n'}\right) + \left(\sum_{i=51}^{70} x_i^2 - \frac{\left(\sum_{i=51}^{70} x_i\right)^2}{n}\right)\right]}{n' + n - 2}$$

$$= \frac{\left[\left(678{,}839.35 - \frac{(5720.1)^2}{50}\right) + \left(266{,}098.85 - \frac{(2255.5)^2}{20}\right)\right]}{50 + 20 - 2}$$

$$S_{xp}^2 = \frac{24{,}448.4698 + 11{,}734.8375}{68}$$

$$= 532.11$$

So, using Eq. 7.13,

$$S_{\bar{y}_{\text{dsri}}}^2 = \left(\frac{1000 - 20}{1000}\right)\left[\frac{569.29 + (1.08978054)^2\,(532.11) - 2(1.08978054)(584.59)}{20}\right.$$

$$\left. + (1.08978054)^2 \frac{532.11}{50}\right]$$

$$= 0.98[-3.6457 + 12.6389]$$

$$= 8.8133$$

The standard error of the mean is

$$S_{\bar{y}_{\text{dsri}}} = \sqrt{8.8133} = 2.9687 \text{ ft}^3\text{/plot}$$

So an approximate 95% confidence interval for cubic feet per plot is

$$\bar{y}_{\text{dsr}} \pm 2S_{\bar{y}_{\text{dsri}}}$$
$$124.7 \pm 2(2.9687)$$
$$\text{LCL} = 118.8 \text{ ft}^3\text{/plot}$$
$$\text{UCL} = 130.6 \text{ ft}^3\text{/plot}$$

Tenth-acre sample plots were used, so the estimated volume per acre is

$$\bar{y}_{\text{acre}} = 124.7(10) = 1247 \text{ ft}^3/\text{acre}$$

The approximate 95% confidence interval is

$$\text{LCL} = 1188 \text{ ft}^3/\text{acre}$$
$$\text{UCL} = 1306 \text{ ft}^3/\text{acre}$$

Recall that the stand is 100 acres. The total tract volume estimate is then

$$\hat{T}_{\text{dsri}} = 100(1247) = 124{,}700 \text{ ft}^3$$

The approximate 95% confidence interval is easily obtained by multiplying the per-acre lower and upper confidence limits by 100 (number of acres) or by multiplying the per-plot lower and upper confidence limits by 1000 (number of tenth-acre plots in 100 acres):

$$\text{LCL} = 118{,}800 \text{ ft}^3$$
$$\text{UCL} = 130{,}600 \text{ ft}^3$$

The forester's uneasiness with the initial cruise would appear to be justified. The original average volume per plot was 114.4 ft^3. With the double sample that value increased to 124.7 ft^3, an increase of 10.3 ft^3/plot, or 103 ft^3/acre. In addition, the confidence interval from the double sample did not include the original estimate.

7.5 SAMPLE SIZES

As with sample size for all other sampling designs, some information on the area to be inventoried is required before a good sample size estimate can be provided. For most sampling designs the requirements are information regarding the variability of the variable of interest *(y)* across the population to be inventoried, the desired bound *(B)*, and the confidence level. In addition to those values, double sampling sample size estimation requires information on the variability of the auxiliary variable *(x)* and how the *x* and *y* variables vary with each other. Usually this information requires a pilot study or a light preinventory where both *x* and *y* are measured.

As noted earlier, the efficiency of double sampling also depends on the relative costs of obtaining data from sampling units in phase 1 ($C_{n'}$) and phase 2 (C_n). Optimum sample size formulas have been derived for the regression estimation methods assuming a cost function of the form

$$C = a + nC_n + n'C_{n'}$$

where:

C = total cost

a = overhead cost

and all other variables are as defined previously.

7.6 SAMPLE SIZES FOR DOUBLE SAMPLING WITH REGRESSION ESTIMATION

Sample sizes for double sampling with regression estimation are the same for dependent and independent phase 2 samples if the sample size is reasonably large. Recall that

$$\rho = \frac{SS_{xy}}{\sqrt{SS_x}\sqrt{SS_y}}$$

To obtain the sample size for a double sample regression estimator, calculate ρ from a pilot study or cruise where information on both x and y are obtained (the same information that would be obtained in phase 2 of a double sample). In addition, calculate S_y^2 as before.

Now calculate

$$a = S_y^2(1 - \rho^2)$$

$$d = S_y^2(\rho^2)$$

Loetsch and Haller (1964) present these equations for optimum sample sizes to obtain a bound B with minimum cost:

$$n' = \frac{\sqrt{\frac{adC_n}{C_{n'}}} + d}{B^2/t^2} \quad (7.16)$$

where:

$t = t$ value (for 95% confidence level $t \approx 2$)

$$n = \frac{\sqrt{\frac{adC_{n'}}{C_n}} + a}{B^2/t^2}$$

It is important to note that only relative costs, not absolute costs, are necessarily required. So, if it is five times more expensive to take phase 2 plots than phase 1 plots, simply use 5 as C_n and 1 as $C_{n'}$.

Table 7.6.1 Percentage of phase 1 plots to include as phase 2 plots for different correlation coefficients and cost relations $(C_{n'}:C_n)$ for double sampling with regression estimation-dependent phases

Relative Cost	Correlation Coefficient (ρ)					
$C_{n'}:C_n$	0.5	0.6	0.7	0.8	0.9	0.95
1:5	77	60	46	36	22	15
1:10	55	42	32	24	15	10
1:15	45	34	26	19	13	8
1:20	39	30	23	17	11	7
1:30	32	24	19	14	9	6
1:50	24	19	14	11	7	5
1:100	17	13	10	7	5	3

For situations where the phase 2 sample is a subsample of the phase 1 sample, the ratio of n/n' can be calculated as

$$f=\frac{n}{n'}=\frac{\left(\dfrac{\sqrt{\dfrac{adC_{n'}}{C_n}}+a}{B^2/t^2}\right)}{\left(\dfrac{\sqrt{\dfrac{adC_n}{C_{n'}}}+d}{B^2/t^2}\right)}=\sqrt{\frac{C_{n'}a}{C_n d}}=\sqrt{\frac{C_{n'}S_y^2(1-\rho^2)}{C_n S_y^2\rho^2}}$$

$$f=\sqrt{\frac{C_{n'}(1-\rho^2)}{C_n\rho^2}} \tag{7.17}$$

Since the optimum ratio of phase 1 plots to include as phase 2 plots depends only on the relative costs and the correlation coefficient, a table can be constructed to indicate what ratio of plots to subsample based on this equation (Table 7.6.1).

EXAMPLE 7.6.1

What sample size in each phase will be necessary to estimate the mean volume in Example 7.2.1 with an approximate 95% bound on the error of estimation of the mean volume per plot of 0.9 ft^3 if it costs five times as much to put in a volume plot as a basal-area-only plot?

Let $C_n = 5$ and $C_{n'} = 1$ since the relative costs are 5 to 1. From Example 7.2.2,

$$S_y^2 = 25.211$$

$$\rho = \frac{SS_{xy}}{\sqrt{SS_x}\sqrt{SS_y}} = \frac{38.38}{\sqrt{6.896}\sqrt{226.9}} = 0.97$$

$$a = S_y^2(1-\rho^2) = 25.211(1-0.97^2) = 1.4899701$$

$$d = S_y^2(\rho^2) = 25.211(0.97)^2 = 23.7210299$$

$$n' = \frac{\sqrt{\frac{adC_n}{C_{n'}}} + d}{B^2/t^2} = \frac{\sqrt{\frac{(1.4899701)(23.7210299)(5)}{1}} + 23.7210299}{(0.9)^2/4}$$

$$n' = \frac{37.0145669}{0.2025} = 182.78 \approx 183$$

$$f = \sqrt{\frac{C_{n'}(1-\rho^2)}{C_n\rho^2}} = \sqrt{\frac{1(1-0.97^2)}{5(0.97)^2}} = \sqrt{\frac{0.0591}{4.7045}} = \sqrt{0.0125624}$$

$$f = 0.112$$

$$n = fn' = 0.112(183) = 20.5 = 21$$

Notice what happens to the allocation if the relative costs change to 10:1:

$$n' = \frac{\sqrt{\frac{(1.4899701)(23.7210299)(10)}{1}} + 23.7210299}{(0.9)^2/4} = 209.97 \approx 210.$$

$$f = \sqrt{\frac{1(1-0.97)^2}{10(0.97)^2}} = \sqrt{\frac{0.0591}{9.4090}} = \sqrt{0.0062812}$$

$$f = 0.0792541$$

$$n = fn' = 0.0792541(210) = 16.6 \approx 17.$$

With a relative cost of 5:1, the proportion of total plots to measure is 21/183 = 11.5%. When the relative cost went to 10:1, the proportion of total plots to measure for volume decreased to 17/210 = 8.0%.

As expected, for a given cost, as the correlation coefficient increases, the percentage of plots to include in the phase 2 sample decreases because information on the value of x provides more information about y. Also, for a given correlation coefficient, the optimum percentage to include in the phase 2 sample decreases as the relative cost increases (that is, as it becomes more expensive to collect information on both x and y, it is optimum to have a smaller percentage of phase 1 sampling units in phase 2).

There may be times when it is not efficient or not possible to take the phase 2 sample as a subsample of the phase 1 sampling units. In this situation, the two phases are said to be independent. To find the optimum sample sizes necessary to use in two independent phases to obtain a given bound use the same equation for n' (Eq. 7.16) as for dependent phases and calculate n as follows:

$$n = \frac{\sqrt{\dfrac{adC_{n'}}{C_n}} + a}{B^2/t^2} \tag{7.18}$$

The sample size equations presented here may also be used if the bound is expressed as a percentage (an allowable error). In order to use the equations, replace S_y^2 in the equations for a and d with the coefficient of variation and replace B with AE.

7.7 EFFICIENCY OF DOUBLE SAMPLING

A reasonable question to ask is, when should double sampling be preferred over simple random sampling or systematic sampling (line-plot cruising)? Cochran (1977) worked with the variance formulas of the different methods and found that double sampling will result in a more precise estimate if

$$\frac{C_n}{C_{n'}} > \frac{\rho^2}{(1 - \sqrt{1 - \rho^2})^2}$$

where:

C_n = cost per sampling unit in the second phase

$C_{n'}$ = cost per sampling unit in the first phase

ρ = simple correlation coefficient between x and y

Essentially this relationship shows that there is a critical value that the ratio of costs in the two phases must exceed before double sampling gives an increase in precision. Table 7.7.1 shows the breakeven points of $C_n/C_{n'}$ for various values of ρ.

Table 7.7.1 Critical values of $c_n/c_{n'}$ which must be exceeded in order for double sampling to be more precise than simple random sampling for the same cost

ρ	$C_n/C_{n'}$
0.5	13.9
0.6	9.0
0.7	6.0
0.8	4.0
0.9	2.5
0.95	1.9

EXAMPLE 7.7.1

Recall Example 7.2.1 and the volume-basal area data. The correlation coefficient ρ was calculated as 0.97. What critical value of ratio of costs must be exceeded for double sampling to be preferred over simple random sampling?

$$\frac{C_n}{C_{n'}} > \frac{\rho^2}{(1 - \sqrt{1 - \rho^2})^2}$$

$$\frac{C_n}{C_{n'}} > \frac{(0.97)^2}{(1 - \sqrt{1 - 0.97^2})^2} = \frac{0.9409}{(1 - \sqrt{0.0591})^2} = \frac{0.9409}{0.5729} = 1.64$$

This means that if it costs 1.64 times or more as much to inventory a plot for volume and basal area as it does to inventory it just for basal area, then double sampling is the more efficient sampling scheme.

7.8 DOUBLE SAMPLING WITH POINT SAMPLING

The high correlation coefficient between volume and basal area, as indicated in Example 7.7.1, is typical for forest stands. Even when volume is in board feet, the correlation between sawtimber-sized tree basal area and board foot volume is relatively high. Since basal area per acre for point sampling can be obtained without measuring trees (with the exception of borderline trees), it represents an efficient, low-cost method of obtaining information on basal area per acre. Use of these basal-area-per-acre values as auxiliary variables in double sampling leads to a very efficient sampling scheme. The procedure can be outlined as follows:

1. On a large number of points, count the in trees as for basal area determination, but do not measure trees unless required for determination of in or out. Call the number of trees counted at each point x_i.

2. On a subsample of the large number of points, measure all trees for volume determination in addition to the tree count. Calculate volume per acre on these points as usual for point sampling. Call this variable y_i. Typically, all trees will be measured for dbh and a subsample for height. A local or single-entry volume equation is then developed to avoid measuring all tree heights. Detailed discussion of local volume table construction is available in mensuration texts (such as Avery and Burkhart, 1994, Chapter 7).
3. The double sampling–point sampling equations provided below are used to estimate volume per acre and its standard error.

This sampling method has been available to foresters almost since point sampling has been available. It was described by Beers and Miller (1964), and estimators were described by Johnson (1961) and Palley and Horwitz (1961). The average volume per acre for this method can be obtained as

$$\bar{y}_{\text{dsps}} = \frac{\sum_{i=1}^{n} y_i}{\sum_{i=1}^{n} x_i} \times \frac{\sum_{i=1}^{n'} x_i}{n'} = \hat{R}\bar{x}' \tag{7.19}$$

where:

$\bar{y}_{\text{dsps}}$ = average volume per acre

y_i = volume per acre for point i worked up as usual for a point sample

x_i = number of trees "in" at point i

n = subsample points on which both tree counts and volume are determined

n' = the large number of points on which tree counts are obtained; includes the subsample of points on which volume and tree counts are obtained plus the additional points on which only tree counts are made

A ratio estimator is used because volume-basal area could reasonably be expected to go through the origin, and volume becomes more variable as basal area per acre increases. These are two assumptions made for ratio estimators to provide unbiased estimates. To calculate the standard error, first calculate S_y^2, the SRS variance, from the subsample points. Then calculate the variance of the ratio as

$$S_{\hat{R}}^2 = \frac{\sum_{i=1}^{n} y_i^2 - 2\hat{R}\sum_{i=1}^{n} x_i y_i + \hat{R}^2 \sum_{i=1}^{n} x_i^2}{n-1} \tag{7.20}$$

Note that the elements in this equation are either already calculated or are very easy to obtain. The first element, $\sum y_i^2$, is the same as the first element in the SRS formula. The last element, $\sum x_i^2$, is simply the number of trees on each point of the subsample squared and summed. $\hat{R}$ was calculated when the mean per acre was obtained, $\sum x_i y_i$ is the number of trees on each point multiplied by the volume per acre on that point and summed over all points. Finally, the estimate of the variance of the mean is

$$S^2_{\bar{y}_{\text{dsps}}} = \frac{S^2_y}{n'} + \frac{S^2_{\hat{R}}}{n}\left(\frac{n' - n}{n'}\right) \tag{7.21}$$

The standard error of the mean is $S_{\bar{y}_{\text{dsps}}} = \sqrt{S^2_{\bar{y}_{\text{dsps}}}}$. An example may help clarify some of the calculations.

EXAMPLE 7.8.1

Suppose a double-sample-point sample was conducted and the following data were collected:

Point	Number of Trees	Point	Number of Trees	Point	Number of Trees	Point	Number of trees
1	10	16	7	31	11	46	10
2	9	17	8	32	9	47	8
3	10	18	9	33	10	48	8
4	10	19	9	34	7	49	9
5	9	20	8	35	8	50	10
6	10	21	9	36	9	51	8
7	6	22	7	37	12	52	9
8	9	23	8	38	9	53	9
9	9	24	9	39	12	54	7
10	8	25	6	40	10	55	8
11	8	26	7	41	8	56	11
12	10	27	8	42	7	57	10
13	12	28	10	43	9	58	9
14	7	29	12	44	10	59	8
15	11	30	10	45	12	60	8
							540

On a subsample of 10 of the points, trees were also measured for dbh and height, and volumes per acre were calculated. The subset information is summarized as follows:

Point	x_i (Number of Trees)	y_i (Volume/Acre ft^3)
3	10	2,000
9	9	1,800
15	11	2,400
21	9	1,700
27	8	1,500
33	10	1,900
39	12	2,500

Point	x_i (Number of Trees)	y_i (Volume/Acre ft^3)
45	12	2,400
51	8	1,700
57	10	2,300
	99	20,200

Estimate the volume per acre in the stand and its standard error. The following sums and sums of squares are needed:

$$\sum_{i=1}^{60} x_i = 540 \qquad \sum_{i=1}^{10} x_i = 99 \qquad \sum_{i=1}^{10} x_i^2 = 999$$

$$\sum_{i=1}^{10} y_i = 20{,}200 \qquad \sum_{i=1}^{10} y_i^2 = 41{,}940{,}000$$

$$\sum_{i=1}^{10} x_i y_i = 204{,}300$$

Now estimate the volume per acre using Eq. 7.19. First

$$\bar{x}' = \frac{540}{60} = 9.0$$

$$\bar{x} = \frac{99}{10} = 9.9$$

$$\hat{R} = \frac{20{,}200}{99} = 204.04$$

Next

$$\bar{y}_{\text{dsps}} = \hat{R}\bar{x}' = 204.04\ (9) = 1836.36 \text{ ft}^3\text{/acre}$$

To calculate the standard error use Eq. 7.21. First calculate S_y^2 and then $S_{\hat{R}}^2$ using Eq. 7.20. Note that all of the values used in calculating the standard error are from the subsample with the exception of n'.

$$S_y^2 = \frac{\sum_{i=1}^{10} y_i^2 - \frac{\left(\sum_{i=1}^{10} y_i\right)^2}{n}}{n-1} = \frac{41{,}940{,}000 - \frac{(20{,}200)^2}{10}}{9} = 126{,}222.22$$

$$S_{\hat{R}}^2 = \frac{41{,}940{,}000 - (2)(204.04)(204{,}300) + (204.04)^2\ (999)}{9}$$

$$S_{\hat{R}}^2 = 17{,}771.70$$

With these variances calculated, the estimate of the variance of the mean can be obtained using Eq. 7.21:

$$S^2_{\bar{y}_{dsps}} = \frac{126{,}222.22}{60} + \frac{17{,}771.70}{10}\left(\frac{60-10}{60}\right)$$

$$S^2_{\bar{y}_{dsps}} = 3584.68\ (\text{ft}^3/\text{acre})^2$$

$$S_{\bar{y}_{dsps}} = 59.87\ \text{ft}^3/\text{acre}$$

The correlation between volume and basal area is so good that rarely will it be necessary to take measurements for volumes on more than 25% to 35% of the total points. From a practical perspective this means that if basal area is known, volume is very nearly known also. An examination of the equation for mean volume per acre reveals how the estimator works.

The numerator of $\hat{R}$ is $\sum y_i$, or the sum of all the volumes per acre on the subsample points. The denominator is the sum of all trees that contributed to the volume in the numerator. $\hat{R}$, then, is an estimate of the average volume per acre represented by one sample tree. In the terminology of Beers and Miller (1964), widely adopted in point sampling, it is the *average volume factor*. The right-hand side of the estimator, $\bar{x}'$, is simply the best estimate possible for the average number of trees per point. The product of average volume per acre per sample tree and average number of sample trees per point gives an estimate of volume per acre. It seems reasonable that if the correlation between volume and basal area is high, it takes very few points to define the relationship, $\hat{R}$. The majority of the time and resources of the inventory can be spent putting in many points on which trees are counted. The result is that sampling errors should be smaller than with typical line-point sampling, where the number of points is necessarily smaller because of cost or time constraints.

Most foresters tally trees by product so that pulpwood trees, chip-n-saw trees, and sawtimber trees are tallied separately. With double sampling, it is necessary to keep the tree classifications separately on count-only points also if separate estimates are needed. When sample trees are broken down into products, the variability from point to point for individual products is larger than what it would be if sample trees were tallied without regard to product. Further, the correlation coefficient between tree count and sawtimber volume is also typically lower than the correlation between tree count and total volume since more trees have obvious defects that affect their sawtimber merchantable volumes. The correlation coefficient is not generally low enough, however, to make double sampling less efficient than regular point sampling. Data from southeastern United States pine stands have correlation coefficients on the order of 0.75 to 0.90 between tree count and sawtimber volume even after defects are considered.

Double sampling modification of the typical point sampling estimator mandates a change in the stand table obtained on the volume points. A reasonable intuitive way to handle this problem is to change the basal area (and by necessity the trees per acre represented) and volume by the percentage that the basal area on the large sample and basal area on the small sample differ. Example 7.8.2 demonstrates this approach. A more elegant approach that leads to an unbiased stand table when regression, rather than ratio, double sampling estimators are used was presented by Matney and Parker (1991). Examples that we have worked indicate very slight differences of no practical significance between the two methods.

EXAMPLE 7.8.2

A double sample-point sample was conducted with a BAF = 10 factor prism in a spruce stand. There were 81 total points placed in the stand with 12 of those being points where both volume and tree counts were made and the remainder (69) being points on which only tree counts were made.

A total of 397 trees were counted on all 81 points, so

$$\bar{x}' = \frac{397}{81} = 4.9012 \text{ trees per point}$$

On the 12 points where volumes were calculated, 65 trees were counted, so

$$\bar{x} = \frac{65}{12} = 5.4167$$

The total of volumes on the 12 points was 119,380 bd ft. The point sample estimator would then be

$$\bar{y}_{ps} = \frac{\sum_{i=1}^{12} y_i}{n} = \frac{119{,}380}{12} = 9948.3 \text{ bd ft/acre}$$

The stand and stock table for the cruise using only the 12 points on which volume was measured was obtained with the tree tally and procedures from Chapter 4:

dbh	Basal Area per Acre (ft^2)	Trees per Acre	Volume/acre (bd ft)
10	0.83333	1.5278	59.6
12	4.16667	5.3052	446.7
14	3.33333	3.1181	504.8
16	6.66667	4.7746	1191.9
18	14.16667	8.0167	2745.5
20	11.66667	5.3476	2305.2
22	6.66667	2.5254	1393.6
24	3.33333	1.0610	641.7
26	3.33333	0.9041	659.5
	54.16667	32.5807	9948.5

The double sample-point sample estimate of volume per acre is

$$\bar{y}_{\text{dsps}} = \frac{119{,}380}{65} \times \frac{397}{81} = 9001.7 \text{ bd ft}$$

Compared with the point-sample-alone volume estimate, this is a decrease of 946.8 bd ft, or $(946.8/9948.5) \times 100 = 9.517\%$. This percentage decrease in volume is the exact same as the percent change in average tree count (from $65/12 = 5.4167$ to $397/81 = 4.9012$, a decrease of 9.517%). To obtain a compatible stand table, reduce volume and basal area (and trees per acre with basal area) for each dbh class by 9.517%. The new stand and stock table is as follows:

dbh	Basal Area per Acre (ft^2)	Trees per Acre	Volume/acre (bd ft)
10	0.7540	1.3825	53.9
12	3.7702	4.8003	404.2
14	3.0161	2.8214	406.8
16	6.0323	4.3203	1078.5
18	12.8186	7.2539	2484.3
20	10.5565	4.8387	2085.9
22	6.0323	2.2851	1261.0
24	3.0161	0.9601	580.6
26	3.0161	0.8181	595.7
	49.0123	29.4804	9000.9

The basal area for dbh class 10 was obtained by taking the basal area for dbh class 10 for the volume points only (0.83333) and reducing it by 9.517% to 0.7540. The trees per acre and volume per acre values were obtained in a similar manner.

The savings in time along with the reduced chance of large sampling error per unit of effort make the combination of double sampling and point sampling a sampling method that deserves much more consideration by foresters than it currently receives.

7.9 DOUBLE SAMPLING FOR STRATIFICATION

The increased precision available for the same sample size through the use of stratified sampling was documented in Chapter 5. Throughout the Chapter 5 discussion, the stratum sizes (N_h) were assumed to be known without error. For many forest properties the total acreage is known, but the acreages in different strata are unknown. Double sampling for stratification is a sampling design that allows for use of stratification and the corresponding benefits when the stratum sizes are unknown and must be estimated.

The first-phase sampling consists of a large sample with the purpose of determining an estimate of acreage in each stratum. As with other double sampling designs, let n' be the number of sampling units in the large first-phase sample. Although other methods of taking the first-phase sample are valid, an efficient method is to overlay a dot grid onto an aerial photograph of the property. The sample size, n', is then the total number of dots that fall on the property. The number of dots that fall into each stratum can be quickly counted and denoted n'_h. The proportion of the property in each stratum, p_h, can then be estimated as n'_h/n'. The N_h values can be estimated as Np_h.

EXAMPLE 7.9.1

A forest property of 80 acres contains three distinct stand types: plantation, natural pine, and hardwoods. Aerial photographs of the property are available. The forester charged with cruising the property places a dot grid over the aerial photograph and counts the number of dots in each stand type with the following results:

Stratum		
1	Plantation	325
2	Natural pine	550
3	Hardwoods	226
	Total	1101

The proportion of the total acreage in each type is then

$$p_1 = \frac{325}{1101} = 0.295 \qquad \hat{N}_1 = 80(0.295) = 23.6$$

$$p_2 = \frac{550}{1101} = 0.500 \qquad \hat{N}_1 = 80(0.500) = 40.0$$

$$p_3 = \frac{226}{1101} = 0.205 \qquad \hat{N}_3 = 80(0.205) = \underline{16.4}$$

$$\sum_{h=1}^{L} p_h = \sum_{h=1}^{3} p_h = 1.000 \qquad \text{Total:} \qquad 80.0 \text{ acres}$$

Once the proportion in each stratum is estimated, proportional allocation may be used to allocate the total number of sample plots or points needed on the ground to the different strata since variance information is not needed for proportional allocation. The number in each stratum is denoted n_h. Total sample size may be approximated by using the estimated stratum sizes, $\hat{N}_h$, in the equations from Chapter 5 for sample size with proportional allocation. Use of these equations, however, requires knowledge of stratum variances to calculate a sample size needed to obtain a desired bound on the error of estimation. Sampling units are measured in each stratum, and stratum means are estimated using the same estimators as for traditional stratified random sampling. This field work, which is identical to the field work for a stratified sample described in Chapter 5, is the second-phase sampling. The means are denoted $\bar{y}_h$. The overall mean is estimated as

$$\bar{y}_{\text{dss}} = \sum_{h=1}^{L} \frac{\hat{N}_h \bar{y}_h}{N} = \sum_{h=1}^{L} p_h \bar{y}_h$$

where:

$\bar{y}_{\text{dss}}$ = overall mean from double sampling for stratification

p_h = proportion of the total acreage in stratum h as estimated in the phase 1 sample

$\hat{N}_h$ = acreage in stratum h as estimated in the phase 1 sample

$\bar{y}_h$ = stratum mean for stratum h obtained from a simple random sample or systematic sample in stratum h

and all other variables are as previously defined.

An estimate for the total is then obtained by

$$\hat{T}_{\text{dss}} = N\bar{y}_{\text{dss}}$$

EXAMPLE 7.9.2

A total of 60 ⅒-acre plots were used to inventory the property described in Example 7.9.1. The plots were allocated to the three strata using proportional allocation. The number of plots and the resulting stratum means for the three strata are shown below:

Stratum	**Type**	n_h	$\bar{y}_h$ **(Cords)**
1	Plantation	$n_1 = 0.295\ (60) = 17.7 = 18$	3
2	Natural pine	$n_2 = 0.500\ (60) = 30.0 = 30$	7
3	Hardwood	$n_3 = 0.205\ (60) = 12.3 = \underline{12}$	5
		60	

To estimate the overall mean in cords on a ⅒-acre plot basis,

$$\bar{y}_{\text{dss}} = \sum_{h=1}^{3} p_h \bar{y}_h = 0.295(3) + 0.500(7) + 0.205(5)$$

$$\bar{y}_{\text{dss}} = 5.41 \text{ cords}$$

On a per-acre basis, $\bar{y}_A = 5.41\ (10) = 54.1$ cords. The total acreage in the property is 80 acres, so $N = 80\ (10) = 800$.

$$\hat{T}_{\text{dss}} = N\bar{y}_{\text{dss}} = 800\ (5.41) = 4328 \text{ cords}$$

Alternatively and equivalently,

$$\hat{T}_{\text{dss}} = 80\ (54.1) = 4328 \text{ cords}$$

Obtaining a standard error and a confidence interval is complicated by the fact that the stratum sizes are estimated rather than being known. There is therefore variability in their estimates in addition to the variability in the other random variables in the equations for variance in typical stratified sampling. Nevertheless, some foresters choose to ignore this variability and use the variance formulas for stratified sampling as if the estimated $\hat{N}_h$ values were N_h. In situations where $\hat{N}_h$ values were obtained from a large sample *(n')*, the difference will probably be small.

An equation to approximate the variance of the mean has been derived for double sampling with stratification (DeVries, 1986) given that both n' and N are large.

$$S^2_{\bar{y}_{\text{dss}}} = \sum_{h=1}^{L} \left(p_h^2 - \frac{p_h}{n'} \right) \frac{S_h^2}{n_h} + \frac{1}{n'} \left[\left(\sum_{h=1}^{L} p_h \bar{y}_h \right)^2 - (\bar{y}_{\text{dss}})^2 \right]$$

where:

$S^2_{\bar{y}_{\text{dss}}}$ = approximate variance of the mean for double sampling for stratification

S_h^2 = variance of y_i for stratum h

N = population size in units of second-phase sample

and all other variables are as previously defined.

The standard error of the mean is

$$S_{\bar{y}_{\text{dss}}} = \sqrt{S^2_{\bar{y}_{\text{dss}}}}$$

and the standard error of the total is

$$S_{\hat{T}_{\text{dss}}} = N S_{\bar{y}_{\text{dss}}}$$

A 95% confidence interval is approximated as

$$\bar{y}_{\text{dss}} \pm 2 S_{\bar{y}_{\text{dss}}}$$

Although the approximate variance formula looks somewhat formidable, it can be broken into parts and calculated, as demonstrated in Example 7.9.3.

EXAMPLE 7.9.3

A variance of the mean, standard error of the mean, standard error of the total, and confidence intervals for both the mean and total will be calculated for the data presented in Example 7.9.1 and continued in Example 7.9.2.

Information on the variances, S_h^2, for each stratum are needed for these calculations:

Stratum	**Type**	S_h^2
1	Plantation	10
2	Natural pine	120
3	Hardwoods	27

Note that the S_h^2 are variances, not variances of the mean. Construction of the following table will provide all elements necessary for calculation of the variance of the mean:

	Stratum			
	1	2	3	Total = $\sum_{h=1}^{L}$
n'_h	325	550	226	1101
$p_h = \frac{n'_h}{n'}$	0.295	0.500	0.205	1.000
$n_h = np_h$	18	30	12	60
$\bar{y}_h$	3	7	5	
S_h^2	10	120	27	
$p_h \bar{y}_h$	0.885	3.500	1.025	$\bar{y}_{\text{dss}} = 5.41$
$p_h \bar{y}_h^2$	2.655	24.500	5.125	32.280
$p_h^2 - \frac{p_h}{n'}$	0.0867571	0.2495459	0.0418388	

Now

$$S_{\bar{y}_{\text{dss}}}^2 = \left[0.0867571\left(\frac{10}{18}\right) + 0.2495459\left(\frac{120}{30}\right) + 0.0418388\left(\frac{27}{12}\right)\right] + \frac{1}{1101}(32.280 - 5.41^2)$$

$$= [0.0481984 + 0.9981835 + 0.0941373] + 0.0027356$$

$$= 1.14$$

$$S_{\bar{y}_{\text{dss}}} = 1.07$$

A confidence interval for the mean is then

$$\bar{y}_{\text{dss}} \pm 2(1.07)$$

$$5.41 \pm 2(1.07)$$

$$\text{UCL} = 7.55 \text{ cords/plot}$$

$$\text{LCL} = 3.27 \text{ cords/plot}$$

On a per-acre basis everything changes by a factor of 10 since plots are 1/10 acres:

$$\bar{y}_{dss} \pm 2(10.7)$$
$$54.1 \pm 2(10.7)$$
$$UCL = 75.5 \text{ cords}$$
$$LCL = 32.7 \text{ cords}$$

For the entire property:

$$\hat{T}_{dss} \pm 2S_{\hat{T}_{dss}}$$
$$S_{\hat{T}_{dss}} = NS_{\bar{y}_{dss}} = 800(1.07) = 856$$
$$\hat{T}_{dss} \pm 2(856)$$
$$4328 \pm 1712$$
$$UCL = 6040 \text{ cords}$$
$$LCL = 2616 \text{ cords}$$

With the increased precision of stratified sampling as compared with systematic sampling without stratification, more foresters should investigate the use of double sampling for stratification. This is even more important for large properties where stratification into distinct types that are easily visible on aerial photographs could result in much more precise estimates. It is important that n' be large enough to avoid serious errors in estimated stratum proportions. Misinterpretation in estimating stratum proportions is cause for concern, and DeVries (1986) has developed a correction procedure for this problem

REFERENCES

Avery, T. E., and H. E. Burkhart. 1994. *Forest measurements.* 4th ed. McGraw-Hill, New York.

Beers, T. W., and C. I. Miller. 1964. Point sampling: Research results, theory and applications. *Purdue University Agricultural Experiment Station Research Bulletin* 786.

Cochran, W. G. 1977. *Sampling techniques.* 3rd ed. Wiley, New York.

DeVries, P. G. 1986. *Sampling theory for forest inventory.* Springer-Verlag, New York.

Johnson, F. A. 1961. Standard error of estimated average timber volume per acre under point sampling when trees are measured for volume on a subsample of all points. *Pacific Northwest Forest and Range Experiment Station Res.* Note No. 201.

Loetsch, F., and K. E. Haller, 1964. Forest inventory: Volume I. *BLV Verlagsgesellschaft*, Münich.

Matney, T. G., and R. C. Parker. 1991. Stand and stock tables from double-point samples. *For. Sci.* 37(6):1605–1613.

Palley, M. N., and L. G. Horwitz. 1961. Properties of some random and systematic point sampling estimators. *For. Sci.* 7:52–65.

PROBLEMS FOR BETTER UNDERSTANDING

1. When a double sample (two-phase sample) is performed, two types of estimators can be used to estimate the population mean: the regression estimator and the ratio estimator. Discuss the differences between these two estimators and explain under what set of conditions each should be applied.
2. When a double sample is performed, the second-phase sample may be dependent on the first-phase sample, or it may be independent of the first-phase sample. Explain how variance estimation is affected for regression and ratio estimators for independent versus dependent second-phase samples.
3. The following information was obtained on 12 1⁄10-acre sample plots:

Plot	Volume Estimated by Eye (ft^3)	Volume Based on Measured Trees (ft^3)
1	230	245
2	180	186
3	190	189
4	220	235
5	250	268
6	190	200
7	240	270
8	180	195
9	160	175
10	210	215
11	220	242
12	170	182

   a. Calculate the slope for the regression of measured volume *(y)* on estimated volume *(x)*.

   b. Calculate the correlation coefficient between measured volume and estimated volume.

4. Refer to Problem 3. Suppose that a total (including the plots referred to in Problem 3) of 85 1⁄10-acre plots had their volume estimated by eye. The average estimated volume for these 85 1⁄10-acre plots was 218 ft^3.

   a. Obtain an estimate of average volume per plot using a double sample regression estimator.

   b. Calculate the variance of the estimate obtained in part a.

c. Suppose the tract from which this sample was taken is 120 acres. Estimate the total tract volume and obtain an approximate 95% confidence interval for the true tract volume.

5. Refer to Problem 3. Plot measured volume versus estimated volume. Do you believe a regression estimator is appropriate for this situation? Why or why not?

6. A 300-acre tract needed to be cruised in a short period of time. Recently, low-level aerial photos were taken of the tract in question. The forester in charge of the cruise decided to use a double sample for which the first-phase sample was 200 1/10-acre sample plots measured on the photos. For each of these photo plots, volume was determined using an aerial photo volume table. A subset of 20 photo plots was randomly chosen, located in the field, and measured for volume determination. The following information is available:

Let

x_i = cubic foot volume on plot i based on photo measurement

y_i = cubic foot volume on plot i based on field measurement

$$\sum_{i=1}^{200} x_i = 47{,}600 \qquad \sum_{i=1}^{200} x_i^2 = 12{,}859{,}324$$

Second-Phase Sample Information

Plot	x_i	y_i
1	210	201
2	235	221
3	180	175
4	225	226
5	230	220
6	240	229
7	230	215
8	225	232
9	205	209
10	245	260
11	240	220
12	190	187
13	170	168
14	215	208
15	225	216
16	240	230
17	250	259

Plot	x_i	y_i
18	245	231
19	215	210
20	220	223

$$\sum_{i=1}^{20} x_i = 4435 \qquad \sum_{i=1}^{20} y_i = 4340$$

$$\sum_{i=1}^{20} x_i^2 = 992{,}625 \qquad \sum_{i=1}^{20} y_i^2 = 951{,}798$$

$$\sum_{i=1}^{20} x_i y_i = 971{,}215$$

a. Use a ratio estimator to estimate the average volume per ⅒-acre plot.

b. Calculate the standard error of the estimate obtained in part a.

c. Plot measured volume (y_i) versus photo volume (x_i). Is a ratio estimator appropriate for these data? Why or why not?

d. Blow up the estimate in part a to the total tract basis and calculate an approximate 95% confidence interval for this estimate.

7. Refer to Problem 6. Suppose that it costs 10 times as much to put in a field measurement plot as a photo plot. What sample size will be required in each phase to estimate the mean volume per plot to within a bound of 3 ft^3 with approximately 95% confidence?

8. Suppose you were going to carry out a double sample in the following manner. On each ⅒-acre circular sample plot, dbh and total height will be estimated by eye for all trees falling on the sample plot. Questionable trees near the plot boundary will be guessed as in or out without measurement of the plot radius. A large number of these guessed plots will constitute the phase 1 sample. On a subset of the phase 1 sample plots, careful measurements will be taken for tree dbh and total height and distance from the plot center to trees near the plot edge will be measured carefully to determine whether the trees are in or out. This subset of plots on which both guessed values and measured values are obtained is the second-phase sample.

a. Discuss advantages that this sampling scheme should have over a sampling scheme for which only measured plots are obtained.

b. Discuss advantages that this sampling scheme should have over a sampling scheme for which only guessed plots are obtained.

c. Suppose there is a correlation of 0.92 between guessed plot volume and measured plot volume. What critical value for the ratio of costs must be exceeded for this double sampling scheme to be preferred over a traditional line-plot cruise?

9. Refer to Problem 8. The coefficient of variation for measured sample plots was 45%. How many sample plots will be required in each phase to estimate the total tract volume with an allowable error of 5% with approximately 95% confidence if it costs five times as much to install a measured plot as it does a guessed plot?

10. A sample of very homogeneous longleaf pine using only six points resulted in the following cubic foot volumes and tree counts:

Point	Number of Trees	Volume/Acre
1	10	3523
2	7	2546
3	6	2201
4	9	3458
5	9	3520
6	9	3404

a. What is the point sampling estimate of volume per acre?

b. What is the standard error of the per-acre estimate in part a?

In addition, tree counts were obtained on 10 additional points. Those counts are

7, 11, 10, 7, 8, 10, 8, 6, 10, 5

c. What is the double sampling estimate of volume per acre.

d. What is the standard error of the estimate in part c?

e. What critical value must $C_n/C_{n'}$ exceed for double sampling to be more efficient than regular point sampling?

11. A large sample ($n' = 200$) of photo plots from a total of 2000 resulted in a mean of the auxiliary variable of 25. A subsample of size 10 resulted in x's and y's as shown below.

Sample	x	y
1	22	2,340
2	26	2,500
3	28	2,660
4	25	2,450
5	24	2,450
6	18	2,100
7	27	2,600
8	27	2,700
9	24	2,350
10	22	2,100
	243	24,250

a. What is the double sampling estimate of the mean? Calculate its standard error.

b. What is the simple random sampling estimate of the mean? Calculate its standard error.

c. What are the relative efficiencies of the two sampling schemes?

d. What is the correlation coefficient?

e. If its costs 25 times as much to put in a ground plot as a photo plot, what correlation coefficient is necessary (minimum) to make double sampling worthwhile?

f. How many plots will be needed in each phase if the relative costs are 25:1 (ground:photo) to obtain a bound on the error of estimation of the mean of 40 with approximately 95% confidence?

12. A forester conducted a double sample-point sample in a 30 acre pine sawtimber stand in south central Arkansas using a BAF-10 prism. He installed a total of 30 points and measured trees for volume on every other point for a total of 15 volume points. On the remaining 15 points he counted the number of sawtimber sample trees. The data for the 15 volume points follows:

Point	Sawtimber Volume (bd ft)	Tree Count
1	4170	4
2	7962	6
3	10,812	7
4	6337	4
5	9307	5
6	1958	1
7	980	1
8	9322	5
9	3900	2
10	6465	3
11	9105	5
12	0	0
13	15,832	8
14	14,050	6
15	14,881	8

The total number of pine sawtimber sample trees counted on all 30 points was 164.

a. Estimate pine sawtimber volume per acre using only the 15 volume points and the traditional point sampling estimator.

b. Calculate the standard error for the estimate in part a.

c. Plot sawtimber volume versus basal area per acre for the 15 volume points.

d. Estimate pine sawtimber volume per acre using all 30 points with the double sampling-point sampling estimator.

e. Calculate the standard error for the estimate in part d.

f. Compare the estimates and standard errors from the two estimators used in parts a and d.

g. Calculate the correlation coefficient between sawtimber volume and tree count.

h. What critical value for the ratio of costs must be exceeded for double sampling to be preferred over simple random sampling?

CHAPTER 8

MULTISTAGE SAMPLING—INVENTORYING LARGE ACREAGES

To this point in the text the timber inventory problem has been approached on a stand-by-stand basis. To obtain estimates of standing volume, dollar value, and so on at the forest level (note that a forest can be composed of any number of individual stands), each stand can be inventoried and resulting estimates summed. It is even possible to obtain an estimate of variability at the forest level by summing the variance estimates for each stand (as with stratified sampling).

In some situations estimates of standing volume, dollar value of standing timber, and so on may be required for a forest and it may not be possible to perform an inventory for each stand. This may be due to monetary constraints, time constraints, or other factors. For example, suppose a 20,000-acre ownership of forest land is up for sale. Further, suppose that a bid that you or your client wishes to submit is due no later than 45 days from the day you find out about the sale. There are several alternatives to consider in order to assign a value to the timber on this ownership. A cruise of every stand could be carried out, but to meet the time constraint many subcontractors would have to be hired at great expense. Each stand could be cruised with a very-low-intensity cruise to minimize expenses, but the resulting estimate would probably be very imprecise. The seller's estimates of standing timber value could be used, but for obvious reasons this may be a risky choice.

The alternatives just presented are actually all less than ideal in this situation. A more reasonable approach to the problem is to use a sampling strategy known as two-stage sampling. Two-stage sampling is carried out by choosing a subset of stands from the total number of stands in the forest and then performing a cruise in each one of the chosen stands. Clearly, this will reduce the time and cost of obtaining the estimate of standing timber volume or value. However, it should be clear that since only a subset of stands are cruised, the final estimate may be more variable than if an adequate cruise was performed in every stand.

8.1 TWO-STAGE SAMPLING

Two-stage sampling is a sampling procedure in which the population is first broken down into units called primary units. Each primary unit is then broken down into secondary units. In the example just mentioned, individual stands are primary units and plots within each stand are secondary units. Sampling proceeds in two stages. First a set of primary units is chosen, and then within each chosen primary a set of secondary units is chosen and measured. Appropriate formulas are used to obtain estimates for the entire population.

It may not be intuitive that a good estimate of an entire forest composed of many stands can be obtained by carrying out a cruise in a subset of the stands. However, this is no less reasonable than assigning a volume or dollar value to a 150-acre stand based on a sample of 150 $\frac{1}{10}$-acre plots chosen from the stand. In both cases the sample data provide for the best estimate of the population of interest.

The problem that is intuitively feared in two-stage sampling is that the stands (primaries) chosen at the first-stage sampling may not be representative of all stands in the forest. Of course, this is possible. This is sampling error (that is, the sample is not representative of the population). However, sampling error is also present in a cruise on a single stand. This problem cannot be avoided, but it can be minimized. One way to reduce sampling error is to run cruise lines perpendicular to elevation contours in the stand. This helps ensure that sample plots are located in all different types within the stand. In two-stage sampling, steps can also be taken to minimize sampling error. For instance, if the age structure or species type of each stand is available, the population can be broken down into appropriate subpopulations (strata), and then a two-stage sample can be done for each subpopulation. The point is that two-stage sampling as just described can provide good estimates of timber inventories for large acreages when it is not possible to cruise every stand. Furthermore, two-stage sampling should be preferred to running a very-low-intensity sample in all stands. That is, good information on a representative set of stands from the forest seems more reasonable than having poor information on all stands in the forest.

Two-stage sampling is actually a special case of the more general sampling scheme known as multistage sampling. In general there can be any number of stages in a multistage sample. In three-stage sampling the population is first divided into primary units. Each primary is divided into secondary units and, in turn, each secondary unit is divided into tertiary units. Four-stage sampling is the next step; it has primaries, secondaries within primaries, tertiaries within secondaries, and quaternaries within tertiaries. Of course, this could go on and on. There are not many situations in which sampling in three or more stages has been applied in forest inventories. However, here is a situation in which three-stage sampling may be applied. A large forestland ownership needs to be inventoried in a short amount of time. Low-resolution aerial photos are available for the entire ownership. Aerial photos are defined as primary sampling units. Within each photo, stands are defined as secondary sampling units. Finally, fixed-area plots within each stand are defined as tertiary sampling units.

It is important to keep in mind that multistage sampling applied in situations similar to those just described cannot provide as precise an estimate as inventories in which each stand is cruised with an adequate intensity. The objective of the multistage sample just described is to provide an estimate for the population in a timely manner so that budget constraints are not exceeded. Of course, there are applications for multistage sampling other than sampling large forest ownerships. For example, to estimate the proportion of trees in a stand that contains one or more grade 1 sawlogs, the following sampling scheme could be used. Primary units are defined to be ⅕-acre fixed-area sample plots. Individual trees within each plot are secondaries. Within each sample plot the trees are counted, and then a predefined number of trees are sampled and the number of grade 1 sawlogs is determined for each.

8.2 SINGLE-STAGE CLUSTER SAMPLING

To understand sampling in two or more stages, it is useful first to study and understand a special case of two-stage sampling known as single-stage cluster sampling.

Single-stage cluster sampling is also referred to as *cluster sampling*. In cluster sampling each sampling unit is composed of a group or cluster of elements. In two-stage sampling, when a primary sampling unit is selected, a subset of elements, referred to as secondary sampling units, is selected and measured for the characteristic of interest. In cluster sampling, once a primary is selected, all elements (that is, secondary sampling units) within the primary are measured for the characteristic of interest.

The reader may recognize that this is exactly what is done when stands are cruised with fixed-area plots. Primaries (that is, a plot) are chosen, and then every secondary (that is, individual tree) within each primary is measured. When estimating characteristics defined on a unit-area basis (such as volume/acre or basal area/acre), the sample is not treated as a cluster sample since unit-area measures have no meaning for an individual tree. However, when estimating an individual tree characteristic (such as average tree dbh, average tree height, or proportion of trees with a disease), the sample should be treated as a cluster sample since the individual tree is the sampling unit, and the trees are selected in clusters.

The estimator of a population mean for all elements in the population, μ, based on a cluster sample, is

$$\bar{y}_{\text{CE}} = \frac{\sum_{i=1}^{n} y_i}{\sum_{i=1}^{n} m_i} \tag{8.1}$$

where:

m_i = number of elements in cluster i

$y_i = \sum_{j=1}^{m_i} y_{ij}$, total of all observations in cluster i

y_{ij} = value of the jth element in cluster i

n = number of clusters in the sample

The numerator of Eq. 8.1 is the total of all elements measured in all clusters in the sample, and the denominator is the total number of elements in the sample. Thus $\bar{y}_{\mathrm{CE}}$ is the sample average per element. In order to estimate the population total using $\bar{y}_{\mathrm{CE}}$, the total number of elements in the population must be known. In forestry situations the total number of elements will rarely be known. The estimator for a population total that proves useful in forest inventory situations is

$$\hat{T}_C = N\bar{y}_{\mathrm{CN}} \tag{8.2}$$

where:

$$\bar{y}_{\mathrm{CN}} = \frac{1}{n}\sum_{i=1}^{n} y_i \tag{8.3}$$

N = number of clusters in the population

Note that $\bar{y}_{\mathrm{CN}}$ is the mean of the cluster totals. Thus in Eq. 8.2 the mean cluster total is multiplied by the number of clusters in the population (N) to obtain an estimate of the population total. This estimator of the population total is the same as the simple random sampling (systematic sampling) estimator presented in Chapter 3. Cluster sampling, as described above, is equivalent to drawing fixed-area plots from the population and determining the plot total (cluster total) for each. Consequently, when fixed-area plot sampling is used to estimate a population total, estimators presented in Chapter 3 are used since they are equivalent to a cluster sampling estimator (Eq. 8.2).

The variance of $\bar{y}_{\mathrm{CE}}$, the mean per element, is

$$S^2_{\bar{y}_{\mathrm{CE}}} = \frac{1}{\overline{M}^2}\frac{S_E^2}{n}\left(\frac{N-n}{N}\right) \tag{8.4}$$

where:

$\overline{M} = \frac{M}{N}$ = average cluster size for the population

M = number of elements in the population

N = number of clusters in the population

$$S_E^2 = \frac{\sum_{i=1}^{n} y_i^2 - 2\bar{y}_{\mathrm{CE}}\sum_{i=1}^{n} y_i m_i + \bar{y}_{\mathrm{CE}}^2\sum_{i=1}^{n} m_i^2}{n-1} \tag{8.5}$$

n = number of clusters in the sample

and all other variables are as defined earlier.

Note that $\overline{M}$ will usually not be known and will be estimated by the average cluster size for the sample:

$$\overline{m} = \frac{\sum_{i=1}^{n} m_i}{n}$$

The variance for the cluster estimate of a population total (Eq. 8.2) is not presented here since it is identical to the variance of the total for a simple random sample (as presented in Chapter 3).

EXAMPLE 8.2.1

The average height of dominant and codominant trees in a 24-acre plantation is to be estimated. A line-plot cruise using 25 1/10-acre sample plots was carried out. On each plot all dominant and codominant trees were measured for total height. Since the characteristic of interest is an individual tree characteristic, the sample is treated as a cluster sample. Each plot is a cluster made up of a number of trees, which are elements. The data are as follows:

Plot	Dominant and Codominant Heights (ft)
1	67, 68, 74, 66
2	66, 65, 67
3	64, 65, 63, 65
4	67, 69, 70, 75, 71
5	61, 63, 62, 63, 64
6	64, 65
7	66, 68, 69
8	71, 72, 73, 75
9	71, 75
10	66, 66, 63
11	60, 62, 63
12	66, 65
13	64, 66
14	75
15	63, 64, 65
16	67, 67, 69

Plot	Dominant and Codominant Heights (ft)
17	69, 75, 71
18	66, 78, 71
19	63, 65, 64
20	62, 63
21	63, 64
22	76
23	71, 72, 73, 72, 71
24	67, 68, 67
25	67, 69, 68

Estimate the average height of the dominant and codominant trees, with y_i and m_i defined as follows:

y_i = total of all observations in plot i (cluster i)

m_i = number of dominant and codominant trees (elements) on plot i

Thus, for plot 1,

$$y_1 = 67 + 68 + 74 + 66 = 275$$
$$m_1 = 4$$

For plot 2,

$$y_2 = 66 + 65 + 67 = 198$$
$$m_2 = 3$$

The y_i and m_i values for each plot are as follows:

Plot	y_i	m_i
1	275	4
2	198	3
3	257	4
4	352	5
5	313	5
6	129	2
7	203	3
8	291	4
9	146	2
10	195	3

Plot	y_i	m_i
11	185	3
12	131	2
13	130	2
14	75	1
15	192	3
16	203	3
17	215	3
18	215	3
19	192	3
20	125	2
21	127	2
22	76	1
23	359	5
24	202	3
25	204	3

Next obtain the following sums:

$$\sum_{i=1}^{25} y_i = 4990 \qquad \sum_{i=1}^{25} m_i = 74$$

$$\sum_{i=1}^{25} y_i^2 = 1{,}134{,}752 \qquad \sum_{i=1}^{25} m_i^2 = 248$$

$$\sum_{i=1}^{25} y_i m_i = 16{,}751$$

The mean height of dominant and codominant trees is now estimated using Eq. 8.1:

$$\bar{y}_{\text{CE}} = \frac{4990}{74} = 67.432 \text{ ft}$$

The variance of this estimate is obtained using Eq. 8.4. Note that $\overline{M}$, the average cluster size in the population (in our application, this would be the average number of trees per 1/10 acre across the stand), is unknown, so it is estimated as

$$\overline{m} = \frac{\sum_{i=1}^{n} m_i}{n}$$

which is the average number of trees per 1⁄10 acre based on our sample of 25 1⁄10-acre plots (clusters). Thus

$$\overline{m} = \frac{74}{25} = 2.96$$

The stand is 24 acres, so

$$N = 10 \times 24 = 240$$

That is, there are theoretically 240 1⁄10-acre plots in the stand. Next, S_E^2, which is given by Eq. 8.5, is calculated

$$S_E^2 = \frac{1{,}134{,}752 - 2(67.432)\,(16{,}751) + (67.432)^2\,(248)}{25 - 1}$$

$$= 138.3184583$$

Finally, use Eq. 8.4 to get the variance of $\overline{y}_{\mathrm{CE}}$ (remember, use $\overline{m}$ in place of $\overline{M}$):

$$S^2_{\overline{y}_{\mathrm{CE}}} = \frac{1}{(2.96)^2} \, \frac{138.3184583}{25} \left(\frac{240 - 25}{240} \right)$$

$$= 0.565697\ (\mathrm{ft})^2$$

The standard error of the mean is

$$S_{\overline{y}_{\mathrm{CE}}} = \sqrt{S^2_{\overline{y}_{\mathrm{CE}}}} = 0.752128$$

An approximate 95% confidence interval for the mean height of dominant and codominant trees is

$$67.4 \pm 2(0.752128)$$

$$67.4 \pm 1.5$$

$$\mathrm{LCL} = 65.9 \text{ ft}$$

$$\mathrm{UCL} = 68.9 \text{ ft}$$

It should be clear how to utilize cluster sampling formulas to obtain valid estimates of a mean value per tree and its associated variance. Another parameter that can be estimated using cluster sampling is a population proportion.

To estimate a population proportion, such as the proportion of trees in a stand with grade 1 sawlogs, using cluster sampling, note the total number of trees on a plot, m_i, and the number of these trees with the desired characteristic, say, C_i. Then the sample estimate of the population proportion is

$$\hat{P}_C = \frac{\sum_{i=1}^{n} C_i}{\sum_{i=1}^{n} m_i} \tag{8.6}$$

The variance of this estimate is

$$S^2_{\hat{P}_C} = \frac{1}{\overline{M}^2} \frac{S^2_C}{n} \left(\frac{N-n}{N} \right) \tag{8.7}$$

where:

$$S^2_C = \frac{\sum_{i=1}^{n} C_i^2 + \hat{P}_C^2 \sum_{i=1}^{n} m_i^2 - 2\hat{P}_C \sum_{i=1}^{n} m_i C_i}{n-1}$$

$\overline{M}$ = average number of elements (trees) per cluster (plot) in the population

N = number of clusters (plots) in the population

n = number of clusters (plots) in the sample

C_i = number of elements (trees) in cluster (plot) i with the characteristic of interest

m_i = total number of elements (trees) in cluster (plot) i

Close inspection of Eqs. 8.6 and 8.7 will reveal that they are identical to the estimators given in Chapter 6 for estimating a population proportion using a ratio estimator. The only difference is the variable names. When the x_i and y_i variables from Chapter 6 are defined to be the total number of trees on a plot (cluster) and the number of trees on a plot (cluster) with the desired characteristic, respectively, the algebraic equivalence is clear. Thus the estimator provided in Chapter 6 for this situation can be referred to as a cluster sample estimator, or this cluster sampling estimator can be referred to as a ratio estimator.

Clearly, cluster sampling is useful and has many applications in forest inventory. Its use is appropriate whenever individual trees are measured on fixed-area sample plots. However, when the characteristic being estimated is defined on a unit-area basis (such as volume/acre), cluster sample estimators are equivalent to simple random sample estimators. Furthermore, when the characteristic of interest is a proportion, cluster sample estimators are equivalent to the ratio estimator discussed in Chapter 6. When the characteristic of interest is an individual tree characteristic (such as average tree diameter or average tree height), the cluster sample estimator $\bar{y}_{CE}$ and its associated variance should be used.

Cluster sampling is most efficient when individual clusters are defined so that the variability within the cluster is high and variability among different clusters is relatively low. This is the opposite of a good definition of strata for a stratified sample. In forest inventory situations fixed-area sample plots may or may not meet this requirement.

8.3 TWO-STAGE CLUSTER SAMPLING

Two-stage cluster sampling is often referred to simply as *two-stage sampling*. Two-stage sampling is a modification of single-stage cluster sampling. Clusters of elements are chosen as before, but only a subsample of elements in each cluster is measured. The idea is to assign a value to each cluster by measuring only a portion of the elements in the cluster. Two-stage sampling is sometimes called subsampling for obvious reasons. If the subsample of elements from each cluster is representative of the entire cluster and the clusters are representative of the population, then clearly the estimates obtained should be representative of the population. Thus two-stage sampling reduces the number of measurements in a given cluster and allows for more clusters to be measured; in certain situations, it makes sampling feasible by reducing the amount of work to a manageable level.

To generalize the discussion of two-stage sampling, new terminology will be used. Sampling units chosen at the first stage will be known as primary sampling units. In single-stage cluster sampling, primary sampling units are called clusters. Within each primary sampling unit there is a number of secondary sampling units from which a subset is chosen to be in the sample at the second stage. In single-stage cluster sampling the secondary sampling units are the elements. In the context of inventorying a stand of trees using fixed-area plot sampling, primary sampling units are the plots and secondary sampling units are individual trees within plots. The main difference between single-stage cluster sampling and two-stage sampling is that in single-stage cluster sampling all secondary sampling units are measured in each selected primary sampling unit, whereas in two-stage sampling a subset of secondary sampling units is measured in each selected primary sampling unit.

There are many potential applications for two-stage sampling in forest inventory work. For example, an individual tree characteristic, such as average height, can be estimated by randomly or systematically locating fixed-area sample plots (primary sampling units) throughout a stand and then randomly or systematically selecting and measuring individual trees (secondary sampling units) within each selected plot.

Another application of two-stage sampling is in estimating biomass (weight) of various components of trees (bole, branches, leaves, and so on). The primary sampling unit will be the individual tree. Secondary sampling units will then be individual branches originating along the main bole of an individual tree selected in the first stage. The characteristic measured might be the total bole weight, total branch weight, or total leaf weight. Total bole weight can be obtained directly by weighing the bole as a whole or in pieces. Total tree branch weight and leaf weight will be obtained by first estimating the averages of these characteristics for branches selected at the second stage and then expanding to the entire tree using the total number of branches along the main bole as an expansion factor.

The most common application of two-stage sampling in forest inventory is obtaining estimates of timber characteristics for large timberland holdings (forests) composed of many stands. As discussed in the introduction of this chapter, the main reason for this application is the need to obtain a reliable estimate of the characteristic of interest (such as volume or dollar value) in a relatively short time frame or with minimal expense. The population of interest is the entire forest, which is made up of many individual stands. Primary sampling units are defined as individual stands. Secondary sampling units are defined as fixed-area plots, or points, within stands selected at the first stage. Individual stands are selected at the first stage randomly, systematically, or with probability proportional to the size of the stand (size can be measured in area, standing volume, dollar value, and the like). Once a stand is selected at the first stage, plots (or points) within stands are usually selected in a systematic fashion (that is, a line-plot cruise). Different estimators of population parameters are required for primaries selected at random (or systematically) and for primaries selected with probability proportional to size. Both cases will be presented and discussed separately.

8.4 TWO-STAGE SAMPLING—PRIMARIES SELECTED AT RANDOM

When primary sampling units are selected at random and secondaries within a primary are selected at random (systematically) the following estimator can be used to estimate the mean value per secondary in the *i*th primary:

$$\bar{y}_{2SR_i} = \frac{1}{m_i} \sum_{j=1}^{m_i} y_{ij} \tag{8.8}$$

where:

y_{ij} = the value of the *j*th secondary in the *i*th primary

m_i = the number of secondaries measured in the *i*th primary

Note that the subscript 2SR indicates that these estimators are for two-stage sampling with primaries selected at random (or systematically).

The total value for the *i*th primary is estimated as

$$\hat{T}_{2SR_i} = M_i \bar{y}_{2SR_i} \tag{8.9}$$

where:

M_i = total number of secondary sampling units in the *i*th primary

and all other variables are as defined earlier.

The mean value for the n primaries selected at the first stage is

$$\bar{y}_{2SR} = \frac{\sum_{i=1}^{n} \hat{T}_{2SR_i}}{n} \tag{8.10}$$

where:

n = number of primary sampling units selected at the first stage

and all other variables are as defined earlier.

The estimated total for the entire population based on a two-stage sample of n primaries selected at random is

$$\hat{T}_{2SR} = N\bar{y}_{2SR} \tag{8.11}$$

where:

N = number of primaries in the entire population

and all other variables are as defined earlier.

When stands are defined as primary sampling units and plots within stands are secondary sampling units, Eqs. 8.8 through 8.11 estimate the following values: Equation 8.8 gives the average of the sample plots measured in stand i; Eq. 8.9 provides a measure of the total of stand i for the characteristic being measured; and Eq. 8.10 gives the average total stand characteristic for the entire population based on the sample of n stands. Finally, it should be clear that Eq. 8.11 provides an estimate of the total for the entire population by multiplying the average total per primary ($\bar{y}_{2SR}$) by the number of primaries in the population (N).

The variance of $\hat{T}_{2SR}$ is

$$S^2_{\hat{T}_{2SR}} = \frac{N^2}{n} S^2_B + \frac{N}{n} S^2_W \tag{8.12}$$

where:

N = number of primaries in the population

n = number of primaries in the sample

$$S^2_B = \left(\frac{N-n}{N}\right) S^2_{BT} \tag{8.13}$$

S^2_{BT} = variation between primaries

$$S^2_{BT} = \frac{\sum_{i=1}^{n} \hat{T}^2_{2SR_i} - \frac{\left(\sum_{i=1}^{n} \hat{T}_{2SR_i}\right)^2}{n}}{n-1} \tag{8.14}$$

$$S_W^2 = \sum_{i=1}^{n} \frac{S_{W_i}^2}{m_i} M_i^2 \left(\frac{M_i - m_i}{M_i}\right) \tag{8.15}$$

m_i = number of secondaries selected and measured in the ith primary

M_i = total number of secondaries in the ith primary

S_{Wi}^2 = variation within the ith primary

$$S_{W_i}^2 = \frac{\sum_{j=1}^{m_i} y_{ij}^2 - \frac{\left(\sum_{j=1}^{m_i} y_{ij}\right)^2}{m_i}}{m_i - 1} \tag{8.16}$$

y_{ij} = value of the jth secondary in the ith primary

Note that the structure of the variance for $S_{\hat{T}_{2SR}}^2$ is different from that for sampling schemes previously discussed. It has two components that are added together. The first component is a between-primary component (S_B^2) and the second is a within-primary component (S_W^2). The within-primary component was used to calculate variances for estimators in single-stage sampling schemes discussed in previous chapters. In fact, for a given primary $S_{W_i}^2$ is calculated exactly the same as S_y^2 values discussed in Chapters 2, 3, 4, and 5. The between-primary component is a component of variation not previously discussed. It comes into play because only a subset of primaries is sampled. It is interesting to note that stratified random (systematic) sampling is a special case of two-stage sampling in which all primaries (strata) are sampled. Since all primaries (strata) are measured in stratified sampling, there is no between-primary (stratum) component of variation in stratified sampling variance formulas.

Two-stage sampling formulas are large and can be intimidating. However, estimates are easily calculated, and if variance calculations are approached in an organized, step-by-step procedure, they are also easy to deal with.

EXAMPLE 8.4.1

An estimate of merchantable standing volume of all pine sawtimber in a 7500-acre forest is needed. The forester in charge of the inventory decides to use two-stage sampling since she does not have enough time or resources to inventory every stand on the forest. She decides to randomly select 12 stands from the total of 110 stands in the forest. In each of the 12 stands, she carries out an approximate 10% line-plot cruise using 1/10-acre circular sample plots. On each plot, total cubic feet of merchantable pine timber is determined. The following information is available for each of the 12 stands that were cruised:

Stand	Acres	M_i	m_i	$\bar{y}_{2SR_i}$ (ft^3/plot)	$S^2_{W_i}$
1	45	450	45	178	12,300
2	110	1100	110	192	13,400
3	150	1500	150	129	14,250
4	32	320	32	225	16,700
5	25	250	25	217	15,400
6	50	500	50	171	13,500
7	95	950	95	253	18,100
8	125	1250	125	189	14,760
9	115	1150	115	163	13,250
10	175	1750	175	179	12,159
11	20	200	20	275	14,259
12	15	150	15	295	13,790

Note that M_i is the total number of 1⁄10-acre plots in stand *i*. Thus, for stand 1,

$$M_1 = 45 \text{ acres} \times 10 \text{ plots/acre} = 450 \text{ plots}$$

Further, m_i is the number of plots that are measured for cubic-foot volume in each stand. A 10% cruise was carried out in each stand, so m_i is simply 10% of M_i. For stand 2,

$$m_2 = 1100 \times 0.1 = 110 \text{ plots}$$

The mean cubic-foot volume per plot for each stand in the cruise is given in the $\bar{y}_{2SR_i}$ column, and the variation among plots within a stand is given in the $S^2_{W_i}$ column. Note that for a given stand, $S^2_{W_i}$ corresponds to the S^2_y values presented and discussed in Chapters 2, 3, 4, and 5 and thus are calculated exactly as shown in those chapters.

To obtain an estimate of the total cubic-foot volume for the entire forest, first calculate the estimates of total volume in each of the stands that were measured, $\hat{T}_{2SR_i}$, using Eq. 8.9. This equation indicates that the total number of sample plots in the stand, M_i, should be multiplied by the average volume per sample plot, $\bar{y}_{2SR_i}$, to obtain $\hat{T}_{2SR_i}$. If this calculation is carried out correctly for each stand, the following values are obtained:

Stand	$\hat{T}_{2SR_i}$ (ft^3)
1	80,100
2	211,200
3	193,500
4	72,000
5	54,250
6	85,500
7	240,350

Stand	$\hat{T}_{2SR_i}$ (ft³)
8	236,250
9	187,450
10	313,250
11	55,000
12	44,250

$$\sum_{i=1}^{12} \hat{T}_{2SR_i} = 1{,}773{,}100$$

Next, using Eq. 8.10, obtain the average total volume per stand based on the sample of 12 stands:

$$\bar{y}_{2SR} = \frac{\sum_{i=1}^{n} \hat{T}_{2SR_i}}{n} = \frac{1{,}773{,}100}{12}$$

$$\bar{y}_{2SR} = 147{,}758.3\overline{3} \text{ ft}^3/\text{stand}$$

Finally, the estimate of the total cubic-foot volume for the entire 7500-acre forest is obtained using Eq. 8.11:

$$\begin{aligned}\hat{T}_{2SR} &= N\bar{y}_{2SR} = 110 \text{ stands } (147{,}758.3\overline{3} \text{ ft}^3/\text{stand}) \\ &= 16{,}253{,}417 \text{ ft}^3\end{aligned}$$

The variance for this estimate is calculated using Eq. 8.12. To make the calculations easier, the equation should be broken into various pieces. First calculate S_B^2 using Eq. 8.13. S_{BT}^2 is calculated using Eq. 8.14:

$$S_{BT}^2 = \frac{\sum_{i=1}^{n} \hat{T}_{2SR_i}^2 - \frac{\left(\sum_{i=1}^{n} \hat{T}_{2SR_i}\right)^2}{n}}{n-1}$$

Using the $\hat{T}_{2SR_i}$ values just calculated,

$$\sum_{i=1}^{12} \hat{T}_{2SR_i} = 1{,}773{,}100 \qquad \sum_{i=1}^{12} \hat{T}_{2SR_i}^2 = 3.557293 \times 10^{11}$$

Thus

$$S_{BT}^2 = \frac{(3.557293 \times 10^{11}) - \frac{(1,773,100)^2}{12}}{12 - 1}$$
$$= 8,521,727,200$$

Then

$$S_B^2 = \left(\frac{N-n}{N}\right) S_{BT}^2 = \left(\frac{110 - 12}{110}\right)(8,521,723,200)$$
$$= 7,592,084,233$$

Now calculate the first half of Eq. 8.12:

$$\frac{N^2}{n} S_B^2 = \frac{(110)^2}{12}(7,592,084,233)$$
$$= 7.655351 \times 10^{12}$$

Next calculate the second part of the variance formula inside the summation sign:

$$\sum_{i=1}^{n} \left[\frac{S_{W_i}^2}{m_i} M_i^2 \left(\frac{M_i - m_i}{M_i}\right)\right]$$

Since 12 stands were included in the first-stage sample, the quantity in square brackets must be calculated 12 times (once for each stand) and then the resulting 12 numbers must be added together. To organize the calculations, use the following table and fill in each column starting from left to right:

Stand	M_i	m_i	$S_{W_i}{}^2$	$\frac{M_i - m_i}{M_i}$	$\frac{S_{W_i}^2}{m_i}$	$M_i^2\left(\frac{M_i - m_i}{M_i}\right)$
1	450	45	12,300	0.9	$273.3\overline{3}$	182,250
2	1100	110	13,400	0.9	$121.\overline{81}$	1,089,000
3	1500	150	14,250	0.9	95.00	2,025,000
4	320	32	16,700	0.9	521.88	92,160
5	250	25	15,400	0.9	616.00	56,250
6	500	50	13,500	0.9	270.00	225,000
7	950	95	18,100	0.9	190.53	812,250
8	1250	125	14,760	0.9	118.08	1,406,250
9	1150	115	13,250	0.9	115.22	1,190,250
10	1750	175	12,159	0.9	69.48	2,756,250
11	200	20	14,259	0.9	712.95	36,000
12	150	15	13,790	0.9	$919.3\overline{3}$	20,250

Now take the two rightmost columns and multiply the numbers for each stand together to obtain the following:

Stand	$\frac{S^2_{W_i}}{m_i} M_i^2 \left(\frac{M_i - m_i}{M_i}\right)$
1	49,814,969.9
2	132,660,000.0
3	192,375,000.0
4	48,096,460.8
5	34,650,000.0
6	60,750,000.0
7	154,757,992.5
8	166,050,000.0
9	137,140,605.0
10	191,504,250.0
11	25,666,200.0
12	18,616,500.0

$$\sum_{i=1}^{12} = 1{,}212{,}082{,}008$$

Now obtain the variance by putting all the components of Eq. 8.12 together:

$$\begin{aligned} S^2_{\hat{T}_{2SR}} &= 7.655351 \times 10^{12} + \frac{100}{12}(1{,}212{,}082{,}008) \\ &= 7.655351 \times 10^{12} + 1.111075 \times 10^{10} \\ &= 7.666461 \times 10^{12} (\text{ft}^3)^2 \end{aligned}$$

As with all other estimates, the square root of the variance of the estimate is the standard error of the estimate. Thus

$$S_{\hat{T}_{2SR}} = \sqrt{S^2_{\hat{T}_{2SR}}} = 2{,}768{,}838 \text{ ft}^3$$

$$16{,}253{,}417 \pm 2(2{,}768{,}838)$$

$$16{,}253{,}417 \pm 5{,}537{,}676$$

$$\text{LCL} = 10{,}715{,}741 \text{ ft}^3$$

$$\text{UCL} = 21{,}791{,}093 \text{ ft}^3$$

This is a fairly wide interval, but it must be kept in mind that only 12 of 110 stands were sampled.

One way to obtain a more precise estimate of the total volume than that obtained in the preceding example is to cruise more stands (that is, choose more primary sampling units). Of course, this will cost more money and will take more time. Another way to obtain a more precise estimate is to use a ratio estimator for the total volume. A great deal of variation exists in the preceding estimate solely because of variability in stand size. For example, the total volume estimate for the 45-acre stand 1 is 80,100 ft^3, and the total volume for the 125-acre stand 8 is 236,250 ft^3. This large variation is reflected in the large between-stand component of variation given by Eq. 8.13 and calculated in Example 8.4.1. In fact, in the previous example the between-stand variation made up over 99.8% of the total variation of the final estimate. This variation can be reduced significantly by using a ratio estimator that takes into account the variable sizes of the stands (primary sampling units) in the sample. The concept is similar to using a ratio estimator to allow for variable-sized strips in a strip cruise (see Example 6.2.5).

8.5 TWO-STAGE SAMPLING RATIO ESTIMATORS FOR POPULATION MEANS AND TOTALS

A ratio estimator for a population mean per secondary sampling unit based on a two-stage sample is

$$\bar{y}_{R2SR} = \frac{\sum_{i=1}^{n} \hat{T}_{2SR_i}}{\sum_{i=1}^{n} M_i} \tag{8.17}$$

where:

$\hat{T}_{2SR_i}$ = total for the ith primary (Eq. 8.9)

M_i = number of secondaries in the ith primary

The subscript R2SR indicates that this is a ratio (R) estimator of the population mean per secondary sampling unit for two-stage (2S) sampling in which the primaries are selected at random (R). The estimator $\bar{y}_{R2SR}$ provides an estimate of the mean per secondary sampling unit for the entire population. Now if M, the total number of secondaries in the population, is known, the following estimator can be used for the population total:

$$\hat{T}_{R2SR} = M\bar{y}_{R2SR} \tag{8.18}$$

where all variables are as previously defined.

The variance of $\bar{y}_{R2SR}$ is

$$S^2_{\bar{y}_{R2SR}} = \frac{N^2}{M^2 n}(S^2_W + S^2_B) \tag{8.19}$$

where:

N = number of primaries in the population

M = number of secondaries in the population

n = number of primaries selected at first stage

$$S_W^2 = \sum_{i=1}^{n} M_i^2 \left(\frac{M_i - m_i}{M_i} \right) \frac{S_{W_i}^2}{m_i} \quad (8.20)$$

$S_{W_i}^2$ = variation within the ith primary (Eq. 8.16)

$$S_B^2 = \left(\frac{N-n}{N} \right) S_{B_i}^2$$

$S_{B_i}^2$ = variation between primaries

$$= \frac{\sum_{i=1}^{n} M_i^2 \bar{y}_{2SR_i}^2 - 2\bar{y}_{R2SR} \sum_{i=1}^{n} M_i^2 \bar{y}_{2SR_i} + \bar{y}_{R2SR}^2 \sum_{i=1}^{n} M_i^2}{n-1} \quad (8.21)$$

and all other variables are as previously defined.

To obtain the variance of the total, multiply $S_{\bar{y}_{R2SR}}^2$ by M^2 since the mean per secondary, $\bar{y}_{R2SR}$, was multiplied by M to obtain the estimate of the total.

Thus

$$S_{\hat{T}_{R2SR}}^2 = M^2 S_{\bar{y}_{R2SR}}^2 \quad (8.22)$$

where all variables are as previously defined.

The equations given above for the variances of these estimators appear a bit intimidating. However, as before, an organized step-by-step approach makes the calculations tractable.

EXAMPLE 8.5.1

The ratio estimator will be used to estimate the total volume for the forest described in Example 8.4.1. The ratio estimate for the mean volume per secondary (1/10-acre sample plot in this case) is calculated using Eq. 8.17:

$$\bar{y}_{R2SR} = \frac{\sum_{i=1}^{n} \hat{T}_{2SR_i}}{\sum_{i=1}^{n} M_i}$$

From Example 8.4.1,

$$\sum_{i=1}^{12} \hat{T}_{2SR_i} = 1{,}773{,}100 \text{ ft}^3$$

and

$$\sum_{i=1}^{12} M_i = 9570$$

Thus

$$\bar{y}_{R2SR} = \frac{1{,}773{,}100}{9570} = 185.2769 \text{ ft}^3/\text{plot}$$

Next estimate the total volume in the population with Eq. 8.18:

$$\hat{T}_{R2SR} = M\bar{y}_{R2SR}$$

M, the total number of secondary sampling units (1/10-acre sample plots) in the population must be determined. There are 7500 acres in the forest, so

$$M = 7500 \text{ acres } (10 \text{ plots/acre}) = 75{,}000$$

Thus

$$\hat{T}_{R2SR} = 75{,}000(185.2769) = 13{,}895{,}767 \text{ ft}^3$$

This estimate is lower than the nonratio estimate by approximately 2.4 million cubic feet.

The variance of this ratio estimate can be obtained using Eq. 8.19:

$$S^2_{\bar{y}_{R2SR}} = \frac{N^2}{M^2 n}\left(S^2_w + S^2_B\right)$$

Now S^2_W is calculated using Eq. 8.20, which is actually the same as Eq. 8.15, which was calculated in Example 8.4.1 as

$$S^2_W = 1{,}212{,}082{,}008$$

Next calculate S_{Bi}^2 using Eq. 8.21 so S_B^2 can be obtained:

$$S_{B_i}^2 = \frac{\sum_{i=1}^{n} M_i^2 \bar{y}_{2SR_i}^2 - 2\bar{y}_{R2SR} \sum_{i=1}^{n} M_i^2 \bar{y}_{2SR_i} + \bar{y}_{R2SR}^2 \sum_{i=1}^{n} M_i^2}{n-1}$$

The following information is available for each stand:

Stand	M_i	$\bar{y}_{2SR_i}$
1	450	178
2	1100	192
3	1500	129
4	320	225
5	250	217
6	500	171
7	950	253
8	1250	189
9	1150	163
10	1750	179
11	200	275
12	150	295

Next fill in all columns of the following table using the information just given:

Stand	M_i^2	$M_i^2 \bar{y}_{2SR_i}$	$M_i^2 \bar{y}_{2SR_i}^2$
1	202,500	36,045,000	6,416,010,000
2	1,210,000	232,320,000	4.460544×10^{10}
3	2,250,000	290,250,000	3.744225×10^{10}
4	102,400	23,040,000	5,184,000,000
5	62,500	13,562,500	2,943,062,500
6	250,000	42,750,000	7,310,250,000
7	902,500	228,332,500	5.776812×10^{10}
8	1,562,500	295,312,500	5.581406×10^{10}
9	1,322,500	215,567,500	3.513750×10^{10}
10	3,062,500	548,187,500	9.812556×10^{10}
11	40,000	11,000,000	3,025,000,000
12	22,500	6,637,500	1,958,062,500
Totals	10,989,900	1,943,005,000	3.557293×10^{11}

Now

$$S_{B_i}^2 = \frac{3.557293 \times 10^{11} - 2(185.2769)\,(1{,}943{,}005{,}000) + (185.2769)^2\,(10{,}989{,}900)}{12 - 1}$$

$$= \frac{1.29974 \times 10^{10}}{11} = 1{,}181{,}595{,}191$$

Next calculate S_B^2:

$$S_B^2 = \left(\frac{N-n}{N}\right) S_{B_i}^2 = \frac{110 - 12}{110}\,(1{,}181{,}595{,}191)$$

$$= 1{,}052{,}693{,}897$$

Thus the variance of $\bar{y}_{\text{R2SR}}$ is

$$S_{\bar{y}_{\text{R2SR}}}^2 = \frac{(110)^2}{(75{,}000)^2\,(12)}\,(1{,}212{,}082{,}008 + 1{,}052{,}693{,}897)$$
$$= 0.000000179(2{,}264{,}775{,}905)$$
$$= 405.9820512$$

Finally, the variance of the total volume, $\hat{T}_{\text{R2SR}}$, is

$$S_{\hat{T}_{\text{R2SR}}}^2 = M^2 S_{\bar{y}_{\text{R2SR}}}^2$$
$$= (75{,}000)^2\,(405.9820512)$$
$$= 2.283649 \times 10^{12}$$

The standard error of the total volume is

$$S_{\hat{T}_{\text{R2SR}}} = 1{,}511{,}174 \text{ ft}^3$$

The approximate 95% confidence interval is

$$\hat{T}_{\text{R2SR}} \pm 2S_{\hat{T}\text{R2SR}}$$

$$13{,}895{,}767 \pm 2(1{,}511{,}174)$$
$$13{,}895{,}767 \pm 3{,}022{,}349$$

$$\text{LCL} = 10{,}873{,}417 \text{ ft}^3$$
$$\text{UCL} = 16{,}918{,}116 \text{ ft}^3$$

The half-width of the confidence interval for the ratio estimator is 3,022,349 ft^3, compared with 5,302,270 ft^3 for the nonratio estimator (from Example 8.4.1). Clearly, the ratio estimator should be preferred in this case. In fact, the ratio estimator should be used whenever the characteristic of interest varies as the size of the primary changes, which is usually the case for a forest composed of many stands.

8.6 TWO-STAGE LIST SAMPLING

Two estimators for a population mean and total have been presented and discussed. For forest inventory applications the ratio estimator is preferred over the nonratio estimator since it will usually lead to a more precise estimate (that is, a more narrow confidence interval). Now a third type of estimator is presented for estimating means and totals for a two-stage sample. This estimator requires that primary sampling units (stands in this application) be selected for inclusion in the sample in such a way that larger stands have a greater probability of being in the sample. In other words, stands are selected with probability proportional to their size. Size is usually an area measurement but it could be a previous estimate of standing volume, basal area, or other parameter that is highly correlated to the current variable of interest. For example, assume that estimating standing merchantable volume for a forest composed of many stands is the objective. Suppose that a list of stands in this forest along with acreages and standing volumes from an inventory 10 years ago is available. From a commonsense point of view, sampling effort should be concentrated in stands with the largest standing volumes. If stands are randomly selected at the first stage, then every stand, regardless of volume, is just as likely as every other stand to be selected. However, if stands are selected at the first stage such that larger stands (in terms of acreage, volume, or basal area) have a higher probability of being in the sample than smaller stands, sampling effort will be concentrated in these types of stands. This is what two-stage list sampling accomplishes. A list of stands in the population is used along with some measure of stand size to select stands so that the larger stands have a higher probability of being in the sample. Two-stage list sampling falls in the general category of probability-proportional-to-size (PPS) sampling. Point sampling (Chapter 4) is another type of PPS sampling in which larger (more valuable) trees have a higher probability of being in the sample than smaller trees. As stated above, it makes sense to concentrate sampling effort in the larger, more valuable stands when carrying out a two-stage sample. In fact, it can be shown that a two-stage list sample will lead to more precise estimates than traditional two-stage sampling if the measure of size used for the primary sampling units is highly correlated with the characteristic of interest. Clearly, measures such as stand acreage, volume 10 years ago, basal area 10 years ago, and the like are all correlated with current standing volumes and/or dollar values. Thus, when this type of information is available prior to sampling, two-stage list sampling should be used in lieu of traditional two-stage sampling.

8.7 SELECTING A TWO-STAGE LIST SAMPLE

Assume that primary sampling units are individual stands and secondary sampling units are fixed-area plots within stands. At the first stage of sampling, stands will be selected with replacement with probability of selection proportional to some measure of size of the stand. As discussed earlier, this measure of size may be area, volume, basal area, or any other characteristic that is highly correlated with the characteristic of interest (such as volume or value) and is also available to the sampler before the inventory is carried out. Unlike most sampling designs discussed in this book, since selection of stands is with replacement, the same stand can be included in the sample more than one time. Once a stand is selected at the first stage, fixed-radius plots (or points) are randomly or systematically located throughout the stand and appropriate measurements are made. If the same stand is selected more than once at the first stage, a second set of plots must be located in the stand. This does not necessarily dictate that the stand must be entered more than once. If a given stand is chosen twice at the first stage, then two systematic cruises can be obtained concurrently by simply changing the grid pattern or by choosing two starting locations in the stand (one for each systematic sample).

To choose stands with probability proportional to their size, a list of all stands in the forest along with their measure of size (area, previous inventory volume, and so on) must be available. Suppose the population of interest is the 15 stands given in the following table. The measure of size available is the stand area (acres), which is given in the second column from the left. Cumulative stand size is given in the third column of this table. To calculate the cumulative size for a given stand, sum the sizes of all stands up to and including the stand of interest.

Stand	Stand Size (Acres)	Cumulative Size (Acres)
1	48	48
2	25	73
3	56	129
4	32	161
5	152	313
6	101	414
7	177	591
8	77	668
9	69	737
10	45	782
11	22	804
12	18	822
13	122	944
14	111	1055
15	29	1084

To select stands with probability proportional to their size, generate random numbers between 1 and the largest cumulative size, which in this case is 1084. A stand is selected if the random number is less than or equal to its cumulative size and greater than the previous stand's cumulative size. For example, suppose the number chosen is 216. Since 216 is less than or equal to the cumulative size of stand 5 and greater than the cumulative size of stand 4, stand 5 is selected to be in the sample. Similarly, if the next random number is 938, stand 13 is selected to be in the sample. This process is followed until the appropriate number of stands has been selected.

8.8 PARAMETER ESTIMATION FOR TWO-STAGE LIST SAMPLING

Once the appropriate number of primaries is selected, fixed-area plots (or points) are randomly or systematically located throughout the stand. After all measurements have been obtained, the following estimator is used for the population mean per secondary sampling unit:

$$\bar{y}_{2SL} = \frac{1}{n} \sum_{i=1}^{n} \bar{y}_i \tag{8.23}$$

where:

$\bar{y}_i = \frac{1}{m_i} \sum_{j=1}^{m_i} y_{ij}$ = mean value per secondary sampling unit (plot or point) in primary sampling unit (stand) i

n = number of primary sampling units (stands) in the sample

y_{ij} = value of the characteristic of interest on secondary sampling unit (plot or point) j in primary sampling unit (stand) i

m_i = number of secondary sampling units in primary i

The subscript 2SL stands for two-stage list sampling. To obtain an estimate for the population total, use the following estimator:

$$\hat{T}_{2SL} = M\bar{y}_{2SL} \tag{8.24}$$

where:

M = total number of secondary sampling units (plots) in the population

and $\bar{y}_{2SL}$ is as defined earlier.

The variance of the mean per sampling unit, $\bar{y}_{2SL}$, is obtained using the following equation:

$$S^2_{\bar{y}_{2SL}} = \frac{S^2_{WB}}{n} \tag{8.25}$$

$$S^2_{WB} = \frac{\sum_{i=1}^{n} \bar{y}_i^2 - \frac{\left(\sum_{i=1}^{n} \bar{y}_i\right)^2}{n}}{n-1} \tag{8.26}$$

Since $\hat{T}_{2SL}$ is simply $\bar{y}_{2SL}$ multiplied by the constant M, the variance of $\hat{T}_{2SL}$ is

$$S^2_{\hat{T}_{2SL}} = M^2 S^2_{\bar{y}_{2SL}} \tag{8.27}$$

Note that the formula for the variance of $\bar{y}_{2SL}$ is much more simple than variance formulas for two-stage sampling procedures with equal probability of selection at both stages. Recall that two-stage sampling estimators presented in Sections 8.4 and 8.5 had a between-primaries component of variance, as well as a within-primary component of variance. In two-stage list sampling, both of these components still exist, but they are estimated simultaneously with Eq. 8.25. If between- and within-primary components of variance are both needed, an additional equation for the within-primary component is used. The between-primary component is then obtained by subtracting the within-primary component from the value obtained using Eq. 8.25 (Murthy, 1967). Of course, most practitioners will not wish to have this information, so Eq. 8.25 is all that is needed to obtain variance estimates. If this breakdown of the variance is needed, Murthy (1967) can be consulted for appropriate formulas.

EXAMPLE 8.8.1

Suppose a reliable estimate of the dollar value for standing merchantable timber is needed very quickly for a 2155-acre forest composed of 21 stands. Two-stage list sampling will be used to obtain the estimate.

In the time available it is determined that eight stands can be cruised. The following table was developed from acreage estimates available prior to the inventory:

Stand	Stand Size (Acres)	Cumulative Size (Acres)
1	240	240
2	129	369
3	175	544
4	38	582

Stand	Stand Size (Acres)	Cumulative Size (Acres)
5	25	607
6	75	682
7	68	750
8	111	861
9	122	983
10	189	1172
11	210	1382
12	138	1520
13	28	1548
14	54	1602
15	99	1701
16	110	1811
17	80	1891
18	70	1961
19	64	2025
20	82	2107
21	48	2155

With a random number table or generator, the following eight random numbers between 1 and 2155 are obtained. The random numbers and stands associated with each one are as follows:

Random Number	Stand
1893	18
1694	15
734	7
268	2
2083	20
1430	12
1474	12
1327	11

Note that stand 18 is selected with the random number 1893 because 1893 is less than or equal to the cumulative size of stand 18 and greater than the cumulative size of stand 17. The same logic is used to select all other stands. Stand 12 was chosen to be in the sample twice. This is acceptable because with list sampling primaries (stands) are sampled with replacement. However, it is imperative that two totally separate and independent sets of secondary sampling units (sample plots) are obtained for this stand.

This may seem counterintuitive, as well as a waste of time and sampling effort. However, to take advantage of the efficiency of the two-stage list sampling estimator, this procedure must be followed. Within each selected stand an approximate 5% cruise will be conducted using ⅒-acre plots on a 4×5 chain grid. Since stand 12 was selected twice, the grid can be cut in half to a 2×5, or two starting points for two separate 4×5 chain grids can be used, or any combination that will give an approximate 10% cruise can be used. Of course, sample plots must be kept in two separate groups, one for each 5% cruise.

After each stand is cruised, the following estimates of average cubic-foot volume per ⅒-acre plot are available:

Stand	$\bar{y}_i$ (ft³/plot)
18	190
15	160
7	220
2	254
20	175
12	162
12	181
11	125

Note that the mean volume per plot was estimated by two independent 5% cruises in stand 12. Now $\bar{y}_{2SL}$ is estimated using Eq. 8.23. First calculate sums and sums of squares for the eight $\bar{y}_i$ values:

$$\sum_{i=1}^{8} \bar{y}_i = 1467 \qquad \sum_{i=1}^{8} \bar{y}_i^2 = 279{,}871$$

Hence

$$\bar{y}_{2SL} = \frac{1467}{8} = 183.375 \text{ ft}^3\text{/plot}$$

To estimate the total volume of the entire forest use Eq. 8.24, which requires M, the total number of ⅒-acre sample plots across the forest. There are 2155 acres in the forest; thus

$$M = 10 \times 2155 = 21{,}550 \text{ plots}$$

So

$$\begin{aligned}\hat{T}_{2SL} &= 21{,}550(183.375)\\ &= 3{,}951{,}731 \text{ ft}^3\end{aligned}$$

The variance of $\bar{y}_{2SL}$ is calculated using Eq. 8.25:

$$S^2_{\bar{y}_{2SL}} = \frac{S^2_{WB}}{n}$$

where:

$$S^2_{WB} = \frac{\sum_{i=1}^{n} \bar{y}_i^2 - \frac{\left(\sum_{i=1}^{n} \bar{y}_i\right)^2}{n}}{n-1}$$

$$= \frac{279{,}871 - \frac{(1467)^2}{8}}{7}$$

$$= 1551.411$$

Thus

$$S^2_{\bar{y}_{2SL}} = \frac{1551.411}{8} = 193.926$$

Next calculate the variance for the total volume using Eq. 8.27:

$$S^2_{\hat{T}_{2SL}} = M^2 S^2_{\bar{y}_{2SL}}$$

$$= (21{,}500)^2\,(193.926)$$

$$= 90{,}059{,}710{,}000$$

The standard error of the total volume is obtained, as always, by taking the square root of the variance:

$$S_{\hat{T}_{2SL}} = \sqrt{90{,}059{,}710{,}000}$$

$$= 300{,}100 \text{ ft}^3$$

An approximate 95% confidence interval for the total tract volume is

$$\hat{T} \pm 2S_{\hat{T}_{2SL}}$$

$$3{,}951{,}731 \pm 2(300{,}100)$$

$$3{,}951{,}731 \pm 600{,}200$$

$$\text{LCL} = 3{,}351{,}531 \text{ ft}^3$$

$$\text{UCL} = 4{,}551{,}931 \text{ ft}^3$$

Assume that the average value per 100 cubic feet is $55. There are 39,517.31 units of 100 cubic feet in the forest. Thus the estimate of the total dollar value is

$$39{,}517.31 \times 55 = \$2{,}173{,}452$$

The standard error of this estimate is calculated by multiplying the standard error of total volume (in units of 100 cubic feet) by the value per 100 cubic feet. Thus the standard error in terms of dollars is

$$3001.00 \times 55 = \$165{,}055$$

Finally, the approximate 95% confidence interval for the total dollar value is

$$\$2{,}173{,}452 \pm 2(\$165{,}055)$$
$$\$2{,}173{,}452 \pm \$330{,}110$$

$$\text{LCL} = \$1{,}843{,}342$$
$$\text{UCL} = \$2{,}503{,}562$$

When secondary sampling units are points rather than fixed-area plots, estimates are obtained much the same as for fixed-area plots. The only difference is that when $\bar{y}_{2SL}$ is calculated from a line-point cruise, the units on the mean will be on a per-acre basis. Thus, when expanding to the total population using Eq. 8.24, simply define M to be the total number of acres in the population.

EXAMPLE 8.8.2

Assume that 10 stands were selected with probability proportional to the acreage of the stands from a 2400-acre forest composed of 42 stands. Within each selected stand a line-point cruise was carried out. At each sample point measurements were made so that Scribner board foot volume of trees larger than 12-in. dbh could be calculated. Average Scribner board foot volume per acre for each sampled stand is as follows:

Stand	$\bar{y}_i$ **(Bd ft/Acre)**
1	1333
2	2400
3	1700
4	990
5	1450
6	1770
7	1667
8	2900
9	1950
10	2200

The average volume per acre for the forest is estimated using Eq. 8.23:

$$\bar{y}_{2SL} = \frac{1}{n} \sum_{i=1}^{n} \bar{y}_i$$

Note that

$$\sum_{i=1}^{10} \bar{y}_i = 18{,}360 \qquad \sum_{i=1}^{10} \bar{y}_i^2 = 36{,}473{,}778$$

Thus

$$\bar{y}_{2SL} = \frac{18{,}360}{10} = 1836 \text{ bd ft/acre}$$

Total board foot volume for the entire forest is obtained using Eq. 8.24:

$$\hat{T}_{2SL} = M\bar{y}_{2SL}$$

Since point sampling was used, M is defined to be the number of acres in the forest.

$$\begin{aligned}\hat{T}_{2SL} &= 2400(1836)\\ &= 4{,}406{,}400 \text{ bd ft}\end{aligned}$$

The variance of $\bar{y}_{2SL}$ is easily obtained with Eq. 8.25:

$$S^2_{\bar{y}_{2SL}} = \frac{S^2_{WB}}{n}$$

$$S^2_{WB} = \frac{\sum_{i=1}^{n} \bar{y}_i^2 - \frac{\left(\sum_{i=1}^{n} \bar{y}_i\right)^2}{n}}{n-1}$$

$$\begin{aligned}S^2_{WB} &= \frac{36{,}473{,}778 - \frac{(18{,}360)^2}{10}}{9}\\ &= 307{,}202\end{aligned}$$

So

$$S^2_{\bar{y}_{2SL}} = \frac{307{,}202}{10} = 30{,}720.2$$

Next the variance of the total forest volume estimate is obtained using Eq. 8.27:

$$S^2_{\hat{T}_{2SL}} = M^2 S^2_{\bar{y}_{2SL}}$$
$$= (2400)^2 (30{,}720.2)$$
$$= 1.769483 \times 10^{11}$$

The standard error of the total forest volume is

$$S_{\hat{T}_{2SL}} = \sqrt{S^2_{\hat{T}_{2SL}}} = 420{,}652 \text{ bd ft}$$

An approximate 95% confidence interval for this estimate is

$$4{,}406{,}400 \pm 2(420{,}652)$$
$$4{,}406{,}400 \pm 841{,}304$$

$$\text{LCL} = 3{,}565{,}096 \text{ bd ft}$$
$$\text{UCL} = 5{,}247{,}704 \text{ bd ft}$$

From the preceding examples it should be clear that two-stage list sampling estimators and variances are less cumbersome than traditional two-stage sampling estimators and variances. Not only does two-stage list sampling provide more precise estimators, it also makes the calculations less complex. Thus, whenever a list of primaries and their sizes is available prior to sampling, two-stage list sampling should be used.

8.9 SAMPLE SIZE DETERMINATION IN TWO-STAGE SAMPLING

Determining sample sizes needed to estimate a population parameter within a given bound for a two-stage sample is not straightforward; in fact, it is actually quite complicated. Knowledge of the costs of sampling primary sampling units and secondary sampling units is needed. It is also necessary to have reliable estimates of variability between primaries and between secondaries within primaries.

In most forest inventory applications this information will not be available and most likely will not be obtained until after the inventory is complete. The information available from previous inventories may be applicable but most likely will not be accurate because of changes in the structure of the population under consideration. However, in general the between-primary component of variation will usually be much larger than the within-primary component of variation (that is, variability between stands is greater than variability between plots within a stand). Thus the goal should be to choose many stands and select a relatively small number of plots within each stand chosen at the first stage. Common sense should be used in such sample size decisions.

It would be unwise to put one or two sample plots in each of a large number of stands because the small sample in each stand will probably yield a poor estimate for the individual stand. Conversely, when it is known that large variation exists among stands, an effort must be made to sample as many stands as possible within time and budget constraints. Those readers interested in a complete discussion of sample size determination for two stage sampling can refer to Sukhatme and Sukhatme (1970), Murthy (1967), and DeVries (1986).

8.10 STRATIFICATION FOR TWO-STAGE SAMPLING

In Chapter 5 it was shown that stratification of a population can be used to obtain more precise parameter estimates. As in single-stage sampling, stratification of primary units prior to a two-stage sample will help increase the precision of parameter estimates (that is, reduce the variability of the estimate). Thus, when using two-stage sampling to estimate timber value or volume for a forest composed of many stands, it would be wise to stratify the stands based on characteristics such as stand origin (natural, old field plantation, cutover plantation, and so on), species composition, stand age, and the like. For example, a forest may be broken into the following strata:

Natural hardwood stands

Natural pine-hardwood stands

Loblolly pine plantations greater than 15 years old

Loblolly pine plantations less than 15 years old

Within each stratum a two-stage sample is obtained and the parameter of interest along with its variance is estimated. The total across all strata is easily obtained by summing the estimates for all strata, and the variance is obtained by summing individual stratum variances. Clearly, stratification as just discussed should help reduce the between-stand variation, which is usually the largest component of variance for a two-stage sample.

EXAMPLE 8.10.1

Suppose a two-stage sample in which primaries were selected with probability proportional to size with replacement and secondaries were selected at random (systematically) without replacement was obtained in each of four strata for a forest composed of 150 stands. The strata and associated estimates of total dollar value of timber along with the variance of the estimates are as follows:

Strata	Timber Value ($)	Timber Value Variance ($^{2})
Natural hardwood stands	1,555,000	40,000,000,000
Natural pine-hardwood stands	2,780,000	23,000,000,000
Loblolly plantation < 15 years	975,000	2,500,000,000
Loblolly plantation > 15 years	4,599,000	11,250,000,000

The total dollar value for the entire forest is obtained by adding the value for each stratum:

$$\hat{T}_{\text{FOREST}} = \$9{,}909{,}000$$

The variance of this estimate is calculated by adding the variances for each stratum:

$$S^2_{\hat{T}_{\text{FOREST}}} = 76{,}750{,}000{,}000$$

The standard error of the total is

$$S_{\hat{T}_{\text{FOREST}}} = \sqrt{S^2_{\hat{T}_{\text{FOREST}}}} = \$277{,}038$$

Thus an approximate 95% confidence interval for the total timber value is

$$\$9{,}909{,}000 \pm 2(277{,}038)$$

$$\text{LCL} = \$9{,}354{,}924$$
$$\text{UCL} = \$10{,}463{,}076$$

Stratification of populations as just described provides a great deal of flexibility for the user so that good estimates can be obtained while reducing overall costs, and it improves the reliability of estimates by simply shifting sampling efforts. For example, plantations less than 15 years old are less variable than natural hardwood stands. Thus a relatively light cruise in a small number of plantations in plantation strata may be all that is required to obtain a good estimate for these strata. This will free up time and money to carry out more intensive cruises of more stands in the more variable natural stand strata.

REFERENCES

Cochran, W. G. 1977. *Sampling techniques.* 3rd ed. Wiley, New York.

DeVries, P. G. 1986. *Sampling theory for forest inventory.* Springer-Verlag, New York.

Murthy, M. N. 1967. *Sampling theory and methods.* Statistical Publ. Society, Calcutta, India.

Sukhatme, P. V., and B. V. Sukhatme. 1970. *Sampling theory of surveys with applications.* 2nd ed. FAO, Rome.

PROBLEMS FOR BETTER UNDERSTANDING

1. Explain or define the following terms:

a. Primary sampling unit

   b. Secondary sampling unit
   c. Multistage sampling
   d. Single-stage cluster sampling
2. The Scribner board foot volume of peeler logs is to be estimated using a line-plot cruise with ¹⁄₁₀-acre plots. Data from 20 plots taken in a 30-acre natural lobolly pine stand are given:

Plot	Volume of Peeler Trees (Scribner Bd Ft)
1	304, 413, 325, 241
2	340, 377, 446
3	240, 413, 272, 377
4	296, 362
5	506, 420, 601, 574, 497
6	340, 402, 548
7	377
8	654, 756, 696
9	330, 420, 574
10	402, 316, 548, 612, 676
11	226, 322, 390
12	284, 428, 475, 316, 229
13	350, 362, 494
14	316, 384
15	342, 540, 594, 515, 322
16	311, 280, 254
17	308, 352, 313, 370
18	294, 407, 473
19	392, 308, 277, 463, 534
20	171, 278, 414

   a. Estimate the average Scribner board foot volume per tree using $\bar{y}_{CE}$ (Eq. 8.1).
   b. Estimate the variance of the estimate obtained in part a.
   c. Estimate the total Scribner board foot volume for peelers in the entire 30-acre stand using $\hat{T}_C$.
   d. Verify the fact that the estimate obtained in part c is exactly the same as would be obtained using simple random sampling Eq. 3.3.
3. Describe two forest resource examples in which three-stage sampling would be useful. Be sure to describe the primary, secondary, and tertiary sampling units.

4. Explain the difference between two-stage sampling and single-stage cluster sampling.

5. A random sample of 10 stands was obtained from a 2500-acre forest composed of 35 stands. In each of the 10 randomly selected stands a line-plot cruise using ⅕-acre circular plots was used to estimate the average weight of sawtimber-sized trees per plot. Stand size (acres), number of ⅕-acre plots sampled in each stand (m_i), the average weight of sawtimber-sized trees per ⅕-acre plot ($\bar{y}_{2SR_i}$), and the variance among ⅕-acre plots within each stand ($S^2_{W_i}$) are given for the 10 randomly chosen stands:

Stand	Acres	m_i	$\bar{y}_{2SR_i}$ (lb)	$S^2_{W_i}$
1	48	24	28,000	158,000,000
2	75	40	34,000	173,500,000
3	105	50	25,500	169,450,000
4	52	25	23,400	131,950,000
5	112	60	29,000	125,675,000
6	42	20	32,500	179,430,000
7	67	30	42,000	172,500,000
8	77	40	36,500	162,000,000
9	83	45	26,000	158,210,000
10	92	50	31,600	179,500,000

a. Estimate the total weight (lb) of sawtimber-sized trees in the entire forest using the nonratio estimator.

b. Calculate the variance of the estimate obtained in part a.

c. Obtain an approximate 95% confidence interval for the estimate obtained in part a.

6. Refer to Problem 5.

a. Estimate the total weight (lb) of sawtimber-sized trees in the entire forest using a ratio estimator.

b. Calculate the variance of the estimate obtained in part a.

c. Compare and discuss the variability of the estimates obtained in Problems 5a and 6a. Which estimate do you prefer? Why?

7. Explain the theoretical advantage associated with two-stage list sampling.

8. Suppose you carry out a two-stage list sample in a forest composed of 20 stands by choosing five stands with probability proportional to size. The measure of size used is merchantable volume (ft^3) present 10 years previously when an inventory of all stands was carried out. None of the stands have been harvested, so you feel comfortable that this measure of stand size is highly correlated to the current standing volume. Volume from 10 years ago for each stand is as follows:

Stand	Volume 10 Years Ago
1	150,000
2	162,000
3	340,000
4	145,000
5	475,000
6	112,000
7	320,000
8	160,000
9	240,000
10	292,000
11	312,000
12	139,000
13	110,000
14	79,000
15	156,000
16	199,000
17	273,000
18	299,000
19	159,000
20	184,000

a. Create a table that gives the cumulative size associated with each stand (keep the stands in the order they are presented).

b. The following five random numbers were generated.

2,388,171
3,792,399
2,431,606
1,738,351
442,206

Based on these random numbers determine which stands should be selected at the first stage of a two-stage list sample.

9. Suppose line-point cruises were carried out in the five stands chosen above. The following summarized data are available:

Stand	$\bar{y}_i$ (ft^3/acre)
3	4350
8	3800

Stand	$\bar{y}_i$ (ft^3/acre)
10	4700
11	5200
18	4650

a. Estimate the total cubic-foot volume in the entire 1750-acre forest.

b. Calculate the variance of the estimate obtained in part a.

c. Obtain an approximate 95% confidence interval for the estimate obtained in part a.

CHAPTER 9

INVENTORY METHODS FOR ESTIMATING STAND GROWTH

A forest is composed of individual trees. Over time those trees grow in diameter and height. Eventually they are either harvested or they die of natural causes. The dynamics of a forest stand can be very complex because the individual trees that make up the stand grow at different rates, and they may die at different times. Unlike tree size, which can be expected to increase over time as the tree grows, stand growth may be either positive or negative. In terms of volume, stand growth may be negative over a period because more volume disappeared from trees dying than grew on the surviving stems. Stand growth can be evaluated in terms of volume, weight, value, or other units.

Before growth is discussed, some commonly used growth components will be defined. *Ingrowth* is the number, volume, weight, value, and so on of trees growing from nonmeasurable size into measurable size classes over a period. For example, many organizations do not measure trees until they become merchantable (say, 4.6 in. for pulpwood). Trees smaller than 4.6 in. that are present in a stand will be ignored until they grow to 4.6 in. or larger. In an inventory, the trees that are now merchantable but were not merchantable at the previous measurement constitute *ingrowth* numbers of trees, weight, volume, and so on. The only way to estimate ingrowth is to mark all trees that are part of the inventory at every measurement. Any currently merchantable tree not marked must be a tree that was too small for measurement and marking at the previous inventory. Ingrowth volume may be a high percentage of total volume growth particularly when many trees in the diameter distribution of the stand are at or near the merchantability threshold.

Mortality is the number, volume, weight, and so on, of trees that die from natural causes during the period from one measurement to another. Natural causes include factors such as old age, insects, diseases, lightning, wind, and ice damage. *Cut,* as distinguished from mortality, is the number, volume, weight, and so on, of trees harvested or salvaged between two measurement periods.

Gross growth consists of the difference between stand characteristic measurements at the beginning and end of the period plus mortality and cut minus ingrowth (Beers 1962):

$$G_g = V_2 + M + C - \mathrm{I} - V_1$$

where:

G_g = gross growth of the characteristic of interest over a period of time

V_2 = value of characteristic of interest at second measurement

V_1 = value of characteristic of interest at first measurement

M = periodic mortality

C = periodic cut

I = periodic ingrowth

Net growth is defined as

$$G_n = V_2 + C - I - V_1$$

where:

G_n = net growth

and other terms are as previously defined.

Obviously, good estimates of gross growth, net growth, and their various components would be useful information for forest managers, regardless of whether they were consultants managing small, private landowner holdings or corporate or government foresters responsible for thousands of acres.

Not all methods of obtaining growth can provide estimates of growth components presented earlier. In fact, only inventory methods that include sample plots with trees tagged for remeasurement can provide this level of detail. Other methods can provide estimates of growth, however, and this chapter will discuss inventory methods and some detail on estimating growth for each of these methods.

There are several established methods for estimating growth. The method chosen usually depends more on the data available than anything else. The most obvious method of estimating growth is to establish a series of permanent sample plots that are remeasured over time. This method will usually result in the growth estimate with the best precision, but establishing, marking, and relocating permanent plots or points is expensive. In addition, foresters who need growth estimates for stands in which permanent plots or points were not previously established cannot use this method. An alternative is to establish some permanent plots along with many temporary plots.

Sampling with partial replacement is a method that uses both permanent and temporary plots to obtain estimates of current volume as well as growth.

Fortunately there are several methods of estimating growth that do not require remeasured plots. Unfortunately, the precision of the growth estimates is typically much lower (the standard error is larger) with these methods. These methods may be summarized as growth from independent inventories, growth from growth and yield systems, and growth from stand table projection. Each of these methods requires different inventory procedures and will be discussed separately.

9.1 GROWTH ESTIMATION FROM PERMANENT PLOTS

Permanent plots are invaluable for obtaining information on changes that occur in a forest. Although there have been many modifications over the years, most permanent plot inventory systems are based on the continuous forest inventory (CFI) system developed by the U.S. Forest Service beginning in the mid-1930s. That system originated as a method of recording growth and mortality as a basis for encouraging sustained timber operations on large industrial and public land holdings (Stott, 1968).

CFI is a system of permanent plots usually laid out systematically over the property on a rectangular grid. When CFI systems were first developed, most sample plots were one-fifth acre in size and circular. Predictably, many different permanent plot systems have copied not only the system, but everything in it, and ⅕-acre circular plots are very popular in these systems.

On each plot, a separate record is maintained for each tree in the plot. Typically all trees greater than some dbh merchantability limit (such as 4.6 in., the lower limit of the 5-in. class) are included. They are numbered in sequence with paint or metal tags or otherwise uniquely identified with plot maps, and at the very least measured for dbh and height. In most systems species, age, and other plot information such as soil characteristics, silvicultural treatments, degree or measure of competing vegetation, and the like are also recorded.

As a result of these intensive measurements and the need to relocate the plot center and exact boundary for the next measurement, CFI systems are expensive, and the sampling intensity is consequently very light (0.03% to 0.1% on a large property). This means that there would be one ⅕-acre plot for every 1000 to 3333 acres. A consequence of this low sampling intensity is that many stands in a forest do not contain a CFI plot. CFI therefore can not be very useful for local managers deciding where to cut since the information obtained does not indicate where volume is located.

CFI has been very useful for documenting overall trends on forest lands. Since changes in individual tree data are measured over time, components of stand growth such as mortality, ingrowth, and cut may be estimated from a properly installed and remeasured CFI system. The system allows planners to answer such questions as "How much volume, weight, or value do we have?" and "Are we cutting more than we're growing?"

A problem for any permanent plot system is that if it is to represent the forest in which it is installed, then any operations that occur in the forest must be uniformly applied to the plots exactly as they are to stands surrounding the plots. If workers doing

TSI work or thinning, for example, notice tags on trees and do a particularly vigilant job on the plot as compared with the rest of the stand, then estimates from the plots will be biased. For this reason many organizations hide their tags at the base of trees and try to disguise the plots, which adds to the expense of relocating plots for remeasurement. Global positioning system (GPS) technology may make relocating permanent plots much simpler and less expensive.

CFI plots were usually remeasured on a 5- to 10-year cycle. Unfortunately, the people in an organization in charge of CFI often change in that amount of time. The new person in charge usually meets with company personnel to decide what measurements should be made to take advantage of the measurement opportunity. Typically the result is a change in the system, sometimes without regard for growth calculations or data analysis. This scenario does not always occur, but it happens often enough to note that the system does not always perform as well as it could if such deficiencies and behavior were recognized.

Finally, it is worth stating that rarely is the silvicultural information obtained in a CFI system useful for developing silvicultural prescriptions based on their correlation with growth. There are so many confounding factors between plots (such as soils, density, site quality, drainage, and competing vegetation) that it is usually impossible to isolate any one factor, such as a site preparation method, for recommendation as a result of overwhelming evidence of good growth from CFI data.

Growth from CFI plots is easily calculated. The volume per acre at the first occasion is subtracted from the volume per acre at the second occasion to obtain the difference or growth. Some textbooks call this the net increase in growing stock. The formulas for calculation are as follows:

$$g_{\mathrm{CFI}} = \bar{y} - \bar{x} \tag{9.1}$$

where:

g_{CFI} = periodic growth per plot

$\bar{y}$ = average of characteristic of interest at time 2

$\bar{x}$ = average of characteristic of interest at time 1

The variance of growth is

$$S^2_{g_{\mathrm{CFI}}} = \frac{S_y^2 + S_x^2 - 2\rho S_x S_y}{n} \tag{9.2}$$

where:

S_x^2 = variance of x

S_y^2 = variance of y

ρ = simple correlation coefficient between plot characteristic at time 1 and time 2

n = number of permanent plots remeasured

Note that since the same plots are measured at both times the volume at time 2 is correlated (related to) with the volume at time 1. Thus, the variance estimate of growth is reduced by the amount $2\rho S_x S_y$. This component of variance is known as the covariance between the characteristic of interest value at time 1 and time 2.

EXAMPLE 9.1.1

A consulting forester established 20 permanent plots on a small acreage to keep up with growth trends. The ⅕-acre plots were established in 1985 at which time trees were measured and volumes were calculated for each plot. In 1990 the plots were measured again and volumes were calculated. Volume data for both measurement times are presented in the following table:

Plot	1985 Volume (ft^3/plot)	1990 Volume (ft^3/plot)
1	147	210
2	508	441
3	561	0
4	426	81
5	12	118
6	261	397
7	599	672
8	433	12
9	492	17
10	163	227
11	294	324
12	387	440
13	266	310
14	134	198
15	143	187
16	112	150
17	14	108
18	155	199
19	256	302
20	187	222

Let y = 1990 volume and x = 1985 volume.

$$\sum_{i=1}^{20} y_i = 4615 \qquad \sum_{i=1}^{20} x_i = 5550$$

$$\bar{y} = 230.8 \text{ ft}^3\text{/plot} \qquad \bar{x} = 277.5 \text{ ft}^3\text{/plot}$$

The estimate for growth is $g_{\text{CFI}} = \bar{y} - \bar{x} = 230.8 - 277.5 = -46.7$ ft^3/plot. On a per acre basis, growth is $-46.7 \times 5 = -233.5$ ft^3.

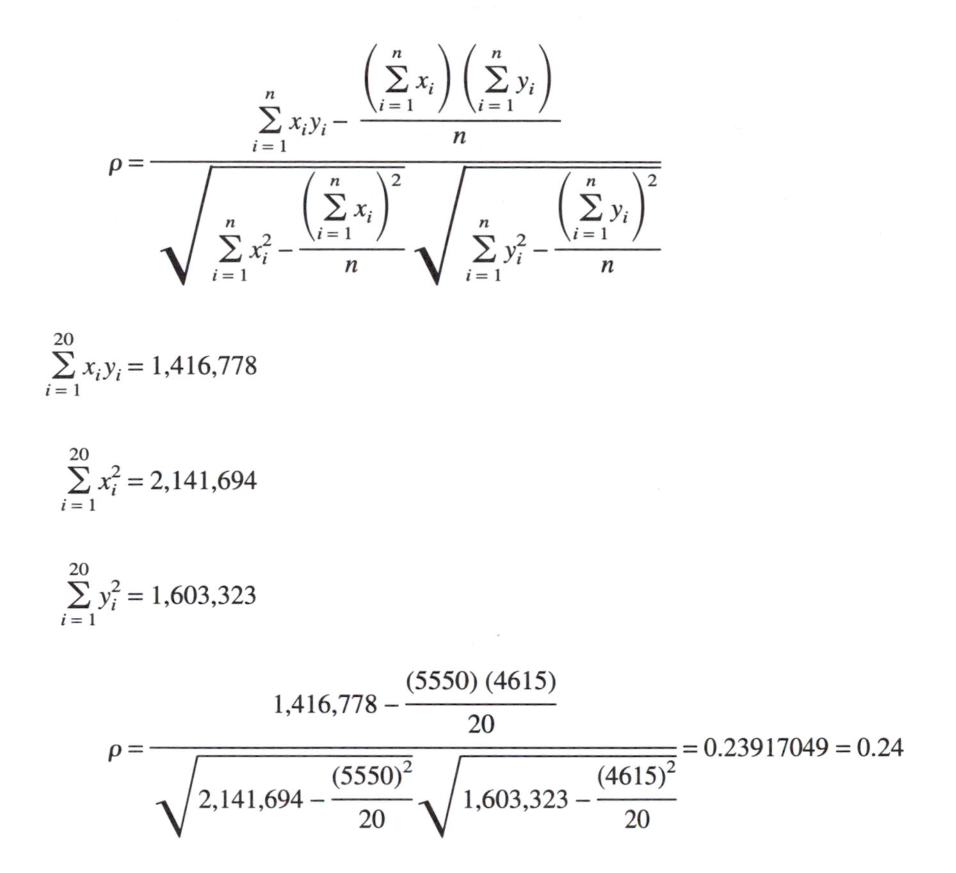

$$\rho = \frac{\sum_{i=1}^{n} x_i y_i - \frac{\left(\sum_{i=1}^{n} x_i\right)\left(\sum_{i=1}^{n} y_i\right)}{n}}{\sqrt{\sum_{i=1}^{n} x_i^2 - \frac{\left(\sum_{i=1}^{n} x_i\right)^2}{n}}\sqrt{\sum_{i=1}^{n} y_i^2 - \frac{\left(\sum_{i=1}^{n} y_i\right)^2}{n}}}$$

$$\sum_{i=1}^{20} x_i y_i = 1{,}416{,}778$$

$$\sum_{i=1}^{20} x_i^2 = 2{,}141{,}694$$

$$\sum_{i=1}^{20} y_i^2 = 1{,}603{,}323$$

$$\rho = \frac{1{,}416{,}778 - \frac{(5550)(4615)}{20}}{\sqrt{2{,}141{,}694 - \frac{(5550)^2}{20}}\sqrt{1{,}603{,}323 - \frac{(4615)^2}{20}}} = 0.23917049 = 0.24$$

A correlation coefficient this low indicates large changes over the growth period. With fewer changes ρ should be closer to one.

$$S_x^2 = 31{,}661.6$$

$$S_y^2 = 28{,}337.5$$

$$S_{g_{\text{CFI}}}^2 = \frac{1}{20}[31{,}661.6 + 28{,}337.5 - 2(0.24)(177.9)(168.3)]$$

$$S_{g_{\text{CFI}}}^2 = \frac{1}{20}(45{,}627.6) = 2281.4$$

$$S_{g_{\text{CFI}}} = 47.8 \text{ ft}^3\text{/plot}$$

The per-acre standard error of growth is $47.8 \times 5 = 239$ ft^3. So the estimate of growth is -233.5 ft^3/acre with a standard error of 239.0 ft^3/acre. Under more typical CFI systems with several hundred plots, the n in the denominator would have a larger impact in reducing the standard error. Since the estimate of growth is negative, there is less volume on the property in 1990 than in 1985. A continuation of forestry operations at the same level as for this five-year period is not sustainable. The negative growth numbers are caused by plots that have been harvested. A check of the records indicates that plots 3, 4, 8, and 9 were all harvested during the five-year period. In addition, the stand in which plot 2 is located had insect-related mortality and the standing volume was reduced.

The forester could remove the harvested plots from the analysis to obtain an idea of how nonharvested areas of the property grew on average for the five years. In addition, a CFI data set would contain more detailed information than the volume summaries presented in Example 9.1.1. The fact that individual trees are tagged allows changes in tree dimensions such as dbh, total height, form, and basal area to be calculated in addition to volumes. Stand structure analysis such as the dynamics of diameter distribution changes over time can be conducted and may form the basis for growth prediction. In addition, the individual tree data form the basis for calculating ingrowth, cut, and mortality.

9.2 GROWTH ESTIMATION FROM PERMANENT POINTS

Point sampling was rapidly accepted by foresters as they recognized it as a probability-proportional-to-size sampling scheme that concentrated effort on the largest and most valuable trees. Since point sampling worked so well for estimating current volume, people naturally began using permanent point samples for growth estimation. Unfortunately, it quickly became apparent that estimation of growth from permanent sample points was not the same straightforward procedure that permanent plots provided.

The problem is that permanent point samples yield incompatible growth estimates when the various components of forest growth are estimated. The various components are S (survivor growth), I (ingrowth), M (mortality), and C (cut or harvest). Compatible estimators are estimators constrained to maintain the equality (Meyer, 1953).

$$\hat{V}_2 - \hat{V}_1 = \hat{S} + \hat{I} - \hat{M} - \hat{C}$$

where:

$\hat{V}_i$ = estimator of the value of interest at time i

and other variables are estimates of growth components just described, with all components expressed in the same units (trees per acre, volume, weight, value, and so on).

Grosenbaugh (1958) was the first to provide estimators of the various components of growth from permanent points. He recommended calculating ingrowth only from trees with ages less than the remeasurement interval. Under this scheme, the additional increase in value from newly qualifying sample trees older than the remeasurement interval is omitted from the growth calculations. In most situations this method reduces ingrowth to negligible amounts. A problem with the method is that age of the trees had to be known.

Beers and Miller (1964) suggested calculating ingrowth from trees that were in at the point but below merchantable size at time 1 and then attained merchantable size by time 2. Their method also omitted growth from trees above merchantable size but out at time 1 and then in at time 2. Note that this method required marking all "in" trees, even those of submerchantable size, so that they could be identified at time 2. All of these estimators are incompatible (that is, $V_2 \neq V_1 + \text{growth}$), which is due primarily to the fact that V_2 includes trees that were out at time 1 but in at time 2, whereas the growth estimates do not include these trees or their growth over the time interval.

Flewelling (1981) provides a thorough review of attempts to estimate growth from permanent points, and he also provides a method of obtaining compatible growth estimates. He describes the problem of compatibility thoroughly. Flewelling's method requires not only the measurement of all sample trees but also the measurement of the distance from the point to each sample tree.

Martin (1982) proposed a method of estimating growth components while keeping the desirable compatibility property. The following classifications of trees are used in this method:

1. Ingrowth trees are those that are below minimum merchantable dbh and in at time 1 but grow and exceed minimum merchantable dbh at time 2.
2. Ongrowth trees are those that are below minimum merchantable dbh and out at time 1 but grow and exceed merchantable dbh and are in at time 2.
3. Nongrowth trees are those that are above minimum dbh and out at time 1 but grow above minimum dbh and are in at time 2. As Gregoire (1993) notes, *nongrowth* is a misnomer since the growth of such trees resulted in their new classification.

Gregoire also discusses compatible estimators by Van Deusen et al. (1986) and Roesch et al. (1989). In all cases, however, it is necessary to take additional measurements at permanent points to disaggregate total growth into compatible components. The alternative is to use Flewelling's (1981) method, which requires measuring and recording distance to each tree. Gregoire (1993) makes the case that incompatible estimates should not be a concern, but realistically the acceptance of estimates by field foresters as well as the general public is more likely if estimates are compatible.

None of these problems is present with permanent plots. The only component of ingrowth is true ingrowth from submerchantable trees or reproduction, which grows into the merchantable size classes. In addition, the point sampling property of selecting trees with probability proportional to size is of less value when plots are remeasured over a long period of time. If a measurement is made when trees are saplings and growing into merchantable size classes, it is important to measure enough trees of this size class to obtain a good estimate of their growth. Similarly, proper management of uneven-aged stands requires good estimates of volume and growth throughout the diameter distribution. As a number of studies have shown, it is possible to estimate growth from permanent points. The U.S. Forest Service currently uses remeasured point clusters in the national survey. It is, however, a method to be used only by those foresters thoroughly familiar with the problems enumerated earlier. Most foresters should probably continue to use permanent plots for their simplicity of measurement and calculation.

9.3 CRITICAL HEIGHT SAMPLING

Before we leave the subject of permanent plots and points, critical height sampling deserves some discussion. In horizontal point sampling, the sweep of the prism or angle gauge at breast height determines which trees are included in the point sample. However, the sweep of the prism or angle gauge could theoretically be made at any height. If the forester could rise directly above the point and examine all sample trees horizontally, at some height a diameter would be found at which the tree would be in the borderline (see Chapter 4) condition. This height is called the critical height.

Kitamura (1962) and, independently, Iles (1979a) expressed volume per acre at a single point as the product of the basal area factor and the sum of the critical heights:

$$v = \text{BAF} \sum_{i=1}^{k} h_{c_i}$$

where:

v = volume per acre at a single point

BAF = basal area factor of the prism or angle gauge

h_{c_i} = critical height of ith tree on the point

k = number of in trees at a given point

Bitterlich (1976) and Iles (1979a) state that critical height sampling is an efficient sampling method because trees are selected with probability proportional to volume. It is also applicable for obtaining cubic-foot volumes in timber types for which no volume equation is available. Iles (1979b) used graphical methods to extend critical height sampling to calculation of stand growth and to support his position that the variance of the growth estimator from successive uses of critical height sampling was less than the variance of the compatible volume to basal area ratio growth estimator. His argument intuitively makes sense, because under successive inventories using critical height sampling, the ongrowth and nongrowth components are smaller than in typical permanent point sampling. Consider nongrowth trees as defined by Martin (1982) as those trees that are above minimum merchantable dbh but out at the first measurement, but that grow and become in at the second measurement. Using the volume-to-basal-area ratio estimator scheme, all of the volume of the tree at the remeasurement is allocated to the volume at the point at the second measurement. Under critical height sampling, the tree would be out at time 1 and in at time 2 as with traditional point sampling, but the volume allocated to the point would be determined by how high on the tree the critical height was located (probably not much higher than dbh unless the time between measurements was very great). The contribution of the tree to ingrowth would therefore be more in line with its actual growth. McTague and Bailey (1985) formally derived variances for critical height estimation and demonstrated the superiority of critical height growth estimators over other compatible growth estimators across a range of assumed dbh growth rates.

The largest impediment to use of critical height sampling is difficulty in measurement of the critical height. For trees at a distance from the point, a Telerelaskop dendrometer, which automatically compensates for angles when used to view up the tree stem, may be used to determine the critical height. For trees closer to the point, the distance to the sample tree should be measured from which the critical diameter can be calculated. The tree can then be viewed from a distance where the vertical angle is not so acute and the critical height determined. Even when this is done, however, it is difficult to determine exactly where on a tree stem a diameter occurs because tree stems are irregular. Unfortunately, accurate critical height determination is crucial; every foot of critical height adds the BAF cubic feet to the volume because $v = BAF\sum_{i=1}^{k} h_{c_i}$.

Many papers have been written on the topic of critical height sampling. A good overview, complete with a comprehensive literature review, is provided by Iles (1990).

9.4 GROWTH ESTIMATION FROM INDEPENDENT SAMPLES

It is sometimes possible to locate previous cruise reports for a property. If this is the case, growth can be estimated by cruising the property again and taking the difference in the two cruise results. Given that previous data are available, this is an inexpensive method of estimating growth, but it results in an estimate with a large standard error relative to remeasured permanent plots. The estimate and its variance are

$$g_i = \bar{y} - \bar{x} \tag{9.3}$$

where:

$\bar{y}$ = average value of characteristic of interest at time 2

$\bar{x}$ = average value of characteristic of interest at time 1

g_i = estimate of growth in the same units as $\bar{y}$ and $\bar{x}$

$$S_{g_i}^2 = \frac{S_y^2}{n_2} + \frac{S_x^2}{n_1} \tag{9.4}$$

where:

$S_{g_i}^2$ = sample variance of growth estimate from independent samples

S_y^2 = sample variance of characteristic of interest at time 2

S_x^2 = sample variance of characteristic of interest at time 1

n_2 = sample size (number of plots) at time 2

n_1 = sample size (number of plots) at time 1

Unlike the remeasured permanent plot estimate, there is no opportunity to subtract a covariance term in the variance calculation since no plots were remeasured. The variance of growth from two independent samples is equal to the sum of the variances of the means used in calculating the growth estimate.

EXAMPLE 9.4.1

A 1983 cruise of a 110-acre tract of timber resulted in cruise estimates of pine sawtimber (PST) and hardwood pulpwood (HPW) as follows:

PST	4.4 MBF/acre	$S_{\bar{y}} = 0.5$ MBF/acre
HPW	5.1 cords/acre	$S_{\bar{y}} = 1.2$ cords/acre

The same area was cruised in 1989 with the following results for the two products plus pine pulpwood (PPW):

PST	7.9 MBF/acre	$S_{\bar{y}} = 0.8$ MBF/acre
HPW	6.9 cords/acre	$S_{\bar{y}} = 0.9$ cords/acre
PPW	4.1 cords/acre	$S_{\bar{y}} = 0.4$ cords/acre

Growth for the PST and HPW products can be calculated as follows:

$$g_{\text{PST}} = 7.9 - 4.4 = 3.5 \text{ MBP/acre}$$

$$g_{\text{HPW}} = 6.9 - 5.1 = 1.8 \text{ cords/acre}$$

$$S^2_{g_{\text{PST}}} = 0.5^2 + 0.8^2 = 0.89 \qquad S_{g_{\text{PST}}} = 0.94 \text{ MBF/acre}$$

$$S^2_{g_{\text{HPW}}} = 1.2^2 + 0.9^2 = 2.25 \qquad S_{g_{\text{HPW}}} = 1.5 \text{ MBF/acre}$$

Since there was no PPW in 1983, the entire amount in 1989 represents growth.

9.5 PERMANENT PLOTS WITH PARTIAL REPLACEMENT

Permanent plots are excellent for growth, but the sampling intensity is typically too low for efficiently estimating current volume because of the cost of permanent plots. Temporary plots, on the other hand, are excellent for estimating current volume, but the growth estimate from temporary plots has a large variance. Recall, too, that one of the problems with CFI systems was that even though current volume was estimated precisely, CFI systems were poor choices for stand management because the broad distribution of plots made it impossible to specify the location of the volume. Moreover, any sampling error caused by the initial location of permanent plots could never be corrected at succeeding measurements unless some permanent plot locations were changed. Sampling with partial replacement (SPR) is a sampling method that has some permanent plots and some temporary plots. Whereas CFI-type systems provide the best estimate of growth and temporary plot cruises provide the best estimates of current volume, SPR allows for good estimates of both growth and current volume.

The difference in SPR and CFI or other permanent plot systems is that only a part of all sampling units are permanent plots to be remeasured at the second occasion. These permanent remeasured plots are said to be matched. In addition, a portion of the plots established at time 1 are temporary plots and are not monumented or remeasured later. At remeasurement, a set of new nonmonumented temporary plots is measured in addition to the matched permanent plots.

The advantage of having matched or remeasured plots for growth has been discussed and is obvious from comparing the variances in Eqs. 9.2 and 9.4. The benefits of remeasured plots in estimating current volume are less obvious, but are related primarily to sample size (many more temporary plots can be measured). Use of both the temporary plots at time 2 and the remeasured (matched) plots provides a current volume estimate of greater precision than using temporary plots alone. This improved current volume estimate is utilized to provide a better growth estimate. Credit for development of sampling with partial replacement in forestry goes to Bickford (1956), and particularly to Ware and Cunia (1962), who provided a unifying theory for the method and compared many different growth estimators.

Although some of the equations used in SPR look complicated, they can usually be broken into parts for computation and then put together. Some needed notation follows:

u = number of temporary sample plots at time 1 (u for unmatched)

m = number of plots at time 1 remeasured at time 2 (m for matched)

n = number of temporary sample plots at time 2 (n for new)

n_1 = total of all plots at time 1 ($n_1 = u + m$)

n_2 = total of all plots at time 2 ($n_2 = m + n$)

Use of these different plot groupings at the different occasions results in six possible sample averages:

$$\bar{x}_u = \frac{\sum_{i=1}^{u} x_i}{u} = \text{average of the unmatched plots at time 1}$$

$$\bar{x}_m = \frac{\sum_{i=1}^{m} x_i}{m} = \text{average of the matched plots at time 1}$$

$$\bar{x} = \frac{\sum_{i=1}^{n_1} x_i}{n_1} = \text{average of all plots at time 1}$$

$$\bar{y}_n = \frac{\sum_{i=1}^{n} y_i}{n} = \text{average of the new temporary plots at time 2}$$

$$\bar{y}_m = \frac{\sum_{i=1}^{m} y_i}{m} = \text{average of the matched plots at time 2}$$

$$\bar{y} = \frac{\sum_{i=1}^{n_2} y_i}{n_2} = \text{average of all plots at time 2}$$

Plot data for each of these estimates have variances calculated in the usual manner for a simple random sample. They will be denoted $S^2_{x_u}$, $S^2_{x_m}$, S^2_{x}, $S^2_{y_n}$, $S^2_{y_m}$, and S^2_{y}. In addition, a sample covariance can be calculated from the matched plots as

$$S_{xy} = \frac{\sum_{i=1}^{m} x_i y_i - \frac{\left(\sum_{i=1}^{m} x_i\right)\left(\sum_{i=1}^{m} y_i\right)}{m}}{m-1}$$

We will first calculate a SPR estimate of current volume ($\bar{y}_{SPR}$). The estimate is a combination of an estimate based on all plots at time 1 and adjusted through regression utilizing matched plots to determine the slope of volume change to the time of remeasurement and an estimate based only on new plots installed at time 2. Ware and Cunia (1962) present these equations in population parameter form. The equations presented here were developed by Scott (1984), and they use sample estimators of the population parameters.

$$\bar{y}_I = \bar{y}_m + \beta_{yx}\,(\bar{x} - \bar{x}_m) \tag{9.5}$$

where:

$\bar{y}_I$ = first component of the sampling with partial replacement current volume estimator

$$\beta_{yx} = \frac{S_{xy}}{S^2_{x_m}}$$

and all other variables are as previously defined.

$\bar{y}_I$ is similar to the double sample regression estimators from Chapter 7 in that the current matched volume is modified depending on the difference between a large estimator of previous average volume ($\bar{x}$) and the matched plot previous average volume ($\bar{x}_m$). An approximate estimator for the variance of $\bar{y}_I$ is

$$S^2_{\bar{y}_I} = S^2_{y\cdot x}\left[\frac{1}{m} + \frac{(\bar{x} - \bar{x}_m)^2}{SS_{x_m}}\right] + \frac{(S^2_{y_m} - S^2_{y\cdot x})}{n_1} \tag{9.6}$$

where:

$S^2_{\bar{y}_I}$ = variance of $\bar{y}_I$

$S^2_{y\cdot x}$ = variance of y given x (see Eq. 6.18)

$S^2_{y_m}$ = variance of y using only matched plots

SS_{x_m} = corrected sum of squares for x using only matched plots

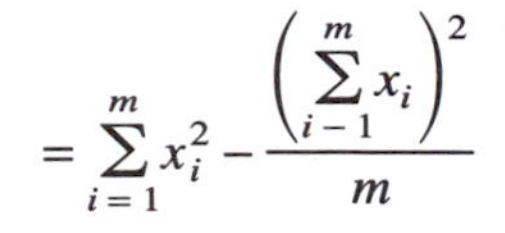

$$= \sum_{i=1}^{m} x_i^2 - \frac{\left(\sum_{i-1}^{m} x_i\right)^2}{m}$$

To obtain an estimate of the current volume using SPR ($\bar{y}_{SPR}$), the following terms are needed:

$$W_I = \frac{1}{S_{\bar{y}_I}^2}$$

$$\bar{y}_{II} = \bar{y}_n$$

This is the average volume at time 2 using only new temporary plots.

$$S_{\bar{y}_{II}}^2 = \frac{\sum_{i=1}^{n} y_i^2 - \frac{\left(\sum_{i-1}^{n} y_i\right)^2}{n}}{n\,(n-1)} = \frac{S_{y_n}^2}{n}$$

$$W_{II} = \frac{1}{S_{\bar{y}_{II}}^2}$$

$$W = W_I + W_{II}$$

Finally,

$$\bar{y}_{SPR} = \frac{W_I\bar{y}_I + W_{II}\bar{y}_{II}}{W}$$

The effect of the Ws in this equation is to weight the estimates inversely proportional to their variances.

$$S_{\bar{y}_{SPR}}^2 \simeq \frac{1 + 4W_I W_{II} \dfrac{\left(\dfrac{1}{(m-1)} + \dfrac{1}{(n-1)}\right)}{W^2}}{W} \tag{9.7}$$

Two estimators of growth are of interest. The first is obtained by taking the best current volume estimate and subtracting the overall estimate at time 1, $\bar{x}$. Obtaining growth, designated g_c by Ware and Cunia (1962), in this manner produces an estimator that makes use of, and is compatible with, the best estimate of current volume, $\bar{y}_{SPR}$. Compatibility means that the volume obtained at the first measurement plus g_c equals the volume obtained at the second measurement.

$$g_c = \bar{y}_{SPR} - \bar{x}$$

$$S^2_{g_c} = \frac{1}{W} + \frac{S^2_x}{n_1} - 2\left(\frac{W_I}{W}\right) \beta_{yx} \frac{\left[mS^2_{x_m} + uS^2_{x_u}\right]}{n_1^2} \tag{9.8}$$

where:

g_c = growth estimate compatible with $\bar{y}_{SPR}$
$\bar{x}$ = estimate of volume at time 1 from all n_1 plots
S^2_x = variance of x from all plots at time 1
$S^2_{x_m}$ = variance of x from only matched plots
$S^2_{x_u}$ = variance of x from only unmatched plots

The other estimator of growth, designated g_b, is not compatible with $\bar{y}_{SPR}$ in that adding growth to $\bar{x}$ does not result in $\bar{y}_{SPR}$. Even so, it is the best linear unbiased estimator (BLUE) of growth. Scott (1984) states that when population parameters are unknown, this growth estimate is biased unless a linear regression is assumed to hold for the population. Calculation of g_b uses four of the means, and can be calculated as follows:

$$g_b = A\bar{y}_m + (1 - A)\,\bar{y}_n + B(\bar{x}_m) - (1 + B)\,\bar{x}_u \tag{9.9}$$

where:

$$A = \frac{m(n_1 + n\beta_{xy})}{(n_1 n_2 - un\rho^2)}$$

$$B = \frac{-m(n_2 + u\beta_{yx})}{(n_1 n_2 - un\rho^2)}$$

$$\beta_{xy} = \frac{S_{xy}}{S^2_{y_m}}$$

$$S^2_{g_b} = A^2 \frac{S^2_{y_m}}{m} + (1 - A)^2 \frac{S^2_{y_n}}{n} + B^2 \frac{S^2_{x_m}}{m} + (1 + B)^2 \frac{S^2_{x_u}}{u} + 2AB \frac{S_{xy}}{m} \tag{9.10}$$

where:

$S^2_{g_b}$ = variance of best linear unbiased estimate of growth
$S^2_{y_m}$ = variance of y for matched plots only
$S^2_{x_m}$ = variance of x for matched plots only
$S^2_{y_n}$ = variance of y for new plots only
$S^2_{x_u}$ = variance of x for unmatched plots only
S_{xy} = sample covariance
ρ^2 = sample correlation coefficient (see Eq. 7.5)

Example 9.5.1 illustrates the computations for current average volume and the two growth estimators.

EXAMPLE 9.5.1

The following volumes (ft^3/acre) were collected on 1-acre plots in 1977 and 1981. Note that 15 plots were matched (remeasured permanent plots), 5 plots initially measured (1977) were not remeasured, and 5 plots were added on the second occasion (1981). Use the data to estimate volume in 1981 as well as g_c and g_b.

Plot	1977	1981
1	3575.2	4882.0
2	2080.6	3361.0
3	5438.1	5925.5
4	1058.3	2127.2
5	4239.7	4803.5
6	4945.8	5268.6
7	1514.1	2296.8
8	3528.5	5187.5
9	1784.5	2625.3
10	2321.0	3882.4
11	1353.5	2484.7
12	2372.4	3736.1
13	2117.6	3018.6
14	1460.2	1821.6
15	1509.7	2738.3
16	2713.3	
17	4560.6	
18	2405.7	
19	2569.2	
20	3480.3	
21		5522.1
22		2682.2
23		3220.3
24		3857.6
25		5418.8

In the calculations that follow, significant digits to eight decimal places are often kept. This is necessary to avoid rounding errors while taking inverses of error variances. It is useful to set up SPR problems on a spreadsheet, which holds all decimal places and allows recalculation quickly in case of error.

$$n_1 = m + u = 15 + 5 = 20$$

$$n_2 = m + n = 15 + 5 = 20$$

$$\bar{x}_u = 3145.82 \qquad S^2_{x_u} = 795{,}205.277$$

$$\bar{x}_m = 2619.95 \qquad S^2_{x_m} = 1{,}924{,}872.271$$

$$\bar{x} = 2751.415 \qquad S_x^2 = 1{,}640{,}319.382$$

$$\bar{y}_m = 3610.61 \qquad S_{y_m}^2 = 1{,}733{,}045.631$$

$$\bar{y}_n = 4140.20 \qquad S_{y_n}^2 = 1{,}649{,}077.085$$

$$\bar{y} = 3743.01 \qquad S_y^2 = 1{,}679{,}510.857$$

$$S_{xy} = 1{,}738{,}631$$

First calculate the current volume estimate. From the matched plots,

$\rho = 0.95192201$ (use Eq. 7.5 or see Example 9.1.1)

$$\beta_{yx} = \frac{S_{xy}}{S_{x_m}^2} = 0.903244674$$

$$\begin{aligned} \bar{y}_I &= \bar{y}_m + \beta_{yx}(\bar{x} - \bar{x}_m) \\ &= 3610.61 + 0.903244674\,(2751.42 - 2619.95) \\ &= 3610.61 + 118.75 = 3729.36 \text{ ft}^3/\text{acre} \end{aligned}$$

$$S_{\bar{y}_1}^2 = S_{y \cdot x}^2 \left[\frac{1}{m} + \frac{(\bar{x} - \bar{x}_m)^2}{\mathrm{SS}_{x_n}}\right] + \frac{(S_{y_m}^2 - S_{y \cdot x}^2)}{n_1}$$

$$S_{y \cdot x}^2 = \frac{\mathrm{SS}_{y_m} - \beta_{yx}^2 \mathrm{SS}_{x_m}}{m - 2} \qquad \text{(see Eq. 6.18)}$$

$$\mathrm{SS}_{y_m} = S_{y_m}^2\,(m - 1)$$

$$\mathrm{SS}_{x_m} = S_{x_m}^2\,(m - 1)$$

$$\begin{aligned} S_{y \cdot x}^2 &= \frac{S_{y_m}^2\,(m - 1) - \beta_{yx}^2 S_{x_m}^2\,(m - 1)}{m - 2} \\ &= \frac{1{,}733{,}045.63\,(14) - (0.9032446742)^2\,(1{,}924{,}872.27)\,(14)}{13} \\ &= \frac{24{,}262{,}638.82 - 21{,}985{,}723.95}{13} \\ &= 175{,}147.2985 \end{aligned}$$

$$\begin{aligned} S_{\bar{y}_1}^2 &= 175{,}147.2985 \left[\frac{1}{15} + \frac{(2751.415 - 2619.947)}{(14)\,(1{,}924{,}872.271)}\right] + \frac{(1{,}733{,}045.631 - 175{,}147.2985)}{20} \\ &= 89{,}572.26 \end{aligned}$$

$$W_{\mathrm{I}} = \frac{1}{S^2_{\bar{y}_{\mathrm{I}}}} = 0.000011164$$

$$\bar{y}_{\mathrm{II}} = 4140.20 \text{ ft}^3/\text{acre}$$

$$S^2_{\bar{y}_{\mathrm{II}}} = \frac{1{,}649{,}077.085}{5} = 329{,}815.4180$$

$$W_{\mathrm{II}} = \frac{1}{329{,}815.4180} = 0.00000303$$

$$W = W_{\mathrm{I}} + W_{\mathrm{II}} = 0.00001419$$

$$\bar{y}_{\mathrm{SPR}} = \frac{0.00001116\,(3729.30) + 0.00000303(4140.20)}{0.00001419}$$

$$\bar{y}_{\mathrm{SPR}} = \frac{0.04162210 + 0.01255308}{0.00001419} = 3817.00 \text{ ft}^3/\text{acre}$$

$$S^2_{\bar{y}_{\mathrm{SPR}}} \simeq \frac{1 + 4W_{\mathrm{I}}W_{\mathrm{II}} \dfrac{\left[\dfrac{1}{(m-1)} + \dfrac{1}{(n-1)}\right]}{W^2}}{W}$$

$$S^2_{\bar{y}_{\mathrm{SPR}}} \simeq \frac{1 + 4(0.000011164)\,(0.000003032) \dfrac{\left[\dfrac{1}{14} + \dfrac{1}{4}\right]}{(0.00001419)^2}}{0.00001419}$$

$$S^2_{\bar{y}_{\mathrm{SPR}}} \simeq 85{,}703.79$$

$$S_{\bar{y}_{\mathrm{SPR}}} \simeq 292.75$$

The current volume estimate is then 3817.00 ft^3/acre with a standard error of 292.75 ft^3/acre.

$$\begin{aligned} g_c &= \bar{y}_{\mathrm{SPR}} - \bar{x} \\ &= 3817.00 - 2751.4 \\ &= 1065.6 \text{ ft}^3/\text{acre} \end{aligned}$$

$$S^2_{g_c} = \frac{1}{W} + \frac{S^2_x}{n_1} - \frac{2W_{\mathrm{I}}}{W}\,\beta_{yx}\,\frac{mS^2_{x_m} + uS^2_{x_u}}{n_1^2}$$

$$= \frac{1}{0.00001419} + \frac{1{,}640{,}319.38}{20} - 2\left(\frac{0.000011164}{0.00001419}\right)(0.903244674)$$
$$\left(\frac{15\ (1{,}924{,}872.271) + 5\ (795{,}205.28)}{20^2}\right)$$

$$= 70{,}472.16 + 82{,}015.969 - 116{,}717.626 = 35{,}770.503$$

$$S_{g_c} = 189.13 \text{ ft}^3/\text{acre}$$

The best estimator of growth, g_b, is calculated as

$$g_b = A\bar{y}_m + (1 - A)\ \bar{y}_n + B\ (\bar{x}_m) - (1 + B)\ \bar{x}u$$

$$A = \frac{m\ (n_1 + n\beta_{xy})}{n_1 n_2 - un\rho^2}$$

$$\beta_{xy} = \frac{S_{xy}}{S^2_{y_m}} = \frac{1{,}738{,}631}{1{,}733{,}045.631} = 1.0032229$$

$$A = \frac{15[20 + 5(1.0032229)]}{(20)(20) - (5)(5)(0.95192201^2)}$$

$$A = 0.994423$$

$$1 - A = 0.0055768$$

$$B = \frac{-m\ (n_2 + u\beta_{yx})}{n_1 n_2 - un\rho^2}$$

$$B = \frac{-15\ [20 + 5(0.903244674)]}{20\ (20) - 5(5)\ (0.95192201)^2}$$

$$B = -0.974552$$

$$(1 + B) = 0.025448$$

$$g_b = 0.994423\ (3610.61) + 0.0055768\ (4140.20) - 0.974552\ (2619.95) - 0.025448\ (3145.82)$$

$$g_b = 980.2 \text{ ft}^3/\text{acre}$$

$$S^2_{g_b} = A^2\frac{S^2_{y_m}}{m} + (1 - A)^2\frac{S^2_{y_n}}{n} + B^2\frac{S^2_{x_m}}{m} + (1 + B)^2\frac{S^2_{x_u}}{u} + 2AB\frac{S_{xy}}{m}$$

$$= (0.994423)^2 \frac{(1{,}733{,}045.63)}{15} + (0.0055768)^2 \frac{(1{,}649{,}077.09)}{5}$$

$$+ (-0.974552)^2 \frac{(1{,}924{,}872.27)}{15} + \frac{(0.025448)^2\,(795{,}205.28)}{5}$$

$$+ \frac{2(0.994423)\,(-0.974552)\,(1{,}738{,}631)}{15}$$

$$= 114{,}251.2761 + 10.2575 + 121{,}876.7014 + 102.9951 - 224{,}658.2301$$

$$= 11{,}583.00$$

$$S_{g_b} = 107.62 \text{ ft}^3\text{/acre}$$

Note that the standard error of the growth estimate for g_b is slightly less than the standard error for g_c (189 versus 107). Even so, this precision comes at the cost of compatibility with the best current volume estimate. That is,

$$\bar{x} + g_c = \bar{y}_{\text{SPR}}$$

but

$$\bar{x} + g_b \neq \bar{y}_{\text{SPR}}$$

even though g_b has the lower variance.

Example 9.5.1 demonstrates the complexity of the estimators used in SPR. Remember, however, that these equations are easily programmable on a computer spreadsheet, so they only have to be entered correctly once. With the advent of personal computers, foresters now have access to inventory and estimation methods that were once not given consideration because of calculation complexity.

SPR provides very good estimates of both growth and current volume. Although estimators have been derived for sampling on more than two occasions (Cunia and Chevrou, 1969), the SPR estimators are dependent on a high simple correlation coefficient (ρ) between volume at the two measurements. In an intensively managed forest ρ may decrease considerably because of harvest and growth changes if time of remeasurement is extended much beyond five years. Thus, as ρ decreases, the benefits of SPR decrease.

9.6 ESTIMATING GROWTH FROM GROWTH AND YIELD MODELS

Permanent plots or permanent plots with partial replacement are preferred for estimating growth. Without permanent plots or two independent inventories, the next best choice for estimating growth is probably a growth and yield system. Not every stand type has had a growth and yield system developed for it, but most plantation systems or even-aged natural stand types in the United States have had a growth and yield system developed for them during the last two decades.

Individual tree growth and yield systems exist and could be used to estimate growth, but comments here primarily relate to stand level models, which require stand values (age, site index, basal area per acre, trees per acre) as inputs. Yield models predict the average expected volume or weight per acre for a given set of stand conditions (age, site index, trees per acre). All that is required to transform a yield system to a growth and yield system is a projection equation for basal area per acre (BA) assuming that the yield model requires BA as an input and/or a survival function if the yield model requires trees per acre *(N)* as an input.

These projection equations and/or survival equations are developed from remeasured permanent plots installed in stands of the type for which the growth and yield systems are developed. As such, they are another step removed from having permanent plots in the stand for which growth estimates are desired. The obvious assumption is that the particular stand in question will grow like the average stand with the same input variable values. Example 9.6.1 illustrates the use of a growth and yield system for estimating growth.

EXAMPLE 9.6.1

Growth information is desired for the last five years in an 18-year-old slash pine plantation with 440 trees per acre and a basal area per acre of 110 ft^2. The stand is growing on site index 62 (base age 25) land. No permanent plots are available for the stand, but a growth and yield system for this population was published by Pienaar et al. (1990). The system utilizes both basal area per acre and number of trees per acre. The survival model presented in the growth and yield system for plantation slash pine is

$$N_2 = \left\{ N_1^{-0.3008} + \left(0.03272 - \frac{0.9628}{S}\right)\left[\left(\frac{A_2}{10}\right)^{0.5245} - \left(\frac{A_1}{10}\right)^{0.5245}\right]\right\}^{-3.3245}$$

where:

N_2 = number of stems per acre at time 2

N_1 = number of stems per acre at time 1

A_2 = age at time 2

A_1 = age at time 1

S = site index (base age 25)

If we want to know how many trees per acre were present five years ago, we can solve for N_2 where $A_1 = 18$, $A_2 = 13$, and $N_1 = 440$. The result is

$$N_2 = \left\{ 440^{-0.3008} + \left(0.03272 - \frac{0.9628}{62}\right)\left[\left(\frac{13}{10}\right)^{0.5245} - \left(\frac{18}{10}\right)^{0.5245}\right]\right\}^{-3.3245}$$

$N_2 = 475.27$, or about 475

Average dominant/codominant height (H_D) is needed to project the basal area per acre. The following equation is presented:

$$H_D = 1.5776 \times S\ [1 - \exp\ (-0.0456 \times A)]^{1.183}$$

where:

H_D = average height of dominant/codominant trees at age A

S = site index (base age 25)

For age 13,

$$H_2 = 1.5776 \times 62\ [1 - \exp\ (-0.0456 \times 13)]^{1.183} = 37.75$$

At age 18,

$$H_1 = 1.5776 \times 62\ [1 - \exp\ (-0.0456 \times 18)]^{1.183} = 49.25$$

The basal area projection equation is

$$\begin{aligned}\ln B_2 = {} & A_1/A_2 \ln B_1 - 4.8066\ (1 - A_1/A_2) + 1.5116\ (\ln H_2 - A_1/A_2 \ln H_1) \\ & + 0.5270\ (\ln N_2 - A_1/A_2 \ln N_1) + 4.1293\ (\ln H_2 - \ln H_1)/A_2 \\ & + 2.4966\ (\ln N_2 - \ln N_1)/A_2\end{aligned}$$

$$B_2 = \exp\ (\ln B_2)$$

For this example $B_1 = 110$, so $\ln B_1 = 4.70048037$.

$$\frac{A_1}{A_2} = \frac{18}{13} = 1.38461539$$

$$\begin{aligned}\ln B_2 = {} & 1.38461539\ (4.70048037) - 4.8066\ (1 - 1.38461539) \\ & + 1.5116\ [\ln (37.75) - 1.38461539 \ln (49.25)] \\ & + 0.5270\ [\ln (475.27) - 1.38461539 \ln (440)] \\ & + 4.1293\ \frac{\ln (37.75) - \ln (49.25)}{13} \\ & + 2.4966\ \frac{\ln (475.27) - \ln (440)}{13}\end{aligned}$$

$$\ln B_2 = 4.42671042$$

$$B_2 = \exp\ (4.42671042) = 83.66\ \text{ft}^2$$

Once the age, height of dominants/codominants, basal area per acre and trees per acre are known, volume per acre can be calculated:

$$\ln V = 2.9939 - 1.1497\ \frac{\ln (H_D)}{A} - 0.3371 \ln (N) + 1.4813 \ln (B)$$

where:

V = per-acre total inside bark stem volume in cubic feet

and all other variables are as previously defined.

$$\ln V_{18} = 2.9939 - 1.1497 \frac{\ln (49.25)}{18} - 0.3371 \ln (440) + 1.4813 \ln (110)$$

$$\ln V_{18} = 7.65596555$$

$$V_{18} = \exp (7.65596555) = 2113.2 \text{ ft}^3$$

Using the values calculated from the projection equations:

$$\ln V_{13} = 2.9939 - 1.1497 \frac{\ln (37.75)}{13} - 0.3371 \ln (475.27) + 1.4813 \ln (83.66)$$

$$\ln V_{13} = 7.15229727$$

$$V_{13} = \exp (7.15229727) = 1277.0$$

The growth from age 13 to age 18 is estimated as

$$V_{18} - V_{13} = 2113.2 - 1277.0 = 836.2 \text{ ft}^3$$

Several points regarding use of growth and yield systems should be emphasized. First, it is important to remember that growth and yield systems are empirically based systems. Their reliability depends on how well the population was represented in the sample plots from which data were taken to develop the system. Extrapolation beyond the range of the data should be avoided, and extrapolation is easy to do when making growth projections. For example, if all plots in a data set used for development of a loblolly pine growth and yield system were between the ages of 10 and 25, the model may not be reliable in projecting to age 35. It is likewise proper to be aware of the range in site quality and stand density present in the yield system database. These extrapolation problems are more acute now that many growth and yield systems have been computerized and users may not have access to documentation spelling out important properties of the database used to derive the models.

In addition to extrapolation, it is important to remember that yields obtained from growth and yield models are average yields for the set of stand conditions used as inputs to the growth and yield system. An actual inventory of a particular stand may result in yields above or below those produced by the system. Over many stands and for forest level planning, the errors tend to average out.

Clutter and Allison (1974) developed a method of projecting an initial stand table through time and Pienaar and Harrison (1988) subsequently revised the algorithm for use in a growth and yield system. They called the procedure *generalized stand table projection.* This should not be confused with the procedure in Section 9.7. The two are very different.

This method is a hybrid of growth and yield methodology and stand table projection methodology that results in a growth projection tailored to a specific stand.

The method uses a stand table obtained from an inventory of the stand. This method is very flexible in that even multimodal stand tables can be modeled easily. The relative size of an individual tree is defined as

$$\frac{b_i}{\bar{b}}$$

where:

b_i = basal area of tree i

$\bar{b}$ = average basal area of all trees on the plot

Pienaar and Harrison (1988) advocate the following relationship between present and future relative size:

$$\frac{b_{2_i}}{\bar{b}_2} = \left(\frac{b_{1_i}}{\bar{b}_1}\right)^{(A_2/A_1)^{\beta}} \tag{9.11}$$

where:

b_{1_i} = basal area of tree i at time 1

b_{2_i} = basal area of tree i at time 2

$\bar{b}_1$ = average basal area of all surviving trees at time 1

$\bar{b}_2$ = average basal area of all surviving trees at time 2

A_1 = age 1

A_2 = age 2

β = a parameter estimated from the data

If β is greater than zero, this relationship implies that trees smaller than the average will become even smaller relative to the average tree size over time, whereas trees that are larger than the average tree size will become larger in relation to the average tree size over time. In addition, a smaller change in relative size will be realized for a given projection length as the initial age increases. These properties are reasonable for even-aged plantations.

The relationship can be algebraically manipulated to obtain the following projection equation:

$$b_{2_i} = \bar{b}_2 \left(\frac{b_{1_i}}{\bar{b}_1}\right)^{(A_2/A_1)^{\beta}} \tag{9.12}$$

This equation could be used to project every tree in the stand along with a stochastic individual tree mortality function. Alternatively, the midpoint diameters of the diameter classes of the present stand table can be projected. The projected stand table is then constrained to have the same trees per acre and basal area per acre as projected by whole stand survival and basal area projection functions. This removes the stochastic nature of the individual tree survival. The following revision of the projection equation ensures compatibility with per-acre basal area:

$$b_{2_i} = \bar{b}_2 n \frac{(b_{1_i}/\bar{b}_1)^{(A_2/A_1)^{\beta}}}{\sum_{i=1}^{n} (b_{1_i}/\bar{b}_1)^{(A_2/A_1)^{\beta}}} \quad (9.13)$$

where:

n = number of survivor trees per acre

and all other variables are as previously defined.

Use of this projection system to obtain growth estimates requires a mortality function, a site index equation, an equation to predict height by dbh class, and a basal area projection equation. All of these are regionwide equations that form the heart of growth and yield systems. The difference between the generalized stand table projection system and typical whole stand growth and yield systems is that the starting point for the projection is modified to be compatible with the current stand table. To the extent that the starting values of basal area and trees per acre are changed from what would have been predicted for them, the stand table projection algorithm is customized to fit the particular stand that had been inventoried. To estimate growth, the current volume is subtracted from the projected volume. For more information on growth and yield systems see Clutter et al. (1983) and Vanclay (1994).

9.7 STAND TABLE PROJECTION

In some situations in which either past growth or projected future growth is needed, there will be no previous cruise information, no permanent plot data, and no growth and yield system. In such cases the only alternative for growth estimation is stand table projection (STP). Stand table projection is an attempt to predict future growth by measuring past growth, usually increment cores, of trees in a stand. An implicit assumption is that future growth over some time interval will mirror past growth over the same time interval. The procedure has shortcomings, which will be detailed, but it also has intuitive appeal since, unlike conventional growth and yield systems, it utilizes data collected in the stand of interest. The method can be applied only in temperate forests where trees typically lay down one growth ring per year.

All stand table projections require that some assumption be made on the amount of future growth as a function of past growth. Typically that assumption has been that diameter growth in the future will be the same as past diameter growth for each diameter class. This constant-diameter-growth assumption is not biologically reasonable except over short intervals. Annual rings on the cross section of any relatively old tree will indicate that trees tend to slow down in diameter growth after their initial fast growth.

Another requirement of STP is estimation of mortality into the future with no historical data on mortality by dbh class on which to base estimates. Finally, estimation of volume or weight per tree in the future stand table requires an estimate of future height by dbh class. Again, there will be no historical data on which to base those estimates.

Most foresters use current local volume equations (based only on dbh) in the future stand table to obtain the future stock table. Some even ignore mortality to obtain higher estimates of volume and then rationalize it by saying that using the current local volume equation compensates for ignoring mortality. It should be clear that STP should be the growth estimation choice of last resort.

Serious errors can be introduced into stand table projection estimates through incorrect selection of sample trees (Clutter et al., 1983). Stand table projection is a method devised to work in individual stands, but often the method is applied over ownerships. Since STP applies growth on a per-tree basis, the sample tree selection method should select sample trees in proportion to trees present, not in proportion to stand type.

Assume that cruisers are taking an increment core tree as the nearest tree along a line at some fixed interval. The tract being inventoried has natural stands with 50 trees per acre and plantations with 500 trees per acre, each occupying 100 acres. Approximately one-half of the increment core trees will come from natural trees and one-half will come from plantation trees. The growth relationship obtained will be applied over both types, although there are 50,000 plantation trees and only 5000 natural trees. Unless trees in the two stand types are growing similarly, which is a highly unlikely assumption, the growth estimate will be biased. In addition, it is likely that mortality will be different for the two stand types. To minimize errors in a method that already requires dubious assumptions, STP should be applied on a stand-by-stand basis or at the very least on a stand-type-by-stand-type basis.

The standard practice, as just described, of selecting an increment core tree as the nearest tree to a fixed interval on a line is seriously biased toward selection of open grown trees. As noted above, trees growing in stands with 50 trees per acre constituted one-half the sample from a tract on which they constituted slightly less than 10% of the population. Even within a stand with density differences caused by random mortality, there will be a tendency to select more open grown trees than the population warrants, thereby contributing to sampling error. This problem can be avoided by taking small, fixed-radius plots at regular intervals along a line and boring all trees on these plots for increment cores. This scheme has the added advantage of selecting sample trees in roughly the same proportion as their presence in the population in terms of dbh class.

A problem also arises with the practice of using point samples to select sample trees for increment cores. If diameter increments are simply averaged within initial diameter classes, the estimates are biased (Lappi and Bailey, 1987) because, for two trees having the same initial diameter, the tree with the larger diameter increment has a higher probability of being chosen as a sample tree since its current basal area is larger. If the increment observations are weighted by the current basal area before averaging within a diameter class, they are unbiased. Practically, this amounts to multiplying each increment by the number of trees per acre (TPA from Chapter 4) represented by the tree from which the increment core was taken, summing these products with each diameter class, and then dividing by the total number of TPA represented by all trees in the dbh class.

Data collected on increment core trees vary but typically look somewhat like the example data in Table 9.7.1. The increment data in the table are all inside bark (ib) measurements. Stand tables, both present and future, require a distribution of trees per acre outside bark (ob). A common assumption is that there is a constant ratio, k, of

Table 9.7.1 Example of data required to carry out a stand table projection

	dbh (ob)	dbh (ib)	Five-Year Increment (ib)	Five-Year Increment (ob) Δdbh (ob)
	9.6	8.0	1.8	2.05
	8.6	7.6	1.2	1.36
	5.4	5.1	1.0	1.14
	9.6	8.2	2.2	2.50
	8.2	6.8	1.2	1.36
	12.3	11.0	1.6	1.82
	13.7	12.0	1.2	1.36
	6.8	5.6	1.0	1.14
	11.2	10.6	1.4	1.59
	10.3	8.8	1.4	1.59
	8.8	7.9	1.2	1.36
	12.9	11.7	1.2	1.36
	10.5	9.1	1.2	1.36
	8.2	7.0	1.8	2.05
	8.7	7.9	1.2	1.36
Total	144.8	127.3		

outside bark diameter to inside bark diameter. Given that assumption, the following mathematics allows estimation of outside bark diameter increment, Δdbh (ob).

Assume dbh (ob) = $k \times$ dbh (ib).

$$\hat{K} = \frac{\sum_{i=1}^{n} \text{dbh (ob)}_i}{\sum_{i=1}^{n} \text{dbh (ib)}_i}$$

where $\hat{K}$ is the empirical estimate of k for the particular stand for which inside bark increment data is available.

For the data in Table 9.7.1,

$$\hat{K} = \frac{144.8}{127.3} = 1.137$$

The outside bark diameter increment, the growth, is obtained by multiplying $\hat{K}$ times the inside bark dbh increment (see the last column of Table 9.7.1).

In most textbook examples (such as Husch et al., 1983), the average growth increment (ob), Δdbh (ob), by dbh class was used to start the STP procedure. The Δdbh (ob) values were obtained by averaging the Δdbh (ob) values obtained from sample trees in the same dbh class. A similar method, more easily applied to computer calculation,

Table 9.7.2 Stand table projection using the constant-diameter-growth assumption

dbh Class	Curent Stand Table	Expected Five-Year Mortality	Remaining Trees	Δdbh (ob)	Classes Moved 1	Classes Moved 2	New Stand Table
6	20	4	16	1.447			
7	32	4	28	1.478	8.848		8.848
8	45	3	42	1.509	14.616	7.152	21.768
9	38	2	36	1.540	20.622	13.384	34.006
10	25	1	24	1.571	16.560	21.378	37.938
11	17	1	16	1.602	10.296	19.440	29.736
12	5	0	5	1.633	6.368	13.704	20.072
13					1.835	9.632	11.467
14						3.165	3.165
	182	15	167				167.000

is to estimate the average periodic dbh growth by dbh class using a simple linear regression model of the form

$$\Delta \text{dbh (ob)} = b_0 + b_1 \times \text{dbh(ob)}$$

The model implies that diameter growth is a function of the current dbh and that diameter growth is constant over time. Values for b_0 and b_1 are obtained from least-squares regression estimation and can be obtained using most spreadsheet programs. As an example, the data from Table 9.7.1 were used to fit this regression model. The resulting model was

$$\Delta \text{dbh (ob)} = 1.26 + 0.03 \times \text{dbh(ob)}$$

The STP for a five-year period from this procedure appears in Table 9.7.2 given a current stand table and expected five-year mortality by dbh class. The Δdbh (ob) value of 1.447 for the 6-in. diameter class row was obtained by using the dbh class midpoint, 6, in the regression model. The 1 in the whole number position indicates that 100% of trees in the 6-in. class will move up at least one dbh class (to the 7-in. class). In addition, .447 of the 16 surviving trees (7.152) will move two classes and will become 8-in. trees. This leaves the remainder (16 – 7.152 = 8.848) in the 7-in. class. This procedure is repeated for each dbh class and the redistributed trees are cumulated to obtain the new stand table. If 2-in. classes are used, the Δdbh value is divided by 2 (the width of the class) to obtain a movement ratio. In this example, 1.447/2 = 0.724, indicates that not all trees in the 6-in. class will move one full 2-in. class. The percentage of trees that will move one class to the 8-in. class is 72.4% and the percentage that will remain in the current 6-in. class is (1 – 0.724) × (100) = 27.6%. This procedure assumes a uniform distribution of trees within a dbh class.

Table 9.7.3 Example of basal area increment calculations using data from Table 9.7.1

Current dbh (ob)	BA (ob)	Five-Year dbh Increment (ob)	dbh Five Years Ago	BA Five Years Ago	BA Increment
9.6	0.50	2.05	7.55	0.31	0.19
8.6	0.40	1.36	7.24	0.29	0.11
5.4	0.16	1.14	4.26	0.10	0.06
9.6	0.50	2.50	7.10	0.27	0.23
8.2	0.37	1.36	6.84	0.26	0.11
12.3	0.83	1.82	10.48	0.60	0.23
13.7	1.02	1.36	12.34	0.83	0.19
6.8	0.25	1.14	5.66	0.17	0.08
11.2	0.68	1.59	9.61	0.50	0.18
10.3	0.58	1.59	8.71	0.41	0.17
8.8	0.42	1.36	7.44	0.30	0.12
12.9	0.91	1.36	11.54	0.73	0.18
10.5	0.60	1.36	9.14	0.46	0.14
8.2	0.37	2.05	6.15	0.21	0.16
8.7	0.41	1.36	7.34	0.29	0.12

The commonly made constant-dbh-growth assumption is not required. The annual growth rings on a cross section of a tree of any size show decreasing ring width over time. At the same time, those decreasing ring widths are laid down over an increasing circumference. The trade-off of these two trends could reasonably produce constant basal area growth. A simple adjustment to the procedure just described allows for a constant-basal-area-growth assumption.

Instead of dbh increment, basal area increment is calculated from the increment core data. Table 9.7.3 details the calculations. The extra steps involved consist of calculating current basal area and previous basal area to estimate basal area increment. Once basal area increment is obtained, the following model assumes constant basal area growth:

$$\Delta \text{BA} = b_0 + b_1 \text{BA}$$

where:

ΔBA = periodic basal area growth

BA = current basal area

b_0 and b_1 = parameters estimated using linear regression

For the data from Table 9.7.3, the fitted equation is

$$\Delta \text{BA} = 0.06910318 + 0.15494370 \text{ BA}$$

Table 9.7.4 Example calculations for traditional stand table projection assuming constant basal area growth over time

$\Delta BA = b_0 + b_1\,BA \quad \Delta BA = 0.06910318 + 0.15494370\,BA$

dbh Class	Stand Table	Expected Five-Year Mortality	Remaining Trees	ΔBA	Δdbh	Classes Moved 1	Classes Moved 2	New Stand Table
6	20	4	16	0.099526	1.365307			
7	32	4	28	0.110512	1.322379	10.2		10.2
8	45	3	42	0.123189	1.305174	19.0	5.8	24.8
9	38	2	36	0.137555	1.306320	29.2	9.0	38.2
10	25	1	24	0.153612	1.320964	25.0	12.8	37.8
11	17	1	16	0.171359	1.345771	16.3	11.0	27.3
12	5	0	5	0.190796	1.378407	10.5	7.7	18.2
13						3.1	5.5	8.6
14							1.9	1.9
	182	15	167					167.0

Table 9.7.4 details the STP using the constant basal area assumption. The only change from the stand table projection in Table 9.7.2 is that ΔBA is calculated using the basal area of the dbh class midpoint (for the first line in the table, this is $0.06910318 + 0.15494370 \times 0.005454154 \times 6^2 = 0.099526$) and then the Δdbh corresponding to that ΔBA must be determined. To obtain Δdbh, calculate the basal area for the midpoint of the dbh class and then add ΔBA to it. For the first line this is $6^2 \times 0.005454154 + 0.099526 = 0.1963 + 0.0995 = 0.2958$ ft^2. Obtain the corresponding dbh as $D = \sqrt{(BA/0.005454154)}$. A tree with a basal area of 0.2958 ft^2 must have a dbh of $\sqrt{(0.2958/0.005454154)} = 7.365307$ in. The growth is then the difference between this dbh and the dbh of the class midpoint for the current stand table. For our example, $7.365307 - 6 = 1.365307$. From this point the STP proceeds as before.

Notice the difference in the new stand tables in Tables 9.7.2 and 9.7.4. Using a constant dbh growth assumption (Table 9.7.2) the diameter distribution is skewed toward more large trees resulting in larger projected future volumes and growth estimates. Since the assumption resulting in that projection, constant dbh growth, is known to be illogical, the constant basal area growth assumption is preferred.

Even with the better constant basal area growth assumption, stand table projection requires many assumptions that are impossible to validate without good long-term permanent plot data. If such data were available, a growth and yield system developed from it would be preferred over STP.

The preference for an inventory system for estimating growth proceeds in much the same order as this chapter. With no information, we are forced to use STP. With no remeasurement data but a growth and yield system, the growth and yield system would be preferred. This is particularly true if it is a growth and yield system that allows input of a current stand table. Any previous data from the current stand, even an independent cruise, should be utilized. Of course, the ultimate resource is permanent plot or point data for the stand for which growth estimates are desired.

REFERENCES

Beers, T. W. 1962. Components of forest growth. *J. Forestry* 60:245–248.

Beers, T. W., and C. I. Miller. 1964. Point sampling: Research results, theory, and application. *Purdue Univ. Agric. Exp. Stn. Res. Bull.* 786.

Bickford, C. A. 1956. Proposed design for continuous inventory: A system of perpetual forest survey for the northeast. U.S. Forest Service Eastern Techniques Meeting, Forest Survey, Cumberland Falls, KY, Oct. 8–13, 1956.

Bitterlich, W. 1976. Volume sampling using indirectly estimated critical heights. *Commonwealth Forest Review* 55(14):319–330.

Clutter, J. L., and B. J. Allison. 1974. A growth and yield model for *Pinus radiata* in New Zealand. *R. Coll. For. Res.* Note 30, pp. 136–160.

Clutter, J. L., J. C. Fortson, L. V. Pienaar, G. H. Brister, and R. L. Bailey. 1983. *Timber management: A quantitative approach.* New York: Wiley.

Cunia, T., and R. B. Chevrou. 1969. Sampling with partial replacement on three or more occasions. *For. Sci.* 15(2):204–224.

Flewelling, J. W. 1981. Compatible estimates of basal area and basal area growth from remeasured point samples. *For. Sci.* 27(1):191–203.

Gregoire, J. G. 1993. Estimation of forest growth from successive surveys. *Forest Ecology and Management* 56:267–278.

Grosenbaugh, L. R. 1958. *Point-sampling and line-sampling: Probability theory, geometric implications, synthesis.* USDA Forest Service, South Forest Exp. Stn. Occas. Pap. 160.

Husch B., C. I. Miller, and T. W. Beers. 1982. *Forest mensuration.* 3rd ed. New York: Wiley.

Iles, K. 1979a. Some techniques to generalize the use of variable plot and line intersect sampling. In *Forest Resource Inventories Workshop Proceedings* (W. E. Frayer, ed.), vol. I, pp. 270–278. Colorado State University, Fort Collins, CO.

Iles, K. 1979b. Systems for selection of truly random samples from tree populations and the extension of variable plot sampling to the third dimension. Unpublished doctoral dissertation, University of British Columbia, Canada (Dissertational Abstract No. 40104B).

Iles, K. 1990. Critical height sampling: A workshop on the current state of the technique. In *State-of-the-art methodology of forest inventory: A symposium proceedings.* USDA For. Serv. General Technical Report PNW-6-TR-263, pp. 74–85.

Kitamura, M. 1962. On an estimate of the volume of trees in a stand by the sum of critical heights. 73 Kai Nichi Rin Ko, p. 64–67.

Lappi, J., and R. L. Bailey. 1987. Estimation of diameter increment function or other tree relationships using angle-count samples. *For. Sci.* 33(3):725–739.

Martin, G. L. 1982. A method for estimating ingrowth on permanent horizontal sample points. *For. Sci.* 28(1):110–114.

McTague, J. P., and R. L. Bailey. 1985. Critical height sampling for stand volume estimation. *For. Sci.* 31(4):899–911.

Meyer, H. A. 1953. *Forest mensuration.* State College, PA: Renns Valley.

Pienaar, L. V., and W. M. Harrison. 1988. A stand table projection approach to yield prediction in unthinned even-aged stands. *For. Sci.* 34(3):804–808.

Pienaar, L. V., W. M. Harrison, and J. W. Rheney. 1990. PMRC yield prediction system for slash pine plantations in the Atlantic coast flatwoods. University of Georgia PMRC Technical Report 1990-3.

Roesch, F., E. J. Green, and C. T. Scott. 1989. New compatible estimators for survivor growth and ingrowth from remeasured horizontal point samples. *For. Sci.* 35:281–293.

Scott, C. T. 1984. A new look at sampling with partial replacement. *For. Sci.* 30:157–166.

Stott, C. B. 1968. A short history of continuous forest inventory east of the Mississippi. *J. Forestry* 834–837.

Vanclay, J. K. 1994. *Modeling forest growth and yield: Applications to mixed tropical forests.* Wallingford, UK: CAB Int'l.

Van Deusen, P. C., T. R. Dell, and C. E. Thomas. 1986. Volume growth estimation from permanent horizontal points. *For. Sci.* 33:583–590.

Ware, K. D., and T. Cunia. 1962. Continuous forest inventory with partial replacement of samples. *Forest Science Monograph 3.*

PROBLEMS FOR BETTER UNDERSTANDING

1. A set of ⅕-acre permanent plots was laid out in a forest in 1985 and remeasured in 1990. The two measurements are as follows:

1985	**1990**
432	550
345	420
115	288
110	222
528	599
610	685
376	489

1985	1990
244	372
632	0
137	245
336	424
364	492
416	550
172	299
202	316

a. If volumes are in cubic feet, estimate the five-year growth in cubic feet per acre using the CFI estimate of growth. Calculate the standard error.

b. Assume that rather than being from permanent plots, the volumes in 1985 and 1990 are from two independent cruises of the forest. Again estimate the growth over the five-year period and the standard error of growth.

c. From identical sets of numbers, why should one estimate of growth be so much more precise than the other?

2. The following increment core data was obtained from all trees on 1⁄100-acre plots in a 50-acre natural loblolly pine stand:

dbh (ob)	dbh (ib)	10-Year Increment (ib)
10.2	9.0	2.2
12.4	10.9	2.1
14.3	12.6	2.1
11.7	10.2	1.9
11.9	10.6	1.7
12.3	10.7	2.1
14.2	12.5	2.3
13.5	11.7	2.2
15.1	13.2	2.5
16.6	14.7	2.6
16.2	14.2	2.5
15.7	13.7	2.4
13.8	12.0	2.2
12.9	11.4	2.1
14.4	12.5	1.9
14.9	13.1	2.0
15.6	13.6	2.4

Here is the present stand table from a cruise of the stand:

dbh Class	Trees per Acre
10	14
11	22
12	24
13	37
14	21
15	10
16	6

a. Assume that stocking is low enough that no competition-related mortality can be expected over the next 10 years. Project the present stand table forward for 10 years using a constant-basal-area-growth assumption.

b. What assumptions must be made to estimate growth from the projected stand table?

3. Discuss problems with using permanent points for growth estimation.

4. A 500,000-acre property has a permanent plot system with 1 plot for every 1000 acres (a total of 500). Plots are remeasured on a five-year cycle and are all ⅕ acre in size. Data for a recent remeasurement cycle are presented with x used to represent measurements made 5 years ago and y used to represent current measurements.

$$\sum_{i=1}^{500} x_i = 173{,}300 \text{ ft}^3 \qquad \sum_{i=1}^{500} y_i = 192{,}400 \text{ ft}^3$$

$$\sum_{i=1}^{500} x_i^2 = 254{,}987{,}655 \qquad \sum_{i=1}^{500} y_i^2 = 354{,}723{,}020$$

$$\sum_{i=1}^{500} x_i y_i = 265{,}506{,}153$$

a. Estimate 5-year periodic growth per acre for the property.

b. Place an approximate 95% confidence interval on your estimate in part a.

c. What steps could be taken to estimate both growth and current volume precisely for the property?

CHAPTER 10

3P AND LINE INTERSECT SAMPLING

Commonly used sampling methods for inventorying forest resources in the absence of a well-defined sampling frame will be discussed in this chapter. First 3P sampling will be discussed. Like point sampling, 3P is a probability-proportional-to-size estimator. Unlike point sampling, 3P sampling involves sampling individual trees rather than clusters of trees.

This chapter will also include a description of line intersect sampling (LIS). Line intersect sampling is a plotless sampling technique that also falls under the general category of probability-proportional-to-size sampling. LIS has been used most often for estimating volume of wood on the ground after logging and for estimating volume of fuelwood on the ground under existing stands.

Assumptions, advantages, and disadvantages of these sampling methods are discussed in this chapter. Another sampling method that falls in the category of plotless sampling is line transect sampling (LTS). This method of sampling, most often used in estimating animal population size, is discussed in Chapter 11.

10.1 3P SAMPLING

3P is a sampling procedure developed for use in forestry by Grosenbaugh (1963). It is a modification of the list sampling procedure described in Chapter 8 for selecting primary units with probability proportional to their size in a multistage sample. Recall that a list of sampling units and their sizes was necessary to use list sampling to select units with probability proportional to their size. The 3P sampling method was developed to efficiently estimate volume of timber in a timber sale. Grosenbaugh was faced with the problem of efficiently determining the volume of all trees when the total number of trees and their sizes were not known prior to sampling. He reasoned that volume of each tree constituting the sale could be quickly estimated by eye and sampling could be conducted with probability proportional to the predicted (estimated) volumes to obtain an efficient estimator of the total sale volume. The term *3P* comes from *p*robability, *p*roportional, and *p*rediction. Grosenbaugh originally suggested using estimated tree volume as the measure of size associated with each tree; however, estimated size can be any tree size characteristic (height, dbh, basal area, and so on).

Grosenbaugh introduced 3P to the forestry profession in a system that included three parts:

1. 3P selection rule for selecting sample trees.
2. Use of optical dendrometers to obtain precise volume estimates of sample trees.
3. A computer program to help in sample tree selection and to process data.

Perhaps because of the way it was introduced and originally used, many foresters think of optical dendrometers and computer programs when they think of 3P sampling. In fact, 3P is simply a sample selection procedure that determines which trees in the sale are actually measured for volume. Anyone with a dbh tape, a hypsometer, and a calculator with a random number key can select trees using the 3P selection rule and subsequently use appropriate estimators to obtain estimates of total or merchantable volume. If a reliable standard or local volume table is available, a dendrometer is not necessary.

Before we go further, it may be helpful to describe a 3P inventory in a step-by-step fashion:

1. *Designate the number of trees to be carefully measured for volume as* n_e (that is, the number of trees to be selected using the 3P selection rule). In practice obtaining exactly n_e sample trees is difficult to do since this number is dependent on random chance as well as the ability of the cruiser to estimate volume consistently. The following sample size formula can be used to estimate n_e:

$$n_e = \frac{4(\text{CV})^2}{(\text{AE})^2}$$

where:

n_e = expected number of 3P sample trees

CV = coefficient of variation of the ratio of measured tree size to estimated tree size expressed as a percent

AE = allowable error (%)

and 4 provides approximately 95% confidence.

This formula is the sample size formula for infinite populations presented in Chapter 3. The n_e depends greatly on CV, which is determined primarily by how consistently the cruiser estimates the size of the trees. Unlike other sampling methods, the CV referred to here is not determined by the variability of the population. It is a measure that quantifies how consistently the cruiser can estimate tree size. Studies have shown that CV values in the 15% to 20% range are realistic for experienced cruisers.

2. *Estimate the total volume of all trees in the population of interest.* Call this $\hat{T}_x$.

$$\hat{T}_x = \sum_{i=1}^{N} x_i$$

where:

x_i = estimated volume of tree i

Note that this requires that the total volume of the population be estimated before any trees are measured. This is usually done during a reconnaissance of the tract. This sampling design is most often used where the population is small (10 trees per acre or so).

3. *Estimate the maximum individual tree volume expected.* Call this value k.

$$k = \max\ y_i$$

where:

y_i = actual measured volume of tree i

If any tree is actually larger than k, it will be measured with certainty. Therefore it is important to estimate k accurately. If it is too low, the sample size will be much higher than expected.

4. *To obtain a sample size close to what is designated in step 1, determine the number z as follows:*

$$z = \frac{\hat{T}_x}{n_e} - k$$

where all variables are as defined previously.

5. *Visit each of the N trees in the population.* At each tree,

   a. Estimate and record the estimated tree volume x_i.

   b. If the estimated tree volume is greater than k (the maximum expected individual tree volume) measure the tree for volume and record as y_i, and then move to the next tree. Otherwise, go to step c.

   c. Draw a random number from the set of integers between 1 to $k + z$. Call this random number KP.

6. *If KP > x_i, move to the next tree and repeat step 5.* If KP $\leq x_i$, measure the tree for volume and record the volume as y_i. Note that the number of trees actually sampled and measured can vary substantially from the expected sample size, n_e, because of the random nature of sample tree selection.

7. *After visiting all N trees on the inventory area, estimate the total volume of the population:*

$$\hat{T}_{3P} = \sum_{i=1}^{N} x_i \left(\frac{\sum_{i=1}^{n} R_i}{n} \right) \tag{10.1}$$

where:

$R_i = \dfrac{y_i}{x_i}$

n = sample size actually obtained

and all other variables are as previously defined.

8. *Calculate the variance.* Because of the random sample size, no exact expression for the true variance exists. Grosenbaugh (1965) suggests the following as an estimate of the variance for a 3P estimator:

$$S^2_{\hat{T}_{3P}} = \frac{\left(\sum_{i=1}^{N} x_i\right)^2}{n} \left[\frac{\sum_{i=1}^{n} R_i^2 - \frac{\left(\sum_{i=1}^{n} R_i\right)^2}{n}}{n-1} \right] \tag{10.2}$$

where all variables are as previously defined.

EXAMPLE 10.1.1

A stand of ponderosa pine is to be inventoried. A reconnaissance of the stand reveals that the largest tree contains approximately 600 bd ft and that there is approximately 200,000 bd ft total volume. Assume that the volume is to be estimated with an allowable error of 5% with approximately 95% confidence. The CV for the cruiser who will be estimating tree volume is assumed to be 20%.

Thus

$$k = 600$$

$$\hat{T}_x = 200{,}000$$

$$n_e = \frac{4(20)^2}{(5)^2} = 64 \text{ sample trees required}$$

$$z = \frac{\hat{T}_x}{n_e} - k = \frac{200{,}000}{64} - 600 = 2525$$

Now using the 3P procedure each tree in the stand is visited, the board foot volume is estimated and recorded, and a random number between 1 and $k + z$ $(600 + 2525 = 3125)$ is drawn. If the random number is less than the estimated volume, the volume of the tree is carefully measured and recorded. A total of 973 trees were visited with the 3P selection rule resulting in 71 sample trees. The following data were recorded or calculated:

$$\hat{T}_x = \sum_{i=1}^{973} x_i = 214{,}500 \text{ bd ft}$$

$$\sum_{i=1}^{71} R_i = \sum_{i=1}^{71} \left(\frac{y_i}{x_i}\right) = 65.32$$

$$\sum_{i=1}^{71} R_i^2 = 66.8039$$

Now using Eq. 10.1,

$$\hat{T}_{3P} = \sum_{i=1}^{N} x_i \left(\frac{\sum_{i=1}^{n} R_i}{n}\right) = 214{,}500\left(\frac{65.32}{71}\right) = 197{,}340 \text{ bd ft}$$

This is a type of ratio estimator. In this case the average ratio was less than 1 (65.32/71 = 0.92), indicating that the cruiser consistently overestimated tree volume. As a result, the estimate of the total volume ($\hat{T}_{3P}$) is a reduction of T_x. An underestimation would have resulted in the opposite adjustment to T_x. The variance of this estimate is calculated using Eq. 10.2:

$$S^2_{\hat{T}_{3P}} = \frac{\left(\sum_{i=1}^{N} x_i\right)^2}{n} \left[\frac{\sum_{i=1}^{n} R_i^2 - \frac{\left(\sum_{i=1}^{n} R_i\right)^2}{n}}{n-1}\right]$$

$$S^2_{\hat{T}_{3P}} = \frac{(214{,}500)^2}{71} \left[\frac{66.8039 - \frac{(65.32)^2}{71}}{70}\right]$$

$$S^2_{\hat{T}_{3P}} = 62{,}113{,}837.51$$

The standard error is $\sqrt{62{,}113{,}837.51} = 7881.23$ bd ft.

3P sampling has obvious intuitive appeal. If every tree is visited and examined, this removes any chance for acreage errors to cause estimation problems as they can and do for line-plot and line-point sampling. Individual trees become the sampling unit rather than fixed areas. The scheme also ensures that large trees, those that will have larger estimated volumes, have a higher probability of being selected. Since large trees tend to be more valuable, this would seem to be a useful property.

Unfortunately, 3P also has undesirable properties, particularly from a sampling theory viewpoint. Schreuder et al. (1968, 1971) developed much of the theoretical basis for 3P sampling and conducted tests of 3P and alternative sampling schemes that could be used in similar situations (in the absence of a well-defined frame). Unfortunately, calculation errors clouded some of their test conclusions (Grosenbaugh, 1976), but their papers are good sources of 3P information.

One undesirable property of 3P sampling is that sample size is a random variable that cannot be known until after the sample is completed. The actual sample size may be larger or smaller than the expected sample size, affecting both cost of sampling and precision. Also, the arbitrary k, the maximum tree size estimated before sampling, has a substantial effect on the estimate. Finally, since no true estimate of the variance exists, there is uncertainty about how precise resulting total volume estimates really are.

In practice, 3P works quite well when utilized for the purpose for which it was originally designed. For situations in which trees are marked for sale and visiting each tree to estimate volume is not a monumental task, the method can provide and has provided accurate estimates of total volume very efficiently. As with many sampling schemes, there was a tendency to try this method in other situations such as for CFI plots and in multistage sampling. The advantages of 3P are less obvious in such situations, and there may be other designs that would perform better in these situations.

10.2 LINE INTERSECT SAMPLING (LIS)

Line intersect sampling (LIS) was developed for forest inventory applications. Specifically, it is used extensively to estimate the amount of slash left on a site after logging or the amount of fuel wood that is present on the forest floor in an actively growing stand (Warren and Olsen, 1964; Van Wagner, 1968). This method is similar to point sampling in that it is a plotless sampling technique in which sample elements are selected with probability proportional to their size. The theoretical development of the sample estimators and associated variances for LIS was presented by DeVries (1973, 1974, 1986).

Estimating the amount of woody material on the ground after a logging operation is of interest for a variety of reasons. It gives an indication of how efficient the logging operation was. The amount of woody material on the ground under an actively growing stand is useful for identifying potential fire hazard as well as for classifying stands into various stages of development or for quantifying habitat of various insects, small mammals, and the like. As may be expected, there is usually a large amount of variability in logging residue and fuelwood lying on the ground. In fact, logging slash or fuelwood may be so thick in some areas that it could be impossible to travel through it. Traditional line-plot cruising could be used to obtain volume estimates of logging slash and fuelwood. However, because of the large amount of variability present in the amount of fuelwood, the number of plots required to obtain reliable estimates is usually very large and consequently prohibitively expensive. Because of this high cost Warren and Olsen (1964) devised the idea of line transect sampling for estimating the amount of logging slash present after a cutting operation.

The basic procedure and subsequent estimators are straightforward. To carry out a line intersect sample,

1. Lay out a line of a given length across the area of interest.
2. Traverse the line (being careful to stay on the initial bearing) and record the diameter of every piece of woody material that crosses (intersects) the line.

Several researchers have investigated the use of various diameters on sample elements. These include diameters at both ends of the bolt, diameter at the midpoint of the bolt, and diameter at the point where the bolt intersects the sample line (Bailey, 1970; Van Wagner and Wilson, 1976). As expected, it is more time-consuming and thus more expensive to measure the diameter at both ends and the midpoint diameter than it is to measure the diameter at the point where the bolt intersects the line. One surprising result is that there is little or no difference in the accuracy of volume estimates for any of the methods. Consequently, all references to the bolt diameter in this section refer to diameter where the line intersects the bolt.

The estimator that is used to estimate the total amount (volume or weight) of slash per unit area is

$$\hat{T} = \frac{\pi}{2L} \sum_{i=1}^{n} \frac{x_i}{l_i} \qquad (10.3)$$

where:

$\pi = 3.141592654 \ldots$

L = length of the sample line

l_i = length of the ith intersecting sample element (bolt)

x_i = characteristic of interest on the ith sample element

If l_i and L are measured in feet, then T estimates volume per square foot. If l_i and L are measured in meters, then T estimates volume per square meter. Let V_i be the cubic volume of bolt i; then

$$V_i = \pi \left(\frac{d_i}{2} \right)^2 l_i \qquad (10.4)$$

where:

V_i = cubic volume of bolt i

d_i = diameter of bolt i where it intersects the line

and all other variables are as previously defined.

At this point the assumption is that d_i and l_i are measured in the same units (feet or meters). Now substitute Eq. 10.4 into Eq. 10.3 in place of x_i:

$$\hat{T} = \frac{\pi}{2L} \sum_{i=1}^{n} \frac{\pi\, d_i^2\, l_i}{4\, l_i}$$

$$\hat{T} = \frac{\pi^2}{8L} \sum_{i=1}^{n} d_i^2 \tag{10.5}$$

where:

T = total volume of slash per unit area (square foot or square meter)

and all else is as previously defined.

It turns out that Eq. 10.5 provides an estimate of the total volume of slash per hectare if L is measured in meters and d_i is measured in cm. To see this, refer to Eq. 10.4:

$$V_i = \pi \left(\frac{d_i}{2} \right) l_i$$

where:

d_i = diameter of bolt i in centimeters

l_i = length of bolt i in meters

V_i = volume of bolt i in cubic meters

and all else is as previously defined.

Now recalling that there are 100 cm/m,

$$V_i = \pi \left(\frac{d_i}{100(2)} \right)^2 l_i$$

$$= \frac{\pi}{4(10{,}000)} d_i^2\, l_i$$

Substitute this quantity into Eq. 10.3:

$$\hat{T} = \frac{\pi}{2L} \sum_{i=1}^{n} \frac{\pi}{4(10{,}000)} \frac{d_i^2\, l_i}{l_i}$$

$$= \frac{\pi^2}{8L\,(10{,}000)} \sum_{i=1}^{n} d_i^2$$

where:

$\hat{T}$ = volume per square meter

Now, noting that there are 10,000 m^2/hectare,

$$\hat{T}_H = 10{,}000\hat{T} = \frac{\pi^2}{8L}\sum_{i=1}^{n} d_i^2 = \frac{1.2337}{L}\sum_{i=1}^{n} d_i^2 \tag{10.6}$$

where:

$\hat{T}_H$ = cubic volume (m^3) per hectare

d_i = diameter of bolt i in centimeters

L = transect length in meters

and all else is as previously defined.

EXAMPLE 10.2.1

Line intersect sampling was used in a small Douglas fir clearcut to estimate the volume of wood with diameters larger than 12 cm left on the site after logging. A 300-m line was laid out and traversed. Each bolt that intersected the line was measured for diameter in centimeters at the point of intersection. A total of 63 bolts were intersected. The sum of the 63 squared bolt diameters is

$$\sum_{i=1}^{63} d_i^2 = 20{,}412$$

Use Eq. 10.6 to estimate volume in cubic meters per hectare with $L = 300$:

$$\begin{aligned}\hat{T}_H &= \frac{\pi^2}{8L}\sum_{i=1}^{63} d_i^2 \\ &= \frac{\pi^2}{8(300)}(20{,}412) \\ &= 83.9 \text{ m}^3/\text{ha}\end{aligned}$$

With a similar derivation it can be shown that cubic foot volume per acre is estimated as

$$\hat{T}_A = \frac{373.2}{L}\sum_{i=1}^{n} d_i^2 \tag{10.7}$$

where:

$\hat{T}_A$ = cubic volume (ft^3) per acre

d_i = diameter of bolt i in inches

L = transect length in feet

The variance of $\hat{T}_H$ and $\hat{T}_A$ cannot be calculated directly for a single transect. However, if several independently located transects are used, then it is possible to estimate the variability of the estimate. Note that one of the assumptions underlying line intersect sampling is that bolts lying on the ground are randomly oriented. When this is true, the estimators given above are unbiased. When this is not true, the estimators above may be biased. To avoid problems with nonrandom orientation of bolts, several transects should be run in different directions. This will help avoid bias and will give several estimates of volume per unit area with which to calculate variability of estimators.

Usually, replicated lines are of different length. When several lines are run through an area, each one results in an estimate of volume per unit area (acre or hectare). Denote the estimate of volume per hectare for the jth line as $\hat{T}_{Hj}$. If a total of m lines are run and a given line j has length L_j, then an overall estimate of volume per hectare is

$$\hat{T}_{H_{\text{LIS}}} = \frac{\sum_{j=1}^{m} L_j \hat{T}_{Hj}}{\sum_{j=1}^{m} L_j} \tag{10.8}$$

where:

$\hat{T}_{H_{LIS}}$ = overall estimate of volume per hectare based on m lines

L_j = length of line j (meters)

$\hat{T}_{Hj}$ = estimate of volume per hectare for line j

m = number of lines

The variance of this estimate is

$$S^2_{\hat{T}_{H_{\text{LIS}}}} = \frac{\sum_{j=1}^{m} L_j (\hat{T}_{Hj} - \hat{T}_{H_{\text{LIS}}})^2}{(m-1) \sum_{j=1}^{m} L_j} \tag{10.9}$$

where all variables are as previously defined.

If English units are used the overall estimate of volume per acre is

$$\hat{T}_{A_{\text{LIS}}} = \frac{\sum_{j=1}^{m} L_j \hat{T}_{Aj}}{\sum_{j=1}^{m} L_j} \tag{10.10}$$

where:

$\hat{T}_{A_{\text{LIS}}}$ = overall estimate of volume per acre based on m lines

L_j = length of line j (feet)

$\hat{T}_A$ = estimate of volume per acre for line j

m = number of lines

The variance of this estimate is

$$S^2_{\hat{T}_{A_{LIS}}} = \frac{\sum_{j=1}^{m} L_j (\hat{T}_{Aj} - \hat{T}_{A_{LIS}})^2}{(m-1) \sum_{j=1}^{m} L_j} \tag{10.11}$$

where all variables are as previously defined.

EXAMPLE 10.2.2

Suppose that eight transects were randomly located in an 80-acre clearcut. The purpose of the sample is to estimate the volume of bolts at least 5 ft in length with diameter greater than 4 in. This will give the forester an idea of how much pulpwood was left lying on the site. Each bolt that intersected a transect was measured for diameter at the point it intersected the transect if it was judged to have a diameter of at least 4 in. and was at least 5 ft long. The resulting estimate of volume per acre and line length of each transect are given in the following table:

Transect	Length (ft)	Volume per Acre ($\hat{T}_{Aj}$)
1	400	255
2	600	362
3	750	490
4	200	350
5	150	500
6	800	378
7	900	290
8	450	525

Use Eq. 10.10 to obtain the overall estimate of volume per acre. The sum of the line lengths is

$$\sum_{i=1}^{8} L_i = 4250$$

The sum of the line lengths times the estimate of volume per acre is

$$\sum_{i=1}^{8} L_i \hat{T}_{Aj} = 1{,}631{,}350$$

Thus, using Eq. 10.10,

$$\hat{T}_{A_{\text{LIS}}} = \frac{1{,}631{,}350}{4250} = 383.8 \text{ ft}^3\text{/acre}$$

The variance of this estimate is calculated using Eq. 10.11. From preceding calculations we know there are eight lines, so

$$m = 8$$

$$\sum_{j=1}^{8} L_j = 4250$$

Now the numerator of Eq. 10.11 is

$$\sum_{j=1}^{8} L_j (\hat{T}_{Aj} - \hat{T}_{A_{\text{LIS}}})^2 = 400\,(255 - 383.8)^2 + 600\,(362 - 383.8)^2 + 750\,(490 - 383.8)^2 + \ldots + 450\,(525 - 383.8)^2 = 34{,}550{,}960$$

Then

$$S^2_{\hat{T}_{A_{\text{LIS}}}} = \frac{34{,}550{,}960}{(8-1)(4250)} = \frac{34{,}550{,}960}{29{,}750} = 1161.4$$

The standard error for this estimate is

$$S^2_{\hat{T}_{A_{\text{LIS}}}} = \sqrt{1161.4} = 34.1 \text{ ft}^3\text{/acre}$$

An approximate 95% confidence interval is easily obtained as follows:

$$\text{LCL} = \hat{T}_{A_{\text{LIS}}} - 2S_{\hat{T}A} = 383.8 - 2(34.1) = 315.6 \text{ ft}^3\text{/acre}$$

$$\text{UCL} = \hat{T}_{A_{\text{LIS}}} + 2S_{\hat{T}A} = 383.8 + 2(34.1) = 452.0 \text{ ft}^3\text{/acre}$$

Line intersect sampling is useful for estimating the amount of slash lying on the ground. It is usually carried out more quickly than a traditional line-plot cruise. However, there is usually quite a large amount of variability associated with estimates resulting from line transect samples. DeVries (1986) has shown that variation in the estimates decreases as line length increases. Thus, in general, it is good practice to use many relatively long lines oriented in various directions to obtain the best estimates of volume per unit area. Pickford and Hazard (1978) and Hazard and Pickford (1986) did computer simulation studies in which they compared line transect sampling done in various ways with fixed-area plot sampling for many different types of populations.

REFERENCES

Bailey, G. R. 1970. A simplified method of sampling logging residue. *Forestry Chronicle* 46:288–294.

DeVries, P. G. 1973. A general theory on line intersect sampling, with application to logging residual inventory. *Mededelingen Landbouwhogeschool* 73(11).

DeVries, P. G. 1974. Multi-stage line intersect sampling. *For. Sci.* 20(2):129–133.

DeVries, P. G. 1986. *Sampling theory for forest inventory: A teach-yourself course.* Berlin: Springer-Verlag.

Grosenbaugh, L. R. 1963. Some suggestions for better sample-tree measurement. *Sor. Am. For. Proc.* 1963:36–42.

Grosenbaugh, L. R. 1965. *Three-pee sampling theory and program "THRP" for computer generation of selection criteria.* USDA For. Serv. Res. Pap. PSW-21.

Grosenbaugh, L. R. 1976. Approximate sampling variance of adjusted 3P estimates. *For. Sci.* 22(2):173–176.

Hazard, J. W., and S. G. Pickford. 1986. Simulation studies on line intersect sampling of forest residue: Part 2. *For. Sci.* 32: 442–470.

Pickford, S. G., and J. W. Hazard. 1978. Simulation studies on line intersect sampling of forest residue. *For. Sci.* 24:469–483.

Schreuder, H. T., J. Sedransk, and K. D. Ware. 1968. 3P sampling and some alternatives, 1. *For. Sci.* 14:429–454.

Schreuder, H. T., J. Sedransk, and K. D. Ware. 1971. 3P sampling and some alternatives, 2. *For. Sci.* 17:103–118.

Van Wagner, C. E. 1968. The line intersect method in forest fuel sampling. *For. Sci.* 15:20–26.

Van Wagner, C. E., and A. L. Wilson. 1976. Diameter measurement in the line intersect method. *For. Sci.* 22(2):230–232.

Warren, W. G., and P. F. Olsen. 1964. A line intersect technique for assuming logging waste. *For. Sci.* 10:267–276.

PROBLEMS FOR BETTER UNDERSTANDING

1. Sample size for a 3P sample is a random variable that is not known until after the sample is complete. What problems might this fact bring about in practice?
2. Estimated tree size in a 3P sample has traditionally been some measure of volume (such as cubic feet or board feet). However, a 3P sample could just as well be carried out by estimating tree dbh, tree height, or maybe even the product of dbh and height.

If a size measure other than volume is used to select 3P sample trees, what will have to be done to calculate $\hat{T}_{3P}$?

3. Suppose that in a given stand the largest merchantable tree has a volume of 35 ft^3. Furthermore, the cruiser can estimate cubic volume with a CV of 15% for the ratio of measured to estimated tree volume. How many 3P sample trees are required to estimate the total cubic-foot volume with an allowable error of 10%? Work at the 95% level of confidence.

4. Refer to Problem 3. It was estimated that there are 40,000 ft^3 of merchantable volume in the tract. What z value should be used when generating random numbers for this tract?

5. Prior to conducting a 3P sample on a marked timber sale, a forester estimates the total volume in the sale to be 600,000 bd ft, and she estimates the maximum tree size to be 550 bd ft. She believes from previous 3P cruises that her coefficient of variation of actual to predicated volume ratio will be about 30%.

a. How many trees should she try to measure to be within plus or minus 10% with approximately 95% confidence?

b. What z value should be used to approximate the sample size?

c. At the end of the inventory the forester had accumulated volumes of 626,000 bd ft. In addition, she measured the following trees (their estimated volumes were included in the 626,000):

Estimated Volume	Measured Volume
280	282
425	440
395	414
400	402
550	545
140	146
104	100
215	227
123	128
305	316
270	288
260	275

The timber sells for $600/MBF. Estimate the total value in the timber sale.

d. Calculate an approximate standard error of the estimate of total value.

6. Line intersect sampling (LIS) is a probability-proportional-to-size sample selection method. Why is this true?

7. Start with Eq. 10.4 and show that total volume per acre is given by Eq. 10.7 when bolt diameter is measured in inches and transect length is measured in feet.

8. A line transect sample was carried out in a recently harvested lodgepole pine stand. An estimate of all slash with minimum diameter of 5 in. and minimum length of 8 ft lying on the area is needed. A single 1250-ft line was laid out and traversed. A total of 49 pieces of slash that met the size specifications were intersected. The sum of squared diameters (measured in inches) is

$$\sum_{i=1}^{49} d_i^2 = 2825$$

Estimate the cubic-foot volume of slash per acre for this stand.

9. Suppose that five more lines were run in the stand discussed in Problem 8. Line length and the estimated volume per acre for each line is

Line	Length (ft)	$\hat{T}_{Aj}$
1	800	455
2	1100	375
3	1600	750
4	950	800
5	700	475

a. Use the estimate from Problem 8 and the data in the preceding table to obtain an overall estimate of the cubic-foot volume per acre of slash in this stand.

b. Calculate the variance of the estimate obtained in part a.

c. Calculate an approximate 95% confidence interval for the estimate obtained in part a.

CHAPTER 11

ESTIMATING WILDLIFE POPULATION SIZES

Estimating the size of a population of a particular animal species is not easily accomplished. There are many reasons for this. Animals are mobile and thus may appear in many different locations in a short span of time. Furthermore, wildlife species tend to be secretive and shy away from humans. Thus population size estimation procedures tend to be somewhat complex. However, there are some basic estimation procedures that are relatively simple to implement.

There are many types of population estimation procedures that are used to estimate the size of a wildlife population. Quadrat sampling, line transect sampling, and capture-recapture methods are three of the methods most often used. In the following discussion it is assumed that the current population size is to be estimated and that there is no interest in obtaining estimates of births, deaths, sex ratios, or other population information. Readers interested in these population parameters should consult the work of Seber (1982) and White et al. (1982).

11.1 QUADRAT SAMPLING

As just discussed, one of the main reasons that estimating the size of wildlife populations is difficult is that the animals are mobile and secretive. This makes getting a reliable count of the number of animals on a given area very difficult. However, in some situations a reliable count can be made on a given area; this may be possible when dealing with easily detectable birds or small mammals with limited home ranges (Seber, 1982).

When fixed-area plots are used in estimating the size of a population, the sampling procedure is usually referred to as quadrat sampling. Quadrats can be any shape; however, for estimating animal population sizes or density they are usually square or rectangular. Once quadrats are laid out in the field, the number of animals in the target population is determined in one fashion or another (such as observation or trapping). Quadrat sampling will vary from one species to another. Smaller quadrats can be used for relatively stationary animals, whereas large quadrats would be required for large, more mobile animals. Ideally, quadrat size should be large enough to ensure that most quadrats have one or more of the animals of interest present.

When using quadrat sampling the population density per unit area, say D, is often of interest. Define M as the total number of elements (animals of interest) in a given area of size A. The total area can be divided into N quadrats each of size a so that

$$A = aN$$

To estimate D, the number of elements on each of n randomly selected quadrats, say m_i on quadrat i, is determined. Then the average number of elements per quadrat is calculated as

$$\overline{m} = \frac{\sum_{i=1}^{n} m_i}{n}$$

Density per unit area is then estimated by

$$\hat{D} = \frac{\overline{m}}{a} \tag{11.1}$$

The variance of this estimate is

$$S_{\hat{D}}^2 = \frac{1}{a^2} \frac{S_m^2}{n} \tag{11.2}$$

where:

$$S_m^2 = \frac{1}{n-1}\left[\sum_{i=1}^{n} m_i^2 - \frac{\left(\sum_{i=1}^{n} m_i\right)^2}{n}\right]\left[\frac{N-n}{N}\right]$$

and all other variables are as previously defined.

It is relatively simple to obtain an estimate of the total number of individuals, M, as

$$\hat{M} = A\hat{D} \tag{11.3}$$

where:

A = total area of interest

and all other variables are as previously defined.

The variance of this estimate is

$$S_{\hat{M}}^2 = A^2 S_{\hat{D}}^2 \tag{11.4}$$

where all variables are as previously defined.

EXAMPLE 11.1.1

A 125-acre area was sampled to determine the number of white-tailed deer. Due to the mobility of the deer, relatively large 5-acre quadrats were used. Ten quadrats were sampled; the number of deer observed on each was as follows:

Quadrat	Number of Deer
1	3
2	2
3	0
4	0
5	5
6	7
7	1
8	0
9	2
10	3

First determine N, the total number of 5-acre quadrats in the area:

$$N = \frac{A}{a} = \frac{125}{5} = 25$$

The average number of deer per quadrat is

$$\overline{m} = \frac{23}{10} = 2.3$$

The density of deer per acre is estimated as

$$\hat{D} = \frac{2.3}{5} = 0.46$$

Next the variance of this estimate is obtained:

$$\begin{aligned} S_m^2 &= \frac{1}{9}\left(101 - \frac{(23)^2}{10}\right)\left(\frac{25 - 10}{25}\right) \\ &= (5.3444)\,(0.6) \\ &= 3.2066 \end{aligned}$$

and

$$S_{\hat{D}}^2 = \frac{1}{5^2}(0.32) = 0.0128$$

The total number of deer on the 125-acre area is estimated to be

$$\hat{M} = 125(0.46) = 57.5 \text{ or } 58$$

and

$$S_{\hat{M}}^2 = (125)^2\,(0.0128) = 200$$

$$S_{\hat{M}} = \sqrt{200} = 14.14$$

An approximate 95% confidence interval is

$$\begin{aligned} \text{LCL} &= 58 - 2(14.14) = 29.7, \text{ or } 30 \text{ deer} \\ \text{UCL} &= 58 + 2(14.14) = 86.3, \text{ or } 87 \text{ deer} \end{aligned}$$

The estimates for D and M given in the preceding example are for any type of population and are equivalent to simple random sampling estimators given in Chapter 3. If it is assumed that the individuals of interest are randomly distributed across the area, then m_i, the number of individuals observed on quadrat i, is a Poisson random variable. In this case the following estimators should be used:

$$\hat{D} = \frac{\overline{m}}{a}$$

$$S^2_{\hat{D}} = \frac{\hat{D}}{an}$$

$$\hat{M} = A\hat{D}$$

$$S^2_{\hat{M}} = A^2 S^2_{\hat{D}}$$

where all variables are as previously defined.

EXAMPLE 11.1.2

Refer to Example 11.1.1. If the deer are randomly distributed (a highly unlikely assumption) across the 125-acre area, then

$$\hat{D} = \frac{2.3}{5} = 0.46$$

$$S^2_{\hat{D}} = \frac{0.46}{5(10)} = 0.0092$$

$$\hat{M} = 125(0.46) = 57.5\text{, or 58 deer}$$

$$S^2_{\hat{M}} = (125)^2(0.0092) = 143.75$$
$$S_{\hat{M}} = 11.99$$

$$\text{LCL} = 58 - 2(11.99) = 34.02 \text{ or 35 deer}$$
$$\text{UCL} = 58 + 2(11.99) = 81.98\text{, or 82 deer}$$

If the shape of the quadrat used is a long, narrow rectangle, it is usually referred to as a strip. When strips are randomly located throughout an area the sampling method is usually known as strip transect sampling. Estimators for density per unit area, D, and the total number of individuals in the population, M, are the same as for quadrat sampling if all strip transects are the same size.

In both quadrat and strip transect sampling, one very important assumption is that all elements of interest that are present on the quadrat or strip are seen and counted. However, for many animal species this is not possible. A sampling procedure that has been developed for such a situation is line transect sampling (LTS).

11.2 LINE TRANSECT SAMPLING (LTS)

LTS falls in a category of sampling known as plotless sampling. It is an extension of the idea of using long, narrow strips as sampling units. The sampling method is carried out by randomly laying out lines of length L across the area of interest. The investigator travels along each line and counts the number of individuals of interest that are sighted up to a distance of w units away from the line in either direction. For each individual sighted along the line, one or more of the following statistics are recorded (Figure 11.2.1) at the time of first sighting

1. Sighting distance = r_i
2. Right-angle distance = y_i
3. Sighting angle = θ_i

The measure of interest is y_i. If y_i is determined in the field directly it is not necessary to obtain r_i and θ_i. Sighting distance and sighting angle are used to determine y_i when it cannot be determined directly in the field.

This sampling method can be used to estimate the density of objects per unit area for any organism (plant or animal) that is distributed across the area according to any unknown stochastic process that has a density per unit area of D. There are four assumptions that must be met to obtain reliable estimates of density from an LTS:

1. Organisms of interest directly on the line are never missed.
2. Organisms are fixed at time of initial sighting (that is, they do not move before detection) and none are counted more than once.
3. Distance (x and r) and angles (θ) are measured exactly.
4. Sightings are independent of one another.

It is very important to design an LTS study to minimize violation of these four assumptions.

Figure 11.2.1 Animal sighted at point P by an observer at point O.

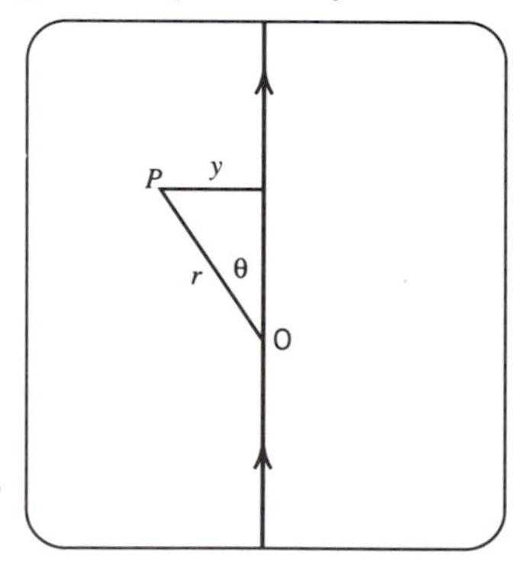

The LTS method assumes that the probability of detecting an organism of interest decreases as its distance from the line increases. Furthermore, LTS does not require that all organisms will be sighted (that is, some organisms present will go undetected). Thus this sampling method is more realistic than quadrat or strip transect sampling for many animal populations. Sightings on either side of the transect can be made no matter how far away the organism is. However, a distance w may be defined as the maximum right-angle distance at which sightings are made. In either case (finite or infinite w) the basic estimator of density per unit area is

$$\hat{D} = \frac{n\hat{f}(0)}{2L}$$

where:

n = number of organisms sighted along the line

L = length of the line

$\hat{f}(0)$ = statistical function evaluated for a distance of 0 ft from the line

Once data are obtained from a line transect sample, the density estimate depends only on estimating $\hat{f}(0)$. This quantity is related to the probability-of-detection function, which is referred to as a detectability curve. The detectability curve is a mathematical function $g(y)$, that provides the probability of detecting an organism at any distance, w, from the line. By definition it will have a value of 1 at a distance of 0 ft from the line (that is, organisms on the line will never be missed). As distance from the line increases, the probability of detection will decrease and approach zero.

There are two major approaches to estimating $\hat{f}(0)$ (and hence D): parametric and nonparametric. The parametric approach requires a statistical probability distribution to describe the detectability curve (such as the negative exponential or Poisson). The right-angle distances are then used to obtain parameter estimates for the selected distribution, and subsequently $\hat{f}(0)$ is obtained. For example, if the exponential probability distribution is used as the model of detectability, then,

$$g(y) = e^{-\lambda_1 y}$$

where:

$g(y)$ = detectability curve

y = distance from transect

λ_1 = parameter to be estimated from the data

Gates et al. (1968) show that for this detectability curve, density is estimated with

$$\hat{D} = \frac{n}{2L\hat{C}} \qquad (11.5)$$

where:

$\hat{D}$ = density per unit area

$$\hat{C} = \frac{\sum_{i=1}^{n} y_i}{n-1}$$

y_i = right-angle distance to animal i

and all other variables are as previously defined.

EXAMPLE 11.2.1

Suppose that a line transect sample was carried out in a forested area to estimate the density of white-tailed deer. A line of 2000 yd was laid out and traversed. The following right-angle distances were obtained for 19 sightings of individual animals:

Animal	Right Angle Distance (Yd) (y_i)
1	10
2	0
3	30
4	25
5	20
6	60
7	50
8	80
9	40
10	10
11	50
12	0
13	25
14	40
15	50
16	75
17	80
18	20
19	10

Use Eq. 11.5 to estimate $\hat{D}$. First

$$n = 19$$
$$L = 2000$$
$$\sum_{i=1}^{19} y_i = 675 \text{ yd}$$
$$\hat{C} = \frac{\sum_{i=1}^{19} y_i}{n-1} = \frac{675}{18} = 37.5$$

and

$$\hat{D} = \frac{n}{2L\hat{C}} = \frac{19}{2(2000)\,(37.5)}$$
$$\hat{D} = 0.0001267 \text{ deer/yd}^2$$

There are 4840 yd^2 per acre, thus density per acre is estimated to be 0.613 deer.
In application it is important to measure L and y_i in the same units.

When there are R replicate lines the overall estimate of density is obtained as

$$\hat{D}_{\text{LTS}} = \frac{\sum_{i=1}^{R} l_i \hat{D}_i}{L} \tag{11.6}$$

where:

$\hat{D}_i$ = density estimate based on transect i
l_i = length of transect i
L = total length of all transects = $\sum_{i=1}^{R} l_i$

The variance from replicate transacts can be estimated as

$$S^2_{\hat{D}_{\text{LTS}}} = \frac{\sum_{i=1}^{R} l_i(\hat{D}_i - \hat{D}_{\text{LTS}})^2}{L(R-1)}$$

$$S^2_{\hat{D}_{\text{LTS}}} = \frac{\sum_{i=1}^{R} l_i \hat{D}_i^2 - L\,\hat{D}^2_{\text{LTS}}}{L(R-1)} \tag{11.7}$$

where all variables are as previously defined.

An approximate 95% confidence interval for the density is obtained as

$$\hat{D}_{\text{LTS}} \pm 2S_{\hat{D}_{\text{LTS}}}$$

where:

$$S_{\hat{D}_{\text{LTS}}} = \sqrt{S^2_{\hat{D}_{\text{LTS}}}}$$

EXAMPLE 11.2.2

Suppose that five lines were laid out and traversed in a forested area. Estimates of the number of white-tailed deer per acre were obtained for each, as shown in Example 11.2.1. Transect length and the estimate of density for each transect are as follows:

Line	Length (Yd)	Density (Deer/yd²)
1	2000	0.0001267
2	1500	0.0002479
3	2500	0.0001550
4	3000	0.0004545
5	1200	0.0004132

To obtain an overall density estimate for this area, use Eq. 11.6. First, we know

$$R = 5$$

Then

$$L = \sum_{i=1}^{5} l_i = 10{,}200 \text{ yd}$$

$$\sum_{i=1}^{R} l_i\hat{D}_i = 2.87209 \text{ yd}$$

So

$$\hat{D}_{\text{LTS}} = \frac{2.87209}{10{,}200} = 0.0002816 \text{ deer/yd}^2$$

which is equivalent to 1.36 deer per acre. The variance of this estimate is obtained using Eq. 11.7.

$$\sum_{i=1}^{R} l_i\hat{D}_i^2 = 0.0010089$$

Then

$$S^2_{\hat{D}_{LTS}} = \frac{0.0010089 - 10{,}200\,(0.0002816)^2}{10{,}200\,(4)}$$

$$= \frac{0.000200184}{40{,}800} = 0.000000005$$

The standard error is

$$S_{\hat{D}_{LTS}} = \sqrt{0.000000005} = 0.000070046 \text{ deer/yd}^2$$

On an acre basis the standard error is 0.34 deer. So an approximate 95% confidence interval for the number of deer per acre is

$$\text{LCL} = 1.36 - 2(0.34) = 0.68$$
$$\text{UCL} = 1.36 + 2(0.34) = 2.04$$

Estimates of density obtained using Eqs. 11.5 and 11.6 rely on the assumption that the probability of detection can be modeled using the negative exponential model $e^{-\lambda x}$. If this assumption is met and care is taken in estimating perpendicular distances, then estimates should be realistic. Seber (1982) discusses procedures to test whether the assumption is supported by the data. Burnham et al. (1980) state that ''the assumption of negative exponential sighting is too restrictive and the estimator is not robust to failure of this assumption. . . . The method has applicability for the analysis of data only if a good test of the assumption is made.'' Other parametric estimators that rely on different detectability curves are available; as with the negative exponential approach, their applicability should be verified. In the nonparametric method right-angle distances or sighting distances and sighting angles are used with more complex mathematical algorithms to obtain an estimate of $\hat{f}(0)$ (Burnham et al., 1980). All of these nonparametric procedures are beyond the scope of this text. Interested readers should consult Burnham et al. (1980) and Seber (1982) for more detailed information on line transect density estimators. A computer program called TRANSECT has been developed for LTS data summarization and density estimation (Laake et al., 1979).

Regardless of which procedure is used to estimate $\hat{f}(0)$, it is imperative that more than one transect be used in any area under study. If possible, several lines should be randomly located and traversed. This allows for better estimates of density as well as for variability estimates to be calculated from the repeated estimates of D (one for each line), as shown in the previous example.

11.3 CAPTURE-RECAPTURE METHODS

The capture-recapture sampling methods to be discussed here fall in the category of single mark-release, single recapture methods. All variations of multiple mark-release, multiple recapture methods are beyond the scope of this discussion. Readers interested in these methods should consult Pollock et al. (1990), White et al. (1982), and Otis et al. (1978).

The basic steps in a capture-recapture sampling procedure for a population of N individuals is as follows:

1. Capture, mark, and release a sample of n_1 individuals.
2. At a later time, after the marked animals have redistributed throughout the population, capture a sample of n_2 individuals and note how many marked animals are recaptured.

The following population size estimators are based on the following assumptions:

1. Marked individuals are redistributed randomly throughout the population after initial capture.
2. Marked individuals retain their marks until recapture.
3. Marking does not affect the probability of recapture.
4. All marks at the second sampling occasion are recorded.
5. The population of interest is closed geographically and demographically.

Most of these assumptions are easily understood. For example, assumption 2 implies that the marks must be present and recognizable throughout the study. The amount of time required for assumption 1 to be met will vary from species to species. The investigator will have to use knowledge of the species' habits to determine how long it will take the marked animals to redistribute throughout the population. Geographic population closure means that an area must be defined within which the population resides. For example, it is not enough to state that the white-tailed deer population size will be estimated. There must be a geographic limit to the population, such as the white-tailed deer population in the northeastern United States or within a certain set of counties in central Pennsylvania. The point is that the geographic limits of the population must be defined. Demographic closure implies that there is no immigration into, emigration out of, or births or deaths in the population during the period of the study. Knowledge of the species' habits must be used to help ensure that this assumption is satisfied.

The most unrealistic and restrictive assumption listed above is that capture probability remains the same from one sampling occasion to the next and is the same for all animals. It is often the case that once an animal is captured it may become trap happy or trap shy. When an animal is trap happy its probability of capture increases, and when an animal is trap shy its probability of capture decreases. Since this assumption is usually violated in capture-recapture studies, estimators based on this assumption provide, at best, only crude estimates of population size. Methods of estimation have been developed for situations in which capture probabilities are not constant. In fact, Otis et al. (1978) have presented estimators for the following situations:

1. Capture probabilities vary with time or trapping occasion due to environmental factors or capture technique.

2. Capture probabilities vary due to behavioral responses (trap happy or trap shy).
3. Capture probabilities vary by individual animal.

Estimators are also available for combinations of these three situations. The estimators used for these more realistic assumptions are very complex and are beyond the scope of this text. Interested readers should consult Otis et al. (1978) and White et al. (1982) for more information.

Single capture–single release capture-recapture studies are classified into direct and inverse procedures. The procedures are identical except for the recapture component. That is, a fixed number of animals, say n_1, is captured at the first sampling occasion. These animals are marked and returned to the population. In direct sampling, a fixed number of animals, say n_2, is recaptured at the second sampling occasion and the number of marked animals, say m, is noted. In inverse sampling, sampling continues at the second sampling occasion until m marked animals are found. Thus in direct sampling the number of animals captured on the second sampling occasion is fixed at n_2, whereas in inverse sampling the number of animals captured on the second sampling occasion is a random variable that is not known until sampling is complete and m marked animals are captured.

Within direct and inverse sampling procedures, sampling at the second occasion can be done with or without replacement. In sampling without replacement, animals captured at the second occasion are excluded from additional recapture (that is, they may be physically removed from the area or are counted only once at the second sampling occasion regardless of how many times they are recaptured). In sampling with replacement an animal can legitimately be captured at the second sampling occasion and recorded as a marked animal more than once. Estimators for the population size differ for direct and inverse sampling as well as for with- and without-replacement sampling.

11.4 DIRECT SAMPLING

A population size estimate for direct sampling without replacement at the second sampling occasion is known as a Petersen estimate or the Lincoln index after work by Petersen (1896) and Lincoln (1930).

The estimator for this type of capture-recapture experiment is

$$\hat{N} = \frac{n_1 n_2}{m}$$

where:

n_1 = number of animals captured, marked, and released at the first sampling occasion

n_2 = number of animals captured at the second sampling occasion

m = number of animals with marks that were captured at the second sampling occasion

This estimator is a biased estimator for N, the population size. Note that bias is not a desirable property for statistical estimators (see Chapter 2). An estimator that exhibits less bias than the traditional estimator given above was developed by Chapman:

$$\hat{N} = \frac{(n_1 + 1)(n_2 + 1)}{(m + 1)} - 1 \tag{11.8}$$

where all variables are as previously defined.

If m is greater than or equal to 7, it can be shown that the bias of this estimator is negligible. However, the user is cautioned that, in general, if fewer than 10 marks are observed at the second sampling occasion, the estimate may fail to give even the order of magnitude of the population. The variance of this estimator is approximated with the following formula (Seber, 1982):

$$S_{\hat{N}}^2 = \frac{(n_1 + 1)(n_2 + 1)(n_1 - m)(n_2 - m)}{(m + 1)^2 (m + 2)} \tag{11.9}$$

where all variables are as previously defined.

To obtain an approximate 95% confidence interval, calculate the bound on the error of estimation as

$$2\sqrt{S_{\hat{N}}^2}$$

and then add and subtract this quantity to $\hat{N}$. Thus

$$\text{LCL} = \hat{N} - 2\sqrt{S_{\hat{N}}^2}$$

$$\text{UCL} = \hat{N} + 2\sqrt{S_{\hat{N}}^2}$$

where:

LCL = lower confidence limit

UCL = upper confidence limit

and all variables are as previously defined.

This confidence interval holds only when the population size is very large. When N is expected to be small, other, more complex methods should be used to obtain confidence intervals (Seber, 1982).

Direct sampling with replacement at the second sampling occasion is usually not preferred to direct sampling without replacement. However, in some capture-recapture studies, with-replacement sampling at the second sampling occasion can not be avoided.

For example, in some bird studies birds are initially captured, marked, and released, and then at the second sampling occasion observers simply look for marked birds rather than recapture them. Obviously, this scheme can lead to the same bird being observed more than once at the second sampling occasion, thus creating a with-replacement sampling scheme. For this situation the following estimator is used to estimate $1/N$ (that is, the inverse of the population size N):

$$\hat{N}^* = \frac{m}{n_1 n_2} = \widehat{\left(\frac{1}{N}\right)} \tag{11.10}$$

where all variables are as previously defined.

The variance of this estimator is

$$S^2_{\hat{N}^*} = \frac{1}{n_2 - 1}\left[\frac{m}{n_1^2 n_2} - \frac{m^2}{n_1^2 n_2^2}\right] \tag{11.11}$$

where all variables are as previously defined.

Since $\hat{N}^*$ estimates $1/N$, the final confidence interval end points should be inverted to obtain a confidence interval in terms of N. As always, 2 will be used as a multiplier on the standard error of $\hat{N}^*$ to obtain an approximate 95% confidence interval.

EXAMPLE 11.4.1

A forester needs to obtain an estimate of the white-tailed deer population on his district. He set up and carried out a capture-recapture study using direct sampling without replacement on the second sampling occasion. A total of 125 deer were captured and marked on the first sampling occasion. After two weeks 100 deer were captured, and 44 of them had marks. Thus

$$n_1 = 125$$

$$n_2 = 100$$

$$m = 44$$

Now, using Eq. 11.8,

$$\hat{N} = \frac{(n_1 + 1)\,(n_2 + 1)}{(m + 1)} - 1$$

$$\hat{N} = \frac{(126)\,(101)}{(45)} - 1 = 281.8$$

$$N = 282 \text{ deer}$$

The variance of this estimate is calculated using Eq. 11.9:

$$S^2_{\hat{N}} = \frac{(n_1 + 1)(n_2 + 1)(n_1 - m)(n_2 - m)}{(m + 1)^2 (m + 2)}$$

$$S^2_{\hat{N}} = \frac{(126)(101)(81)(56)}{(45)^2 (46)} = 619.7$$

The upper bound on the error of estimation is

$$2\sqrt{S^2_{\hat{N}}} = 49.8, \text{ or } 50$$

An approximate 95% confidence interval for N is

$$\text{LCL} = 282 - 2(50) = 182$$
$$\text{UCL} = 282 + 2(50) = 382$$

Next assume that the second sampling occasion was done with replacement (that is, marked animals could be counted more than once). Thus the sampling scheme is direct sampling with replacement at the second sampling occasion. The appropriate estimator to use for this situation is Eq. 11.10. For this example,

$$\hat{N}^* = \frac{44}{(125)(100)} = 0.00352$$

Inverting this estimate yields a population estimate of 285 deer. The variance of this estimator is obtained with Eq. 11.11:

$$S^2_{\hat{N}*} = \frac{1}{n_2 - 1}\left[\frac{m}{n_1^2 n_2} - \frac{m^2}{n_1^2 n_2^2}\right]$$

$$S^2_{\hat{N}*} = \frac{1}{99}\left[\frac{44}{(125)^2 (100)} - \frac{(44)^2}{(125)^2 (100)^2}\right]$$

$$= 0.000000159$$

The upper bound on the error of estimation is

$$B^*_{\hat{N}} = \sqrt{0.000000159} = 0.00079822$$

Thus an approximate 95% confidence interval for $1/N$ is

$$\text{LCL} = 0.00352 - 2(0.00079882) = 0.00192359$$
$$\text{UCL} = 0.00352 + 2(0.00079882) = 0.00511644$$

In terms of N the approximate 95% confidence interval is obtained by taking the inverse of each endpoint (LCL and UCL) of the interval. When this is done the LCL for $\hat{N}^*$ becomes the UCL for N and the UCL for $\hat{N}^*$ becomes the LCL for N. The endpoints of the confidence interval for N are

$$\text{LCL} = 195$$
$$\text{UCL} = 520$$

As should be expected, the confidence interval for with-replacement sampling is wider than the interval for without-replacement sampling.

11.5 INVERSE SAMPLING

As discussed earlier, inverse sampling differs from direct sampling in the recapture phase of a capture-recapture study. In inverse sampling the decision is made prior to recapture that sampling at the second occasion will continue until m marks are observed. Thus m is fixed and the sample size at the second sampling occasion, n_2, is a random variable that is not known until after the sampling is complete. On average, inverse sampling is more efficient than direct sampling, although differences are negligible. Furthermore, it may turn out to be more expensive and less convenient to carry out an inverse sample. This is so because sampling continues until m marks are captured. It is possible in some populations that these m marks may never be recaptured, thus causing a major setback in the study.

For inverse sampling without replacement on the second sampling occasion the following estimator is used:

$$\hat{N}_{\text{I}} = \frac{(n_1 + 1)n_2}{m} - 1 \tag{11.12}$$

where all variables are as previously defined.

The approximate variance for this estimator is

$$S^2_{\hat{N}_I} = \frac{(n_1 - m + 1)\,(N + 1)\,(N - n_1)}{m(n_1 + 2)} \tag{11.13}$$

where N should be replaced by $\hat{N}_1$ and all other variables are as previously defined. Inverse sampling with replacement is a somewhat more complex estimation problem. The estimator for N is

$$\hat{N}^*_{\text{I}} = \frac{n_1 n_2}{m} \tag{11.14}$$

where all variables are as previously defined.

The variance of this estimator is estimated by

$$S^2_{\hat{N}_I^*} = \frac{n_1^2 n_2 (n_2 - m)}{m^2(m+1)} \tag{11.15}$$

where all variables are as previously defined.

Interval estimates for this estimator are not straightforward. In fact, for large sample sizes numerical methods are required, and for small samples the chi-square distribution is required. Interested readers should consult Seber (1982) for more information.

EXAMPLE 11.5.1

A forester was given the opportunity to estimate the bobcat population on a large forest district in southern North Carolina. She decided to employ a capture-recapture approach using inverse sampling without replacement at the second sampling occasion. At the first sampling occasion 20 cats were captured and tagged. At the second occasion, sampling continued (without replacement) until five marks were observed. A total of 40 cats had to be captured to find the five marks. Thus

$$n_1 = 20$$
$$n_2 = 40$$
$$m = 5$$

Now, using Eq. 11.12,

$$\hat{N}_I = \frac{21(40)}{5} - 1 = 167 \text{ bobcats}$$

The variance of the estimator is calculated with Eq. 11.13:

$$S^2_{\hat{N}_I} = \frac{(20 - 5 + 1)(168 + 1)(168 - 20)}{5(20 + 2)}$$

$$= \frac{(16)(169)(148)}{110}$$

$$= 3638.1$$

The estimated standard error is

$$S_{\hat{N}_I} = \sqrt{3638.1} = 60.3$$

An approximate 95% confidence interval is

$$\text{LCL} = 167 - 2(60.3) = 46.4, \text{ or } 47 \text{ cats}$$
$$\text{UCL} = 167 + 2(60.3) = 287.6, \text{ or } 288 \text{ cats}$$

REFERENCES

Burnham, K. P., D. R. Anderson, and J. L. Laake. 1980. Estimation of density from line transect sampling of biological populations. *Wildlife Monographis* No. 72.

Gates, C. E., W. H. Marshall, and D. P. Olson. 1968. Line transect method of estimating grouse population densities. *Biometrics* 24:135–145.

Laake, J. L., K. P. Burnham, and D. R. Anderson. 1979. *User's manual for program TRANSECT.* Logan, UT: Utah State University Press.

Lincoln, F. C. 1930. *Calculating waterfowl abundance on the basis of banding returns.* Circ. U.S. Dept. Agric. No. 118:1–4.

Otis, D. L., K. P. Burnham, G. C. White, and D. R. Anderson. 1978. Statistical inference from capture data on closed animal populations. *Wildlife Monographis* No. 62.

Petersen, C. G. J. 1896. The yearly immigration of young plaice into the Limfjord from the German Sea. *Rep. Danish Biol. Sta.* 6:1–48.

Pollock, K. H., J. D. Nichols, C. Brownie, and J. E. Hines. Statistical inference for capture-recapture experiments. *Wildlife Monographs* No. 107.

Seber, G. A. F. 1982. *The estimation of animal abundance and related parameters.* New York: Macmillan.

White, G. C., D. R. Anderson, K. P. Burnham, and D. L. Otis. 1982. Capture-recapture and removal methods for sampling closed populations. LA-8787. Los Alamos, NM: NERP (Los Alamos National Laboratory).

PROBLEMS FOR BETTER UNDERSTANDING

1. Why should forest resource managers be interested in estimating wildlife population sizes?
2. Suppose that 10 ½-acre quadrats were randomly located throughout a 50-acre stand of timber. On each quadrat the number of gray squirrels was determined. The following data are available:

Quadrat	Number of Squirrels
1	8
2	6
3	10

Quadrat	Number of Squirrels
4	1
5	2
6	0
7	7
8	12
9	9
10	4

a. Estimate the per-acre density of squirrels in this stand.

b. Calculate the variance of the density estimate from part a and then obtain an approximate 95% confidence interval for the estimate.

3. Refer to Problem 2. Assume that the squirrels are randomly distributed throughout the stand.

a. Estimate the per-acre density of squirrels in the stand.

b. Calculate the variance of the density from part a and then obtain an approximate 95% confidence interval for the estimate.

4. What four assumptions are made so that reliable estimates are obtained from a line transect sample?

5. There are two main ways to go about estimating density from a line transect sample. Both methods are used to estimate a detectability curve. Explain what a detectability curve is.

6. A forester wants to estimate the per-acre density of woodcock in a 150-acre hardwood stand. He has decided to use line transect sampling to obtain the estimate. One line that he laid out and traversed was 750 yd long. The following data were obtained from this line:

Woodcock	Right-Angle Distance (Yd)
1	15
2	25
3	10
4	3
5	0
6	17
7	20

Assume that the detectability curve is negative exponential.

a. Estimate the per-acre woodcock density in this stand.

b. Estimate the number of woodcock in the 150-acre stand.

7. Seven line transects were laid out in various directions in a 900- hectare mixed pine hardwood stand in east Texas. Observers walked the lines and estimated right-angle distances to each coyote that was observed. Line length (meters) and estimated coyote density per square meter for each line are as follows:

Line	Length (m)	Coyote Density (per m^2)
1	500	0.000050
2	800	0.000100
3	1000	0.000025
4	400	0.000120
5	250	0.000075
6	790	0.000200
7	950	0.000080

a. Estimate the per-hectare density of coyotes represented on each line.

b. Obtain a single overall estimate of the per-hectare density of coyotes represented in this stand using all available data.

c. Calculate the variance of the estimate obtained in part b.

8. Refer to Problem 7. Calculate an estimate of the total number of coyotes on the 900-hectare tract. Further, obtain an approximate 95% confidence interval for this estimate.

9. List the assumptions made for single mark release single recapture capture-recapture studies. What assumption is the most unrealistic?

10. Suppose a capture-recapture study was carried out to estimate the number of raccoons on a forest district. Initially, 75 raccoons were captured, marked, and released. At a second sampling occasion 50 raccoons were captured without replacement. Twenty-five of the animals captured at the second sampling occasion had marks.

a. What type of sample is described in this problem?

b. Estimate the number of raccoons on the district.

c. Estimate the standard error of the estimate obtained in part b.

11. Refer to Problem 10. Assume the second sampling occasion was carried out with replacement.

a. Estimate the number of raccoons on the district.

b. Obtain an approximate 95% confidence interval for the estimate in part a.

ANSWERS TO ASSORTED PROBLEMS FOR BETTER UNDERSTANDING

CHAPTER 2

1. **a.** 2168
b. 496,990
c. 216.8
d. 2996.4
e. 299.64
f. 17.31
g. 25.2%

2. **a.** 64
b. 460
c. 5.6
d. 6.4
e. 0.75
f. 37.0%

3. **a.** 320
b. 11,500
c. 140

   d. 32
   e. 3.74
   f. 37.0%

4. **a.** 1289
   b. 570
   c. 154,633
   d. 31,300
   e. 69,390
   f. 1,661,521
   g. 324,900
   h. 734,730
   i. 47.5
   j. 107.4

5. **a.** 1850; 171,062
   b. 74
   c. 1,423.42
   d. 56.94; 7.55
   e. LCL = 58.9; UCL = 89.1
   f. 15.1
   g. 20.4%
   h. 51.0%

6. If we sample a given population a large number of times (assuming each sample is different) and calculate a 95% confidence interval for each sample, then 95% of the samples will lead to intervals that contain the "true" parameter being estimated and 5% of the samples will lead to intervals that do not contain the "true" parameter being estimated.

Chapter 3

1. **a.** 532.7 ft^3/acre
   b. LCL = 469.0 ft^3/acre; UCL = 596.4 ft^3/acre
   c. 13,317.5 ft^3
   d. LCL = 11,725 ft^3; UCL = 14,910 ft^3
   e. If we sample this stand a large number of times (assuming each sample is different) and calculate a 95% confidence interval for total tract volume, then 95% of the samples will lead to intervals that contain the "true" tract volume and 5% of the samples will lead to intervals that do not contain the "true" tract volume.

2. **a.** \$346.25/acre

b. LCL = \$304.85/acre; UCL = \$387.66/acre

c. \$8656.25

d. LCL = \$7621.25; UCL = \$9691.50

3. **a.** 899,969 bd ft

b. 46,289.52 bd ft

c. LCL = 807,389.95 bd ft; UCL = 992,548.05 bd ft

d. 49.6%

e. \$238,492

f. LCL = \$213,958; UCL = \$263,025

4. **a.** 49.4 ft^2/acre

b. 37.4 ft^2/acre

c. Pine: LCL = 40.2 ft^2/acre; UCL = 58.6 ft^2/acre
Hardwood: LCL = 30.9 ft^2/acre; UCL = 43.9 ft^2/ac

d. 86.8 ft^2/acre
LCL = 73.5 ft^2/acre; UCL = 100.1 ft^2/acre

5. 262 plots

6. 147 plots

7. **a.** Binomial random variable

b. 0.44

c. 0.0011

d. LCL = 0.374; UCL = 0.506

8. **a.** 2¾ chain × 2¾ chain

b. 2 chain × 4 chain

9. ¼ acre plots have smallest total average cost.

10. Sample sizes, *n*, required to achieve various AE percentages in stands with different CVs.

	AE(%)					
	5	**10**	**15**	**20**	**25**	**30**
CV(%)			*n*			
20	64	16	8	4	3	2
40	256	64	29	16	11	8
60	576	144	64	36	23	16
80	1024	256	114	64	41	29
100	1600	400	178	100	64	45

CHAPTER 4

1. 0.83, 1.18, 0.65, 0.73, 0.38, 0.14, 0.10, 1.52, 2.59, 2.12

2. BAF = 5
6.06, 4.24, 7.72, 6.81, 13.31, 35.25, 51.97, 3.29, 1.93, 2.36
BAF = 10
12.12, 8.48, 15.43, 13.63, 26.62, 70.49, 103.94, 6.57, 3.86, 4.72
BAF = 20
24.24, 16.97, 30.86, 27.25, 53.23, 140.99, 207.88, 13.15, 7.72, 9.45

3. 11.00, 13.75, 16.50, 19.25, 22.00, 24.75, 27.50, 30.25, 33.00, 35.75, 38.50, 41.25, 44.00, 46.75, 49.50, 52.25, 55.00, 57.75, 60.50, 63.25, 66.00, 68.75

4. 7.76, 9.70, 11.64, 13.58, 15.52, 17.46, 19.40, 21.34, 23.28, 25.22, 27.16, 29.10, 31.04, 32.98, 34.92, 36.86, 38.80, 40.74, 42.68, 44.62, 46.56, 48.50

5. 2807

6. 3270

7. 186.45; 90
205.01; 110

9. **a.** 2148

b. 1726.4 to 2569.6

c. 68,736

d. 55,246.1 to 82,225.9

e. 49%

f. $18,092.40

g. $14,382.68 to $21,802.12

10. 2, 3, 5

11. Total volume = 226,369 ft^3
Total trees = 11,396
Total basal area = 5820 ft^2
Average volume/acre = 4527.39 ft^3

12. Average cubic foot volume/acre = 4525.2

13. Average cubic foot volume/acre = 4525.2

14. Average cubic foot volume/acre = 4525.4

15. 225

CHAPTER 5

4. $N_1 = 1250$; $N_2 = 1900$; $N_3 = 500$; $N = 3650$

5. **a.** 666.51; 598.54; 1348.62

b. 343,750; 592,800; 89,000

c. 1.04×10^9; 2.16×10^9; 3.37×10^8

6. a. 279,207.86 to 408,292.14; 499,832.70 to 685,767.30; 52,276.44 to 125,723.56

b. 1,025,550

c. 3.537×10^9

d. 906,604.63 to 1,144,495.3

8. a. 2000 cords; 750 cords; 10,000 cords

b. 300 cords; 75 cords; 1250 cords

c. $20,000; $225,000; $200,000

d. $3000; $2250; $25,000

e. $191,940.63 to $293,059.37

f. 101

9. a. 2611 and 126; 1280 and 61.3; 240 and 72.6

b. 4131 and 158

c. $n_1 = 34$; $n_2 = 9$; $n_3 = 8$

d. 166

e. $n_1 = 117$; $n_2 = 34$; $n_3 = 17$

f. $34,655 and $1330

10. $\bar{y} = 13$; $s_{\bar{y}}^2 = 0.35$ with fpc

11. a. $\hat{T} = 571{,}241$ ft^3 and $S_{\hat{T}} = 29{,}283$ ft^3

b. $\hat{T}_{\text{sawtimber}} = 504{,}155$ ft^3 and $S_{\hat{T}(\text{sawtimber})} = 33{,}824$

c. $N = 12{,}857$; $S_N = 857$

d. $n_1 = 1129$; $n_2 = 1612$; $n_3 = 666$; $n_4 = 1564$

e. 5442

12. a. 532,000 m^3
417,318.92 to 646,682.08 m^3

b. Proportional allocation would be preferable even with no knowledge of variability differences.
$n_{ES} = 100$
$n_{GR} = 40$
$n_{CS} = 10$

c. *Grevillea robusta,* because the variance is larger.

13. $n = 17$

14. a. 1800; $S_{\hat{T}} = 185.97$

b. 30

c. $n_1 = 16$; $n_2 = 9$; $n_3 = 6$

15. a. $\bar{y}$/acre = 8.86; $S_{\bar{y}_{\text{acre}}} = 0.28$

b. $\hat{T} = 443{,}107$; $S_{\hat{T}} = 14{,}140$

CHAPTER 6

3. 50%

5. **a.** 815,924

b. 896,200

6. **a.** 2.1686×10^9

b. 2.9135×10^8

7. **a.** 821,937

b. 3.1383×10^8

9. 192,901; 7731

10. 191,482; 3514

11. **a.** 17,958

b. 1744

12. **a.** 18,061

b. 1848

13. **a.** 151,231

b. 13,802

CHAPTER 7

3. **a.** 1.1435

b. 0.9786

4. **a.** 200.1

b. 17.02

c. 240,072; LCL = 230,171; UCL = 249,973

6. **a.** 232.9

b. 17.8

c. 698,700; LCL = 591,918; UCL = 805,482

7. 63

8. **c.** 2.26

9. $n' = 12$; $n = 3$

10. **a.** 3108.7

b. 237.4

c. 3077.6

d. 151.5

e. 1.59

11. **a.** 2469.6; 28.9

b. 2425; 66.0

c. 2.26

d. 0.923

e. $\rho > .385$

f. $n' = 288$; $n = 25$

12. **a.** 7672

b. 1277

c. 9679

d. 949.8

e. 0.947

f. 1.95

CHAPTER 8

2. **a.** 402.1

b. 467.96

c. 416,145

5. **a.** 404,092,500 lbs

b. 1.2286294×10^{15}

c. LCL = 333,988,870 lbs; UCL = 474,196,120 lbs

6. **a.** 383,316,733 lbs

b. 4.0974936×10^{12}

8. **a.** 3, 8, 10, 11, 18

9. **a.** 7,945,000 ft^3

b. 1.6185312×10^{11}

c. LCL = 7,140,380 ft^3; UCL = 8,749,619 ft^3

CHAPTER 9

1. **a.** 310.67 ft^3; 250.3 ft^3

b. 310.67 ft^3; 1224.6 ft^3

2. **a.**

dbh	Trees per Acre
11	6.2
12	15.7
13	20.6
14	24.1
15	32.2
16	19.3
17	9.8
18	5.5
19	0.7
	134.0

4. **a.** 191 ft^3/acre

b. LCL = 14.2 ft^3/acre; UCL = 367.8 ft^3/acre

CHAPTER 10

3. 9

4. 4410

5. **a.** 9

b. 1082

c. $386,433.94

d. $3,398.00

8. 843.4 ft^3/acre

9. **a.** 644.3 ft^3/acre

b. 6843.07

c. LCL = 478.8 ft^3/acre; UCL = 809.7 ft^3/acre

CHAPTER 11

2. **a.** 11.8

b. LCL = 6.95; UCL = 16.65

3. **a.** 11.8

b. LCL = 8.73; UCL = 14.87

6. **a.** 1.5058

b. 226

7. **a.**

Line	Density per hectare
1	0.5
2	1
3	0.25
4	1.2
5	0.75
6	2
7	0.8

b. 0.918

c. 0.05393

8. 827; LCL = 409; UCL = 1245

10. **a.** 149

b. 16.3

11. **a.** 150

b. LCL = 117; UCL = 211

INDEX